Franciscans and American Indians in Pan-Borderlands Perspective

Franciscans and American Indians in Pan-Borderlands Perspective: Adaptation, Negotiation, and Resistance

Edited by

Jeffrey M. Burns and Timothy J. Johnson

Essays from a Conference Hosted by Flagler College St. Augustine, Florida

The Academy of American Franciscan History
Oceanside, California
2018

Table of Contents

Foreword

In 2014, Flagler College hosted an international conference entitled,"Franciscan Florida in Pan-Borderlands Perspective: Adaptation, Negotiation and Resistance" from March 13th–15th. The collected essays of this volume evince the important efforts of emerging and established scholars from Argentina, Germany, and the United States. The contributions from the members of Hopi, Navajo, and Native California tribes are particularly noteworthy.

From the outset, I called on the interdisciplinary expertise of Dr. David Hurst Thomas from the American Museum of Natural History to assist in defining the purpose and parameters of our conference. His extensive network of colleagues in the fields of archaeology and anthropology assured an impressive representation of experts for our conference sessions. My longtime colleague, Dr. Gert Melville from the Technische Universität Dresden, was instrumental in organizing a significant "Old World" contribution to our "New World" gathering. Our efforts were sustained by Dr. Jeffrey Burns, the indefatigable director of the Academy of American Franciscan History. I am most pleased that he agreed to co-edit this volume with me. Thanks are due as well to the Academy of American Franciscan History and the Saint Augustine Foundation for their generous financial support.

As with our previous conference in 2011, "From La Florida to La California: Franciscan Evangelization in the Spanish Borderlands," the Flagler College campus in historic Saint Augustine served as an idyllic point of cultural encounter and exchange. The college community excelled in providing a warm and welcoming atmosphere marked by gracious and professional service.

The dream of this conference would have remained just that had our former president, Dr. William T. Abare, Jr., not endorsed the initiative together with our Vice President of Academic Affairs, Dr. Alan Woolfolk. The dedication of several specific individuals continues to remind me that Flagler College is a community comprised of remarkable people. Ms. Laura Stevenson Dumas (College Affairs), Pattie Bibb (formerly of Dining Services), and William Jackson (Technology Services) were remarkable in their willingness to assist conference planners and participants. Ms. Jan Cheney (Academic Affairs) stands front and center as my nominee for the title "Best College Conference Coordinator." Decidedly enthusiastic and deft with details, she makes me even consider planning another conference at Flagler College.

Surely a college's identity is ultimately molded and marked by faculty and students. I want to thank my colleagues, Dr. John Young (History) and Dr. John Diviney (formerly of Spanish and Latin American Studies), for their willingness to chair conference sessions. Not only did students attend some sessions, three of my research assistants, Ms. Angelina DeVincenzo, Ms. Carie Levy, and Mr. Zachary Moore, played a key role in bringing this book into being through their editing efforts. Ms. Catherine Provenza demonstrated her professional skills and sensitivity to the humanities by producing a wonderful image for our conference poster and the cover of this book.

Finally, I find myself at the point where I can thank Professor Agnieszka (Aggie) Johnson. None of the comments above would have ever found a page if this *mulier fortis* was not there for every step of this journey at Flagler College.

Dr. Timothy J. Johnson
Craig and Audrey Thorn
Distinguished Professor of Religion

Introduction
Franciscan Florida in Pan-Borderlands Perspective: Adaptation, Negotiation, and Resistance

David Hurst Thomas

The papers in this volume[1] were presented on March 13–15, 2014 at a conference held at Flagler College (in downtown St. Augustine) entitled *Franciscan Florida in Pan-Borderlands Perspective*,[2] an event specifically designed to commemorate and observe the 450th anniversary of the founding of St. Augustine (Florida).[3] Universally hailed as the oldest continuously inhabited European settlement in the continental United States,[4] St. Augustine served for nearly two centuries (1565–1763) as the capital of La Florida, a small Spanish military outpost guarding the northern margin of Spain's vast empire. In the aftermath of the Seven Years' War, the British ruled St. Augustine for two decades (1763–1784), after which Florida again

1. I am grateful to Jeffrey Burns and Diana Rosenthal for assistance in preparing this introduction.

2. The 2014 Flagler conference was an outgrowth of a previous conference, also held at Flagler College, entitled *From La Florida to La California: The Genesis and Realization of Franciscan Evangelization in the Spanish Borderlands.* On March 24–26, 2011, anthropologists, archaeologists, historians, linguists, and theologians from both sides of the Atlantic gathered to explore the Franciscan impact on the political, cultural, and spiritual geographies of the American Borderlands. These conference essays comprised the first systematic study of Franciscan efforts throughout the Spanish Borderlands. Beyond the obvious connection to St. Augustine and La Florida, the present volume also expands the scope from the earlier effort; see Timothy J. Johnson and Gert Melville, eds. *From La Florida to La California: The Genesis and Realization of Franciscan Evangelization in the Spanish Borderlands* (Berkeley: Academy of American Franciscan History, 2013).

3. Sponsoring partners included the Academy of American Franciscan History, Arizona State University, Franciscan Institute at Saint Bonaventure University, the Saint Augustine Foundation, Research Centre for Comparative History of Religious Orders, Germany, St. Augustine Historical Society, and the Saxon Academy of Sciences, Leipzig.

4. See, for instance, J. Michael Francis, *St. Augustine, America's City: A Story of Unbroken History and Enduring Spirit* (Strassbourg, France: Éditions du Signe, 2015).

reverted to Spanish rule as a consequence of the American Revolution. The short-lived Second Spanish period ended in 1821, when Florida was ceded to the United States. Remaining a territory until 1845, Florida became the twenty-seventh state in the United States of America. "St. Augustine's history," argues historian Michael Francis, "is a fascinating blend of triumph and tragedy, a complex tapestry of human interactions."[5]

The Flagler Conference specifically addressed the evolution and nature of the Franciscan mission system that originated at St. Augustine and soon extended west to Tallahassee and northward along the Georgia coastline. Recent ethnohistorical and archaeological research demonstrates that the sixteenth- and seventeenth-century Franciscan missions of La Florida differed dramatically from mission systems operated in Texas, the American Southwest, and California.

To effectively explore the similarities and differences among the various North American missions, *Franciscan Florida in Pan-Borderlands Perspective* deliberately adopted the "cubist" perspective proposed a quarter-century earlier to frame *Columbian Consequences,* a three-volume consideration of the 500th anniversary of Columbus' arrival in the Caribbean.[6] In both cases, a diverse range of stakeholders was invited to marshal their expansive theoretical perspectives to address issues of acculturation, political and economic relations, religious conversion, and the nature of multiethnic relationships across the Spanish Borderlands.[7] The *Franciscan Florida in Pan-Borderlands Per-*

5. Francis, *St. Augustine, America's City,* back cover.

6. David Hurst Thomas, "The Spanish Borderlands in Cubist Perspective" in *Columbian Consequences, vol. 1, Archaeological and Historical Perspectives on the Spanish Borderlands West,* ed. David Hurst Thomas (Washington, D.C.: Smithsonian Institution Press, 1991), 1–14; David Hurst Thomas, "Cubist Perspectives on the Spanish Borderlands: Past, Present, and Future," in *Columbian Consequences, vol. 3, The Spanish Borderlands in Pan-American Perspective,* ed. David Hurst Thomas (Washington, D.C.: Smithsonian Institution Press, 1991), xiii–xx; David Hurst Thomas, "The Life and Times of Junípero Serra: A Pan-Borderlands Perspective," *The Americas* 71 (2014): 185–225. The cubist perspective has also been recently advocated by Kent G. Lightfoot, "A Cubist Perspective of Indigenous Landscapes and Spanish Missions," in *Indigenous Landscapes and Spanish Missions: New Perspectives from Archaeology and Ethnohistory,* eds. Lee M. Panich and Tsim D. Schneider (Tucson: University of Arizona Press, 2014), 191–208.

7. Such "cubist" conversations are grounded in analogies from art history. Since the Renaissance, Western artists have labored to perfect techniques for rendering three-dimensional visual reality into their artificial two-dimensional medium. Traditionally, such artists have relied on various illusionist devices including perspective, foreshortening, the use of color, and modeling to convince their viewers that reality could be comprehended by a spectator viewing a scene from a fixed position. The early twentieth-century cubist movement rejected this time-honored single perspective, enlarging their spectator's vision to include multiple, simultaneous views of the subjects—as if one could translocate—instantaneously moving from point to point, and up and down. In place of the familiar Renaissance vantage point, cubists substituted the radical notion that perspective could (and

spective symposium set out to extend the cubist gaze to deliberately foreground indigenous landscapes, particularly encouraging conversations directed at the interrelated issues of adaptation, negotiation, and resistance.

Franciscan Missions of La Florida

Gert Melville (chapter 2) dissects the earliest sixteenth-century European interest in Native America, which ranged from treasure seeking, to trade opportunities, to a chance to propagate Christian beliefs through missionary work. All three motivations are evident in the earliest Spanish attempts to colonize the Florida peninsula.

Pedro Menéndez de Avilés founded the colony of La Florida in 1565 as a strategic Spanish coastal foothold to safeguard the treasure-laden fleets of the Indies passing through the Old Bahama channel and sailing back to Spain. Not only did King Philip II need to prevent the French and British from capturing the cargoes of silver, gold, and other valuables, but La Florida would provide a base to shelter shipwrecked mariners, to rescue survivors, and to salvage goods that sank offshore. This permanent base could also facilitate launching further expeditions to explore the interior. The overarching strategic significance of La Florida ensured a relatively stable source of royal funding, but also required that Spanish colonists rely heavily on coastal Native American populations to buffer against interruptions in external supply lines.

When Pedro Menéndez de Avilés was granted the rights to establish the towns of St. Augustine and Santa Elena, Spanish King Philip II also insisted on a number of conditions, including assurances that the Adelantado attend to the spiritual welfare, not only of Florida's European colonists, but also the Indians already living there. Governor Menéndez first entrusted the evangelization of La Florida to the upstart Jesuit Order (founded only three decades earlier). The first Jesuit priests arrived in St. Augustine in September 1566, but five years later Jesuit General Francisco de Borja informed Menéndez de Avilés that he was pulling all Jesuits out of La Florida, admitting that "one can count on the fingers of the hand the number of converts made."[8] Declaring that La Florida "is not for the Society of Jesus," the first Jesuit attempt to missionize the New World ended in utter failure.[9]

---

should) be shifted at will. In the cubist epistemology, heads, noses, and eyes could be depicted concurrently in profile and full-face view. Because the final statement still transpired within a two-dimensional plane, cubists infused their subjects with an analytic form showing front, side, and even backside elements at once.

8. Nicholas P. Cushner, *Why Have You Come Here? The Jesuits and the First Evangelization of Native America* (New York: Oxford University Press, 2006), 47–48.

9. David J. Weber, *The Spanish Frontier in North America* (New Haven: Yale University Press, 1992), 54; see also J. Michael Francis and Kathleen M. Kole, *Murder and*

Helmut Flachenecker (chapter 3) tracks this and subsequent Jesuit missionary efforts in North America, which ultimately led to the canonization of Kateri Tekakwitha, the first Native American saint. He emphasizes that the degree to which the models employed in missionization efforts throughout French- and Spanish-dominated North America were initially developed during the evangelization of medieval Europe, concluding that whether "in Ireland or Pomerania like in Florida or New France, saints had the very important task of convincing people to change their religion. But this was not only a Christian phenomenon. . . . Both conquerors and conquered people influenced one another and both cultures are forever transformed. . . . This lesson learned is not only true in the United States, but everywhere that evangelization took place."

Following the Jesuit departure, Menéndez turned over missionary work in La Florida to the Franciscan Order, already well established in America. Two Franciscans who sailed with Christopher Columbus in 1493 were specifically charged by the Spanish Crown to bring Catholicism to the natives of the New World. Franciscans said the first New World Mass at Santo Domingo (Hispaniola) and brought the missionary vanguard to the newly discovered Caribbean islands. King Carlos V sent—at the request of Hernán Cortés—the first Franciscan friars to New Spain in May 1524 with a mandate to establish missions throughout the country.

Stephanie Righetti-Templer (chapter 4) discusses how these mendicant Franciscan friars—the so-called Twelve Apostles of Mexico—staged a colloquium with Aztec leaders to determine the meaning and effectiveness of this initial conversion effort. Although the Franciscan colloquium was certainly convened with the intention of convincing the Aztecs of the true faith, Righetti-Templer observes that the subsequent report "actually served as a catechism for generations to come and outlined the exemplary image of the 'good pagan' who, after all, can be converted by the arguments of the Franciscans and his own common sense."

Similarly, Constanza Ceruti (chapter 6) sees a similar "creative syncretism" in defining how the beliefs and rituals of Andean peoples were "rooted in ancestral views of mountain landscapes that were modified under the rule of the Incas, challenged during the Spanish conquest, and modeled by Catholic missionaries." Considerable tension characterized colonial interactions between Andean communities and most Catholic missionaries, particularly when traditional Andean rituals and "idolatry extirpation campaigns" were promulgated by Augustinian, Dominican, and Mercedarian Orders. By contrast, Ceruti points out the degree to which Franciscan spirituality and Andean religiosity

---

Martyrdom in Spanish Florida: Don Juan and the Guale Uprising of 1597, Anthropological Papers of the American Museum of Natural History 95 (New York: American Museum of Natural History, 2011), 30–34.

shared a common emphasis on simplicity and an extraordinary sensitivity toward the natural world. She concludes that the "active process of syncretism . . . has been ongoing in South America for five hundred years [and] the Franciscans should be acknowledged for building cultural bridges that are now available to native ritual experts and Catholic priests and missionaries, to work together for the well-being of the Quechua and Aymara peoples of the Andes."

In other words, by the time their friars arrived in La Florida, the Franciscan Order were amassing, quite literally, a world of missionary experience, building upon the early Aztec experience, extended by additional persuasive strategies developed in Peru and even the fourteenth-century Franciscan mission to the Mongols. As I argue in chapter 1, this emergent "theo-vision" stressed the value of flexibility, adaptability, and heterogeneity in their administration of Christian doctrine.[10]

Chapter 1 emphasizes how the missions of sixteenth- and seventeenth-century La Florida represented a unique blending of Franciscan and Mississippian spaces. By accepting conversion to Christianity and accepting resident Franciscans within their jurisdictions, native chiefs both retained the authority reckoned through ancient Mississippian hereditary bloodlines and also drew on the largesse of the Catholic Church and the Spanish crown. This is why, in part, Christian conversion in Spanish Florida stood in stark contrast to practices in both Alta California and the American Southwest. In the Franciscan missions of La Florida, a policy of *conquest by compact* ensured mutual defense and exclusive trade within the Spanish sphere of influence. In return, the indigenous leaders tendered a promise of obedience to the governor and a willingness to receive missionaries, undergo indoctrination, and become part of a mission province. The ritualized architecture of La Florida reflected the material consequences of a hybrid blend of Franciscan ideals played out in the context of continuing Mississippian beliefs and motivations.

Several other chapters add significantly to our understanding of how the Franciscan missions of La Florida operated. With respect to literacy, Mark Christensen (chapter 5) has already documented the importance of long-term writing systems among the Mayan society of the Yucatan peninsula. For centuries, the classic Maya employed a hieroglyph-based format, which continued into the colonial period, when the Maya perpetuated this tradition of literacy by switching to the Roman alphabet. Although classic Mayan hieroglyphs have been translated to a large degree, Christensen emphasizes the ambiguity that still surrounds the Mayan Christian copybooks of the nineteenth- and twentieth-century colonial period.

---

10. The term "theo-vision" derives from Fr. Joseph P. Chinnici, O.F.M., "Theo-history and the California Frontier," *Boletín: The Journal of the California Mission Studies Association* 21: 2 (2004): 55–63.

In a stunning pair of papers, Timothy Johnson (chapter 8) and George Aaron Broadwell (chapter 9) extend the discussion of colonial-period indigenous literacy to North America by tracking the extraordinary Franciscan commitment to literacy among the Mississippian populations of La Florida. Johnson and Broadwell focus particularly on the earliest indigenous writers in North America, including Francisco Pareja's *Confessionario* and other texts by "shadow authors." Broadwell argues that Pareja was not the sole author of these texts—multiple dialects are evident throughout the *Confessionario* and the Timucua passages contain multiple divergences from the Spanish that Pareja could not possibly have intended.

This unexpected orthographic diversity, Broadwell argues, demonstrates that early seventeenth-century Timucuan people themselves were writing their own language, literally becoming native co-authors to the *Confessionario*. Pareja apparently served more as an editor who assigned appropriate sections to qualified Timucuan converts for translation, then assembled and polished the final product for printing: "The Spanish intention in translating these documents in Timucua was to have native people read them in their own language. Thus Spanish mission education included training Timucuas to read and write. We do not know how extensive Timucua literacy was, but Native people wrote letters to each other and to Spanish authorities. . . . The seventeenth-century Timucua authors . . . were part of a larger literate population of Timucua people." Chapter 1 develops further the implications of such literacy across the Spanish Borderlands.

Four chapters address the persistence of indigenous identity within (and around) the seventeenth-century Franciscan missions of La Florida. Keith Ashley (chapter 7) emphasizes that "contrary to popular views, there was no such thing as a single historic Indian identity, even among the missionized Indians of La Florida." Mocama, Guale, and Timucua people not only maintained ongoing identities different from one another, and but also likely within individual communities as well, as reflected in the maintenance of council houses, agricultural organization, and overall mission community structure.

Elliot Blair (chapter 10) develops parallel themes by tracking various episodes of population relocation and aggregation that transpired throughout mission-period La Florida, variously at the behest of Franciscans, secular authorities, and indigenous leaders. The initial translocations often involved access to the trade goods critical to the conversion process. Following a half-century interval of relative peace, raiding and slaving parties attacked the Guale communities and mission towns, where unconverted refugees began to coalesce at the missions, and an infantry garrison was established on St. Catherines Island to protect them. Toward the end of the mission period, people moved to offset population loss due to epidemic disease and protection against slaving expeditions from the north.

Similarly, Richard Jefferies and Christopher Moore (chapter 11) detail the specific population aggregation and relocation with respect to mission settlements on Sapelo Island where, by the early seventeenth century, Mission San Joseph de Sapala, had emerged as a regional center, becoming the only Guale town on the island. But increasing frequency and intensity of Chichimeco attacks on Guale towns caused additional contraction of Guale settlements into communities crowded by migration from the mainland to the barrier islands. Although the four towns were aggregated on Sapelo Island, John Worth suggests they maintained politically, and likely spatially, discrete populations.[11]

Denise Bossy (chapter 12) explores persistence of indigenous identity in La Florida with specific reference to the Tamas who moved into the Apalachee mission province in the 1670s. The movement of hundreds of Tama Yamasees into Apalachee reflected an overarching strategy of splintering and living in dispersed, if interconnected, settlements. Employing a long-term Mississippian strategy of migrating, yet maintaining diplomatic networks with other communities in La Florida, the Yamasees generated a "web of communities" spread across the entire Southeast. Individual Yamasee settlements negotiated strategic alliances with outsiders, maintaining a flexibility that both protected traditional lineages and their leadership while simultaneously seeking new opportunities for the Yamasees in general.

Elaborating the concept of *spiritual diplomacy*, Bossy examines the degree to which the Mississippian polities across La Florida "sought out or welcomed Franciscan missionaries and expressed interest in Catholic rituals, stories, songs, and theological principles"—understood by both parties to be both religious and political. Whereas the Tama Yamasees could see definite spiritual, political, and practical advantages included in converting to Catholicism, the Spanish and Tama Yamasees often differed in what conversion and alliance actually entailed. Once the Spanish tried to claim spiritual and political dominion, many Tama Yamasees abandoned mission life altogether, following up ties in the overall Yamassee network to relocate to the north. Never severing their ties with the Spanish completely, some Tamas did return to La Florida in 1715 after the failure of their alliance with the British in South Carolina. Bossy emphasizes the unusual degree to which the Tama Yamasees engaged with the Franciscans, but also stresses how Tama-Spanish interactions fell into the overall pattern of Yamasee dispersal, migration, and alliance.

---

11. John Worth, *The Struggle for the Georgia Coast* (Tuscaloosa: University of Alabama Press, 2007), 12.

Franciscan Missions in the American Southwest

Franciscan missionization strategies in the American Southwest shifted markedly over the centuries, and so did Native American attitudes toward those missions (see chapter 1). During initial Franciscan missionary efforts in New Mexico (roughly 1610 and 1645), Franciscans treaded lightly when introducing churches into the Southwest to avoid triggering a backlash among the Pueblos. By choice and necessity, such Franciscan mission architecture reflected both architectural and technological realities; colonial officials even approved the use and construction of kiva-like structures within the missions. But by the early 1660s, Spanish colonial policy stiffened and Franciscans moved to suppress *katsina* activities, sometimes smashing "indigenous idols" and deliberately destroying kivas—policy shifts that contributed to the Pueblo Revolt of 1680.[12]

Evaluating the post-Revolt reconquest of the American Southwest, Jim Norris has argued that Franciscan authority broke down due to inadequate language training, their inability to adapt to the difficulties of life on the frontier, frequent transfers among the southwestern missions, and their overall willingness to accept indigenous Pueblo practices.[13]

Modern studies of the Pueblo Revolt and its aftermath are hampered because so many written records were destroyed in the 1680 takeover of Santa Fe, although colonial perspectives are extensively documented through the Spanish *autos* and Franciscan correspondence. The Pueblos left no written records and the Spanish records fail to report on nuances of social behavior among radically different Pueblo groups. After the Spanish reconquest of 1692, many Pueblos were interrogated about their pre-revolt relationships with the Franciscans and other Spaniards, but there remains the problem of listening to Pueblo voices as filtered through Spanish interlocutors and translators.

The Hopi History Project, a formal collaboration between the Hopi Tribe and the University of Arizona, is an attempt to redress this imbalance. In chapter 18, Thomas E. Sheridan and Stewart B. Koyiyumptewa address various narratives of conquest and resistance by comparing and contrasting available written accounts in the Spanish documents against contemporary Hopi oral histories of the same events. Sheridan and Koyiyumptewa emphasize how those oral traditions, passed down from generation to generation for more

---

12. David J. Weber, ed. *What Caused the Pueblo Revolt?* (Boston: Bedford/St. Martin's, 1999), v; see also Susan Deeds, "Pushing the Borders of Latin American Mission History," *Latin American Research Review* 39: 2 (June 2004): 211–220.

13. Jim Norris, *After The Year Eighty: The Demise of Franciscan Power in Spanish New Mexico* (Albuquerque: University of New Mexico Press in cooperation with the Academy of American Franciscan History, 2000).

than four centuries, narrate a pattern of missionary abuses, some generalized, others specific. They believe that such abuses drove the Hopis to rebellion and forced them to destroy one of their own communities, Awat'ovi, in 1700 to prevent the return of the missionaries.[14]

A number of indigenous archaeological programs have also attempted to redress the historical imbalance created by the heavy reliance on Spanish written documents to understand the Pueblo Revolt.[15] Matthew Liebmann (chapter 13) addresses the changing nature of Franciscan architecture in New Mexico's Jemez Valley. At first glance, the nature and architecture of the Franciscan churches might seem to reflect the changing nature of Franciscan power and influence during the seventeenth century: "Early on the explicit policy of the Order of Friars Minor was one of domination and control, and this is reflected in the architectural elements that mark these churches as different, ascendant, and authoritative. Following their widespread martyrdom and expulsion in the Pueblo Revolt of 1680, the Franciscans changed their policies to become more tolerant, assimilative, and less obtrusive."

Exploring an alternative perspective, Liebmann argues that the architectural patterns of these churches "seem counterintuitive." During the peak of Franciscan missionary power and authority in the early seventeenth century, when friars were experiencing their greatest successes, church architecture was militaristic and defensive, looking quite like medieval castles. But with the mid- and late-seventeenth-century crackdown on *katsina* activities—when tensions between the friars and neophytes accelerated—church architecture became less defensive and more smoothly integrated into the surrounding Pueblo communities.

Liebmann suggests that, with the construction of early seventeenth-century militaristic-style churches, "the Franciscans protested too much." In their attempt to dominate Pueblo life, the priests contributed to conditions that ultimately brought about their downfall in the Pueblo Revolt of 1680. "These churches shaped the events of the latter seventeenth century as much as they were shaped by the Pueblo people who built them."

---

14. See also Thomas E. Sheridan and Stewart B. Koyiyumptewa, "*Moquis, Kastiilam,* and the Trauma of History: Hopi Oral Traditions of Seventeenth-Century Franciscan Missionary Abuses," in *New Mexico and the Pimería Alta: The Colonial Period in the American Southwest*, eds. John G. Douglass and William M. Graves (Boulder: University of Colorado Press, 2017), 239–262.

15. See also Matthew Liebmann, *Revolt: An Archaeological History of Pueblo Resistance and Revitalization in 17th-Century New Mexico* (Tucson: University of Arizona Press, 2012); Mike V. Wilcox, *The Pueblo Revolt and the Mythology of Conquest: An Indigenous Archaeology of the Pueblo Revolt of 1680* (Berkeley: University of California Press, 2009); Robert W. Preucel, ed., *An Archaeology of the Pueblo Revolts* (Albuquerque: University of New Mexico Press, 2002).

The *Franciscan Florida in Pan-Borderlands Perspective* conference concluded with a roundtable discussion among four experienced missionaries, three Franciscan friars, and a Sister of the Blessed Sacrament who has spent a number of years working with Franciscan friars: Gilbert Schneider, O.F.M. (Pastor of Our Lady of the Blessed Sacrament Parish, Navajo Indian Reservation), Blane Grein, O.F.M. (Retired Pastor of Our Lady of Fatima Parish, Navajo Indian Reservation), Theresa Chato, S.B.S. (Navajo, Former Missionary on the Navajo Reservation), and Maynard Shurley, O.F.M. (Navajo, Case Worker with the Navajo AIDS Network). Sr. Chato and Br. Shurley are Navajo Indians (see Chapter 19).

Franciscan missionary efforts among the Navajo began in 1902 when Fr. Leopold Ostermann, O.F.M., was first sent out from the base at St. Michaels to begin ministering. With community and federal approval, land was set aside for a mission, and the first church and friary was built 1905–1906. When the growth required a new church, in the 1980s, both the Pope and American bishops encouraged clergy to embrace other cultures while they spread the gospel.

Much of this panel centered on the Franciscan church architecture at Our Lady of Fatima Catholic Church constructed in the Navajo community of Chinle (Arizona). Built in the shape of a Navajo hogan, the church at Chinle reflects this wish.[16] Although considerably larger than traditional Navajo dwellings, Our Lady of Fatima church is six-sided with an east-facing entrance, patterned after its smaller counterparts. The church contains a sky hole in the top center of the building and a 6-foot hole in the center of the floor to expose the sacred earth. The purpose is to remind Navajo people of the creation of the Earth (because in their story of creation, all forms of life came forth from such a hole).

The inside entry doors have Navajo images of the Yeis, the holy people of the Navajo (and a reminder to the people to walk a holy path). The baptismal font is situated directly beneath the stylized roof opening, atop the hole in the center of the floor. The four stages of life are shown in the baptismal bowl: A baby on a cradleboard, a young woman awaiting the future, a woman weaving a rug, and an elderly man watching his sheep. Paintings inside the church sanctuary depict the Stations of the Cross, hung adjacent to Navajo statues and figurines. The panel reiterates that integration of the two belief traditions makes it easier for parishioners to accept both without divisiveness.

These case studies dramatically underscore that throughout the several

---

16. Fr. Blane Grein and Charlotte J. Frisbie, *Blessings Brought, Blessings Found: Annunciation Mission, 1905–2005, Our Lady of Fatima Parish, Celebrating 100 Years of Franciscan and Church Presence in Chinle, Arizona* (Albuquerque: Cottonwood Printing, Inc., 2005).

centuries of Franciscan practice in the American Southwest, the friars enjoyed a considerable degree of social agency—in both constructing their generation of mission architecture and their preferences about how Catholic rituals should be conducted. The friars' plans for designing the new mission structures reflected personal experiences in the churches they attended as children, the colleges where they had studied, the other missions they might have visited, and sometimes, the explicit wishes of the indigenous congregations. Contemporary Franciscans use the term "inculturation" to describe their freedom to express their individuality in architecture.[17]

Franciscan Missions of Alta California

Although the latest of the Franciscan mission systems to be established along the Spanish Borderlands, Alta California was in many ways the most medieval in both design and execution—specifically with respect to corporal punishment, concern over false conversion and the sacrament of baptism, and church control of Indian affairs (particularly indigenous governance and literacy).

Fr. Junípero Serra's medieval Mallorcan missionary identity was grounded in the belief that gentile Native Californians, whom he viewed as children, sincerely wanted to be in the Franciscan missions.[18] Serra's personal devotion to the Immaculate Conception was reinforced by the mystical writings of María de Jesús de Ágreda, whose "bilocation" from her Spanish convent to the American Franciscan frontier permitted her to address Indians of the Borderlands in their own tongue, urging them to find friars who could convert them to the holy Catholic faith. In Serra's theo-vision, missionizing Alta California was facilitating what had already been preordained by others.

Serra attempted to protect his church and Spanish society from crimes, heresies, and false conversions. Despite formal complaints alleging harsh treatment of mission Indians in both the Sierra Gorda and Alta California missions, Serra was comfortable with floggings and armed patrols sent out to return fugitives as consistent with his evangelical beliefs in "paternalistic rigor." "Serra wanted absolute control over the missions and the Indians who lived in them . . . [he did not] want Indians to learn that the Spanish governor, not

---

17. I am grateful to Fr. Jack Clark Robinson O.F.M. for clarification on this point.

18. The term "medieval" is employed judiciously. James A. Sandos, *Converting California: Indians and Franciscans in the Missions* (New Haven, CT: Yale University Press, 2004). Sandos writes of Serra's "carefully cultivated medievalism" within a missionary philosophy rooted in "scholastic thought and medieval practice" (38, 69). This usage appropriately situates Serra as a pre-Enlightenment figure opposed to the Bourbon reforms and the people who brought them to California. In this sense, "medieval" should not be read as a synonym for intolerant, close-minded, and dismissive of alternative points of view.

the Franciscans, had ultimate civil and judiciary authority over them."[19] These beliefs distanced Junípero Serra and colleagues from the majority of Franciscans practicing elsewhere in the Spanish Borderlands.

Several chapters highlight new directions in the study of Alta California missions. Lee Panich (chapter 15) examines how indigenous Californians and Franciscans negotiated their divergent, but deeply held views about appropriate death, burial, and mourning practices. Prior research of these customs tends to downplay or ignore the presence of large colonial-era cemeteries, leaving invisible not just the tragic toll that the missions exacted on indigenous peoples in colonial California, but also the complex processes of resistance, negotiation, and accommodation that unfolded there.

The Franciscans, for their part, clearly intended to alter Native Californian beliefs and customs to conform with Roman Catholic practices. But the friars also appear to have accommodated certain indigenous customs regarding death and mourning. Evaluating evidence from Franciscan documents, early anthropological writings and mission-period archaeological deposits, Panich demonstrates that, whereas Franciscans varied somewhat in their attitudes toward the endurance of indigenous mortuary practices, neophytes in the missions of Alta California persistently honored their deceased in long-term, culturally appropriate ways.

Within the missions of Alta California, for instance, most neophytes were buried in the extended position in the *campo santo* adjacent to the mission church—fully consistent with long-standing Franciscan practice. But contrary to Franciscan customs, neophytes throughout Alta California clearly continued the precontact ritual practice of placing grave goods (such as beads and seeds) during burials at many missions. Individual Franciscans appear to have either tolerated the practice or at least turned a blind eye to its persistence. Native people also continued other aboriginal mourning practices, including wailing, bodily adornment, and dietary restrictions, eliciting variable reactions from the Franciscans.

Two additional papers address scalar issues in the study of Spanish missions of Alta California. Tsim Schneider (chapter 16) emphasizes the importance of addressing the larger landscapes that situated indigenous behaviors directed toward the missions, those places "where Indians—while also visiting and negotiating the challenges wrought by the missions—returned to seek refuge and reconvene in the company of people, places, and traditions."

Schneider emphasizes that both within mission compounds and away from them, neophytes were forced to recontextualize their own ways of know-

19. Steven W. Hackel, *Junípero Serra: California's Founding Father* (New York: Hill and Wang, 2013), 214. There is also the overarching issue of whether Serra's Alta California missions were actually missions (in the technical sense), or whether they had become *doctrinas* under the control of secular (rather than Franciscan) authority.

ing and of doing things. Many of the historical accounts of the San Francisco Bay missions, for instance, demonstrate that administrative passes were frequently issued to permit neophytes to conduct hunting and gathering far beyond the mission compounds. He stresses the importance of "repositioning" archaeological investigations to look for mission-era evidence within the indigenous hinterlands—far beyond the walls surrounding specific missions. Schneider concludes that "approved and illicit returns to old villages—like some shell mounds—facilitated reconnections to significant places, gathering areas, and sacred sites and, in doing so, these settings provided contexts for reinvesting in tradition and reordering shattered worlds."

Kent G. Lightfoot and Ann E. Danis (chapter 17) expand this theme to the international borders of Alta California, highlighting the importance of the broader Franciscan mission landscape as a place for understanding the nature of relationships and interactions that transpired among the friars, neophytes, and other colonial and native peoples. Like Schneider, Lightfoot and Danis emphasize the importance of conducting research beyond the immediate church-convento complex, setting out a four-zone "spatial-sonic model" for the Alta California missions: the mission quadrangle, proximal zone (within in the soundscape of the mission bell), the outlying hinterlands, and the interspaces of colonial regimes (international zones). This geosensory framework, they argue, can facilitate a clearer understanding of the social, political, and economic relationships that existed between people in these pluralistic colonies and in the outlying peripheries.

Unlike missions elsewhere along the Spanish Borderlands, the Franciscan missions of Alta California comprise a unique and integral part of contemporary local identity. This public appeal is not new. A 1984 poll, taken in the bicentennial of Serra's death, showed that two-thirds of Californians considered him the most important person in the history of the state.[20] Others point out that these very mission settlements devastated indigenous California populations. Some even see Serra's Franciscan missions as death camps ("Auschwitz with roses") reflecting an imperialist policy of genocide and ethnic cleansing.[21] The recent canonization of Saint Serra has attracted global attention to the life and works of Junípero Serra and the California missions.[22] The final two papers in this volume address rather different aspects regarding the public perception of Alta California's Franciscan missions.

---

20. Steven W. Hackel, *Junípero Serra,* cover flap.

21. Rupert Costo and Jeannette Henry Costo, eds. *The Missions of California: A Legacy of Genocide* (San Francisco: Indian Historian Press, 1987); James A. Sandos, "Junípero Serra's Canonization and the Historical Record," *American Historical Review* 93: 5 (December 1988): 1253–1269.

22. See also Jeffrey M. Burns, "Serra's Sainthood: A Cause for Healing or Controversy," *America Magazine* (August 31–September 7, 2015).

Franciscan mission history has long been a staple of the fourth-grade California curriculum.[23] In an essay directed largely toward California educators, Marie Christine Duggan (chapter 14) tackles the controversial issue of whether or not Spanish missions should be viewed as slave-holding plantations. Beginning with a quote from a website for teachers, Duggan emphasizes the degree to which mission Indians have been perceived, in the popular mind, as enslaved people. "By the 1990s," she believes, "few argued any more that mission Indian status was fundamentally distinct from slavery."

Duggan's essay concentrates on the 1769–1810 period, when California was part of the Spanish empire. From the perspective of socio-economic history, Duggan systematically deconstructs the slavery argument, concluding that slavery did not exist in Spanish California because the Franciscan mission—as opposed to a slave plantation—was designed for social control rather than profit. Although mission Indians, like slaves, had no effective recourse to the law, Indians were integral within the mission hierarchy, and mission Indians were the first line of defense to retrieve fugitives. She argues that Indians in California missions failed to produce much beyond their own subsistence because the Spanish did not invest in equipment capable of raising productivity or move Indians to the location of profitable tasks. Duggan concludes that, "whatever mission Indians were, they were not slaves—if only because Indians were not property and African slaves were."

Andrew Galvan and Vincent Medina (chapter 20) wrestle with a different problem. Both descend from a lineage of mission Indians that extends back centuries, perhaps millennia. Their ancestors were baptized, lived and died at Mission Dolores, where they were buried after funerals in the Old Mission Church. As the present Curator and Assistant Curator of Mission Dolores, respectively, Galvan and Medina struggle to find a way to effectively (and truthfully) recognize the 5700 Indian people in unmarked graves buried in the Mission Dolores Cemetery. They argue, in effect, that these mission Indians are largely written out of the overarching history of Franciscan missions in Alta California.

Nearly 70,000 indigenous Indians are buried within the mission cemeteries of Alta California and, except for the occasional wooden marker, explicit acknowledgment of these native peoples is nearly non-existent. But Galvan and Medina point out an exemplary exception—the memorial for the Native American Mission neophytes buried at Mission San Francisco de Solano (popularly known as Mission Sonoma). Bronze tablets in the street adjacent to the mission recount the 800+ names of the population of mission Indians buried there (as researched from the mission period death records), demonstrating

23. Quite literally, my fourth-grade exposure to Californian missions started my own career path in history and archaeology.

to visitors the multitude of native burials present: "Each person has a name, a story, and a presence."

Galvan and Medina are attempting to do something similarly respectful at the Mission Dolores cemetery: "Time and time again we emphasize at Mission Dolores that people came to the missions in order to survive and that the mission was built by Indians, and for Indians. We are determined to tell that neglected history."

* * * * *

With a cubist gaze in mind, a broad range of stakeholders participated in *Franciscan Florida in Pan-Borderlands Perspective.* The 2014 symposium and this resulting publication involved roughly three dozen individuals, representing a diverse range of backgrounds, indeed, with a number of overlapping identities. By profession, 15 are archaeologists and six are historians; the group also includes three Franciscans, one cultural anthropologist, one economist, one archivist, and one professor of religion. One-quarter of the participants are Native Americans. Two-thirds are faculty members at North American universities, three teach at European universities, and one is a professor in South America. Four are museum curators, two serve as tribal cultural preservation officers, and two are missionaries.

This multifocal group attempted to compare and contrast the Franciscan missions of Spanish Florida with those established in the American Southwest and Alta California, also drawing upon relevant case studies throughout the rest of the New World. The emphasis throughout remained diversity and difference—not only between the major components of the Spanish Borderlands, but among perceptions of various stake-holding communities. Rather than attempting to forge a normative consensus of "what the Franciscan missions were like," the explicit goal was to explore the diversity of practice across time and space.

Chapter 1
Social Agency in the Franciscan Mission Borderlands

David Hurst Thomas[1]

Herbert E. Bolton (1917) published his now-classic paper, "The Mission as a Frontier Institution in the Spanish-American Colonies," nearly a century ago.[2] In sharp contrast to prevailing perspectives of the day, Bolton argued, "in the English colonies the only good Indians were dead Indians. . . . [L]acking Spaniards to colonize the frontier, [Spain] would colonize it with the aborigines. . . . In the Spanish colonies it was thought worthwhile to improve the natives for this life as well as for the next." Bolton emphasized that "[t]he central interest around which the mission was built was the Indian. . . . [T]he Spanish sovereigns, from the outset, had three fundamental purposes. They desired to convert him, to civilize him, and to exploit him."[3]

Although generally dismissive of any meaningful indigenous role in their own missionization, Bolton recognized that the nature of the local Indians—ranging from "the more advanced tribes . . . [to] California, were of the most barbarous"—notably conditioned the configuration of the mission as a pioneering agency.[4] This chapter compares and contrasts the Franciscan mission complexes in Alta California, the American Southwest, and Spanish Florida, focusing particularly on the role of indigenous governance, the divergences in baptism and conversion, the nature of tribute, and the differential practice of literacy. In each case, it is clear that indigenous people and local culture exerted a major impact on the Franciscan missions established in their communities.[5]

---

1. I am grateful to Robert Bettinger, Lorann Pendleton Thomas, and Diana Rosenthal for assistance in preparing this manuscript.

2. Herbert E. Bolton, "The Mission as a Frontier Institution in the Spanish-American Colonies," *The American Historical Review* 23 (1917): 42–61.

3. Bolton, "The Mission as a Frontier Institution," 43, 52, 61.

4. Ibid., 61.

5. This essay expands on several topics recently developed in David Hurst Thomas's "The Life and Times of Junípero Serra: A Pan-Borderlands Perspective," *The Americas* 71 (2014): 185–225.

Deconstructing the Grand Narratives

Spanish Borderlands historiography has long been dominated by perspectives of informed (if occasionally heavy-handed) readings of textual evidence—in the process skewing colonial historiography toward a history of Europeans along the northern frontier of New Spain at the expense of the indigenous populations already living there. The resulting grand narratives variously define a Spanish colonial period that witnessed the nearly complete disruption of indigenous lifeways. Constructed centuries after the fact, such conventional wisdoms recreated colonial America mostly in terms of culture clash, encouraging investigators to dwell almost exclusively on themes of conquest, disease, assimilation, and loss—too often resulting in so-called "terminal narratives."[6]

"In the last decades of the twentieth century," observed David J. Weber, "American historians discovered America."[7] By this, he meant the colonial interval was being contextualized, that is, broadened to embrace new geographical areas and freed from over-simplistic models of dependency, assimilation, and cultural extinction. Susan Deeds writes of the so-called new mission history in Latin American studies,[8] taking note of similar trends in historiography that emphasize more detailed understandings of individual missionaries and the native peoples they encountered. These broad-based investigations have explored the differential impacts of conquest, the comparative demographies and epidemiologies, and the nature of shifting ethnicities and identities. This more enlightened discourse attempts to transcend the simplistic dualisms of dominant cores/dominated peripheries, active colonizers/passive colonized, and widespread misperception of indigenous survivals and extinctions.[9]

---

6. Michael V. Wilcox, *The Pueblo Revolt and the Mythology of Conquest: An Indigenous Archaeology of Contact* (Berkeley: University of California Press, 2009), 11–15.

7. Quoted in Juliana Barra and Edward Countryman, "Maps and Spaces, Paths to Connect and Lines to Divide," in *Contested Spaces in Early America*, eds. Juliana Barra and Edward Countryman (Philadelphia: University of Pennsylvania Press, 2014), 1; see also Neal Ferris, *The Archaeology of Native-Lived Colonialism: Challenging History in the Great Lakes* (Tucson: University of Arizona Press, 2009); Mark D. Mitchell and Laura L. Scheiber, "Crossing Divides: Archaeology as Long-term History," in *Across a Great Divide: Continuity and Change in Native North American Societies, 1400–1900*, eds. Laura L. Scheiber and Mark D. Mitchell (Tucson: University of Arizona Press, Amerind Studies in Archaeology, 2010), 1–22.

8. Susan Deeds, "Pushing the Borders of Latin American Mission History," *Latin American Research Review* 39 (2004): 211–220.

9. Matthew Liebmann and Melissa S. Murphy, "Rethinking the Archaeology of 'Rebels, Backsliders, and Idolaters,'" in *Enduring Conquests: Rethinking the Archaeology of Resistance to Spanish Colonialism in the Americas*, eds. Matthew Liebmann and Melissa S. Murphy (Santa Fe: School for Advanced Research Press, 2010), 3–18.

Indigenous Governance and Franciscan Missionizing Strategies

Franciscan custom employed long-established architectural conventions that played out, in one form or another, in the missions of the Spanish Borderlands. The entire mission complex—not just the church and friary, but also the offices, storerooms, workshops, sheds, barns, pens, herds, and fields—became a virtually self-contained community. This utopian plan reflected deliberate designs derived from more than eight hundred years of monastic tradition and four centuries of Franciscan development. But within this general plan resides a remarkable flexibility concerning local circumstances. Modern Franciscan friars sometimes speak of their self-perception as "amiable anarchists," willing to modify established rules and protocols to achieve the ultimate goal of salvation. Perhaps reflecting this contemporary sense of "inculturation," the Franciscan plan varied considerably across medieval Europe and in Renaissance Mexico, where individual friars traveling into the Spanish Borderlands carried with them accumulated monastic experiences.[10] Individual Franciscan friars were empowered with a degree of social agency in constructing their generation of mission architecture and the way in which the Catholic rituals would be conducted—all based on personal experience in the churches attended as a child, the mission colleges, and the other missions visited, all of which molded idealized plans in the minds of friars that influenced what was built at the new missions.

Franciscans encountered diverse Native American landscapes with contrasting institutional behaviors ranging from extreme organizational authority to striking degrees of individual autonomy. It is difficult to overemphasize the deep contrasts in decision making and social agency that characterized the Franciscan experiences in Alta California, the Pueblo Southwest, and the Mississippian Southeast.

Engaging the Mississippian Southeast

Spanish explorers entering the deep American South encountered indigenous hierarchical and authoritarian structures not so different from their own, with social status defined along a complex system of racial gradients and classifications. Mississippian governance maintained relatively short-term, brittle federations of chiefdoms characterized by long-distance trade networks and centralized leadership.[11] Centuries before these Europeans arrived, Mississip-

10. Contemporary Franciscan usage of "amiable anarchists" and "inculturation" is discussed in Thomas, "The Life and Times of Junípero Serra," 223.

11. John Worth, "Spanish Missions and the Persistence of Chiefly Power," in *The Transformation of the Southeastern Indians, 1540–1760,* eds. Robbie Ethridge and Charles

pian societies defined their own hereditary birthrights grounded in genealogical descent from a single noble ancestor. The privileged chiefly class was accorded considerable status and wealth. Mississippian subordinates supplied the labor and material resources underwriting this hereditary inequality, sometimes risking their lives in chiefly warfare.[12] The Spanish newcomers insisted on direct negotiations with paramounts and the subordinates were expected to fall into line. Individual chiefdoms identified closely with their *micos* and were protective of chiefly authority. When disputes arose between towns and lineages, they sometimes split to acquire distinctive social identities, each maintaining its own ceremonial center and suite of ritual practices.

The economy of seventeenth-century Spanish Florida defined an exchange network, with indigenous populations channeling maize and labor into colonial St. Augustine. Several Timucua, Mocama, and Guale caciques pledged allegiance and obedience to Spanish officials, but others refused to do so. Those paramounts siding with the Spanish not only enjoyed a powerful military ally, but they also gained access to new tools and technologies.[13]

Ethnohistorian and archaeologist John Worth compares the roles of Franciscan friars stationed in La Florida to modern Peace Corps workers functioning among indigenous communities as cultural brokers and agents of collaborative change. To do this, the southeastern missions deliberately embodied elements of local Mississippian architecture in the form of council houses capable of sheltering thousands inside; several missions also sported ball courts, where *pelota* games pitted traditional rivals in sometimes-violent combat. The ritualized architecture of La Florida thus reflected the material consequences of a hybrid blend of Franciscan ideals played out in the context of continuing Mississippian beliefs and motivations.

Hudson (Jackson: University Press of Mississippi, 2002): 39–64; Worth, "Catalysts of Assimilation: The Role of Franciscan Missionaries in the Colonial System of Spanish Florida," in *From La Florida to La California: The Genesis and Realization of Franciscan Evangelization in the Spanish Borderlands*, eds. Timothy J. Johnson and Gert Melville (Berkeley: Academy of American Franciscan History, 2013), 131–142; Worth, "Inventing Florida: Constructing a Colonial Society in an Indigenous Landscape," in *Native and Spanish New Worlds: Sixteenth-Century Entradas in the American Southwest and Southeast*, eds. Clay Mathers, Jeffrey M. Mitchem, and Charles M. Haecker (Tucson, University of Arizona Press, 2013), 198–204.

12. David Hurst Thomas, "Honor and Hierarchies: Long-term Trajectory in the Pueblo and Mississippian Worlds," in *Native and Spanish New Worlds: Sixteenth-Century Entradas in the American Southwest and Southeast*, eds. Clay Mathers, Jeffrey M. Mitchem, and Charles M. Haecker (Tucson: University of Arizona Press, 2013), 251–273.

13. David Hurst Thomas, "War and Peace on the Franciscan Frontier," in *From La Florida to La California: Franciscan Evangelization in the Spanish Borderlands*, eds. Timothy J. Johnson and Gert Melville (Berkeley, CA: The Academy of American Franciscan History, 2013), 105–130.

Engaging the Pueblo Southwest

Initial Franciscan prospects for missionization in the Southwest were optimistic because the local Indians seemed to dwell in permanent towns. The Spanish characterized both the buildings and the people who lived there as *los pueblos*, to distinguish them from the more mobile Apache and Navajos. But Hispano settlers soon realized that Pueblo settlements were actually quite fluid, with households frequently relocating among villages' annual cycles of seasonal dispersal and aggregation. Not only did Franciscans prefer full-time sedentary populations, they were likewise confounded by the nature of decision making and governance within Pueblo society. Although numerous egalitarian ideologies existed in Pueblo life, these polities were not egalitarian in practice. Status differences (especially those between the ceremonially rich and ceremonially poor) have deep roots in Pueblo societies organized on theocratic principles. "To the extent that pueblos are governed at all, they are governed by priests—members of secret societies who exercise authority over ritual and, in many communities, secular aspects of life."[14]

Pueblo leadership and decision making involved differential access to esoteric knowledge and ceremonial objects, social duties and family/lineage alignments, and inequities in wealth and power. Hierarchies of priests belonging to secret sodalities exercised considerable authority over ritual, political, and often-mundane matters. A sense of endemic, inherent opposition to indigenous authorities characterized many Pueblo communities throughout the mission period.[15] For Spanish newcomers, such embedded decision making posed endless problems as native communities negotiated their new colonial world, which was structured to foster factionalism and resistance to top-down authority figures (including members of the Franciscan order). Because Pueblo power and authority were exercised by groups rather than individuals, great confusion arose when civil and church authorities appointed new leaders. "Did [the Spanish] know that the individuals they installed in new leadership roles would be answerable to war captains who were the instruments of the secret religious hierarchy?"[16]

---

14. John A. Ware, *A Pueblo Social History: Kinship, Sodality, and Community in the Northern Southwest* (Santa Fe, NM: School for Advanced Research, 2014), 40–41.

15. A case can be made that Pueblo opposition to hierarchical power structures can be traced back a millennium to a time when the ancient Chacoan Southwest fell apart because Pueblo people deliberately rejected social inequities, heritable leadership, and complex tribute networks. If so, then the post–A.D. 1300 migrations that characterized the Pueblo Southwest may represent a "devolution" from politically complex structures into more corporate "syncretic" forms that characterize historic and modern Pueblos; see Thomas, "War and Peace," 128, and the references cited therein.

16. Ware, *A Pueblo Social History*, 181.

Because Franciscans erected their missions along the margins of existing Pueblo villages, they were inevitably drawn into the day-to-day realities of indigenous factionalism. So situated, many friars working among the Pueblos found it necessary and appropriate to accommodate local indigenous customs in a way never experienced in places like Alta California.[17] Pueblo communities typically developed pro- and anti-Franciscan factions, with the resulting conflicts reflecting a pervasive social agency that privileged decisions by factions of actors who were simultaneously operating within contemporary colonial contexts, yet making critical decisions for their own future. While such social agency did sometimes embrace innovation and change, there were endless options to reiterate (in whole or in part) what had been done in the past. Friars working in New Mexico soon realized that the inherently segmented sociopolitical structure of the Pueblos both embraced and resisted the sweeping changes brought about by colonial authority.

The realities of the Pueblo Southwest ensured that many local practices persisted, sometimes virtually unaltered from pre-Contact times. Although precise histories of each southwestern mission community are difficult to discern, it is clear that some indigenous Pueblo practices had close similarities and parallels to the Catholic rites introduced by Franciscans during colonial times.[18] Franciscan Catholicism was seen among some Pueblos as a counterbalance to the inequities of the indigenous *katsina* (often transcribed as *kachina)* religion, likely perceived as an add-on "to an already rich and complex ceremonial system."[19]

Katsina ritualism is "an inclusive sodality" present in virtually all contemporary Pueblo societies and, today, most evident at the western Pueblos of Hopi, Zuni, and Acoma.[20] The rituals predominantly enhance masculine ritual power, and provisions were usually made to include young males in the ritual organization, an inclusion formalized at puberty. Disaffected young single males (especially those accorded lower rank and status than the headmen of the medicine societies, sodalities, and *katsina* societies) formed the core of neophyte Franciscan enlistees throughout several Pueblo communities.[21]

---

17. Jim Norris, *After the Year Eighty: The Demise of Franciscan Power in Spanish New Mexico* (Albuquerque: University of New Mexico Press in cooperation with the Academy of American Franciscan History, 2000), chapter 5.

18. William L. Merrill, "Indigenous Societies, Missions, and the Colonial System in Northern New Spain," in *The Arts of the Missions of Northern New Spain, 1600–1821*, eds. Clara Bargellini and Michael K. Komanecky (Mexico: Antiguo Colegio de San Ildefonso, 2009), 122–153.

19. Carroll L. Riley, *The Kachina and the Cross: Indians and Spaniards in the Early Southwest* (Salt Lake City: University of Utah Press, 1999), 21–65; see also John A. Ware, *A Pueblo Social History.*

20. Ware, *A Pueblo Social History,* 165.

21. James F. Brooks, "Women, Men, and Cycles of Evangelism in the Southwestern Borderlands, A.D. 750–1750," *American Historical Review* 118 (2013): 738–764.

Catholic saints and Pueblo *katsinas* are "reasonably compatible concepts and the material benefits that came with the new religion . . . were likely welcomed by Pueblo ceremonialists and commoners alike."[22] But problems arose when the missionaries punished Pueblos for taking part in millennia-old marriage practices. After a few decades, Spanish forces raided kivas, destroying altars and *katsina* icons. These disjunctions were confusing to Pueblos and ultimately contributed to the Pueblo Revolt of 1680.[23]

Women were prohibited from acquiring *katsina* knowledge among the eastern Pueblos, at Zuni, and to some degree at Hopi. The Pueblo Revolt further reflected the chasms separating traditionalists from those drawn to Catholicism, pulling not only on religious sympathies but also cross-cutting longstanding power relations in Pueblo society.[24] It is a small wonder that many Pueblo women were attracted to a Franciscan catechism that not only emphasized the importance of the Virgin Mary and Guadalupe, but honored the lives and suffering of other female saints as well.[25] During the post-Revolt era in the Rio Grande area, there are repeated representations of the Virgin Mary in rock art associated with refugee Pueblos.[26]

Engaging Alta California

Franciscans faced other challenges in Alta California, where maize cultivation never took hold and acorn harvesting drove indigenous subsistence instead. This remarkably productive and reliable resource base made territorial defense worthwhile, and it is often forgotten that, at the time of European contact, Alta California was the most densely populated aboriginal landscape in North America, with a bewilderingly rich and diverse mix of languages, cultures, and environmental adaptations.

Robert Bettinger has recently characterized the sociopolitical organization of indigenous Alta California as "orderly anarchy"—the term *anarchy* referring to "an absence of leaders" (rather than implying any kind of chaos or disorder).[27]

22. Ware, *A Pueblo Social History*, 181.

23. Thomas, "War and Peace on the Franciscan Frontier."

24. Brooks, "Women, Men, and Cycles," 756.

25. Repeated representations of the Virgin Mary in rock art are associated with refugee Pueblos dating from the post-Revolt era in the Rio Grande area. Matthew J. Liebmann, "Signs of Power and Resistance: The (Re)Creation of Christian Imagery and Identities in the Pueblo Revolt Era," in *Archaeologies of the Pueblo Revolt*, ed. R.W. Preucel (Albuquerque: University of New Mexico Press, 2002), 132–144; Matthew J. Liebmann, *Revolt: An Archaeological History of Pueblo Resistance and Revitalization in 17th-Century New Mexico* (Tucson: University of Arizona Press, 2012), 136–142.

26. Liebmann, *Revolt,* 136–142.

27. Robert L. Bettinger, *Sociopolitical Evolution in Aboriginal California: The Rise of Orderly Anarchy* (Berkeley: University of California Press, 2014).

Despite remarkably high population densities, most California Indians lived in very small sociopolitical groups—patrilineal and landholding, frequently coalescing for mutual protection into larger organizations known as *tribelets.* But because stored food was regarded as private property (with key resource tracts owned by individual families), the power of the tribelets and their chiefs was severely limited. As increasing population size limited available opportunities for movement and alliance making, individual- and family-level organization strengthened among California Indians. In effect, argues Bettinger, the power and grip of tribelet organization was seriously constrained in favor of small, "inward-looking" groups who devised their own ingenious solutions to the challenges of California's environmental, technological, and social obstacles to resource intensification.

The "orderly anarchy" of indigenous Alta California was strangely well suited to the "amiable anarchy" of Franciscan missionization, as imported by Fr. Junípero Serra and his colleagues.[28] From his earliest Franciscan training in Mallorca, Fr. Serra was a firm believer in the experiences of María de Jesús de Ágreda (1602–1665). María de Ágreda wrote in *The Mystical City of God* about her personal audience with the Virgin Mary, who revealed the true nature of heaven and confirmed her own Immaculate Conception. Although never leaving her convent in Spain, Sor María had "bilocated" to America by flying on the wings of Saint Michael and Saint Francis, sometimes making multiple trips in a single day. Protected by angels and dressed as a friar, María de Ágreda spoke to the Indians in their own language, urging them to seek out a Franciscan to perform their baptisms. Serra thought he was that Franciscan and fully expected to be greeted as such in America. Profoundly influenced by *The Mystical City of God*, Serra took a copy to the Sierra Gorda in Mexico, and his companion Francisco Palóu carried one to Alta California.[29]

Serra's diary of his journey to Alta California reiterates his belief that the bilocating María de Ágreda had preceded him (although he did not know exactly where), and he thought that "at the mere sight of the Franciscans, the

28. There is a certain irony evident in casting Fr. Serra as an "amiable anarchist" who missionized among the "orderly anarchists." As noted, contemporary Franciscans indeed do stress their willingness to be flexible in the specifics to ensure their ultimate objective, that of saving souls. While this was certainly true of Serra to some degree, one must likewise take into account Fr. Junípero Serra's late-medieval Mallorcan mindset, his "theo-vision." An amiable anarchist in some respects, Serra was also among the most conservative, least flexible friars practicing in the Spanish Borderlands; see the discussions and references in Steven W. Hackel, *Junípero Serra: California's Founding Father* (New York: Hill and Wang, 2013), 1–28, and Thomas, "Life and Times," 186–190, 211–216.

29. Maynard Geiger, *The Life and Times of Fray Junípero Serra, O.F.M. or, The Man Who Never Turned Back, 1713–1784, a Biography* (Washington, D.C.: Academy of American Franciscan History, 1959), 11–115; James A. Sandos, *Converting California: Indians and Franciscans in the Missions* (New Haven, CT: Yale University Press, 2004), 191, no. 12.

'gentiles' would be converted to 'the holy Catholic' faith."[30] Convinced that Sor María had prepared the Indians to seek salvation, paving the path for him to spread Christianity, Serra pursued a *reducción* settlement strategy grounded in convincing gentiles to abandon their natal villages for life in Spanish-style mission complexes. In other words, Serra's remarkably successful, bottom-up missionizing philosophy played directly upon the innate "anarchical" tendencies of Native Californians, urging them to make decisions grounded in individual and family considerations rather than the wishes of the tribelets and their chiefs.

Not surprisingly, Serra found himself at odds with Spanish military authorities in Alta California who insisted on local elections to facilitate Indian *alcaldes* instituting Hispanic-style politics locally. Serra strenuously opposed this plan, insisting instead upon "absolute control over the missions and the Indians who live in them. . . . [He did not] want Indians to learn that the Spanish governor, not the Franciscans, had ultimate civil and judiciary authority over them."[31] Serra also wanted to ensure that the elected Indian officials remained subject to corporal punishment in the event they needed correction by the padres.

Divergences in Conversion and Baptism

The sacrament of baptism was pivotal in the Franciscan approach to conversion, given friars' belief that once a child was conceived and born into the world, the rebirth in Christ and the life of the spirit could be achieved through baptism. Demonstrating the primacy of the spirit over the flesh, this act of spiritual regeneration could rival (and even surpass) the importance of physical generation.

Baptism as a universal sacrament came into play in rather different ways across the Spanish Borderlands. In Alta California, Serra and his colleagues frequently baptized Indians at the initial encounter—drawing the indigenous away from their home villages into the new mission complexes. Not only were the Franciscans firm in their belief that María de Ágreda already paved the way for those seeking salvation, but the friars needed a Christian labor force to build the mission structures and farm the fields to feed the flock.

Considerable debate persists about whether Serra literally equated baptism with conversion to Catholicism (thereby implying a tacit pledge to reject all non-Christian beliefs as false).[32] Franciscans in Alta California perceived them-

---

30. Hackel, *Junípero Serra: California's Founding Father* (New York: Hill and Wang, 2013), 158.

31. Ibid., 214.

32. Sandos, *Converting California*, xiv–xv; Steven W. Hackel, "Junípero Serra's California Sacramental Community," in *"To Toil in that Vineyard of the Lord": Contemporary Scholarship on Junípero Serra*, eds. Rose Marie Beebe and Robert M. Senkewicz (Berkeley: Academy of American Franciscan History, 2010), 75–94.

selves as parents or guardians of baptized Indians, who they regarded as children. If the willingness to be baptized also signaled a neophyte's acceptance of Roman Catholic principles, then the friars would have seen disobedience and backsliding among these "disobedient children" as behaviors requiring correction by parental physical discipline, including the use of whips, shackles, and imprisonment in stocks. James Sandos describes this practice in Alta California as "spiritual debt peonage."[33] Other scholars question this interpretation, arguing instead that conversion among California Indians took much longer, with the friars only gradually replacing native beliefs with Catholic ritual, practice, and, eventually, belief in Christianity.[34] So viewed, although corporal punishment was certainly employed, this was not because the neophytes had converted and were backsliding (hence breaking their vows), but rather because, at baptism, they were not fully pledged to live as Christians, and bad behavior imperiled their souls.[35]

However interpreted, the Alta California approach to baptism and physical discipline contrasts with sixteenth- and seventeenth-century practices elsewhere in the Spanish Borderlands, where Franciscans permitted indigenous people "to live autonomously beyond the bounds of empire."[36] Across the American Southwest, for instance, the more enthusiastic "wet-heads" (the Pueblo term for baptized Christians) rapidly allied themselves with the Franciscans, sometimes placing crosses and deerskin paintings in public spaces to reinforce their own baptism. But at the same time, other Pueblos displayed a decided "coolness" toward such outward signs of conversion, expressing some confusion as to whether baptism was somehow related to labor drafts and death.[37]

Franciscans working in the southwestern missions attempted to allay some of this confusion and concern over conversion by incorporating traditional

---

33. James A. Sandos, "Junípero Serra's Canonization and the Historical Record," *American Historical Review* 93 (1988): 1253–1269; Sandos, *Converting California*, xv, 108.

34. See also Hackel, *Children of Coyote, Missionaries of Saint Francis: Indian–Spanish Relations in Colonial California, 1769–1850* (Chapel Hill: University of North Carolina Press, 2005), 228–271, and Hackel, *Junípero Serra,* 220–223.

35. For another view of baptism, conversion, and corporal punishment, see Joseph P. Chinnici, O.F.M., "Theo-history and the California Frontier," *Boletín: The Journal of the California Missions Studies Association* 21 (2004): 55–62.

36. David J. Weber, "Bourbons and Bárbaros: Center and Periphery in the Reshaping of Spanish Indian Policy," in *Negotiated Empires: Centers and Peripheries in the Americas, 1500–1820*, eds. Christine Daniels and Michael V. Kennedy (New York: Routledge, 2002), 79–103; Sandos, *Converting California*, xiv–xv; Hackel, "Junípero Serra's California Sacramental Community," 75–93.

37. Ramón A. Gutiérrez, *When Jesus Came, the Corn Mothers Went Away: Marriage, Sexuality, and Power in New Mexico, 1500–1846* (Stanford, CA: Stanford University Press, 1991), 65, 241; see also Riley, *The Kachina and the Cross*, 124–125; Wilcox, *The Pueblo Revolt*, 138–140, 208.

Pueblo architecture into the new missions. Coronado's 1540 *entrada* into the American Southwest encountered unique "ritually charged" underground religious chambers they called *estufas* (better known today as *kivas*). These underground chambers served multiple functions in the Pueblo world—not only venues for *katsina* dance and ritual, but also for clan and social group meetings. Although multiple historical sources suggest that missionary pressure forced the kivas to be abandoned from 1630 to 1680, Hopi oral tradition maintains that kivas were used throughout this period.[38] Early in the Franciscan missionary effort in New Mexico (between about 1610 and 1645), colonial officials approved the use and construction of kiva-like structures within the missions. These so-called "*convento kivas*" may have provided familiar-yet-Franciscan spaces where children and others could be taught the basics of Christianity, the catechism, and Spanish culture. Historian David Weber supported this view, pointing out that (at least during the early seventeenth century) Franciscans introduced churches into the Southwest only "gingerly" to avoid triggering a backlash among the Pueblos, who vastly outnumbered the newcomers, thereby demonstrating "restraint and flexibility that had long European antecedents."[39] Convento kivas would seem to rank among the many "creative architectural provisions" employed by Franciscans throughout the New World, including the construction of sixteenth-century "Franciscan mosques" in Mexico.[40]

In the early missions of New Mexico, then, Franciscans pursued a plan of "careful integration" when establishing new mission churches. This practice tolerated (perhaps even encouraged) the persistence of certain indigenous religious practices, but convento kivas seem to have gone out of use about 1645, in part because the missions of New Mexico were outgrowing their initial phase of proselytization. Spanish colonial policy stiffened further in the early 1660s when Franciscans moved to suppress *katsina* activities at Isleta and Pecos, where indigenous idols were smashed and kivas deliberately destroyed—surely contributing to the animosities that surfaced in the Pueblo Revolt of 1680. During the post-Revolt era, Franciscan authority broke down due to inadequate language training, their inability to adapt to the difficulties of life on the frontier, frequent transfers among the southwestern missions, and their overall willingness to accept traditional Pueblo practices.[41]

---

38. Watson Smith, "Prehistoric Kivas of Antelope Mesa, Northeastern Arizona," *Papers of the Peabody Museum of American Archaeology and Ethnology* 39 (1972), 75–76; Harold Courlander, *The Fourth World of the Hopis* (Albuquerque: University of New Mexico Press, 1971), 160.

39. Weber, *The Spanish Frontier*, 10–11.

40. James E. Ivey, "Convento Kivas in the Missions of New Mexico," *New Mexico Historical Review* 73 (1998): 121–152.

41. David J. Weber, ed., *What Caused the Pueblo Revolt?* (Boston: Bedford/St. Martin's, 1999), v; see also Morris, *After the Year Eighty*; see also Deeds, "Pushing the Borders," 215.

In stark contrast to both Alta California and the American Southwest, Christian conversion in Spanish Florida proceeded as *conquest by compact*, in which "promises of mutual defense and exclusive trade [produced] a Spanish sphere of influence; a promise of obedience to the king in the person of his appointed governor, extending the king's realms and bringing a new district into the ecumene; and a promise to receive missionaries, undergo indoctrination, and become part of a mission province."[42]

Explicitly enmeshing themselves within the top-down dynamics of stratified Mississippian society, friars working among the Timucua, Guale, and Apalachee concentrated initially on converting the hereditary caciques to Christianity. Any cacique requesting baptism announced his willingness to accept the law of God and practice of Christian worship by raising a cross in the town plaza—thereby symbolically granting Franciscans permission to build churches and convert the entire community, with the blessing of the paramount. By doing so, Franciscan missionaries working in La Florida did so squarely within the context of chiefly authority.[43] Bushnell emphasizes that in Florida "conversion was unquestionably voluntary, for whole regions rejected the gift of the gospel and membership in the republic of Indians."[44]

The Multiple Roles of Tribute

Tribute in the Alta California missions was primarily in the form of indigenous labor, part of a system variously characterized as communal, slavery, and/or feudal.[45] Friars organized neophytes by occupation, roughly rank-ordered from skilled artisans to fishermen, stockmen, and horticulturalists, followed by laborers and field hands. Neophytes were to be kept busy, not only for the fruits of their labor, but also to ward off idleness and to keep

42. All quotes in this paragraph derive from Amy Turner Bushnell, "'These people are not conquered like those of New Spain': Florida's Reciprocal Colonial Compact," in "500 Years of Florida History—The Seventeenth Century," ed. Jane Landers, special issue of the *Florida Historical Quarterly* 92 (2014): 530.

43. By contrast, any cacique rising in rebellion against Spanish authority (church and state being defined as inseparable) was judged to be guilty of breach of contract. "He could be deposed, stripped of his inherited privileges, and sent into exile. To be restored, he must undergo ritual humiliation. . . . [T]hose who followed his lead forfeited the status of Christians conquered by the gospel and entered the ranks of nations conquered by the sword, subject to forced labor." Turner Bushnell, "These people are not conquered," 531.

44. Ibid. See also Turner Bushnell, "Ruling the Republic of Indians in Seventeenth-Century Florida," in *Powhatan's Mantle: Indians in the Colonial Southeast*, eds. Gregory A. Waselkov, Peter H. Wood, and Tom Hadley (Lincoln: University of Nebraska Press, 2006), 195–213.

45. Kent G. Lightfoot, *Indians, Missionaries, and Merchants: The Legacy of Colonial Encounters on the California Frontiers* (Berkeley: University of California Press, 2005), 66–68.

them from returning to the woods.[46] As presidios and Pueblos became increasingly dependent on the missions for food, labor demands increased significantly after 1810. The hide and tallow industries came to dominate the economic activities of the missions during the Mexican period (post-1821), coupled with a dramatic decline in the overall number of neophytes living in the missions.

The tribute system imposed in the American Southwest required that Pueblo people assume the burden of producing foodstuffs and textiles for the newcomers. *Encomenderos* required tribute levels of one *fanega* of maize (about 100 pounds) twice annually from each Pueblo household, plus 5.6 square feet of cotton textiles.[47] Seasonal abundance of maize stores were often misread by the Spanish as "surplus," whereas the Pueblos saw these caches as insurance policies against the inevitable dry and lean years of the southwestern landscape.[48] To the Spanish, such tribute was an expected means of colonial exchange, but for the Pueblos, there was an expectation of reciprocity, leading to deep-seated mistrust and resentment—two very different perceptions of the same tribute system. The situation was exacerbated by constant conflict between secular authorities and missionaries over Pueblo labor for construction of churches, conventos, fields, ranches, and gardens.[49]

The role and significance of tribute played out quite differently in the missions of Spanish Florida, where coastal Mississippian people had paid and received tribute for centuries. Traditional caciques, deliberately empowered within the mission system, had long held important offices in local political and religious hierarchies, with tangible social, political, and economic advantages. While inherited status was a necessary condition for leadership, *micos* found themselves constantly required to shore up their power base through effective manipulation of ritual, access to scarce trade items, and hospitality. These paramounts had long maintained large-scale, regional systems of tribute, traveling extensively to conduct war, diplomacy, ritual, and to participate in complex, rank-enhancing marriage alliances.

The trappings of chiefly office included clothing, adornment, and regalia—long staples in the pre-Columbian Mississippian world.[50] The preexisting emphasis on appropriate chiefly attire and the exchange of exotic luxury items such as conch shell, polished greenstone, high-quality chert, and

---

46. Sandos, *Converting California*, 9–10, 101; Hackel, *Junípero Serra*, 164–166.

47. Wilcox, *The Pueblo Revolt*, 137.

48. Joe S. Sando, "The Pueblo Revolt" in *Po'pay: Leader of the First American Revolution*, eds. Joe S. Sando and Herman Agoyo (Santa Fe: Clear Light, 2005), 5–53.

49. David J. Weber, ed., *What Caused the Pueblo Revolt of 1680?* (Boston: Bedford/St. Martin's, 1999), 5.

50. John E. Worth, *The Timucuan Chiefdoms of Spanish Florida, Volume 1: Assimilation* (Gainesville: University Press of Florida, 1998), 12–13.

native copper were particularly important between neighboring chiefdoms in transactions that were more symbolic than economic.

The colonial system in Spanish Florida reinforced such long-standing Mississippian power structures by channeling access to indigenous land and labor through hereditary chiefs. By participating in the external colonial Spanish markets, traditional Guale leaders transformed agricultural surpluses, land, and labor—all commodities under their control—into military backing and, perhaps more importantly, the symbolically charged Spanish goods including cloth, tools, and beads. In this way, the caciques positioned themselves to receive tribute from both the Spaniards and their own people.

The importance of material goods and native labor thus carried over from pre-Contact to colonial times, with selected *micos* now enjoying exclusive access to new tribute and prestige items to enhance their chiefly authority.[51] Early in the colonial era, gifts to caciques included fine woolen friar's cloth, Asian cotton cloth, pressed linen, stockings, silk buttons and braids, Chinese taffeta, and even firearms such as arquebuses (despite Spanish colonial prohibitions elsewhere).[52] Fray Francisco de Ávila was taken captive during the Guale uprising of 1597; his ransom consisted (almost entirely) of ritually charged items of symbolic tribute: six knives with yellow handles, three bundles of glass beads, six hatchets, one dozen iron axes, four muskets, and a single white blanket.[53] In the 1670s, Governor Hita Salazar reported that the Indians preferred to be paid weekly with items of European manufacture, which he judged to have curiously low monetary value—hawks bells in two sizes, knives with black or white hafts, blue or multicolored beads, sheet brass, lengths of blue or red cloth, razors, and scissors.[54]

Whereas some Spanish leaders scoffed at these tribute items as simply trifles and trinkets being circulated among naïve indigenous leaders, to the Mississippian *micos* and their subordinates, these "trinkets" were not merely tokens of Spanish largesse. In many ways, such gifts "represented the 'cement' for the colonial system, providing local and regional caciques with visible symbols of chiefly rank and status by way of access to exotic Spanish clothing, food, and other items. Chiefs who failed to return from St. Augustine with

51. Joseph M. Hall, Jr., *Zamumo's Gifts: Indian–European Exchange in the Colonial Southwest* (Pittsburgh: University of Pennsylvania Press, 2000); J. Michael Francis and Kathleen M. Kole, *Murder and Martyrdom in Spanish Florida: Don Juan and the Guale Uprising of 1597*, Anthropological Papers of the American Museum of Natural History 95 (New York: American Museum of Natural History, 2011), 91.

52. Worth, *The Timucuan Chiefdoms*, 24.

53. Francis and Kole, *Murder and Martyrdom*, table 6.

54. Amy Turner Bushnell, *Situado and Sabana: Spain's Support System for the Presidio and Mission Provinces of Florida*, Anthropological Papers of the American Museum of Natural History 74 (New York: American Museum of Natural History, 1994), 122.

such gifts might have been far less likely to overlook the more insidious consequences of missionization."[55]

In effect, the knives with special handles, the lengths of blue and red cloth, and multicolored beads had become sanctified and ritualized out of the Spanish world of *commodities* and into the Mississippian realm of *priceless non-commodities.* This process of "singularization" reflects the need for societies "to set apart a certain portion of their environment, marking it as 'sacred.'"[56] Through ritual practice, such commodities no longer belonged to the usual economic sphere. In the modern Western world, such symbolically sacred things include public lands, monuments, state art collections, paraphernalia of political power, royal residences, chiefly insignia, and ritual objects. As non-commodities, they became *priceless* "in the full possible sense of the term, ranging from the uniquely valuable to the uniquely worthless." Symbolic authority typically asserts itself by reserving and exercising the right to "singularize" objects through an extension of sacred power as projected onto "sacralized objects . . . [and] biographies of things can make salient what might otherwise remain obscure."[57]

The centrality of tribute items and their role in maintaining the Mississippian chiefly order contrasts vividly with the intra-Puebloan factional egalitarianism and the "orderly anarchy" of Alta California. Paramount chiefs of La Florida competed with one another—sometimes violently—to enter into the Franciscan mission system; by courting the Spanish newcomers, they defined novel ways to maintain and continue their Mississippian practices—employing ostentatious displays of wealth and status items to reinforce their hereditary status. Oddly enough, the Franciscan mission system provided Mississippian polities a way of projecting past practices into an uncertain future.

Language as Power

The role of language, long a staple of missionary practice, reflects the variability and sometimes-conflicting nature of the pace of assimilation and acculturation. On the one hand, Fr. Serra wanted to obliterate California Indian culture, but not necessarily right away. Because he could control the California Indians within their mission environment, but not in the greater Hispanic world springing up in California, he wished to moderate how they were brought into that world. There is, of course, the overarching issue of whether

55. Worth, *The Timucuan Chiefdoms*, 137.

56. Igor Kopytoff, "The Cultural Biography of Things: Commoditization as Process," in *The Social Life of Things: Commodities in Cultural Perspective*, ed. Arjun Appadurai (Cambridge: Cambridge University Press, 1986), 64–68.

57. Both quotes are from Kopytoff, "The Cultural Biography of Things," 67, 73–75.

Serra's Alta California missions were actually missions (in the technical sense) at all, or whether they had become *doctrinas* under the control of secular (rather than Franciscan) authority.[58] To this point, Marie Duggan has argued for a certain linguistic conservatism on the part of friars in the missions of Alta California, noting that presidio commanders complained that the neophytes were not being taught Spanish quickly enough. "So long as the linguistic barrier remained [missionaries] were the indispensable intermediaries between the Indians and the civil officers. . . . [T]hey were the lords and masters of their parishioners. . . . They did not relish the prospect of giving it all up."[59]

In stark contrast, scholars are only now beginning to understand and appreciate the extraordinary Franciscan commitment to literacy among the Timucua, Guale, and Apalachee neophytes living in the missions of Spanish Florida.[60] Among the pieces of writing from that time is Fr. Francisco de Pareja's well-known 1613 *Confesionario*, which was written (at least in part) while he served at San Juan del Puerto (coastal Florida). Fr. Gerónimo de Oré's account from this same area in 1614 documents the presence of various books in the possession of local neophytes, including the *Confesionario*. Fr. Francisco Alonso de Jesús also recorded that Spanish Florida could claim more than 20,000 baptized indigenous Christians as well as 50,000 male and female catechumens who were literate and learned with great ease.[61] Fr. de Jesús also recorded the presence of schools in each *doctrina*, where instruction went far beyond rote memory, emphasizing instead the acquisition of grammar, syntax, and vocabulary. There survives a clear record of written communication among neophyte leaders in their native language, demonstrating their involvement in active textual communities, translating various European and native languages, interpreting liturgical texts, and actively engaging in their own evangelization.

Concluding Thoughts

Franciscan friars encountered remarkably different Native American constructs of political power and social identity across the Spanish Borderlands—from the hierarchical, tightly stratified Mississippian chiefdoms to the complex, ritually embedded leadership in the egalitarian southwestern Pueblos to

---

58. Hackel, *Junípero Serra*, 214–215; see also Hackel, *Children of Coyote*, 228–271.

59. Marie Christine Duggan, "Moving Beyond Slavery: The Institutional Status of Mission Indians," this volume.

60. Timothy J. Johnson, "Fray Francisco Pareja and the Cultures of Confession," this volume.

61. John H. Hann, "1630 Memorial of Francisco Alonso de Jesús, on Spanish Florida's Missions and Natives," *The Americas* 50 (1993): 85–105; quotation as translated in Johnson, "Fray Francisco Pareja and the Cultures of Confession," this volume.

the densely populated Alta California landscape of "orderly anarchists" who privileged individuality and family-level control over tribal authority. Although universally adhering to an overarching Spanish plan for the New World—to convert, to civilize, and to exploit—the resulting Spanish missions as Boltonian "frontier institutions" differed greatly with respect to indigenous governance, rites of baptism and conversion, the nature of tribute, and the degree of literacy among neophyte communities.

As historian Michael Witgen has recently argued, the time has come to take "indigenous social formations seriously," to recognize the self-representations of indigenous peoples as political and diplomatic actors in the colonial world.[62] This task is complicated by the recognition that many of the social and political constructions of the Native American landscape lacked readily translatable equivalents in European parlance.

While the friars believed without question in the power of their Catholic religion to save souls, the overarching ideology of salvation became deeply enmeshed in perceived differences between the civilized and the savage. While the focus of interaction centered on the Catholic religion, on-the-ground realities of the mission experience became deeply entangled, with all parties attempting to figure out how to disentangle expectations from realities on the part of "the other." The challenge for the modern Borderlands scholar would seem to lie in augmenting and balancing the grand narratives of Bolton and his Borderlands students with more contemporary understandings of relevant Native American "counternarratives."[63]

62. Michael Witgen, *An Infinity of Nations* (Philadelphia: University of Pennsylvania Press, 2012), 26.

63. Ibid., 16.

Chapter 2
The Native American Perception of Europeans in Early Travelogues of the 16th Century

Gert Melville

What actually was it the Europeans wanted in that newly discovered world they later called "America?" Their primary concern probably was to look for the gold of India that was already talked of constantly during the Middle Ages. Columbus already searched for it on Tortuga (or Turtle) Island and even looked for Baneque, the island of gold itself, which the natives had told him about and which was said to have a mountain of pure gold.[1] But the Europeans also saw the agricultural resources that Columbus already noticed on the island of Hispaniola when he said: "In all of Castile there are no lands that could be compared to the fertility and loveliness of this country."[2] Others, in turn, believed in undreamt-of opportunities of trade, when they noticed the high profit margins already in the first barter deals with European trinkets and Native American products like gold jewelry. Meanwhile, pious people recognized the chance to propagate the Christian belief through missionary work; others needed adventure, the foundation of dominions, to give free rein to their violence. . . . They all needed, hoped for, used or took something from that continent—and they did not ask if this was their right. They did not ask because they were convinced they possessed the right.[3] They had the true faith, and the only true God was with them. They

1. Cecil Jane, ed., *The Voyages of Christopher Columbus* (Amsterdam and New York: Israel, 1970), 29. Regarding the motives of Columbus' voyage, of which gold occupied the most prominent place, see the overview in John Dyson and Peter Christopher, *Columbus: For Gold, God and Glory* (Sevenoaks: Hodder & Stoughton/Madison, 1991).

2. Jane, ed., *The Voyages*.

3. Regarding this aspect see my article "Medieval Understandings of Foreign Cultures as Conditions for the Early Modern Takeover of America," in Timothy J. Johnson and Gert Melville, eds. *From La Florida to La California. Franciscan Evangelization in the Spanish Borderlands* (Berkeley: The Academy of American Franciscan History, 2013, 47–60, here 49–50). Regarding the overall development cf. Tzvetan Todorov, *The Conquest of America: the Question of the Other* (New York: Harper Perennial, 1992).

had the better weapons, had horses, bigger ships, higher knowledge, more practical technology, more efficient politics. The others, the natives, were the heathens, the savages, the primitives, the weak, whose structures immediately fell apart when they were attacked. Columbus still envisioned them as the future subjects of his king and the soon-to-be baptized Christians,[4] but time brushed him aside quickly. The acts of violence of Cortés and Pizzaro, the massacres, the enslavements, the epidemics were the cruel symbols of a divergence of civilizations that led to the enslavement and annihilation of millions of people. They were not symbols of a communication that would have embraced and united both sides—like it was still the case in the beginning with that Caribbean chieftain who wanted to share all his lands with Columbus because he had been sent to him from heaven.[5] The chieftain was the victim of a misunderstanding that prevented any genuine communication from the start. The mutual ignorance, the prejudices and the inability to understand or want to understand each other's nature had created a chasm that could drive both sides to nothing else but confrontation—a very unbalanced one, as we know.

Yet at least the side of the European invaders was not without speech or reflection. From the beginning—that is, in the 16th century—there was a considerable number of observers who recorded exactly what they experienced, saw and heard and who were quite capable of fathoming the foreign peoples of the New World. At first glance, they sometimes may appear like dime novels when they tell of their author's great adventures, of their fights against man-eaters and monsters, of long military campaigns through swamps, jungles, deserts and mountain ranges, of pillages, defilements and killings. Yet they also provided exact descriptions of the customs, living conditions, diet, rituals and structures of the natives' society. They had two different purposes: to inform the Europeans at home and to induce admiration for the author. True communication, however, always comprised the opposite perspective as well. Thus, one has to ask if the authors revealed something about the appearance of the Europeans in the eyes of the natives. In order to be able to state something about another person's behavior towards oneself, one also ought to have a vague notion of how the other person perceives oneself.

My short contribution will deal with exactly this problem. For this purpose, I used the following seven works as examples:

- The log book Columbus wrote during his first journey, which led him to the Bahamas, to Cuba and Hispanola in 1492/93.[6]

4. Jane, ed., *The Voyages*, 149.
5. Ibid.
6. Ibid.

- The *Indianische Historia* [Indian History] by Niclaus Federmann from Augsburg in Southern Germany, who worked for the trading company of the Welser family in the north of South America. In this work, he wrote about his military expedition into the heart of Venezuela in 1530.[7]

- The *Wahrhafte Historie einer wunderbaren Schifffahrt* [True History of a Wondrous Boat Journey], which was authored by Ulrich Schmidel from Bavaria. It gives an account of the Spanish campaign of conquest from the Rio de la Plata to Paraguay, in which he took part as a mercenary from 1534 to 1554.[8]

- The *Historia del Mondo Nuovo* [History of the New World] by Girolamo Benzoni, an adventurer from Milan who traveled in the Western Caribbean, Central America and Peru from 1541 to 1556 and wrote an autobiographical account of these journeys.[9]

- The *Historia von den nackten, wilden Menschenfressern* [History of the Naked, Wild Man-Eaters]. It is an account by Hans Staden from Hesse of his stay in Brazil as bombadier in Portuguese service in the years 1548 to 1555, during which he fell into the hands of man-eaters and was their prisoner for a prolonged time.[10]

---

7. Niclaus Federmann, *Indianische Historia. Ein schöne kurtzweilige Historia Niclaus Federmanns des Jüngern. Faksimile-Ausgabe nach dem Original in der Österreichischen Nationalbibliothek [von] 1557* (Wien: Volkstum-Verlag, 1994); Karl Klüpfel, ed., *N. Federmanns und H. Stades Reisen in Südamerica: 1529 bis 1555*, Stuttgart: Verlag des Literarischen Vereins in Stuttgart, 1859. The text is easily accessible online at https://books.google.de/books?id-Fq0LAAAAIAAJ&pg-PA1&hl-de&source-gbs_toc_r&cad-2#v-one page&q&f-false.

8. *Wahrhafte Historie einer wunderbaren Schifffahrt, welche Ulrich Schmidl von Straubing von 1534 bis 1554 in Amerika oder Neue Welt bei Brasilia oder Rio de la Plata getan*, ed. Fernardo Amando Aymoré (Wiesbaden:Edition Erdmann in der marixverlag GmbH, 2010); in English translation: *The Conquest of the River Plate (1535–1555). Voyage of Ulrich Schmidt to the Rivers La Plata and Paraguai*, ed. by Luis L. Dominguez (London: Hakluyt Society, 1981): https://www.gutenberg.org/files/48058/48058-h/48058-h.htm.

9. Girolamo Benzoni, *History of the New World Shewing His Travels in America, from A. D. 1541 to 1556: with Some Particulars of the Islands of Canary*, ed. William H. Smyth (London: Hakluyt Society, 1857; reprint Cambridge: Cambridge University Press, 2009. The historical edition from Venice 1572 is accessible as facsimile online at https://books.google.de/books?id-1vZzhmtdPQkC&printsec-frontcover&dq-Girolamo+Benzoni&cd-5&hl-de#v-onepage&q-Girolamo%20Benzoni&f-false.

10. Hans Staden, *Brasilien 1548–1555. Historia von den nackten, wilden Menschenfressern*, ed. Gustav Faber (Lenningen: Edition Erdmann GmbH, 2006). The text can be accessed online at http://gutenberg.spiegel.de/buch/warhaftige-historia-5531/1.

- The *Histoire d'un voyage fait an la terre du Bresil*, the erudite story of a journey to Brazil by Jean de Léry, a Calvinist theologian from Burgundy, in the year 1557.[11]
- *A brief and true report of the new found land of Virginia, authored by the Englishman Thomas* Hariot, in 1588, in which he gave an eyewitness account of the attempt to establish a settlement on Roanoke Island in what is now North Carolina under Sir Richard Grenville in 1584.[12]

My aim was to select accounts that cover the complete pertinent range from the Rio de la Plata to the East coast of what is now the United States and that were written very early. In this way, I wanted to obtain reactions that were indeed as primary and fresh as possible. Above all, it seemed important to me to draw upon authors who foregrounded their personal experience of every-day life. It is to be expected that one of the topics will be the way one's own actions and behavior are reflected in the natives, since the awareness of this can simply ensure one's survival.

But let it be said right away: the pickings are remarkably small. Even though the travel reports are exhaustive and occasionally exhibit remarkable observational faculty regarding the lifestyle of the natives, in rare cases, it is reported that natives made explicit comments on Europeans as well. For the most part, there are only the authors' remarks on the behavior of natives, which we can then use to draw conclusions about their opinion of the Europeans. Presumably, this result of my studies is already the most important answer to our question: European observers, who had intensive contact with the daily life of the native population, but still only remained on the new continent for a certain amount of time, hardly succeeded in putting themselves into the position of the natives' understanding far enough to be able to fathom the extent to which their own world, in turn, had to appear strange and incomprehensible.[13]

---

11. *Jean de Léry, Brasilianisches Tagebuch 1557* (Tübingen: Horst Erdmann Verlag, 1967). Cf. Franz Steinkohl, *Die gottlosen Guten Wilden. Das Bild der Sauvages in Jean de Léry's „Histoire d'un voyage fait en la terre du Brésil* (Rheinfelden and Berlin: Schäuble Verlag, 1996).

12. Thomas Hariot, *A briefe and true report of the new found land of Virginia* (Frankfurt: Typis Ioannis Wecheli, 1590). Leicht zugänglich auf der Internet-Seite: https://www.gutenberg.org/files/4247/4247-h/4247-h.htm.

13. Deeper insights into the perception of the natives by the Europeans might be detected in observers who settled permanently in the "New World" and had to engage the natives' way of thought professionally—that is especially the missionaries. But also in this instance, scholarship has not yet sufficiently considered the facts. Promising avenues can, however, be found in Stephanie Rhigetti's "The Indians and the Mendicant Friars: A Colloquium on Religion. A Study of the First Meeting of the Twelve Mexican Apostles with the Aztecs in Mexico" in this volume. It would be worth pursuing this line of questioning even further; here a call to do so has to suffice.

In most cases, this was limited to remarks on how the Native Americans did not believe what the Europeans told them about themselves and that they, therefore, rather wanted to retain their amazement about the Europeans' incredible appearance. There are indeed some significant examples for this. One of them is found in Columbus' log book on the occasion of the visit of a Native American chieftain on the Spaniards' ship, during which Columbus wanted to explain the power of the king of Castile. It reads: "Yet neither the Indians who acted as interpreters on board of the caravels nor the chieftain himself believed even a single word I said as they were all firmly convinced that we Christians had descended from heaven and that the kingdom of Castile was located in heaven and not on earth."[14] This may have been attributable to the sudden appearance with big ships and menacing weapons that suggested superiority and was absolutely inscrutable at first glance. Due to this, the Europeans induced great fear, as e.g. Nikolaus Federmann stated on the behavior of the Venezuelan natives, which was generally characterized "by the fear, the fright and horror at the strange, never-before-seen, clothed and bearded people and their steeds."[15] It was a fear that could easily shift to the soothing feeling of supernatural significance like with those village dwellers who cried at the sight of Columbus' crew: "Now look at the men who have descended from heaven and bring them some food and drink."[16] Yet another passage in Columbus decidedly rebutted the unexpectedness as a reason for this false explanation again: "They were profoundly convinced that I and my people had come down from heaven. Those Indians I have taken on board from the other islands—namely, from the Bahamas—did not abandon this belief either, although they had been informed about this accordingly."[17] Such uncertainty in appraising the Europeans or this numinous quality that seemed to adhere to them is probably also the explanation for the circumstance that the Europeans could rely on such a swift acceptance of their dominance again and again—an acceptance that rendered the military successes possible in the first place. I will come back to this again in a moment.

Yet in matters of belief, if one wants to proselytize and reach people's souls, one should penetrate the other's understanding more deeply. The countless remarks in the European writings stating that the natives were utterly incapable of the recognition of one God or of a life after death clearly show what a misunderstanding was at hand there. So, it comes as no surprise that Girolamo Benzoni related how once, in what is Nicaragua today, a Spanish grandee wanted to explain the merits of heaven, which was opened up by

14. Jane, ed., *The Voyages.*
15. Klüpfel, ed., 19.
16. Jane, ed.
17. Ibid.

the Christian belief, to present Native Americans. The Native Americans listened to all of this and agreed with the elucidations. Yet they went away unimpressed because, according to their belief, they already expected a happy life after death as well.[18] What ideas of the Europeans' religion were there on the Native Americans' side—apart from the aforementioned identification of the Europeans themselves with gods? Were these ideas only present as a result of missionary activity?[19] Or were the Europeans not also perceived in their religious behavior in the frequency of entirely profane encounters?

Hans Staden is an outstanding crown witness for this since he lived in the extreme situation of being a prisoner of ritual man-eaters on the Brazilian coast for months. According to his tale, "his" god saved him from the fate of being eaten—or more precisely: he was saved by the god the natives considered to be "his." That is to say, after he had once prayed to God for help before a storm and the tempest had withdrawn at that, the natives, ironically enough, again and again asked him to call on "his" god for help, such as e.g. "At that, they came into my hut and demanded I should speak to my god in order that the rain would cease again. If it did not cease soon, they would be unable to plant."[20] The natives saw the benefit of their prisoner's personal connections to a god and they also saw the technology of communication in the form of prayer. "Now I saw that you have talked to your god",[21] he was told time and again. Yet the power of this god was also perceived as one that surpassed that of all other gods. When Staden had to prove he was not one of the hated Portuguese, "his god," as it were, helped him in the eyes of the natives again. Namely, "his" god sent an epidemic to the people of the natives because Staden had allegedly been tortured by them. Thereupon he was told: "We have already caught a number of Portuguese and also eaten them but their god never became as angry as yours. This shows us that you are no Portuguese."[22] A splendid conclusion that shows that, according to those natives' point of view, by no means all European nations whose representatives (besides the Portuguese, Frenchmen and Spaniards as well) had appeared off the Brazilian coast possessed the same gods.

Therefore, the Native Americans projected their own worlds of imagination on the Europeans very consciously, too: here, the structure of tribes each with their own gods whose greater powers directly competed in each

18. Girolamo Benzoni, ed. Smyth.

19. See Righetti's contribution in this volume.

20. Hans Staden, ch. 51 (http://gutenberg.spiegel.de/buch/warhaftige-historia-5531/51).

21. Hans Staden, ch. 52 (http://gutenberg.spiegel.de/buch/warhaftige-historia-5531/52).

22. Hans Staden, ch. 39 (http://gutenberg.spiegel.de/buch/warhaftige-historia-5531/39).

case just like the people did among each other as well. Consequently, it was not quite that wrong when a learned man like Jean de Léry compared these religious structures with the realm of the gods of antiquity.[23] On the other hand the natives did very well perceive quotidian things of the Europeans, which were foreign to them as such, and oftentimes saw in them—because they could not explain them—products of the super-natural. Jean de Léry for example reports that the natives, who themselves did not comprehend the function of a script, thought it was magic when he took notes and later read from them. Literally he reports, "The Indians knew that the Spaniards could communicate with each other without seeing each other by sending letters from one place to another. Because of that, the Indians believed that the Spaniards either possessed the gift of prophesy or that the letters could speak." [24]

Yet such worlds of imagination definitely also referred to the perception of the codes of social behavior. One example for this: When, after his capture, it was revealed to Staden that he soon was to be roasted and eaten, he was overcome by terrible fear. He later described the natives' reaction in his *Historia*. The natives had watched him closely as he was praying a psalm with tears in his eyes, and they said: "Look now how he fears for his life."[25] This gains particular importance in view of the fact (which Jean de Léry describes in the same way) that captured natives with the same prospect of death behaved in a completely different way: namely, proud, even positively happy because of the certainty of revenge by their fellow tribesmen, and relishing the participation in the preparation of their killing in the form of a ritual celebration. For the natives, Staden—like the other Europeans with the same fate, too—was a peculiar type of man who did not have any clue what pleasures he missed out on due to his behavior.

Yet in reviewing all those accounts of the travelers one finds that, undisputedly, one topic was always in the foreground: the utilizing, taking and hoping for something from the new continent as if it was one's own from the first. More than all other undertakings, those raids, conquests and land seizures undoubtedly were the activities of the Europeans that were most striking to the people concerned. This becomes particularly clear as regards the account by Ulrich Schmidel about the seizure of the area north of the Rio de la Plata, during which tribe by tribe was ticked off as conquered. Such undertakings generated cruelty and ignominy on both sides but sometimes also

---

23. Jean de Léry, *Brasilianisches Tagebuch*, ch. 17, 276–298 ("Which, among the wild, one could call religion").

24. Ibid.

25. Hans Staden, ch. 20 (http://gutenberg.spiegel.de/buch/warhaftige-historia-5531/24).

signs of brotherliness. "We stayed four days among them and these men imparted to us of their poverty and we did the like by them," Schmidel wrote about a small tribe in the wasteland of the Mato Grosso.[26] However, he noted on another one, "they approached us in the way of peace but received us with a false heart."[27]

There, in the south of the continent, the natives also came to know the Europeans in another way: even though they were strong, they were vulnerable nevertheless. The natives were able to destroy Buenos Aires and the ships moored there in 1541, and with that the nimbus of the invincibility of Europeans had been lost.[28] However, we know nothing about how the natives thought about this or to what extent this had changed their image of the Europeans. Schmidel had his hands full with imparting his own experiences.

Yet there were other depictions that also allowed room for the natives' feelings in view of the oppressive politics of the Europeans. Girolamo Benzoni, for instance, was an author who did not withhold the most severe criticisms by the natives. As a reply to the reading of a peace offering from the Spanish king, he had American natives from the Columbian Cartagena answer "that they did not want the friendship of the king of Castile, and bade them [the king's envoys] return whence they came. They only wanted good people to come to their country, and not such as did nothing but evil."[29] In another passage, Benzoni uses an even more drastic way to present the disdain for Europeans. A captured chieftain told the governor of the same area, "he could not imagine how Christians could be such a generation of vipers, committing such great evil wherever they went; he only wondered how the earth could bear them."[30]

From a god to the devil, a remarkable transformation for the image of the Europeans in America in the course of only a few decades. The American natives did not draw this image with their own hands. Before the verdict of history, they had to rely on their observers to do this for them, observers who came from the circle of their enemies and destroyers. Yet these only did that in passing and, in most cases, entirely unintentionally. However, as we were able to see, some things could be read from this: initial reverence, misunderstandings, speechlessness, anger and self-humiliation—and it is certain that it will be possible to find more once our question is pursued completely and systematically. Maybe this will bring to light more clearly what was a hope to some observers of the New World when they were thinking about the natives'

26. *Wahrhafte Historie einer wunderbaren Schifffahrt,* ed. Aymoré, 78.
27. Idem, 99.
28. Cf. idem, 64–65.
29. Benzoni, ed. Smyth, 55.
30. Idem, 129.

opinion of the foreign Europeans—namely, what Thomas Hariot, for instance, said about the Native Americans in North Carolina after his arrival there:

> *For although they haue no such tooles, nor any such craftes, sciences and artes as wee; yet in those thinges they doe, they shewe excellencie of wit. And by howe much they vpon due consideration shall finde our manner of knowledgeš and craftes to exceede theirs in perfection, and speed for doing or execution, by so much the more is it probable that they shoulde desire our friendships & loue.*[31]

History has falsified such a vision. This is the actual tragedy.

31. Thomas Hariot (https://www.gutenberg.org/files/4247/4247-h/4247-h.htm).

Chapter 3

Reciprocity and Relationship: Encounters between Missionaries and Evangelized Peoples in the Spanish Borderlands and Europe

Helmut Flachenecker

An Indian prophecy, recorded in the nineteenth century in the Mount St. Helens region, struggles with the worst that could happen in the future: "Soon there will come from the rising sun a different kind of man from any you have yet seen, who will bring with him a book and will teach you everything, and after that the world will fall to pieces."[1] The "book" and its influence, which would destroy this Indian world forever, could very well be interpreted as the Bible. In other words, Christianity will change the culture of the conquered people forever, but will the conquerors be affected as well in the same measure? In this chapter I explore this question by using information passed from sixth-century Ireland and seventeenth-century New France. Developments there may cast light on what transpired during encounters between indigenous peoples and Franciscans in the Spanish Borderlands in the U.S. East and West from the sixteenth through the nineteenth centuries.

Religious Organizations as Nonmonolithic Entities

Religious organizations are not monolithic entities; instead they react to external influences. They are subject to continuous change by having contact with different kinds of people and their beliefs. The more distant a religious organization's headquarters or center, the more heterogeneous and rooted in local cultures the newly evangelized communities will become. Very often decision making on whether to convert was made in the context of internal power struggles. Members of the unsuccessful party or group in the confrontation had to change their religious behaviors, go into exile, or suffer vio-

1. Cited in Colin G. Calloway, *New Worlds for All: Indians, Europeans, and the Remaking of Early America* (Baltimore: John Hopkins University Press, 1998), xiii.

lence. It is worth noting here that the spread of political power, which supported certain religions, was not in every way concordant with the spread of faith. Conquest via force of arms alone does not guarantee acceptance and commitment ("taking it into their hearts") by indigenous people such that they themselves proselytize future generations.

Clergy members usually attempt to uphold beliefs and values in a strict and precise way, while the lay population is more open-minded. Perhaps the greatest theological issues in Christianity are the nature of Christ—divine or human or both—or the description of the nature of the Trinity. This was an enormous challenge for every missionary of all proselytizing religions. Richard Foltz highlights some of the consequences in his magnificent book, *Religions of the Silk Road*.[2]

Further evidence of the relationship and reciprocity between missionaries and natives is illustrated by Jerry Bentley. He mentions that in the course of cross-cultural contacts there are sometimes signs of a "conversion by voluntary association."[3] People who lived in a remote area wanted to raise their social prestige by adopting the religious beliefs of more cosmopolitan foreigners, such as merchants. Such converts believed themselves to be linked to a greater outer world.

The success of an active proselytizing process depended on rewarding preaching efforts and translating the religious texts in respective vernacular languages. The quicker and more sophisticated the translations, the more successful the missionaries were. Trying to convert indigenous people and proselytize them not only depended on the persuasiveness of the missionaries, but also on indigenous women. In brief, the enormous influence that mothers have on the cultural and thus religious education of their children cannot be overestimated.[4]

These abovementioned examples from Bentley and Foltz result from research conducted in Inner Asia. The question that arises at this juncture is whether these findings are also applicable to the proselytizing processes in Europe's Early Middle Ages as well as in Florida, New Mexico, or elsewhere in the New World.

New France

France was a Catholic monarchy, which took part in evangelizing the native peoples of North America, mainly in what now comprises Canada and

---

2. Richard Foltz, *Religions of the Silk Road: Premodern Patterns of Globalization* (New York: Palgrave Macmillan, 2010), 9, 22.

3. Jerry Bentley, *Old World Encounters: Cross-Cultural Contacts and Exchanges in Pre-Modern Times* (New York: Oxford University Press, 1993), 184.

4. Foltz, *Religions of the Silk Road*, 17–20.

the United States. France considered itself to be "the most Christian of nations" (*la nation la plus chrétienne*). For this reason, New France was a place for refashioning its entitlements, since the French kings were continually engaged in power struggles with Spain and England in Europe. These disputes were also evident in the evangelization process. But foreigners were not the only enemies of French clergymen in the New World, as they were often at loggerheads with French traders whose behavior was motivated by profit rather than faith.[5]

Samuel de Champlain (1570–1635), who lived in a French settlement on the St. Lawrence River, and is remembered as the "father of New France," played an important role in establishing relationships with natives. In 1615, the first Récollect (Franciscan) missionaries sailed with him to the New World. They tried to break up the monopoly of the Jesuits with their missionary task. In 1620 they erected their first church and seminary in Québec. They were—as was everyone in New France in this time—very enthusiastic about proselytizing the Indians. Due to their small numbers as well as indigenous resistance, their missionizing attempts failed. Ten years later, in 1625 Champlain convinced the Jesuits to continue the proselytizing task.[6] Champlain had a vision of creating a new Catholic colony, where Natives and French settlers would live together in harmony, including marrying each other.[7] This example shows that the vision of a new Catholic society occurred not only in the Spanish colonies in the first half of the sixteenth century but also in the French colonies.

Evangelization efforts were hindered by numerous misunderstandings, especially when the missionaries did not tolerate certain indigenous religious rituals. For most Christian missionaries, Indian beliefs and practices were not considered religious. Consequently, all Indian spirits or beliefs regarding nature, plants, and animals were incomprehensible.[8] In a report from Champlain about the religious ceremonies of indigenous tribes (1603), some patterns of the early preaching methods are described: the native myth of the origin of mankind was confronted with the Christian creation myth. The Natives had no idea what the Christian "credo" and the "divine trinity" really meant. On the other side, and this was astonishing for the missionaries, some

---

5. Brian Brazeau, *Writing a New France, 1604–1632: Empire and Early Modern French Identity* (Burlington, Vermont: Ashgate Publishing Company, 2009), 98–100; Cornelius J. Jaenen, *Friend and Foe: Aspects of French-Amerindian Cultural Contact in the Sixteenth and Seventeenth Centuries* (New York: Columbia University Press, 1976), 46–47.

6. Brazeau, *Writing a New France*, 102–106.

7. Gayle K. Brunelle, *Samuel de Champlain, Founder of New France: A Brief History with Documents* (Boston/New York: Bedford/St. Martin's, 2012), 2, 5, 17, 20–21, 125–126.

8. Colin G. Calloway, *New Worlds for All: Indians, Europeans, and the Remaking of Early America* (Baltimore: Johns Hopkins University Press, 1998), 68. For the *katsina* dances of the Hopis in New Mexico, see Page, *Uprising*, 47.

Indian nations believed in an immortal soul and/or a divine creator. The Hurons also had a myth similar to the story of Cain and Abel.[9] On the other hand, Champlain couldn't understand why the Natives had no liturgy; instead "everyone prayed in his heart as he thought best."[10] And the Indians also believed that prayers are effective. But for all that the native's belief was devilish for the French. By the way, one can find this conviction by the Spaniards as well. As Juan Ortiz wrote in 1539, "Indians are worshippers of the Devil."[11]

Most interesting was the reaction of the Huron tribe, after hearing the homilies of Champlain and the Récollet missionary Father Joseph: "You say things that pass our understanding and that we cannot comprehend by words, as something beyond our intelligence." Instead of listening to the new principles and simply believing them, the Natives wanted to experience the routines of Christian life. The Hurons wanted to share their lives with French settlers: "Seeing this we shall learn more in one year than hearing your discourses in twenty." As an alternative to the proposal of mixed settlements, the Hurons proposed to send their children, as the next generation would surely be more open-minded and able to gain a sense of the new religion.[12] The Hurons urged the Christians to exemplify their beliefs to them by showing them their way of life rather than relying exclusively on sermons and homilies.

The clash of civilizations was tough for the Indians: diseases, famine, alcohol, and violence devastated their numbers and social structures collapsed. There were numerous ways to deal with the new circumstances. Some blamed the chaotic situation on the new beliefs[13]; others became desperate and converted hoping for safe harbor to live under the new circumstances. Some decided to engage in active resistance by fighting the intruders, while others agitated in a more passive manner, as they listened to the missionaries but did not agree with their doctrines.[14]

---

9. Jaenen, *Friend and Foe*, 42–43.

10. "Observations and Mutual Incomprehension at Tadoussac (1603)," in Brunelle, *Samuel de Champlain*, 71–75. See also "On the Founding of Québec and Observations of the Montagnais Living Nearby (1608)," in Brunelle, 76–79, esp. 78; and "Finally: A Journey into Iroquois Territory and a Battle at Lake Champlain (1609)," in Brunelle, 80–87, esp. 82.

11. Luis Hernandez de Biedma, *Narratives of the Career of Hernando de Soto in the Conquest of Florida*, 2 vols., ed. Edward G. Bourne, trans. Buckingham Smith (New York: Allerton Books, 1922), vol. 1:29–30.

12. "Huronia—Observations and a Military Alliance (1615–1616)," in Brunelle, *Samuel de Champlain*, 89–99, esp. 96.

13. Jaenen, *Friend and Foe*, 63.

14. Calloway, *New Worlds for All*, 71–74.

Evangelization—Saints—Conversion

The type of evangelization illustrated above had to be part of the general efforts toward conversion. Conversion is generally a time-consuming process comprised of at least three levels:

1. First is the formal mission being supported by the ruling group of the target population (formal conversion): clergy provide sermons and baptism.
2. Next, Church institutions must be erected (institutional Christianization): diocese with a cathedral, establishment of a parish system. But how does the Church deal with this institutional frame in the context of a nomadic people who are not sedentary in a specific place?[15]
3. The third level is Christianization of the population (pastoral Christianity): Better understanding of the new rules with the help of synods and canons, in addition to internalization of Christian beliefs via assistance of syncretistic forms.

These structural phases will differ according to time and place. Thus, the goals of missionary work are not exactly the same in the Early Middle Ages and the seventeenth and eighteenth centuries. In the context of medieval Europe, a lot more time was needed for successful missionizing than in New Mexico during the eighteenth century and Alta California in the eighteenth and nineteenth centuries.

This process also signifies a "cross-cultural conversion"[16] of each individual person, which is very difficult to explain in detail. Foltz develops three categories to define this complex process:

1. Conversion through voluntary association
2. Conversion by political, social, or economic pressure
3. Conversion by assimilation[17]

Of course this is an ideal picture of how conversion could work structurally. Quality and sustainability of conversions are of paramount importance. Teaching doctrines to people who cannot understand the language of the missionaries could, indeed, generate a huge number of neophytes. But how deep is the new faith anchored in their lives?[18] In addition, the objectives and politi-

15. Jaenen, *Friend and Foe*, 54–55.
16. Foltz, *Religions of the Silk Road*, 6–8.
17. Ibid., 9–15.
18. See the discussions noted in the Jesuit "Relations" for New France in Jaenen, *Friend and Foe*, 66–67.

cal-economic environment of missionizing efforts changed radically over the centuries. Perhaps in the case of Christopher Columbus, in addition to political and economic goals, there was also an "apocalyptic legacy" in Columbus's efforts to explore the New World.[19]

In any case, there will be resistance as well as remarkable cultural diffusion. For instance, on rare occasions even a saint arose from the Christianized indigenous population. The very first Native woman Catholic saint in Northern America was Catherine Tekakwitha (Tegahkouita) from the Mohawk tribe, who lived in the second half of the seventeenth (1656–1680). Her biography was written by a Jesuit named Pierre Cholenec who describes her as follows: Catherine was born in 1656 and orphaned as a child. As a survivor of the smallpox epidemic, her body and face were marked with scars. She lived a short life as a devout Christian and ascetic woman. According to her *Vitae*, she struggled to avoid marriage and to live as a crypto-Christian until French Jesuits arrived in her village to baptize her.

It is remarkable that the author emphasizes the difference in preaching and baptism received by the majority of the tribe members and the special treatment that Catherine obtained in that context. The reason for this was her ongoing special dedication to Christian beliefs. She lived an isolated life in the background unlike Holy Brigid in Ireland. The first missionaries who visited Catherine's village were not very interested in her as an individual. An accident drew the attention of missionary Father Jacques de Lamberville to her. Instantly, he felt that she was an outstanding proselyte and provided her with intensive religious lessons. It was difficult for the missionaries to understand and cope with the "conduct and morality" of the Indian village. According to the *Vitae*, in contrast to the common cross-cultural misunderstandings among Natives, Catherine was a "soul filled with the most precious gifts of Heaven who had been guided in the most sublime spiritual ways."[20] Of course, this was likely a pious fiction, but the *Vitae* helps us to understand a bit more about what could have occurred in the interaction between missionaries and their proselytes. Catherine had problems with her cross-cultural lifestyle: she resisted being married, and she was attacked for conserving her chastity and purity, she was pressured because she didn't work on Sundays,

---

19. Timothy J. Johnson, "The Apocalypse in St. Augustine: Christopher Columbus, Religion, and the New World," in Culturally La Florida: Spain's New World Legacy, Proceedings of the Conference, May 3–6, 2012, Flagler College, St. Augustine. For New France, see Jaenen, *Friend and Foe*, 48.

20. An English translation of the *Vita* of Catherine appears in Allan Greer, *The Jesuit Relations: Natives and Missionaries in Seventeenth-Century North America*, The Bedford Series in History and Culture (Boston/New York: Bedford/St. Martins, 2000), 172–185, esp. 176. See also Allan Greer, *Mohawk Saint: Catherine Tekawitha and the Jesuits* (New York: Oxford University Press, 2005).

and she was accused of adultery.[21] As a result, she wished to leave her native village, but her uncle, who was responsible for her, would not allow that. With the help of her adoptive sister, who was already married to a Christian Indian, both fled to a French mission and miraculously the uncle couldn't stop them. Catherine's life as a bride of Christ ended in early 1680. Her death was allegorized in a perfect Christian way: she received the sacred anointing and then passed with a certain self-certitude and calm countenance.[22] Catherine is a rare example of successful pastoral Christianity. In general, Catherine's *Vita* demonstrates the difficulties inherent in changing cultural patterns, and particularly in the context of cross-societal religious behaviors.[23] In addition, the *Vita* also shows the mysticism and piety of the French missionaries.[24] Thus, the *Vita* is a description about of an Indian reflection on French mysticism, or what appears more likely, a French idealistic picture of Catherine as both a devout French virgin and as a pious and devout savage.

Mission and Christianization in Ireland

Missionary activities in the French- and Spanish-dominated areas in North America are always linked to the evangelization processes in medieval Europe which gave the models for this development. It is a mediator influence that could help us better understand the proselytizing processes during the sixteenth to eighteenth centuries on the western side of the Atlantic.

For purposes of providing a comparison, we will examine a transformation process from the fifth century in Ireland. It seems that the first Christians lived in the south of Ireland, where Palladius performed basic missionary work in 431. Christianity spread to the north, where Patrick is known to have worked as a messenger of the faith. We do not know the exact geographical area where he preached, baptized, and ordained priests; however, tradition fixes all of this work in the Armagh area.[25] Patrick (†461/491) was British and therefore a stranger in Ireland. He had difficulties in understanding Celtic behaviors.

21. Greer, *The Jesuit Relations*, 174–176.

22. Ibid., 183–184.

23. Catherine was the first North American Indian to be beatified in 1980 and then canonized by Pope Benedict XVI in October 2012. The efforts aimed at declaring her a saint began in 1884. Catherine was the unofficial patroness of Montreal, Canada and for many Indian people. To make her life accessible to a broader audience, a well-illustrated book was published as a "commemorative canonization edition": Giovanna Paponetti, *Kateri: Native American Saint. The Life and Miracles of Kateri Tekawitha* (Ranchos de Taos, New Mexico: Captured Moments, 2012).

24. Jaenen, *Friend and Foe*, 49.

25. Kathleen Hughes, "The Church in Irish Society," in *A New History of Ireland*, vol. 1, *Prehistoric and Early Ireland*, ed. Dáibhí Ó Cróinín (Oxford: Oxford University Press, 2005), 301–311.

Saint Patrick's "Letter to Coroticus" and his "Confession" written in the 470s are considered authentic and provide a vague description of the early Church in Ireland or, as Patrick suggested, of the Church at the "end of the world."[26] In the proselytizing process (formal conversion), he presumably used the following order: preaching, baptizing, and giving confirmation to "the people."[27] We do not know, as in many other cases, the details of how conversion was accomplished and how social division worked in this process. Patrick tells us only generally that he baptized "thousands" and that he preached "for the strengthening and confirming" of faith.[28] Many questions remain unanswered, such as: Who was "the voice of the Irish"? Did Saint Patrick target already Christianized people or real heathens? In what language did he or Palladius preach? The need for interpreters is as old as the need to proselytize, as in other religions, such as Buddhism. The vocabulary of the proselytizing religion must have an entry into the language of the proselytized people.[29] It is a fundamental task of Christianity since the early days in Jerusalem. We can trace proselytizing efforts across the centuries. The Delaware Indians in Ohio and Moravian missionaries in the eighteenth century comprise another example at a different place and time.[30]

Patrick saw himself as an "ambassador" of Christ (*pro quo legationem fungor*) who had the task of bringing Christian law.[31] He, like his Celtic successors, did not acquire a special mandate from the pope to missionize. Patrick's mission was grounded on the mandate in the Bible that encourages the faithful to "preach the Gospel to all of creation" and to save every soul—similar to his Franciscan and Jesuit successors in North and South America.[32] For this reason, he left his former episcopal see in Britain, which caused a lot of trouble. Instead, he chose lifelong peregrination, a self-imposed exile and

26. Dáibhí Ó Cróinín, "Hiberno-Latin Literature to 1169," in *A New History of Ireland*, vol. 1:372.

27. "Confession," in *Saint Patrick's World*, ed. Liam de Paor (Dublin: Four Courts Press, 1996), 106. For a Latin version with a French translation, see *Saint Patrick: Confession et Lettre à Coroticus*, eds. Richard P. C. Hanson and Cécile Blanc, Sources Chrétiennes 249 (Paris: Les Èditions du Cerf, 1978), 70–133.

28. "Confession," ed. de Paor, 105.

29. Not only by the Christian religion, also by Buddhism. See Bentley, *Old World Encounters*, 73, 77. For New France, see Jaenen, *Friend and Foe*, 51–53.

30. Calloway, *New Worlds for All*, 83.

31. "Letter against Coroticus," in *Saint Patrick's World*, ed. Liam de Paor (Dublin: Four Courts Press, 1996), 110; "Confession," ed. de Paor, 107; *Saint Patrick: Confession et Lettre à Coroticus*, ed. Hanson and Blanc, 128, 134–153, esp. 138.

32. "Confession," ed. de Paor, 101 ("now the salvation of others is my care and concern"); *Saint Patrick: Confession et Lettre a Coroticus*, eds. Hanson and Blanc, chapter 28, p. 102: "*ut ego curam haberem aut satagerem pro salute aliorum, quando autem tunc etiam de me ipso non cogitabam.*"

wandering for the love of God.[33] He did not charge anything for his services, a behavior that did not coincide with lacking money. He received payments, especially from "religious women, who would spontaneously offer[ed] me [Patrick] small gifts or throw some of their personal ornaments on the altar."[34] Is this a sign of a successful pastoral Christianity?

Whenever it was necessary, Patrick gifted and paid fees to kings and chiefs. Additionally, he granted their sons "stipend(s)" if they wanted to join him and the new religion.[35] In doing so, he attempted to persuade the youth to convert to the new belief system. He also tried to redeem baptized captives.[36] The principal targets of Patrick, as well as Bishop Otto of Bamberg in Pomerania during the twelfth century, were women, young noblemen, prisoners, and merchants, as in New France and New Mexico. Moreover, in Ireland there were several monks and nuns ("virgins of Christ"). These early Irish clergy were not exclusively monastics. These men and women, who wanted to live an extremely different lifestyle, came from noble families, that is, from families of the "chieftains."

Patrick approached the leading groups with a special focus on the younger generation, as they were essential for a Christian future.[37] It takes a long time for missionary work to succeed, and according to Patrick, perseverance granted by God pays off eventually. Similar tactics were manifest in the New World centuries later.

The first synods with their canons led to the establishment of a full Church hierarchy in Ireland. Institutional and pastoral Christianization could then proceed. However, various clergymen built a separate institution that at first had no links to pagan society and its laws. During the first half of the sixth century, this newly founded Irish Church struggled for acceptance. Supporters of the old religion fought hard against the new Christian beliefs and the ongoing change in society's rules. It became clear that clergy was necessary in order to convince people that what they longed for and what they needed could be found in the new faith.[38] Another crucial matter was defining the

33. "Confession," ed. de Paor, 104; *Saint Patrick*, eds. Hanson and Blanc, chapter 43, 116.

34. "Confession," ed. de Paor, 106; *Saint Patrick*, eds. Hanson and Blanc, chapter 49, 122: "*mulieribus religiosos, quae mihi ultronea munuscula donabant et super altare iactabant ex ornamentis suis.*"

35. "Confession," ed. de Paor, 107; *Saint Patrick*, eds. Hanson and Blanc, chapter 52, 124.

36. Letter against Coroticus, ed. de Paor, 109; *Saint Patrick*, ed. Hanson and Blanc, 136.

37. Letter against Coroticus, ed. de Paor, 111; *Saint Patrick*, ed. Hanson and Blanc, 144.

38. "Confession," ed. de Paor, 103; *Saint Patrick*, eds. Hanson and Blanc, chapter 40, 112: "*et ubique essent clerici qui baptizarent et exhortarent populum indigentem et desiderantem.*"

exact date for the annual Easter feast. One of the early Easter tables was very convincing and made it possible to agree on a date; this table may have belonged to Palladius.[39]

Muirchú's book, *Life of St Patrick*, written around 680, enables us to draw several conclusions about the presumably first Easter feast in Ireland. It was celebrated in Tara, a pagan center, and Patrick is known to have had an intended confrontation with the Druids.[40] Furthermore, Muirchú underlines the difficulties of convincing rural people not to work on Sundays.[41] This statement shows similarities not only between the nature of disputes of the Christian missionary and the Celtic Druids, but also of missionaries in North America and the indigenous shamans. For the Indians, the missionary was a type of shaman.[42] This perception could have been the same in the fifth century for Irish society.

According to Dáibhí Ó Cróinín, conversion intended for Irish societies consisted of new laws, new religion, new Church institutions, new language (Hiberno-Latin), and, as a final result, a new culture resulting from a transformed society.[43] At this point only cross-cultural links and a syncretic integration of the new faith into old forms of fundamental beliefs could provide a modern solution: both sides must be ready for change.

After the first mission phase, the third step, "pastoral Christianization," began in Ireland with the establishment of synods. The so-called "First Synod of St Patrick," a text from the seventh century that includes presumably former synodic decisions, emphasizes efforts aimed at a solid hierarchy of bishops, clerics, and monks. Some canons also mention pagan ideas concerning witchcraft, such as consulting seers about marriage prospects. The commandments provide insights into mixed forms of diverse beliefs: some pagans gave alms to Christian churches.[44] This leads to the following question: Are people practicing syncretic forms of faith still pagans, or newly converted Christians, or possibly something in between? Cross-cultural relationships changed people on both sides with respect to their religious faith.

Monastic reforms in Ireland in the second half of the sixth century included asceticism, a celibate and more religious life, as well as a new form of ecclesiastical institution. The monasteries belonged either to a *paruchia*, or to a network of monasteries attached to a single abbey. It is said that the

39. Dáibhí Ó Cróinín, "New Light on Palladius," *Peritia* 5 (1986), 276–283; Ó Cróinín, *Early Irish History and Chronology* (Dublin: Four Courts Press, 2003), 28–34.

40. "Muirchú's Life of St Patrick," ed. de Paor, 182–187.

41. Ibid., 191.

42. Calloway, *New Worlds for All*, 73: The Hurons believed that the Jesuits were a type of sorcerer in the 1630s and 1640s.

43. Ó Cróinín, "Hiberno-Latin Literature," 371.

44. "The First Synod of St Patrick," ed. de Paor, 136.

newly established networks overrode old dependencies to bishops and their dioceses. As an important part of their identity, each monastic group needed a saint who was their spiritual patron and leader. The abbess Brigid (†523) is a famous example. She ruled over a monastery in Kildare with a bishop at her side.[45] Abbots and abbesses had close links to the founder, who gave the monastery land as an economic base.[46] Church organizations and society were closely linked. This new form of interrelationship is sometimes called "inculturation" or syncretism. The monasteries were now the gathering places for baptism and burials, and their members were responsible for the pastoral care of the people. For a long time, Pagans and Christians lived side by side.[47] The newly created holy places were often situated at old pagan sites. Hence the new faith demonstrated a kind of continuity. This could be another form of "inculturation."[48]

As suggested previously, the spread of Christianity would have been unthinkable without the veneration of saints. Their miracles illustrate a great deal about societies and their social values according to which the holy women and men lived. As a precondition for baptism, the Christian god had to act mightier than a pagan god. For example, St Ailbe (†second quarter of the sixth century) resurrected the sons of a king who were killed during a war with another dynasty. Therefore, he enabled the newly baptized king in a successful revenge. In the *Vitae* of St Ailbe, some hints of preceding pagan mythology can be found: Ailbe was fostered by wolves; furthermore, he had power over lions.[49]

Similar to St Ailbe, the descriptions about Abbess Brigid, written from Cogitosus (†650), are also very instructive for a better understanding of the process of "inculturation" of Christianity in a society with very close links to nature. For instance, Brigid's well-known closeness to animals and nature, the flocks of cows and sheep she kept, and her fear of animal theft should be named. According to the *Vitae* she would dry her wet cloak on a sunbeam[50], and offer hospitality and support for the poor. Incidentally, there is a striking resemblance between the Indians of North America and their relationship to nature with that of the Irish pagans.[51] Brigid liked to drink beer and was engaged in a constant search for salt to preserve food as well as make it more flavorful. Furthermore, she was said to have miraculously interrupted an unde-

45. "Cogitosus's Life of St Brigid," ed. de Paor 205, 208. The bishop was a former hermit.
46. Hughes, "The Church in Irish Society," 311–315.
47. See the "diabolic cult" in "Cogitosus's Life of St Brigid," ed. de Paor, 216.
48. Hughes, "The Church in Irish Society," 313.
49. "The Life of St Ailbe," ed. de Paor, 228–230.
50. "Cogitosus's Life of St Brigid," ed. de Paor 210, 211.
51. Calloway, *New Worlds for All*, 72–73; Jaenen, *Friend and Foe*, 43.

sired pregnancy.[52] She helped a woman who wanted to live a pure life as a virgin, but the "devilish lust," which was part of pagan society according to Christian texts, defeated her.

Women in Irish societies had two general choices. Brigid asked a number of women "whether she wished to take the veil and remain a virgin or whether she preferred to be given in marriage."[53] All of her marvelous behaviors—whether her closeness to dangerous beasts like wolves or wild ducks or to protect a woman from the "evil lust" of men—were important for people to achieve a deeper sense of Christianity. The miracles demonstrate the grace and power of God.[54] Places for veneration of a saint developed as an early center comparable to a marketplace, a location for refuge or a safe haven for the worldly treasure of kings.[55] Brigid is also a symbol for the role of women in the Christian world. In a changing society, gender roles must be re-cast and one crucial point of discussion was monogamous marriage. This was a general theme not only in Ireland.[56] Some indigenous women on the east coast of the United States felt that Christianity offered them a means to learn reading and writing—and perhaps have more independence from men.[57]

To summarize, in Ireland or Pomerania like in Florida or New France, saints had the very important task of convincing people to change their religion. But this was not only a Christian phenomenon. Even Mahayana Buddhist sects had certain special believers who could help others find enlightenment.[58]

Trade and Missionary Activities

A very interesting connection with conversion is economic progress. For some Indian nations, allowing missionaries to preach in their villages meant that they had an opportunity to trade for certain foodstuffs and supplies from merchants, who followed the clerics.[59] This trade potential existed in the Early Middle Ages as well, and not only in Europe. One of the major assumptions in Foltz's book about the Silk Road and religious influences was the relationship between trade and missionizing. The Muslims in particular developed this connection.[60]

---

52. "Cogitosus's Life of St Brigid," ed. de Paor, 211.
53. Ibid., 212.
54. Ibid., 215.
55. Ibid., 223.
56. For examples from New Mexico, see Page, *Uprising*, 56.
57. Calloway, *New Worlds for All*, 75–76.
58. Bentley, *Old World Encounters*, 76.
59. Jaenen, *Friend and Foe*, 67–68.
60. Foltz, *Religions of the Silk Road*, 85–89.

Coins were an ideal information carrier or symbol of power and faith. Caliph Abd al-Malik, member of the Umayyad dynasty, who reigned from 686 to 705,[61] minted a gold dinar, on which the following quotation was engraved on one side: "There is no God except God alone. He has no partner."

A similar approach could be seen in the coinage of Charlemagne. Christian symbolism such as a cross is also found on coins minted during his reign.[62] Thus, both rulers of empires under different religions adopted a similar means of propaganda.

The message reached people within and outside the empire, believers as well as non-believers, as the means of communication were trade routes. Trade serves as a relatively unobtrusive channel through which people become acquainted with a new religion—all without missionaries, churches, or church organization. Traders were hardly missionaries—they never preached or baptized. But their efforts facilitated conversion by slow "economic pressure." The trade itself via merchants was the propagator. In this manner, Islam stretched "from the Atlas Mountains of northwest Africa to the Hindu Kush" during the seventh and eighth centuries.[63] In the same way, the Nestorian faith was disseminated between Persia and China during the same period.[64]

But of course understanding a coin's inscription required literacy by consumers. Another limitation is that traders were not tasked to proselytize people; their behavior and attitudes only provided a glimpse of their own faith. So the spread of Christianity to Inner Asia was not a missionizing process like in the New World. Traders were often feared by Franciscans because of their bad manners—there could be a huge gap between profit-making and faith. Even when there were many stable trade links between the Near East and Asia, the number of Christians in Inner Asia and China seemed to be very low. In brief, trade alone could not bring about large-scale missionizing success.

Nonetheless, the connection between trade and missionary work was important for the spread of Christianity in Europe. Regarding Pomerania, for example, trade links to the Baltic Sea were already established during the twelfth century in a temporally parallelism with missionizing efforts. Later on

61. Hamilton Alexander Rosskeen Gibb, *Abd al-Malik b. Marwān*, in *The Encyclopaedia of Islam*, new ed., vol. 1, eds. H. A. R. Gibb, J. H. Kramers, E. Lévi-Provençal, and J. Schacht, assisted by S. M. Stern, 1–320, and eds. B. Lewis, Ch. Pellat, and J. Schacht, assisted by C. Dumont and R. M. Savory, 321–1359 (Leiden, Boston, Tokyo: Brill, 1998), 76a–77b.

62. Rosamond McKitterick, *Charlemagne: The Formation of a European Identity* (New York, Cambridge University Press, 2008), 274–275; Ildar H. Garipzanov, "The Image of Authority in Carolingian Coinage," *Early Medieval Europe* 8 (1999), 197–215.

63. Bentley, *Old World Encounters*, 90.

64. Ibid., 106.

the Hanseatic League emerged and influenced Pomeranian cities at the mouth of the Odra River.[65] This is illustrated by the story of a merchant, one of the first to become Christian in Pomerania. In addition to his personal efforts, missionaries were available. In Spanish America, establishing new trade routes alongside the spread of Christianity were also observed. Missionary activities in parallel with mercantile efforts demonstrate an early form of globalization. For instance, the worldwide trade in glass beads from China via the Philippines, Venice, France, Spain, the Netherlands and Bohemia to the Americas could be considered an indicator of this development.[66]

Correlations between long-distance trade and missionary activities are strikingly similar to those between political structure and religion. New dynasties needed confirmation by proselytizing religions. This is obvious for the major world religions—Buddhism, Islam, and Christianity. Emperors from Central Europe to Central Asia supported these religions and their possibilities to make new beliefs more understandable through syncretism.[67] These connections and resulting identity changes evolved in Asia and Europe, and then in the Americas. The following example illustrates this: The "long-held notions of what it meant to be French" were modified in New France through conversion, inculturation, and trade. However, this change brought problems as well. Marc Lescarbot (ca. 1570–1642), who wrote the *History of New France*, once asked rhetorically what was the most important for New France's development—"the Christian religion and the spread of the French name or the private gain of a merchant who does nothing for the service of God or of the King?"[68] Similar argumentation is found in Champlain: The merchants are only "driven by pure malice" and not by the glory of God and the French king.[69] These quotes illustrate that the trader's influence was ambivalent. On the one hand, they were motivated by self-interest, and on the other served

65. Helmut Flachenecker, "Companions and Guides: Saints as Models for Missions," *From La Florida to La California: Franciscan Evangelization in the Spanish Borderlands*, eds. Timothy J. Johnson and Gert Melville (Berkeley, CA: Academy of American Franciscan History, 2013), 83–103, esp. 97–102; Flachenecker, "Bischof Otto von Bamberg und die Christianisierung Pommerns," in *Credo: Christianisierung Europas im Mittelalter*, vol. 1, *Essays*, ed. Christoph Stiegemann, Martin Kroker, and Wolfgang Walter (Petersberg: Michael Imhof Verlag, 2013), 417–426.

66. Peter Francis Jr., Bead Manufacture and Origins, in: *The Beads of St. Catherines Island*, ed. Elliot H. Balir, Lorann S. A. Pendleton, Peter J. Francis Jr. (New York: American Museum of Natural History, 2009), 53–100.

67. Bentley, *Old World Encounters*, 68.

68. Marc Lescarbot, *The History of New France/Histoire de la Nouvelle-France (1611–12)*, eds. Henry Percival Biggar, trans. William Lawson Grant (Toronto: The Champlain Society, 1907), vol. 2:481.

69. Samuel de Champlain, *The Works of Samuel de Champlain/Oeuvres*, ed. Henry Percival Biggar (Toronto: The Champlain Society), 1922–1935, 6 vols., see vol. 2:218.

as a special kind of missionaries in that they were practitioners of a specific faith and represented a specific nation.[70]

Conclusion

The relationship between missionaries and evangelized people changed religious behaviors on both sides and therefore the religion itself. The consequences are specific forms of syncretism that change according to time and place. The missionary experiences in Florida and California are unique in their regional peculiarities, but not in a more structural sense. The missionaries, if they were to be successful and make their efforts sustainable, always had to deal with local symbols of veneration and worldviews of the affected people. From this perspective, events in early medieval Ireland are similar to the situation missionaries and other outsiders faced on the Silk Road or in New France. Richard Foltz underlines this process as follows: "Getting new ideas accepted in traditional societies usually requires camouflaging their 'newness.'" The new belief has to be made "compatible with people's traditional understanding."[71] A conceptual syncretism occurred in China, when Buddhism, Nestorianism, and Manichaeism formed a unique new religious identity in the eighth century[72]; Catholicism and Celtic culture in Ireland interfered with each other beginning in the fifth century. Furthermore, interaction between Slavic religious behaviors in Pomerania and Christian ones took place in the early twelfth century as well.

"New syncretic cultural configurations" also resulted of interaction between an empire and long-distance trade: the conquest of a country was easier for the conquerors with the support of a proselytizing religion.[73] An exception to this conjunction was the transfer of Christianity to Ireland, as mentioned by Patrick. He did not seek to change political structures and was not sent to the isle by a mighty king. This meant that the Irish missionaries working on the continent later had no support from Irish kings. However, the Irish along with Anglo-Saxon missionaries received support from the Frankish kings establishing a connection between the new religion and the empire in this way. Conversion and syncretism, fostered by political pressure, were the main drivers in the spread of Christianity across Europe. This model would "travel" to the New World centuries later.

There are many examples of syncretism and adaptations that could not be mentioned in this paper. The missionaries had to cope with indigenous

---

70. Brazeau, *Writing a New France*, 106–113.

71. Foltz, *Religions of the Silk Road*, 72.

72. On syncretism by the Uighurs who were in contact with Buddhism, Manichaeism, and Nestorian Christianity, see ibid., 80–84; and Bentley, *Old World Encounters*, 75.

73. Bentley, *Old World Encounters*, 73, 78 (Buddhism), 89, 90 (Islam).

peoples from Florida to New Mexico; otherwise, they would probably not have survived. They had to live for years in Indian villages. This situation alone "could produce new levels of tolerance among previously intolerant missionaries."[74] When missionaries had to learn the languages of their proselytes, they also acquired a greater understanding of the indigenous culture.[75] It was a challenge to translate the parables of the Holy Scriptures in languages that had no appropriate terms or notions for words like "sin," "evil," "Holy Trinity," and "transubstantiation." This lack of words in the vernacular languages can be viewed as a sign for a necessary cultural change among the new evangelized societies, not only in the language but also in behaviors.

Indigenous people offered resistance sometimes for decades. This problem brings language into focus as a major reason for the long road to pastoral Christianity after relatively quick formal conversion.[76] But there could be another interpretation as well. Was the so-called "lack of language" by missionaries an excuse for "blaming the victim" (pagan societies)? Perhaps Indian languages in New France (for instance) showed/contained a variety of expressions that the Europeans could not understand. Thus, the absence of words or concepts as an explanation for the failure of (or weak) pastoral Christianity rings false. We know now that the Indian languages were not as deficient as the missionaries asserted.[77]

In many cases Christianization failed, that is, Christianity was never spread by the natives themselves.[78] These cases are fundamentally different from the Irish example, where in the end the Celts themselves spread Christianity to new regions of the Continent. In Florida, most of the people weren't proselytized until the mid-1700s. In New Mexico many Hopis rejected the new belief system for centuries—and continue to do so to the present. This means that the certain groups of natives never achieved "level 3" or "pastoral Christianity" because they did not want it. There was a lot of formal conversion, and even rare forms of Church institutions existed, but this does not signify conversion of the heart. The natives in Florida did not convert through "voluntary association," but "by political, social and economic pressure," to use Foltz's categories. What we see is also a huge difference between the diverse Indian nations and their kind of faith in this Christianization process between the East and West coasts. All things considered, there seems to be no great success for the missionaries at all, especially in the West. The romantic tableau of the pious savage has no real place in this history. The level of syncretism

74. Calloway, *New Worlds for All*, 88.
75. Ibid., 75, 86–87.
76. As a summary see Bentley, *Old World Encounters*, 104–105.
77. Jaenen, *Friend and Foe*, 52–53.
78. Ibid., 75.

shows the level of success as well. Were the proselytes more Christian or more heathen? This is still the decisive question in many cases. We must also keep in mind that changing Indian religions always meant a complete transformation of indigenous culture.[79] In the European Middle Ages, the influence of politics as well as tolerance of other religions were quite different. And the abovementioned Christians in China and Islamic countries around the year 1000 were always tiny minorities. The influence of the official religion was too strong for the new to have had a chance to convert the majority of people (even superficially, as in the quick formal conversion discussed previously).

In the Spanish Borderlands, the blame for each individual setback was, according to Spanish commentators, settled firmly on the shoulders of the respective heathens. Daniel Murphree shows how Europeans developed a process of racializing ("idiom" of describing physical differences) in reaction to ongoing failure in conquest and settlement in the colonial Floridas between 1566 and 1763. These descriptions were used to devise a unique European Floridian identity rooted in distinction from indigenous peoples.[80]

In conclusion, I return to the initial question raised in this chapter: Christianization will change the culture of the conquered people forever, but will the conquerors also be affected? The answer is a clear affirmative. Both conquerors and conquered people influenced one another and both cultures are forever transformed.[81] There are always cross-cultural encounters—perhaps mysticism is the "cultural bridge"—that alter the protagonists.[82] This lesson learned is not only true in the United States, but everywhere that evangelization took place.

79. Ibid., 56.

80. Daniel Murphree, "Race and Religion on the Periphery: Disappointment and Missionization in the Spanish Floridas, 1566–1763," in *Race, Nation, and Religion in the Americas*, ed. Henry Goldschmidt and Elizabeth McAlister (Oxford: Oxford University Press, 2004), 35–59, esp. 36–37, 43.

81. A comparable conclusion is found in Calloway, *New Worlds for All*.

82. Jaenen, *Friend and Foe*, 70; Bentley, *Old World Encounters*, passim; also 69.

Chapter 4
The Indians and the Mendicant Friars: A Colloquium on Religion—A Study of the First Meeting of the Twelve Mexican Apostles with the Aztecs in Mexico

Stephanie Righetti-Templer[1]

Hernán Cortés, the conqueror of the Aztec kingdom, explicitly requested in his fourth report that Carlos V send brothers of the Franciscan and Dominican orders—that is, mendicant friars and not prelates or bishops—to Mexico.[2] The Christian faith should not appear theatrical but rather the true content of Christianity should be spread. Shortly after the arrival of the twelve brothers, Cortés suggested that a symposium on religion should be maintained in which the brothers could speak with Aztec leaders. Some years later, the redoubtable Bernardino de Sahagún reconstructed and put this conversation into writing.

Colloquiums on Religion

Debates among representatives of the three revealed religions (Jewish, Christian, Islam) or of different currents within respective religions were

---

1. I would like to thank my doctoral adviser Prof. Dr. Gert Melville and Dr. Timothy J. Johnson, Agnieszka Johnson, Taylor Logeais and Flagler College in Saint Augustine Florida for their kind support and facilitation. Further thanks goes to the Graduierten-akademie of the TU Dresden for enabling my participation at the symposium and the presentation of my research project there.

2. Hernán Cortés: *Cartas de Relación*, edited by A. Delgado Gómez (Madrid: Ed. Castalia, 1993) Carta de Vera Cruz-Quinta relación:

> „*... que estas partes venieren, uno de la orden de San Francisco y otro de la orden de Santo Domingo, los cuales tengan los más largos poderes que Vuestra Majestad pudiere, porque por ser estas tierras tan apartadas de la Iglesia Romana y los cristianos que en ellas residimos y residieren tan lejos de los remedios de nuestras conciencias y como humanos tan subjetos a pecado, hay necesidad que en esto Su Santidad con nosotros se estienda en dar a estas personas muy largos poderes. . . .*"

common in the Middle Ages. Already in the third century after Christ there were christological disputations as well as in the eighth century between the Western and Eastern Churches referring to iconoclasm.[3] In the twelfth century, there were acknowledged debates in Christianity between representatives of currents considered heretical and representatives of the ecclesiastical doctrine. Likewise, various disputations with Judaism and Islam are documented, as are internal disputes within Judaism and Islam. Because certain basic knowledge about other religions was acquired, genuine dialogues did occur in the twelfth century. By expanding the missionary work of the mendicant orders, the dialogue between Christians and Muslims peaked in the thirteenth and fourteenth centuries. Through the effects of growing missionary fervor as demonstrated by the Mendicant Orders, the thirteenth and fourteenth century saw a virtual heyday of Christian-Islamic dialogue. Most of these controversies, however, are fictional and literary narrations. But there are also concrete ones to be found, the most famous of which happened according to the accounts of the Franciscan William of Rubruck in the second half of the thirteenth century in Karakorum. Upon the Great Khan's initiative, Rubruck participated in a dialogue with a Nestorian, a Muslim, and even Buddhists. The religious dialogues were often realized in a context of coercion, particularly between Christians and Jews. Although Christian and Muslim zealotry continued throughout the Middle Ages (e.g., the crusades and jihads, respectively), such dialogues were nonetheless evidence of a certain curiosity and preparedness to approach a different religion on the basis of reasonable arguments.[4]

The Participants

Indigenous People

The Aztecs arrived in the Valley of Mexico in the twelfth and thirteenth centuries and settled on an island in Lake Tetzcuco. Soon after, via alliances and conflicts with neighboring cities, the Aztecs gained hegemony in the valley. When the young ruler of the Tepanec tribe initiated aggressive expansion, the cities of Tetzcuco, Tenochtitlán, and Tlacopán established a triple alliance in 1428 against the Tepanec city-state and brought an end to its hegemonic ambitions. After other conflicts, the Aztecs became the most important traders of Mesoamerica. In subsequent years, the triple alliance extended its influence toward the southeast, reaching today's Guatemalan border. Last, they also conquered other independent eastern states. Due to internal con-

---

3. Iconoclasm: the debate about the destruction of religious icons for religious reasons.

4. U. Mattejiet, *Religionsgespräche*, in *Lexikon des Mittelalters*, CD-ROM edition (Metzler, 2000). 7, 691–692.

flicts, Tenochtitlán eventually became dominant. The governor of the Aztecs, Montezuma II, claimed the right of control over all the territories and achieved the status of a god-king.[5] Ten years before the Spaniards arrived, eight unusual events (e.g. comets, lightning) and prophecies were recorded. Thus, when the Spaniards arrived at the Mexican coast for the first time, Montezuma II assumed that the god Quetzalcoatl had come. A long and bloody struggle ensued and on August 13, 1521 the Aztecs, led by Quauhtémoc, surrendered to Cortés.[6]

As can be deduced from the prologue, the "people of New Spain,"[7] who were later named "princes and gentleman,"[8] took part in the colloquium on religion. At the beginning of the colloquium they were divided into tribes: Mexican, descendants of Tenoch, peoples of Acolhuacan, Tepanec, Tlaxcala, Michoacán, and Huaxteca.[9] Hereafter, I use the term "Aztec" for all indigenous participants.

Franciscans

Through his words and actions, Francis of Assisi showed how important mission work was for him. In the chapter on missions in the First Rule of 1221 (*Regula non bullata*), he issued a clear mandate, considered similar to the one Jesus declared to his apostles: The friars should go into the world, live in poverty and trust God, heal the sick, exorcise the devil, proclaim the kingdom of God, and bring peace. Francis himself was a missionary in Syria, Morocco, Egypt, and Spain. Francis's followers began to travel the world as missionaries during his lifetime. Shortly after his death, in response to the Mongol invasion in Eastern Europe, the popes sent Franciscan heralds to Asia to learn the intentions of the Great Khan. Consequently, the evangelization of America cannot be considered the Franciscans' first major challenge.

For the Franciscans, the European discovery of America meant a new beginning for old ideas in the New World. Their hope was to return to a life like that of Jesus, in poverty, evangelization of daily life, and rebirth of humanity in Adam's innocence and simplicity. The Native Americans seemed to be ideal for this purpose. They dreamed of a utopia, a millennial kingdom in per-

---

5. H. J. Prien, *Die Geschichte des Christentums in Lateinamerika* (Göttingen: Vandenhoeck & Ruprecht, 1978), 45–47.

6. B. Riese, *Der Untergang der Sonnengötter. Die Hochkulturen des alten Amerikas* (Freiburg im Breisgau: Herder, 2010), 241–251.

7. Bernardino de Sahagún, *Colloquios y doctrina christiana*. In *Sterbende Götter und christliche Heilsbotschaft. Wechselreden indianischer Vornehmer und spanischer Glaubensapostel in Mexiko 1524, "Colloquios y doctrina cristiana" des Bernardino de Sahagún aus dem Jahre 1564,* edition and translation by W. Lehmann (Stuttgart: Kohlhammer, 1949). 73.

8. Ibid., 73.

9. Ibid., 77.

fect peace, a paradise on earth, the kingdom of the Apocalypse, and unsurpassed theocracy.

In the late fifteenth and early sixteenth centuries, the Observants and the Conventual friars in Spain were engaged in bitter disputes. The Observants, who required strict adherence to the rules of Saint Francis, were growing in influence. At the same time, a movement emerged that would play an important role in the evangelization of the New World through the Friars Minor. This group, called "Holy Gospel," were devoted to the ideals and lifestyle of Saint Francis. Accordingly, they adhered to strict rules for diet, attire, and surroundings; their convents were austere, and they slept on planks and went barefoot. It is no wonder that the missionary brothers selected to go to Mexico would derive from this movement.[10]

The Setting

Soon after the conquest of Mexico, Cortés requested that a conversation on religion take place between Aztec nobles and Franciscans. For this colloquium Cortés wanted the twelve brothers to represent Christianity, and thus he eschewed the pomp and glory of secular clerics. This corresponds well with how he received the brothers. To the surprise of the indigenous nobles, he knelt on the floor in front of the brothers and kissed their hands. Subsequently, a dialogue on religion took place. Not only did the Aztecs get a word in this, they were also allowed to consult each other and to then return to the Franciscans with a more competent speaker. Significantly, at first Cortés did not want to force conversion via the Spaniards' superior weaponry.[11]

Forty years later Bernardino de Sahagún, a Franciscan missionary in Mesoamerica, reconstructed the colloquium on religion of the twelve brothers with Aztec leaders in Spanish and Náhuatl, the generally shared idiom of all the Aztec groups. Sahagún's first thirteen chapters and a portion of chapter fourteen are currently housed in the Vatican Archives. The rest of the remaining thirty chapters have not survived, although the titles of the missing chapters are preserved. The colloquium consisted of two parts: the first relates to the content of the conversation, while the second presents brief information in the form of a catechism for baptismal candidates.

The colloquium report describes a specific conversation in 1524 between two people on the subject of religion.[12] Although Sahagún wrote about the

---

10. Antonio Rubial, *La hermana pobreza: El franciscanismo de la Edad Media a la evangelisazión novohispana* (Mexico City: Universidad Nacional Autónoma de México, 1996), 63–67.

11. Hans Wißmann, *Die "Colloquios" des Padre Fray Bernardino de Sahagún als religionsgeschichtliche Quelle* (PhD diss., University of Heidelberg, 1977), 122–123.

12. Ibid., 112–-116.

conversation forty years after the event took place, it provides perspective on the Christianization that took place during those years. Sahagún also reported on the conversation with a specific intent explained in the prologue: the report was intended for use in teaching Christianity.[13]

The Colloquium

Franciscan Point of View

The Franciscans begin the conversation with a "word of teaching,"[14] after which they immediately clarify that they, like the inhabitants of Mexico, are human and not divine. They explain that pope Adrian VI had commissioned them at the request of the Spanish king. The pope sent them to the New World as teachers[15] so that they could bring the Christian religion to its inhabitants,[16] since what they perceived as God was in reality the Devil.[17]

At the beginning of the first chapter the Franciscans refer explicitly to their mortality.[18] As previously mentioned, Cortés received the Franciscans by kneeling and kissing them in the presence of the Aztec leaders. That this choreography was effective is evident in the Aztecs' statement: the Spaniards had just taken control of the governing body of their people, and Montezuma II had publicly asserted that he believed Cortés to be Quetzacoatl, who had returned to Earth. Cortés took advantage of this belief during the reception of the Franciscans and in so doing retained his alleged divinity. Nevertheless it has to be kept in mind that the Aztecs used the identification of powerful people with deities as a religious and political topic, i.e. that they did not really believe in the Spaniards' divinity. Regardless of precisely what the Aztec nobles believed at that moment, the Franciscans rejected such identification at the beginning of the conversation. What induced the Franciscans to effectively dismiss this comparison, which would have supported their authority, was likely an attempt to create proximity to the natives whom they wanted to convert and distance themselves from the conquerors.[19]

Sahagún's document then describes the pope's power to open the way to the kingdom of heaven. Through this power "to open" the pope has the authority to rule over earthly sovereigns.[20] To attain the kingdom of heaven, the Aztecs

13. Ibid., 116–118.
14. Sahagún, *Colloquios y doctrina christiana*, 73.
15. Ibid., Sahagún, 76 (77).
16. Ibid., 76.
17. Ibid., 76.
18. Ibid., 74.
19. Wißmann, *Die "Colloquios,"* 42–48.
20. Sahagún, *Colloquios y doctrina christiana*, 91–92.

had to give up their erroneous beliefs, described as an affront to the true God. Thanks to the Franciscans' priestly function, the Aztecs need not appear before the pope[21]; the missionaries could assist them on the path to the kingdom.[22]

This chapter draws attention to the Franciscans who purposely avoided any association with the Aztecs' concept of the afterlife. There is no term in the Aztec language for God's earthly kingdom except the Holy Catholic Church. The description of the pope as a human being who possesses the key to enter the other world is a very powerful image since, as a consequence, he makes decisions regarding access to God's kingdom. According to the Aztec belief system, one's access to the afterlife is solely determined by the way in which one dies. The most important difference between the two concepts of the afterlife is that the Aztecs considered the other world to be the realm of the dead, while in Christianity, the union of the two kingdoms (living and dead) is extraordinarily important. In Christianity the realm of the dead does not exist since the Church and kingdom of God are one. The two dimensions are described as simultaneous transcendence and immanence. Through their priestly function resulting from the pope's authorization, the Franciscans had the power to allow or prohibit access to the kingdom of heaven. Consequently, they also had the key to the kingdom of God in their hands. This chapter specifically defines the consequences of conversion, or access to the kingdom and thus to glory.

After the Aztecs responded to the aforementioned ideas, the Franciscans expressed their opinion on the sin of believing in the Aztec gods. The Franciscans emphasized that the Aztec gods could not be true gods because if they were, the Franciscans would worship them. They then invoke the authority of God's Word and its universal validity.[23] The Aztecs may have been deceived by tricksters and/or believed in false gods only because they had not yet received news of the true God. Moreover, this state of affairs allowed the Franciscans to absolve the indigenous people of their serious sins. But if the Aztecs, now that they knew the God's Word, continue to worship false gods, they would become guilty and God would allow the Spaniards to continue their extermination program.[24] After this threat, the Aztecs asked for more information about the Christian God.[25] At this point the Franciscans use the disaster of the Conquest as a means of pressure to convince the natives of the true faith. We must stick to the fact that after the aforementioned threat, those who showed interest in the Christian faith were the Aztec nobles and not the priests.[26]

21. Ibid., 76.
22. Ibid., 94; Wißmann, *Die "Colloquios,"* 70–75.
23. Sahagún, *Colloquios y doctrina christiana*, 108–109.
24. Ibid., 109.
25. Ibid., 109–110.
26. Wißmann, *Die "Colloquios,"* 85–87.

The following chapters continue with the detailed explanations promised to the Aztecs. The brothers talked about the fall of the angels from which demons originated.[27] The Aztec gods were said to be among the demon ranks.[28] At this point the Franciscans mentioned names of the Aztec gods and in this way their stories became plausible. They showed that they considered the Aztec gods absolutely real and they did not doubt their existence. To what extent this recognition helped the missionizing effort is difficult to determine as the Aztecs had already been conquered at the time. Again, the only alternative for the Aztecs was to become Christians.[29]

The thirteenth chapter describes the creation the world in seven days and simultaneously introduces the days of the week in Spanish. This is a very clever move to promote conversion, since the calendar was very important in the Aztec worldview and cosmology. As both the Aztec religion and Christianity had a pair of first parents, the Franciscans replaced these figures by the Christian variants of Adam and Eve. Nevertheless, they are careful to use language that prevents Aztecs from mistakenly believing that these are the same people with different names. The Franciscans explicitly emphasized that Aztec beliefs and those of Christianity were not similar with only superficial differences, as only Christianity was true.[30]

Aztec Point of View

The sixth chapter of the colloquium records the speech of the great Aztec nobles. After a formal greeting to the Franciscans, they addressed the issue of their confusion about the Spaniards' origin. The Aztecs suggest that Aztec sovereignty had been destroyed even before the arrival of the brothers, although they administered the territory until the arrival of the real rulers. Eventually they think that the vanquished aztec kings and their predecessors would have been much more able to answer to the Spaniards. They doubt that they even have the authority to give up their traditions as demanded by the Christians. For this reason they hand over the task to the aztec priests who alone have the authority to decide on such matters, i.e. the elimination of the society's traditions was formally transferred to the priests.

Next was the priests and their tasks were presented, such as givers of fire, those with the title "plumed snake" and others educated in the scriptures.[31] The latter described were as those who wear the Tleutatolli—this concept can

27. Sahagún, *Colloquios y doctrina christiana*, 115–116.
28. Ibid., 117–118.
29. Wißmann, *Die "Colloquios,"* 89–95.
30. Ibid., 97–99.
31. Ibid., 96–97.

be translated as "bearer of the divine word" or "bearer of divine stories."[32] The aztec priests replaced now the ancient kings in their authority to lead. Since the nobles were mainly warriors who were responsible for warfare and tax collection, they felt incompetent for tasks required by the Spaniards.[33] The only ones who still had the authority to negotiate the acceptance of Christianity were priests. However, the nobles were aware that all worthy of veneration from their ancestors, that is, customs, laws, rules, and so on, would be destroyed in time with the acceptance of Christianity.[34] The acceptance of another religion entailed renunciation of their own traditions and thereby their identity. They deliberated at length with the aforementioned priests who should have made the decision, or at least, acted as advisers.[35]

After an address by the Franciscans, the Aztecs' response followed in the form of a speech by the "plumed serpent" priest. The priest community questioned whether they as subjects, in fact, might be capable of having their own opinions since the rejection of the Christianity would bring their demise.[36] However, they nevertheless contradicted the Franciscans in this sense. With the following words the Aztec priests show that they had nothing to lose: "We commoners [subjects] . . . are perishable, we are mortal. Even if we did not die. . . , but our gods would be dead."[37] At this point, one can see that the Aztecs cultivated different type of relationship with the divine than the Christians: failure was attributed to the impotence of the gods. Thus, if they accepted the protection of new lords, their gods die. But the entire identity of the Aztecs and other tribes was related to the gods. The gods had always been worshiped and they deserved veneration because they provided wealth, and because traditionally, they had always been worshipped by the ancestors.

The Mexican people drew their strength from ancient ties to the gods. This implies one more indication that accepting Christianity would result in complete annihilation of Mexican identity. For that reason the priests must contradict the Franciscans. The priest expressed this in following ominous words: "Our Lords, do not do anything to your tail, your wing [i.e., your people], that would cause it disgrace, that would make it perish. So also for the elderly men and women, it was their education, their formation. Do not let us bring the wrath of the gods upon us, do not let us be under their fury. . . . [D]o with us whatever you want. Our lords, this is our answer, this is our response to your revered breath, to your revered word."[38] The Aztec priests

32. Ibid., 97.
33. Ibid., 97–98.
34. Ibid., 96.
35. Ibid., 98; Wißmann, *Die "Colloquios,"* 97–99.
36. Sahagún, *Colloquios y doctrina christiana*, 101.
37. Ibid., 102.
38. Ibid., 106–107.

did not render a judgment on the Franciscan claim that their beliefs were false because they associated the beliefs with the cultural and religious traditions of the Mexican people. Again, I stress here that Aztecs beliefs are inseparably linked to their cultural identity.

The Franciscans reiterated that they wanted to save the souls of the natives[39] and do not see that the Aztecs had to give up all that was theirs. The Aztec priests were very aware of the consequences of conversion. They showed dismay and anger that the Franciscans discredited their gods but did not go into detail, nor did they attempt to defend their gods with arguments. While the Franciscans strictly separated politics and religion by intentionally distancing themselves from the conquerors, this separation did not exist for the Aztecs. It was not possible for the Aztecs to have a conversation about objects or concepts from religion because they do not separate state, politics, tradition, and culture from religion. Not only did they fail to understand the differentiation, but they also refused to do so. This was connected with the fact that as the conquered, they do not want to take their sovereignty from the people along with their identity. Neither side understood the other side's arguments. This is evident in the fact that the Aztecs worshiped a higher being but for them this was not inconsistent with the worship of other gods as well. The Franciscans had presented the Christian God with the ancient Aztec name, while at the same time they called the other gods idols. Consequently, the Aztecs did not understand the meaning of the Franciscans' innovations since they already worshiped the God above, which did not involve a contradiction to their polytheism. They rejected this argument of the Franciscans because for them there was no contradiction and, therefore, there was no reason to reject the other gods. So we see that the Franciscans' attempt to accommodate their theory with Aztec imagery and names did not actually work.[40]

In a section of Chapter 16 that has been reconstructed through the extant titles, the Aztecs did not agree with each other on whether they should accept the Christian faith. In Chapter 21, they finally declared their willingness to convert.[41]

Discussion and Conclusion

The Franciscans held the colloquium with the intention of convincing the Aztecs of the true faith. There could be no alternative to ending the conversation other than acceptance of Christianity by the defeated. It follows, furthermore, that the Franciscans saw the Aztecs as humans and able to accept

39. Ibid., 77.
40. Wißmann, *Die "Colloquios,"* 78–85.
41. Ibid., 100–110.

Christianity, meaning that they possessed sufficient capacity to judge and recognize the true faith through discussion. The Franciscans were convinced that their logical argument could lead to the acceptance of Christianity. In their opinion, the fact that the Aztecs also worshiped a diety above showed a remarkable capacity for religious thought. Accordingly, a connection of their missionary efforts with the monotheism of Christianity was very promising. Although in the colloquium there is hardly room for the Aztecs' views, its intention is clear. Because religion in their society is inextricably linked to culture, history, politics, and tradition, conversion to Christianity means the loss of identity. For this reason, first the nobles and then the priests attempted to resist Christianity.[42] The Christians did not reproach the paganism of the Aztecs; rather they believed that their ignorance of the true God led to a "mistaken faith." The Franciscans had very little interested in the essence of the Aztecs' religion; they did not attribute any significance to the most serious objection of the Aztecs, the loss of their identity. From a purely theological perspective, they judged that idol worship was prohibited, regardless of its strong link to the indigenous people's identity. But precisely because their history and gods were inseparable, the priests considered their gods to be dead. In short, we can say that the Franciscans had, in fact, a religious conversation with Aztec cultural leaders (in effect, political and religious specialists) speaks in favor of the Franciscans who saw the people of Mexico as capable of reasoning. However, the colloquium barely left room for contrary arguments, at least according to existing sources. Only conversion to Christianity was acceptable; the Aztecs never had the opportunity to convince a Spaniard of the legitimacy of their faith. Instead, the colloquium consisted of a talk between the winners and losers, the outcome of which was determined from the beginning.

The fact that years later Sahagún reconstructed this colloquium demonstrates the importance of this endeavor for missionary work. The report actually served as a catechism for generations to come and outlined the exemplary image of the "good pagan" who, after all, can be converted by the arguments of the Franciscans and his own common sense.

---

42. Ibid., 124–127.

Chapter 5
Maya Christian Copybooks and the Teabo Manuscript

Mark Christensen

For years the Maya and their writings have captured the attention of the general public and scholars alike. The drawings of nineteenth-century explorer Frederick Catherwood depicting the great buildings and monuments of the ancient Maya laced with hieroglyphs ignited the Western world's fascination with this "lost culture." It seemed as though the Maya had been busily writing for centuries, but what did they write about? Although scholars have since made astounding achievements in "breaking the Maya code" to read the hieroglyphs, today the question remains in the minds of scholars and public alike and even provided fodder for the recent 2012 doomsday craze.[1]

Although forced to share the Yucatan Peninsula with the Spaniards, the colonial Maya nevertheless continued their tradition of writing, albeit in the Roman alphabet. Scholars have made important inroads into understanding what the colonial Maya wrote by uncovering documents ranging from the mundane bill of sale to the seemingly esoteric writings found in what have been termed the Books of Chilam Balam (Maya-authored manuscripts relating various topics important to Maya culture). Yet despite such progress, whenever a scholar approaches a Maya document, the basic question resurfaces: "What did they write about?" It was this question that bounded through my mind as I held a curious Maya manuscript in the summer of 2012.

While visiting family in Utah, I decided to spend some time at Brigham Young University (BYU) to visit with some of my undergraduate professors

*An expanded version of this paper eventually became published in the introduction of my book *The Teabo Manuscript: Maya Christian Copybooks, Chilam Balams, and Native Text Production in Yucatan* (Austin: University of Texas Press, 2016) and appears here with permission.

1. I am referencing, of course, Michael D. Coe's seminal *Breaking the Maya Code* (New York: Thames & Hudson, 1992). For more on the Maya and their supposed doomsday prophecy regarding 2012, see Matthew Restall and Amara Solari, *2012 and the End of the World: The Western Roots of the Maya Apocalypse* (New York: Rowman & Littlefield, 2011); and David Stuart, *The Order of Days: The Maya World and the Truth about 2012* (New York: Harmony Books, 2011).

and explore the L. Tom Perry Special Collections. I was particularly interested in a collection titled, "Biography of William E. Gates, 1863–1940" (MSS 279). Throughout his career studying the Maya, Gates collected an impressive amount of material that included Maya manuscripts from the colonial period. During his life and upon his death, this collection found its way into various universities including Princeton, Tulane, and Brigham Young. The latter purchased a portion of the collection in 1946 that today consists of 117 boxes of documents, manuscripts, photocopies, grammars, personal correspondence, and other materials. Included in this collection is a manuscript written in Yucatec Maya of forty-four pages, originally (mis)cataloged as a "Christian doctrine." Upon closer examination of the text to see what its Maya author(s) was saying, I discovered that it was much more.

Like many manuscript copybooks of its time, this particular manuscript is a collection of discourses written on large sheets of paper. The size was certainly not uniform, but the rough size of the eleven sheets is 21 cm × 33 cm, folded in half to create a sewn gathering of forty-four pages with each folded page measuring 21 cm × 16.5 cm approximately.[2] The manuscript has various thematic sections. The first contains a redaction of the creation of the world and the Fall of Adam and Eve. Following is the genealogy of Christ taken from the Bible, and eschatological material including a Maya rendition of the European apocalyptic text *The Fifteen Signs before Doomsday*. The manuscript then contains a devotional anthem and invocation to both Mary and Christ—discourses that readily appeared throughout European books of hours—and a passage on indulgences that loosely resembles the "Papal instructions for avoiding purgatory" found in the Chilam Balam of Kaua. Finally, the manuscript concludes with a few medicinal remedies for common ailments that seem to have been appended in the early twentieth century, one of which includes the entry "Teabo 8 de Enero de 1911." This paper offers preliminary findings that begin to bring to light this unstudied Maya manuscript, referred to hereafter as the "Teabo Manuscript," a complete analysis of which is found in my recently published *The Teabo Manuscript: Maya Christian Copybooks, Chilam Balams, and Native Text Production in Yucatan*.[3]

Colonial Maya Texts

Although Spaniards had contact with the Yucatec Maya with some regularity beginning in 1517, the military conquest of Yucatan was a lengthy

2. I thank Russ Taylor, Chair of Perry Special collections at Brigham Young University, for providing me with the specific measurements.

3. Mark Christensen, *The Teabo Manuscript: Maya Christian Copybooks, Chilam Balams, and Native Text Production in Yucatan* (Austin: University of Texas Press, 2016).

process involving various *entradas* that did not end until the establishment of Yucatan's capital, Merida, in 1542. This is not to say that the Maya were then "conquered" or that subsequent "revolts" were not actually products of an unfinished conquest, or even that the Yucatan Peninsula was entirely secured by the Spanish. Much of the area would remain unconquered, or what the Spanish preferred to refer as territory *despoblado* (uninhabited) to disguise their inability to subdue the area.[4]

This delay in military subjugation also delayed evangelization efforts. The Franciscans dominated such efforts and waited until 1545 to obtain a firm foothold in Yucatan, although their numbers remained low throughout the colonial period with Yucatan receiving only 2.9 percent of all friars sent from Spain by the Crown.[5] Once there, they immediately began establishing convents and schools, the latter comprising an essential component in converting the Maya.[6] In his *Historia de Yucatán*, Juan Francisco Molina Solís poetically stated:

> In the shadow of the cathedral, and in each one of the monasteries scattered throughout all the territory of the peninsula, schools (for the Maya) were opened; and this was not an accidental or isolated work, but premeditated and carried out with a thoughtful and shrewd plan.[7]

Molina Solís further claims that even the smaller towns, the *pueblos de visita*, had schools equipped, among other things, with a Maya instructor or *maestro*.[8] In the colonial schools the youth of the Maya nobility were taught how to read and write in the Roman alphabet, and also instructed in the Christian

4. For more on the Conquest of Yucatan and, particularly, the natives' role in it, see Matthew Restall, *Maya Conquistador* (Boston: Beacon Press, 1998); John F. Chuchiak IV, "Forgotten Allies: The Origins and Roles of Native Mesoamerican Auxiliaries and Indios Conquistadores in the Conquest of Yucatan, 1526–1550," in *Indian Conquistadores: Indigenous Allies in the Conquest of Mesoamerica*, eds. Laura E. Matthew and Michel R. Oudijk (Norman: University of Oklahoma Press, 2007); Michel R. Oudijk and Matthew Restall, "Mesoamerican Conquistadors in the Sixteenth Century," in *Indian Conquistadores: Indigenous Allies in the Conquest of Mesoamerica*, eds. Laura E. Matthew and Michel R. Oudijk. For a succinct overview, see Victoria Bricker, *The Indian Christ, the Indian King: The Historical Substrate of Maya Myth and Ritual* (Austin: University of Texas Press, 1981), 13–24.

5. John D. Early, *The Maya and Catholicism: An Encounter of Worldviews* (Gainesville: University Press of Florida, 2006), 133.

6. Sergio Quezada argues for three determining factors when deciding where to place the first convents: political and administrative importance, pre-Hispanic religious significance, and density of Indian population. Sergio Quezada, *Maya Lords and Lordship: The Formation of Colonial Society in Yucatán, 1350–1600*, trans. Terry Rugeley (Norman: University of Oklahoma Press, 2014), 50.

7. Juan Francisco Molina Solís, *Historia de Yucatán durante la dominación Española*, vol. 1 (Mérida: Imprenta de la Lotería del Estado, 1904), 322.

8. Ibid., 324.

doctrine.[9] Scattered throughout the late sixteenth-century reports of *encomenderos* given in response to Philip II's questionnaire, and known as the *Relaciones Geográficas*, is the general phrase "In this town there is a school for young boys where they are taught to read and write and who have their *maestro*."[10]

Some of the Maya trained in the schools left to become *maestros* in their own towns charged with the responsibility of instructing the youth in the Catholic doctrine and even of serving as surrogate priests in the frequent absence of the ecclesiastic. Documents from the early Franciscans and ecclesiastics testify to their reliance on these native assistants whose responsibilities could include baptizing the sick and dying infants, hearing confessions of those in their last extremity, delivering sermons and conducting church business on Sundays, and the general policing of the community's spiritual nature.[11] These trained *maestros* also assisted ecclesiastics in composing religious texts in Maya such as catechisms, sermons, and doctrinal treatises.[12] Per-

---

9. Mendieta indicates that occasionally there was "carelessness" regarding the restriction of the schools to noble youth and that at times non-noble natives were admitted "especially in the small towns where there are few people." Jerónimo de Mendieta, *Historia eclesiástica indiana* (Barcelona: Linkgua Ediciones, 2007), 432. However, the *Códice franciscano* (1889) encourages ecclesiastics to not make such a mistake as it would be inappropriate to make commoners the rulers of towns where the nobles had traditionally governed (62–63).

10. For example, see *Relaciones Histórico-Geográficas de la Gobernación de Yucatán: Mérida, Valladolid y Tabasco*, vol. 2 (Mexico City: Universidad Nacional Autónoma de México, 1983), 199, 226, 246, 299, 336. The topic of native education is covered in other works and I refer the reader to those, including Robert Ricard, *The Spiritual Conquest of Mexico: An Essay on the Apostolate and the Evangelizing Methods of the Mendicant Orders in New Spain: 1523–72*, trans. Lesley Byrd Simpson (Berkeley and Los Angeles: University of California Press, 1966), 96–101; *Martín Ramos Díaz*, "Idólatras y mentores: Escuelas en el Yucatán del siglo XVI," *Estudios de Historia Novohispana* 28, no. 28 (2003); Mark Z. Christensen, *Nahua and Maya Catholicisms: Texts and Religion in Colonial Central Mexico and Yucatan* (Stanford: Stanford University Press, 2013), 54–56; Mark Z. Christensen, *Translated Christianities: Nahuatl and Maya Religious Texts* (University Park: Pennsylvania University Press, 2014), 7–8; William Hanks, *Converting Words: Maya in the Age of the Cross* (Berkeley: University of California Press, 2010), 59–84; Anne C. Collins, "The Maestros Cantores in Yucatán," in *Anthropology and History in Yucatán*, ed. Grant D. Jones (Austin: University of Texas Press, 1977); *Códice franciscano, siglo XVI: Nueva colección de documentos para la historia de México*, ed. Joaquín García Icazbalceta (Mexico City: Imprenta de Francisco Díaz de León, 1889), 62–73.

11. *Códice franciscano*, 82–84; France Scholes, et al., *Documentos para la Historia de Yucatán*, vol. 2, *La iglesia en Yucatán* (Mérida: Compañía Tipográfica Yucateca, 1938), 25–34.

12. For more details on the role of *maestros* and religious texts, see Christensen, *Catholicisms*, 74–80. Interestingly, John F. Chuchiak has argued that *maestros* could also serve in the role of a pre-Contact priest, or *ah kin*. See his "Pre-Conquest *Ah Kinob* in Colonial World: The Extirpation of Idolatry and the Survival of the Maya Priesthood in Colonial Yucatán, 1563–1697," in *Maya Survivalism*, eds. Ueli Hostettler and Matthew Restall (Markt Schwaben, Germany: Verlag Anton Saurwein, 2001); also Laura Caso Barrera, *Caminos en*

haps the most famous example is Gaspar Antonio Chi who in a *probanza de mérito* (proof of merit) he sent to the king of Spain stated:

> [I have] performed great services for God and Your Majesty in order to bring about the conversion of the natives of this province . . . and, as requested by the said friars, translated and wrote sermons in the Indians' language in order to preach to them.[13]

Prior to the arrival of the Spanish, the Maya nobility maintained the spiritual and physical well-being of their *cahob* through various positions including that of the *ah kin* or Maya priest. Many of these individuals saw opportunity in the new colonial structure to maintain their positions of religious authority as *maestros*. Indeed, in the eighteenth-century ecclesiastical officials would complain that many towns had too many native officers stipulating that there should be only two instructors of the doctrine and both over the age of fifty.[14]

Overall, the schools instructed the next generation of Maya rulers in the doctrine and details associated with a Spanish/Catholic colonial world. The Maya students learned how to compose bills of sale, testaments, and even religious texts. They became versed on how to maintain reports, financial records, and compose petitions. Moreover, they had access to European texts—the extent of which depended on the size of the church's library. Perhaps most importantly, these schools endowed the Maya with the tools to negotiate a world filled with new actors, rules, and religious beliefs. And these tools helped construct a Maya Christian worldview evinced in the documents, both religious and mundane, that they would produce.

Elsewhere I have grouped native-language religious texts into three general categories.[15] Category 1 texts are printed texts composed by either ecclesiastics, native aides, or both, and intended for a readership of ecclesiastics and natives alike. Category 2 texts concern handwritten texts authored by ecclesiastics, native aides, or both, and designed for a local readership of primarily ecclesiastics and at times natives. Category 3 regards texts written by natives for natives. Although it is possible that some ecclesiastics, certainly those of a more lenient nature, were aware of such texts or even assisted in their composition at some stage, they were not the intended users or audience, nor did they play a role in the texts' preservation, recopying, and iteration.

---

la selva: migración, comercio y Resistencia, mayas yucatecos e itzaes, siglos xvii–xix (Mexico City: El Colegio de México, Fondo de Cultura Económica, 2002), 109–122.

13. Cited in Matthew Restall, "Gaspar Antonio Chi: Bridging the Conquest of Yucatán," in *The Human Tradition in Colonial Latin America*, ed. Kenneth J. Andrien, 2nd ed. (Lanham, MD: Rowman & Littlefield, 2013), 19.

14. Juan Gómez de Parada, *Constituciones sinodales del obispado de Yucatán*, ed. Gabriela Solís Robleda (Mérida: Universidad Nacional Autónoma de México, 2008), 288.

15. Christensen, *Catholicisms*, 53–89.

Because of the strict editorial scrutiny of printed texts in Category 1 and the involvement of ecclesiastics as either authors or audience for Category 2 texts, the literary products of both categories generally contained little or no unorthodox content.[16] However, the general autonomous nature of Category 3 texts afforded them greater opportunity to contain unorthodox contents as a product of either cultural adaptations, personal/local preferences, or both.

Ecclesiastical authorities, however, were not naïve to this, and they took steps to try and regulate the content and quality of religious texts. Indeed, they were aware of the potential errors and misunderstandings that could arise from allowing native assistants too much autonomy with regards to translating and composing religious texts. Thus, the initial leniency granted toward native involvement in the translation and composition of Christian texts ended. The First and Second Mexican Provincial Councils of 1555 and 1565, respectively, both restricted severely the natives' involvement in the translation process and even their possession of native-language Christian texts. Generally speaking, natives were not to translate nor possess any religious text without direct authorization from an ecclesiastic, and they were not to create their own, personal religious texts.

Reflecting this concern for natives writing autonomously and possessing religious texts is a 1570s Inquisition questionnaire regarding, among other things, whether or not to prohibit the natives' possession of translated texts. The questionnaire was given to a few select ecclesiastics chosen for their language abilities. Regarding the possession of religious texts, fray Domingo de la Anunciación responded saying "handwritten [books] should be totally prohibited from them because we have experience that all of the native-authored handwritten books have a thousand errors both in the writing and in the material they relate." However, ecclesiastics were more trusting of Category 1 printed texts and Anunciación states that certain ones, such as Molina's confessional manuals and his own large and small *doctrinas* (catechisms), could "confidently" be left among natives.[17] In a word, natives were not officially authorized to compose and maintain autonomously their own Christian texts, those of Category 3.[18]

---

16. Printed texts required various approvals from ecclesiastical authorities. For example, one of the reasons Beltrán dedicated his *Novena* to the bishop Francisco Pablo Matos Coronado was to achieve the bishop's endorsement according to the dictates of such councils. CAIHY, SM-46, photostat reproduction of Fray Pedro Beltrán de Santa Rosa, *Novena de Christo crucificado con otro oraciones en lengua maya* (Mexico City: Don Francisco de Xavier Sánchez, 1740), "Dedicatoria."

17. AGN, Inq., vol. 43, exp.4, f. 137.

18. Francisco Antonio Lorenzana, *Concilios provinciales primero, y segundo, celebrados en la muy noble y muy leal ciudad de México, presidiendo el Illmo. Y Rmo. Señor D. Fr. Alonso de Muntúfar, en los años de 1555, y 1565* (Mexico City: 1769), 143–144, 201–202. See also Christensen, *Translated Christianities*, 9–11. The increased scrutiny of native-language

But this does not mean that such texts ceased to exist. Indeed, Yucatan and its evangelization depended heavily on native-authored manuscripts—an understandable trait when considering that, unlike Mexico City, a printing press would not be available until 1813.[19] Various religious authorities reported confiscating Maya-authored religious texts of a Category 3 nature. Late sixteenth-century Inquisition reports from Yucatan indicate that translated religious texts were found "in the possession of some Indians who know how to read."[20] Diego López de Cogolludo and Pedro Sánchez de Aguilar both recount instances where handwritten *cartapacios* (copybooks) were confiscated from the Maya. And Fray Diego de Landa mentioned that he had collected various handwritten sermons in Maya whose contents displeased him.[21] The same occurred in the highlands of Guatemala where the K'iche' Codex—a colonial manuscript containing three calendar sequences modeled after the hieroglyphic screenfold books of the Maya—was penned. Commenting on the author of the Codex, Archbishop Cortés y Lárraz stated, "I am informed that he was a choirmaster (*maestro*)."[22] Such texts are invaluable to

---

religious texts by ecclesiastical authorities and the Inquisition, and the divided opinions among the religious orders regarding such scrutiny is well-documented in Martin Nesvig's *Ideology and Inquisition: The World of the Censors in Early Mexico* (New Haven, CT: Yale University Press, 2009), 155–160; David Tavárez's *The Invisible War: Indigenous Devotions, Discipline, and Dissent in Colonial Mexico* (Stanford, CA: Stanford University Press, 2011); 67–68; Christensen, *Catholicisms*, 84–88; Jaime González Rodríguez, "La difusión manuscrita de ideas en Nueva España (siglo XVI)," *Revista complutense de historia de América* 18 (1992): 89–116. For more on the Inquisition and its censorship of printed texts, see Patricia Manning, *Voicing Dissent in Seventeenth-Century Spain: Inquisition, Social Criticism and Theology in the Case of El Criticón* (Leiden: Brill, 2009).

19. Christensen, *Translated Christianities*, 4–7.

20. AGN, Inq., vol. 141, exp.86, reproduced in Francisco Fernández del Castillo, *Libros y libreros en el siglo XVI* (Mexico City: Archivo General de la Nación, Fondo de Cultura Económica, 1982), 319.

21. AGN, Inq., vol. 90, exp. 42. René Acuña suggests that some of these sermons found their way into Fray Juan Coronel's 1620 *Discursos predicables*. See his "Escritos Mayas inéditos y publicados hasta 1578: testimonio del obispo Diego de Landa," *Estudios de cultura Maya* 21 (2001): 169.

22. Barbara Tedlock, "Continuities and Renewals in Mayan Literacy and Calendrics," in *Theorizing the Americanist Tradition*, ed. Lisa Philips Valentine and Regna Darnell (Toronto: University of Toronto Press, 1999), 197. For more on the influence of hieroglyphs on colonial writing, see Victoria Bricker, "The Last Gasp of Maya Hieroglyphic Writing in the Books of Chilam Balam of Chumayel and Chan Kan," in *Word and Image in Maya Culture: Explorations in Language, Writing and Representation*, ed. William F. Hanks and Don S. Rice (Salt Lake City: University of Utah Press, 1989), 39–50; Kerry M. Hull, "Poetic Tenacity: A Diachronic Study of Kennings in Mayan Languages," in *Parallel Worlds: Genre, Discourse, and Poetics in Contemporary, Colonial, and Classic Maya Literature*, ed. Kerry M. Hull and Michael D. Carrasco (Boulder: University Press of Colorado, 2012), 73–122; Matthew Restall, "Heirs to the Hieroglyphs: Indigenous Writing in Colonial Mesoamerica," *The Americas* 54, no. 2 (1997): 239–267; John F. Chuchiak, "The Images

modern scholars for their ability to reveal a Maya interpretation of a colonial Christian world. Moreover, because of the role of the Maya in their creation and preservation, and due to their lack of direct ecclesiastic supervision, Category 3 texts illustrate what the Maya chose to record, or better, what aspects of Christianity they deemed important enough to preserve and incorporate. Today, these texts are limited in number, but to this corpus the Teabo Manuscript adds one more.

Maya Texts, Ethnohistory, and Copybooks

Having established that the Maya composed a wide variety of colonial texts, including those religious, we now return to the question we began with: "What did they write about?" Ralph Roys was among the first to answer such a question though his transcriptions and translations of myriad colonial Maya texts that enabled him to produce numerous articles and books between 1920 and 1965. His transcriptions and translations of colonial Maya documents ranging from medicinal and botanical treatises to mundane land sales are still employed by scholars today. Anthropologists such as Munro S. Edmonson and Victoria Bricker at Tulane took up the torch and employed "the [Maya's] literary documents of the sixteenth century and later" as a "primary window open on the America of aboriginal times."[23] The Books of Chilam Balam attracted the most attention during this time—particularly in the 1980s.[24] Although such studies furthered the use of colonial Maya texts, the texts were largely used as a source of information on the precolonial past with the colonial era receiving secondary attention. Emphasis was placed on Maya science, medicine, and calendrics. Linguistic and anthropological studies dominated this era and pioneering breakthroughs occurred in our understanding of colonial Yucatec Maya as a language and writing system and its relationship to past and present generations.[25] Yet a social history of the colonial Maya obtained primarily from their sources had yet to be achieved.

To be sure, the colonial period won attention from scholars throughout the 1970s and 1980s to produce a variety of seminal works on Maya colonial

---

Speak: The Survival and Production of Hieroglyphic Codices and Their Use in Post-Conquest Maya Religion, 1580–1720," in *Maya Religious Practices: Processes of Change and Adaptation*, eds. Daniel Graña Behrens, et al., Acta Mesoamericana, vol. 14 (Markt Schwaben, Germany: Verlag Anton Saurwein, 2004), 71–103.

23. Edmonson, "The Princeton Codex," 138.

24. For a summary of the work of earlier scholars on the Chilam Balams, see Alfred M. Tozzer, *A Maya Grammar* (1921; New York: Dover, 1977), 182–194.

25. In particular, William Hanks produced notable work in this area. See, for example, his "Authenticity and Ambivalence in the Text: A Colonial Maya Case," *American Ethnologist* 13, no. 4 (1986): 721–744; and his "Grammar, Style, and Meaning in a Maya Manuscript," *International Journal of American Linguistics* 54, no. 3 (1998): 331–369.

society such as Robert Patch's 1979 dissertation that would later become his 1993 *Maya and Spaniard in Yucatan, 1648–1812*, Nancy Farriss's *Maya Society under Colonial Rule* (1984), and Grant Jones's *Maya Resistance to Spanish Rule* (1989). Yet the focus remained on Spanish sources. An important analytical re-creation of colonial Maya culture through their colonial texts appeared with the 1978 dissertation of a Bricker student, Philip C. Thompson. His study utilized a large corpus of Maya testaments and bills of sale originating from the eighteenth-century town of Tekanto to produce an ethnography of the town and its people. Importantly, Thompson used the sources to uncover inheritance patterns, kinship terminology, and class structure and its relationship to political office.[26]

Thompson's study was seminal in another way: it cast a brighter spotlight on the importance and utility of mundane Maya texts. Certainly scholars knew of their existence—Roys made this clear with his 1939 *Titles of Ebtun*. Yet, generally speaking, they were overshadowed by more monumental, seemingly interesting works such as the Chilam Balams or the Ritual of the Bacabs. Like Thompson, Matthew Restall exploited the benefits of mundane documentation in his 1992 dissertation "The World of the Cah," later to become *The Maya World* (1997). Whereas Thompson examined the town of Tekanto, Restall expanded his scope to employ a wide variety of documentation from various regions throughout Yucatan to expose the centrality of the Maya's sociopolitical unit, the *cah*, in the lives of the colonial Maya. It represents the first social history employing native-language sources to encompass the Yucatec Maya as a whole, or as James Lockhart would put it, to "see the general within the particular."[27]

Twenty-first-century studies utilizing Maya documentation involve a wide range of texts from Chilam Balams to testaments, and although the precolonial Maya still receive attention, particularly from anthropologists, the colonial Maya increasingly appear. For example, Victoria Bricker and Helga-Maria Miram's important study on the Chilam Balam of Kaua (2002) and Laura Caso Barrera's work on the Chilam Balam of Ixil (2011), while detailing colonial connections to the precolonial past, also explore a colonial world where Spanish systems had significantly influenced Maya culture. Along with

26. The dissertation would later be augmented by additional sources and published as *Tekanto, A Maya Town in Colonial Yucatán* (New Orleans: Middle American Research Institute, Tulane University, 1999).

27. James Lockhart, "The Social History of Colonial Spanish America: Evolution and Potential," *Latin American Research Review* 7, no. 1 (Spring 1972): 36. Restall's work can be seen as a product of the school known as the "New Philology" and pioneered by his mentor, James Lockhart. For more on the new philology and its impact on Mesoamerican social histories, see Matthew Restall, "A History of the New Philology and the New Philology in History," *Latin American Research Review* 38, no. 1 (2003): 113–134.

the continued works of Restall (1995, 1997, 1998, 1998, 2005), John Chuchiak has also made good use of both Spanish and Maya texts to produce an impressive collection of articles and book chapters detailing the contributions of the Maya in colonial society.[28] Moreover, the increase of known and accessible Maya texts has allowed for comparisons among the texts themselves; the works of Timothy Knowlton (2008, 2010) and myself (2013, 2014), among others, both fall into this category. Finally, in 2010 Hanks produced his seminal *Converting Words*, which examines the formation and spread of a *Maya reducido* or Christianized Maya. Significantly, his chapter examining the Chilam Balams "reverses a long scholarly tradition in which these works are read for their pre-Columbian content, not for their value as an index of colonial transformation."[29]

It is in this general vein of thought that I place my work on the Teabo Manuscript. Although precolonial connections are noted, my work will concentrate more on what the Teabo Manuscript can tell us about the colonial Maya, their writing, and their religious worldview. Among its other contributions, the manuscript calls attention to a category of Maya manuscripts I term the "Maya Christian copybook." Most *cah*-preserved manuscripts containing various religious or historical entries have fallen into the nebulous category of Chilam Balam texts. Scholars differ in their qualifications of what makes a text a "Chilam Balam." Originally, the term applied to colonial Maya manuscripts that contained the prophecy of a Maya prophet, or *chilam*, with the surname Balam who lived during the eve of the Spanish arrival, an event he reportedly prophesied. Certain works, such as the Chilam Balams of Tizimin and Chumayel, contain the prophecies of the prophet. Yet over the years, the term became applied to most of the town-preserved codices scholars discovered regardless of whether or not they contained the prophecy of Chilam Balam.[30] As a result, the majority of manuscripts granted the name "Chilam Balam" make no mention of the prophet whatsoever.

---

28. Such works include, but are not limited to "*Ah Kinob*"; "Secrets Behind the Screens: Solicitantes in the Colonial Diocese of Yucatan and the Yucatec Maya, 1570–1785," in *Religion in New Spain*, ed. Susan Schroeder and Stafford Poole (Albuquerque: University of New Mexico Press, 2007), 83–109; "The Sins of the Fathers: Franciscan Friars, Parish Priests, and the Sexual Conquest of the Yucatec Maya," *Ethnohistory* 54, no. 1 (Winter 2007): 69–127; "*De Descriptio Idolorum*: An Ethnohistorical Examination of the Production, Imagery, and Functions of Colonial Yucatec Maya Idols and Effigy Censers, 1540–1700," in *Maya Worldview at Conquest*, eds. Timothy Pugh and Leslie Cecil (Boulder: University Press of Colorado, 2009), 135–158; "Writing as Resistance: Maya Graphic Pluralism and Indigenous Elite Strategies for Survival in Colonial Yucatán, 1550–1750," *Ethnohistory* 57, no. 1 (Winter 2010): 87–116.

29. Hanks, *Converting Words*, xix.

30. I thank Victoria Bricker for her insight into this occurrence. Personal communication, July 29, 2013.

The Teabo Manuscript itself provides an apt example of the tendency to award the Chilam Balam label to such codices. Although Teabo produced the Chilam Balam of Na and perhaps even the Tekax, rumors have long existed of Teabo having produced other unknown Chilam Balams. In the 1920s, Jean Genet and Pierre Chelbatz described a Chilam Balam for Teabo of twenty pages that contained historical accounts and whose location is unknown.[31] In their 1948 work examining the Chilam Balams, Alfredo Barrera Vásquez and Silvia Rendón indicated that rumors existed regarding the possible existence of lost Chilam Balams of Teabo, Peto, Nabula, Tihosuco, Tixkokob, Hocaba, and Oxkutzcab.[32] Moreover, at one point Munro Edmonson commented that while examining the Gates material—from whence came the Teabo Manuscript—he had come across several Chilam Balam texts from Teabo.[33] Although it is uncertain what specific texts these scholars were referring to when making such claims, it is likely, particularly in the case of Edmonson, that the Teabo Manuscript was initially referred to as a Chilam Balam.

So what, then, are the Books of Chilam Balam? Simply put, they are manuscript compilations of various topics deemed important enough by their authors, likely including *maestros*, and *cah* to record in writing. In a way, these books are bound portions of a larger archive of material available to the Maya authors and/or *cah*. This, then, allows for a *cah* to have multiple copies of any given text circulating in various manuscripts. Due to the central nature of the *cah* in producing these texts, most Chilam Balams carry the name of the town from which they originated. Because the Maya rewrote and amended the manuscripts multiple times throughout the colonial period, the versions available to scholars today are commonly late eighteenth- to nineteenth-century issues of early colonial originals.

The content of the Chilam Balams vary from text to text and can include anything from town histories, to calendrics, to medicinal remedies, to doctrinal tracts.[34] Many Chilam Balams derived their content from similar texts allowing,

---

31. Jean Genet and Pierre Chelbatz, *Histoire des peuples Mayas-Quichés (Mexique, Guatemala, Honduras)* (Paris: Les Editions Genet, 1927), 42, 145, 147. Charles Gibson and John B. Glass use Genet and Chelbatz's work to include the *Chilam Balam of Teabo* in their "A Census of Middle American Prose Manuscripts in the Native Historical Tradition," in *Handbook of Middle American Indians*, vol. 15, *Guide to Ethnohistorical Sources*, part 4 (Austin: University of Texas Press, 1975), 385–386.

32. Alfredo Barrera Vásquez and Silvia Rendón, *El libro de los libros de Chilam Balam* (Mexico City: Fondo de Cultura Económica, 1974 [1948]), 12.

33. One of which was certainly the Na. Bricker, personal communication, February 12, 2013; Munro S. Edmonson, trans. and ed., *The Ancient Future of the Itza: The Book of Chilam Balam of Tizimin* (Austin: University of Texas Press, 1982), xi.

34. Hanks, *Converting Words*; Timothy Knowlton, *Maya Creation Myths: Words and Worlds of the Chilam Balam* (Boulder: University Press of Colorado, 2010); Victoria Bricker, "The Last Gasp," 39–50; Bricker and Miram, *Kaua*; Timothy Knowlton, "Dynamics of

for example, the Teabo Manuscript, the Morley Manuscript, and the Chilam Balams of Kaua and Chan Kan to all share cognate passages on the creation of the world. Because ecclesiastical officials technically forbade natives from possessing and creating their own religious texts, these manuscripts remained hidden from questioning eyes and only nine are known to scholars today.[35]

Yet not all texts compiled and preserved by Maya towns can or should be classified as Chilam Balams. In recent years, scholars have increasingly recognized the existence of handwritten religious manuscripts that contained compilations of selected religious texts deriving from Christianity. Maya trained in writing and the Christian religion in the schools compiled these religious copybooks that were subsequently rewritten and amended over the course of the colonial period. Interestingly, some of the material in such works also appears in Chilam Balam texts. Perhaps the most well-known religious copybook is the Morley Manuscript initially examined by Gretchen Whalen. Timothy Knowlton describes the work as "sort of a 'missing link' between the Books of the Chilam Balam and Christian doctrinal works produced by the Franciscans."[36] Due to their importance and maintenance by local Maya within the *cah*, the books occasionally contain annotations in the final pages or the margins of the book detailing death records and, at times, a few medicinal remedies. Just as someone might record the baptismal date or death of a loved one in the first or last pages of their Bible, so too did the Maya utilize these texts for such purposes.

Although it is tempting to define these Maya-authored religious copybooks as Chilam Balams, particularly when considering their various cognate passages with existing Chilam Balam texts, it would not tell us much about them due to the wide variety of texts the Chilam Balam category encompasses. Moreover, although the compilers of Maya Christian copybooks were surely aware of the Chilam Balam manuscripts, they chose to select and include in their works only texts of a religious nature, thus differentiating them from Chilam Balam texts.

And there are other manuscripts besides that of the Morley and Teabo that likewise testify to a genre of Maya Christian copybooks distinct from Chilam Balams (see Table 1). The Garrett-Gates Mesoamerican Manuscripts

---

Indigenous Language Ideologies in the Colonial Redaction of a Yucatec Maya Cosmological Text," *Anthropological Linguistics* 50, no. 1 (Spring 2008); Laura Caso Barrera, *Chilam Balam de Ixil: Facsmiliar y estudio de un libro maya inédito* (México: Artes de México y del mundo, 2011).

35. Portions of this discussion on the Chilam Balams derive from Christensen, "The Teabo Manuscript," *Ethnohistory* 60, no. 4 (2013): 749–753. For an excellent examination of the Chilam Balams, see Hanks, *Converting Words*, 338–364. Admittedly, it is possible, as Hanks suggests, that ecclesiastics were aware of the Books of Chilam Balam.

36. Knowlton, *Creation Myths*, 48.

TABLE 1. Extant Examples of Maya Christian Copybooks

Manuscript	Origin	Religious Texts	Death Records	Author
Teabo Manuscript	Teabo	Genesis commentary, 15 signs, other	Yes	Unknown
Morley Manuscript	Unknown	Genesis commentary, 15 signs, other	No	Unknown
"Maya Sermons," GGMM no. 65	Unknown	Exempla, 15 signs, other	No	Unknown
"Passion text," GGMM no. 66	Teabo	Passion, discursos sobre la missa, indulgence	Yes	Baltasar Mutul
GGMM no. 70a	Teabo	"Arte de bien morir"	Yes	Unknown
GGMM no. 71	Teabo	Various prayers, other	Yes	Unknown
GGMM no. 72	Tekom (Chichimila?)	Various prayers, other	Yes	Unknown
Harvard Manuscript	Unknown	Passion	No	Unknown

collection at Princeton University (GGMM) contains several examples, all of which date from the eighteenth to nineteenth centuries. Two are Maya books containing various prayers; one—no. 71—is from Teabo, the other—no. 72—has death records from Tekom and makes references to Chichimila. The latter contains a section with instructions written in a Maya hand on how to help someone in the last extremity. The Maya reader is instructed to immediately call for a priest authorized to confess, and that if it were an emergency he should read the prayers included in the text.[37] The intended reader and owner of such a work was surely a Maya *maestro* charged with such duties. In fact, in his instructions to ecclesiastics, the sixteenth-century bishop of Yucatan, fray Francisco de Toral, outlined the role of *maestros*, who he calls in Maya *ah cambeçah* (he who teaches), in helping other Mayas to die well. Due to their importance in this regard he stated, "And the *ah cambeçah* and others who likewise help [the sick] to die well are highly valued before our lord God."[38] This role for *maestros* continued throughout the colonial period.[39]

37. Princeton University Library, Department of Rare Books and Special Collections, Garrett-Gates Mesoamerican Manuscripts (C0744) (hereafter GGMM), no. 72, "Yucatec Prayers," 31r.

38. France Scholes, et al., eds. *Documentos para la historia de Yucatán*, vol. 2, *La iglesia en Yucatán* (Mérida: Compañía Tipográfica Yucateca, 1938), 30.

39. In 1722 ecclesiastics were again admonished to use "ah cambeçahs" to help others die well. Gómez de Parada, *Constituciones sinodales*, 110.

Another example, but from an unknown town, is a likely eighteenth-century copybook (GGMM no. 65, hereafter referred to as "Maya Sermons") of seventy-two folios containing a variety of Christian texts that includes a "*libro de matrimonio de predicasiones de pariende*" and portions of the *Flos sanctorum*, a popular hagiography in Spain. One of the texts is a Maya version of the text *The Fifteen Signs before Doomsday*. Interestingly, cognate passages of this text can also be found in the Teabo and Morley Manuscripts, and the Chilam Balam of Tusik. Also fascinating, pages five through eighteen of this over 140-page manuscript correspond very closely with the first twenty-three pages of the Tusik that recounts the moralistic tales of "A Soldier," "St. Julian," "Coronado," "Pilate," and "St. Paul," *The Fifteen Signs*, and a subsequent discussion of the Final Judgment. The Maya stories and eschatological discussion derived from hagiographies and texts popular throughout the Middle Ages such as Jacobus de Voragine's *The Golden Legend* (ca. 1260)—with the *Flos sanctorum* being the Spanish version—and the Bible.[40]

An additional Maya Christian copybook from Teabo is a manuscript that consists of a Maya redaction of the Passion (GGMM no. 66, hereafter "Passion text"), followed by instructions for the Mass that has cognate texts in the Kaua and Chan Kan.[41] Still another small manuscript text from Teabo and bound in leather is a Maya translation of the seventeenth-century *Ramillete de divinas flores* (Bouquet of Divine Flowers) (GGMM no. 70a), which is an *Arte de bien morir* by don Bernardo Sierra that apparently experienced some popularity among the Maya.[42] The final pages contain death records from mid to late nineteenth-century Teabo and some, including one from 1882, contain the name and signature of Secundino Na—most definitely the same person as the José Secundino Na who helped compose the Chilam Balam of Na from Teabo, and who was an active author in that town until his death on May 15,

---

40. The story of St. Julian can be found in Jacobus de Voragine, *The Golden Legend of Jacobus de Voragine*, trans. and eds. Granger Ryan and Helmut Ripperger (New York: Longmans, Green and Co., 1941), 130–131.

41. Bricker and Miram, *Kaua*, 301–306. Marla Korlin Hires, "The Chilam Balam of Chan Kan" (Ph.D. dissertation, Tulane University, 1981), 130–135. The manuscript receives brief attention in *Maya Research (Mexico and Central America)*, ed. Frans Blom, vol. 2, no. 3 (New York: Alma Egan Hyatt Foundation, 1935), 300–301. The Passion theme continued strong among the Maya beyond the colonial period. See Victoria Bricker, *The Indian Christ, the Indian King: The Historical Substrate of Maya Myth and Ritual* (Austin: University of Texas Press, 1981), 155–162.

42. For example, once trained in reading and writing, the Maya Miguel Canchan was reportedly seen always with the work. Caso Barrera, *Caminos*, 295. This genre of text was popular and numerous authors produced works with similar names, although some fell under the prohibition of the Inquisition. In fact, the convents of sixteenth-century Merida contained the prohibited *Ramillete de flores espirituales* by Manuel de Gaya. Fernández del Castillo, *Libros y libreros*, 325.

1885.[43] Indeed, the rubrics are an exact match. One final example is a manuscript of unknown provenance of which various images were found among the Mayanist Ian Graham's papers at the Peabody Museum in Harvard.[44]

As mentioned, many of these manuscripts have cognate texts with various Books of Chilam Balam. But their selective religious content sets them apart. Thus, I have classified such manuscripts as the Teabo and Morley, and those mentioned above, as "Maya Christian copybooks." Of course, I realize that such classifications and distinctions were not employed by the colonial Maya in such a way and that they are for the main convenience of modern researchers who, like myself, have an insatiable need to categorize everything. The content matter of both Chilam Balams and Maya Christian copybooks appeared equally important to the Maya and oftentimes flowed freely between one genre of texts to another. Yet the fact remains that Maya manuscripts containing purely Christian content exist today, and for the sake of convenience, I have chosen to classify them as Maya Christian copybooks.

These copybooks provide valuable information on colonial text production, culture, and religion. Their compilers, preservers, and audience were certainly Maya, thus making them Category 3 texts. However, it cannot be said for certain that local ecclesiastics were not aware of their existence. Recently Hanks challenged the idea that Chilam Balam texts were kept "hidden" from priests.[45] Regarding Maya Christian copybooks, I would offer the possibility that such texts were kept hidden from "certain" priests, but perhaps allowed to be seen by those more lenient. Regardless, because they were technically forbidden and maintained by local Maya within their communities, these copybooks provide a rare insight into what aspects of Christianity the Maya deemed important enough to record. With rare exception, these copybooks have gone largely unstudied and represent a significant gap in the historiography concerning Maya evangelization, religion, and text production in the colonial period.[46] My forthcoming work endeavors to begin to fill that gap.

---

43. These final pages are missing from the original copy in Princeton, but are included in the photostatic copy held at Brigham Young University, L. Tom Perry Special Collections (LTPSC), MSS 279, box 74, folder 2, "Para ayudar a buen morir en lengua yucateca." For the signature of Na, see Gubler and Bolles, *Na*, 224–225, 237.

44. I thank Victoria Bricker for alerting me to and providing digital images of this manuscript.

45. Hanks, *Converting Words*, 346.

46. Knowlton, *Creation Myths*; Gretchen Whalen, "An Annotated Translation of a Colonial Yucatec Manuscript: On Religious and Cosmological Topics by a Native Author," Foundation for the Advancement of Mesoamerican Studies, 2002, http://www.famsi .org/ reports/ 01017.

General Observations about the Teabo Manuscript

The surviving corpus of Maya texts, particularly Maya Christian copybooks, point to Teabo as an active producer of colonial manuscripts. That said, is seems unlikely that the number of texts available today from Teabo was due to any additional ecclesiastical presence or the superior religiosity of its residents. Most likely, Teabo produced similar quantities of texts to that of other comparable Maya towns, but collectors, such as Gates, had the most luck in acquiring those from Teabo.

Regarding the Teabo Manuscript itself, the paper appears to be that of the eighteenth or early nineteenth century, but the orthography extends into the twentieth century. Moreover, a number of dates appear throughout the text from 1802 to 1925. Thus the manuscript has been copied and amended multiple times, the final occurrence being in the twentieth century, until somehow it fell into Gates's possession. Fortunately, the line "Teabo 8 de Enero de 1911" appears in the final pages of the manuscript to confirm its origin.

Concerning its author(s), many Maya Christian copybooks and Books of Chilam Balam lack an identifiable author. Some authors, like José Secundino Na and José María Na openly took responsibility. Others invented their sources out of whole cloth or simply allude to them. The Chilam Balam of Ixil provides examples of both. The book declares that its medicinal remedies were "given by a moor, by his own voice, Ruy Díaz de Vivar (El Cid)."[47] El Cid was a Spanish nobleman and the great military leader of medieval Spain and his published legend was popular, although prohibited, reading throughout New Spain. Here, the Maya of Ixil obviously knew of the legend and elected the Campeador as the source of the remedies while obscuring the true author. Moreover, inserted at the bottom of one of its pages is the line, "*yo proveye junn yPolito Pech* (rubric)" (I supplied the paper/book, Hipólito Pech).[48] Although we cannot be certain as to the specific role of Hipólito, the insertion indicates the role of the Pech *chibal* (lineage) in the book's composition. In the end, when no clear assertions are available we are left to surmise the identity of the author(s). However, analyses of orthography, prose, and hand can be used to assist in making observations, and such is the case with the Teabo Manuscript.

The following appears at the end of the Teabo Manuscript's redaction of *The Fifteen Signs before Doomsday*:

---

47. Caso Barrera, *Ixil*, 29, 98, 99.
48. Ibid., 17.

> *dia 11 de Desienbre de 1803 años caa ti ɔoci yn canbal hoksic hunpel libro Gensis u kaba u tial txocol Ca u sates ten yn yum Max bin y ylic ua yan Kasite ten u...*[49]
> The 11th of December 1803, when I finished learning to manifest a book called Genesis in order for it to be read. That he forgives me, my lord who will see if there are errors, I the...

An extremely similar phrase is also found in another Teabo text, the "Passion text," which redacts the Passion of Christ:

> *Teabo y Nobi 22 de 1803 años Ca ti ɔoci yn canbal hoksic hunꝑel Libro fasion u kaba u tial txocol Ca u sates ten yn yumob hemax bin ylic ua yan Kasite ten u ɔeɔil u Palilob Uay ti Cah Teabo lae Baltħaseͬ Mutul* (rubric)
> *esno*
> *Ten Baltasar Mutul tialtic libro fasion lae esno* (rubric)[50]
> Teabo, November 22, 1803, when I finished learning to manifest a book called Passion in order for it to be read. That they forgive me, my lords who will see if there are errors, I who am the least of their servants. Here in this *cah* of Teabo. Baltasar Mutul, notary (rubric)
> I who am Baltasar Mutul possess this Passion book, notary (rubric)

The incomplete statement from the Teabo Manuscript lacks its author. Although, the statement by Baltasar Mutul in the Passion text is a near verbatim match to that in the Teabo Manuscript, the handwriting differs, suggesting a different author and the use of a common concluding statement. Given that the entry in the Teabo Manuscript appeared less than one month after that in the Passion text, and that both originate from Teabo, it seems very plausible that Baltasar Mutul was aware of the Teabo Manuscript's compilation although his hand is difficult to locate in the manuscript itself. That said, changes in orthography, prose, and ink throughout the text suggest the hands of various contributors. Although inconsistencies in any given author's calligraphy and orthography make such analyses an inexact science, it appears that at least two Maya authors penned the doctrinal texts of the Teabo Manuscript. Moreover, the death record and the random medicinal remedies appear in different hands.

Thus, like other Maya Christian copybooks, the Teabo Manuscript had multiple contributors. That such copybooks were preserved by the *cah* and exchanged hands is also made clear by the Passion text. Although Baltasar Mutul was the self-proclaimed author and owner, death records amended in

---

49. LTPSC, MSS 279, box 74, folder 3, "Christian doctrine" (hereafter Teabo MS), 35. The sentence appears incomplete.

50. GGMM no. 66, "Discourses on the Passion of Christ and Other Texts," 44.

the final pages range throughout the late nineteenth century. Two entries recording the 1875 death of "Mª Bictoriana Na" (María Victoriana Na) and the 1882 death of Juan Pech were signed by Secundino Na, certainly the same person as the José Secundino Na who composed the Chilam Balam of Na from Teabo and who added some death records in the previously mentioned Maya translation of *Ramillete de divinas flores* also from Teabo.[51] It would seem likely that Mutul and his successor, Na, both composed and had access to a variety of Maya Christian copybooks in their town of Teabo.

In sum, the Teabo Manuscript was one of several Maya Christian copybooks extant today from Teabo. Two or more Maya authors likely compiled the work in the early nineteenth century from various existing sources, and it was then preserved and appended throughout the early twentieth century until it fell into the possession of Gates. The intention was seemingly to compose a work of Christian texts the authors and/or the *cah* deemed important. The texts and topics the Maya authors and the *cah* of Teabo deemed important enough to record in the Teabo Manuscript are the subjects of my forthcoming work.

51. The Passion text exists in its original form in GGMM no. 66, "Passion of Christ," and also in photostats at LTPSC, MSS 279, box 74, folder 10, "Pasión de Jesucristo." Interestingly, when Jóse Secundino Na signed the Chilam Balam of Na, he used a phrase similar to Baltasar Mutul's: "Here I have finished copying the notebook on the 15th day of August of the current year of 1863. It is I who will see if there is anything forgotten or wrong. It is not my fault because my education is not complete. This I swear by my word, I José Secundino Na." Gubler and Bolles, *Na*, 224–225. Gubler and Bolles use the date 1873. However, this seems to be an error as the manuscript reads "mil ochocientos sesenta y tres años."

Chapter 6
Andean Ritual Experts and Native Views on Sacred Mountains and Priests

Constanza Ceruti

Beliefs and rituals in South America are the result of millennia of cultural traditions and centuries of creative syncretism. The religiosity of the native people of the Andes is rooted in ancestral views of mountain landscapes that were modified under the rule of the Incas, challenged during the Spanish conquest, and modeled by Catholic missionaries.

The Andes mountains are the abodes of ancestors' spirits, which are known as *achachilas* among the Aymara people in the highlands of Bolivia. The Kallawayas in the Eastern Andes see their mountains as places of origin or *pacarina,* a belief that is shared among the Quechua communities in the Colca region in southern Peru. Mountain spirits (*apus, wamanis, mallkus*) are related to Mother Earth (Pachamama) and Pachacamac (Lord of Earthquakes). In the time of the Incas, mountains were used as altars to present offerings to the state deities Inti (Sun), Viracocha (Creator), and Illapa (Lightning). The sacred geography of the Andes nurtures beliefs in "dangerous places" such as *salamancas* (haunted caves) and *lagunas bravas* (haunted lagoons). Occasional references to mermaids and golden-horned bulls attest to the Hispanic influences on Andean mythology.

High-altitude archaeology has made a significant contribution to the understanding of mountain worship in the ancient Andes, by means of the study of Inca shrines erected on summits over 20,000 feet in elevation. Their extraordinarily preserved artifacts and frozen mummies of sacrificial victims have added a unique archaeological dimension to religious studies that were primarily based on ethnohistorical sources.[1] Ethnographic expe-

1. María Constanza Ceruti, *Cumbres Sagradas del Nororeste Argentino* (Buenos Aires: Editorial de la Universidad de Buenos Aires, 1999); Ceruti, *Llullaillaco: Sacrificios y Ofrendas en un Santuario Inca de Alta Montaña* (Buenos Aires: Ediciones de la Universidad Católica de Salta, 2003); Johan Reinhard and María Constanza Ceruti, *Inca Rituals and Sacred Mountains: A Study of the World's Highest Archaeological Sites* (Los Angeles: Cotsen Institute of Archaeology, University of California–Los Angeles, 2010).

riences on mountain pilgrimages have also deepened our understanding of Andean religiosity.[2] Although the Inca ceremonies of *capacocha* that carried messengers and offerings to the highest mountains did not survive the European invasion, the cultural legacy of the Inca civilization has been successfully kept alive in the religious traditions shared by native groups throughout the Andes.

In this chapter we will consider Andean traditional religious experts of Ecuador, Peru, Bolivia, northern Chile and Argentina, and their role in pilgrimages, initiation, divination, and healing rituals, as well as sorcery and witchcraft. We will extend the analysis to briefly cover the traditional Andean views on Catholic priests and Franciscan missionaries.

An Overview of Andean Ritual Experts

Modern Andean ritual experts have been described as a combination of priest and shaman[3] and sorcerer and diviner.[4] Nonetheless, they are likely to lead fairly ordinary lives, performing their sacred duties in harmony with the usual activities that provide daily subsistence. Magic and healing rituals are performed at night; offerings and sacrifices are presented at sunrise; and the most demanding tasks, such as the healing trips of the Kallawaya medicine men, are scheduled to take place in winter (which do not interfere with agricultural activities).

Andean ritual experts owe their vocation and power to the sacred mountains in the landscape that surrounds them. The Quichua healers work at the mercy of the volcanoes Chimborazo and Cotopaxi, in Ecuador. The Quechua *altomisayocs* in Peru are capable of speaking directly to the *apus* of the mountains Ausangate and Salcantay, which were also considered sacred in times of the Incas. Aymara ritual experts and Kallawaya medicine men are under protection of the highest peaks of the Royal Range in Bolivia, the *achachilas* of mounts Illimani and Illampu. In northern Argentina, the traditional healers invoke powerful volcanoes such as Llullaillaco and Quehuar.

The ritual praxis in the Andes is regulated, among other things, by the weekly calendar, in which certain days are believed to be auspicious for particular kinds of ceremonies. Wednesdays and Thursdays are appropriate to

2. Ceruti, "Qoyllur Rit'i: Etnografía de un peregrinaje ritual de raíz incaica por las altas montañas del sur de Perú," *Scripta Ethnologica* (Centro Argentino de Etnología Americana, Buenos Aires) 29 (2007): 9–35; Ceruti, *Procesiones andinas en alta montaña* (Salta, Argentina: Editorial de la Universidad Católica de Salta, 2013).

3. Guillermo Cock, "Sacerdotes o chamanes en el mundo andino," *Historia y Cultura* (Lima) 16 (1983): 135–146.

4. Juan Alberto Vellard, *La medicina indígena sudamericana* (Museo Etnográfico de la Facultad de Filosofía y Letras de la Universidad de Buenos Aires, 1983), 12.

perform healing and agricultural rituals; Saturday and Sunday are destined for Catholic rituals and Tuesdays and Fridays for sorcery and witchcraft.[5]

Quechua Ritual Experts

The Quechua ritual experts are generically known as *paqos*. *Paqos* do not engage in witchcraft, which is in the sphere of the sorcerers (*layqa*). Quechua medicine men are known as *hampiq*, and the diviners as *wataq*.[6] Ritual experts who invoke mountain spirits are called *misayocs* and *sonqoyocs*, which can be translated, respectively, as "those who have the offering assemblages" and "those who have the heart."

The *altomisayocs* are Quechua ritual experts of higher rank, selected by lightning and capable of conversing directly with the *apu* spirits in the highest mountains. They are sometimes in possession of a particular stone that helps them in their ritual praxis. The power and status of the *altomisayoc* reside in the number and hierarchy of the *apus* that they can summon.[7] According to their age and prestige, Quechua ritual practitioners are comparatively categorized as "major" or *kurak*, and "minor" or *sulka*.

The Quichuas in the area of Chimborazo recognize local healers known as *jambidores*. They cast away evil spells from houses and help cure people who have been negatively affected by the wind whirlpool.[8]

Kallawaya Medicine Men

Kallawaya ritual experts who diagnose and cure by "feeding" the sacred places in the landscape are considered to be "wise." The "wise man" is a *qari yachaj* and the "wise woman" is a *warmi yachaj*.[9] A ritual expert in divination with coca leaves (*coca qhawaq*) intervenes to identify the *yachaj* who has been chosen for each particular ceremony. Ritual practitioners selected through divination with coca are known as *tupachisqa*, whereas those elected by the community are called *acllasqa*.[10]

The Kallawaya who becomes an intermediary before the mountain spirits in collective ceremonies is called with the same names that are used to desig-

5. Joseph Bastien, *La montaña del cóndor: metáfora y ritual en un ayllu andino* (La Paz: Hisbol, 1996), 101.

6. Manuel Marzal, "La experiencia religiosa quechua," in *Rostros indios de Dios*, ed. Manuel Marzal, pp. 27–80 (La Paz: Hisbol, 1992), 53.

7. Efraín Morote Best, "Espíritus de montes," in *Letras* 56/57 (Lima: Palma, Néstor Homero, 1956), 303.

8. Federico Aguiló, *El hombre del Chimborazo* (Quito: Ediciones Abya-Yala, 1992), 19.

9. Bastien, *La montaña del cóndor*, 92.

10. Ina Rosing, *Rituales para llamar la lluvia* (La Paz: Editorial Los Amigos del Libro, 1996), 273.

nate ancestral mountain spirits: *machula, apu*, and *achachila*.[11] High-ranking ritual experts present offerings to the most important sacred places in the landscape; whereas messengers are recruited to carry bundles of offerings (prepared by the experts) to the sacred places that are considered secondary in the hierarchy.[12]

The young messengers who carry offerings to the sacred summits are known as "those who go upwards" or *pata puriqkuna*.[13] Those who climb the mountains to perform the sacrifices and offerings on the summits are called *orco puriquna*, and those who go to the mountains to call the rain are known as *paraman puriqkuna*. In addition, ritual experts can work for "the feminine side" or "the masculine side." Those on the feminine side have power over the rain; whereas the ones on the masculine side are said to have "hot hands" and to hold power over lightning.[14]

Aymara Ritual Experts

The *yatiri* is an Aymara ritual expert of the highest rank who has been selected by lightning and is therefore able to contact the mountain spirits. He is often described as a native priest specialized in the religious affairs of his community.[15]

Yatiris are expected to fulfill their ritual role at home, working with whoever comes to them but without explicitly promoting their skills. In contrast, Kallawaya healers go from house to house and travel to other villages selling their medicine.[16]

Andean advisors whose wisdom is based on an intellectual experience are known as *amautas* and may be conceived as philosophers, whereas *yatiris* are diviners whose knowledge is intuitive and derives from their relationship with the lightning, mountain spirits, and auxiliary skulls or *riwutus*.[17]

In contrast, the *chamakanis* are the equivalent of the Quechua *altomisayoqs*, those who can communicate directly with the spirits of the higher mountains[18]; whereas the *laykas* are sorcerers who perform witchcraft.[19] Other Aymara ritual experts include the *uñiri*, who performs divination by consult-

11. Ibid., 64.
12. Ibid., 273.
13. Ibid., 154.
14. Ibid., 144–154, 354–362.
15. Domingo Llanque, *Medicina aymara* (La Paz: Hisbol, 1994), 25–26.
16. Tomás Huanca, "El yatiri," in *La comunidad aymara* (La Paz: Ediciones CADA, 1989), 70.
17. Ibid., 40–41.
18. Juan Alberto Vellard, *El Hombre y los Andes* (Buenos Aires: Ediciones Culturales Argentinas 1981), 159.
19. Huanca, "El yatiri," 24.

ing the coca leaves; the *aysiri*, who deals with atmospheric phenomena; the *luqtiri*, who is an expert in offerings for health and success; the *quwachiri*, who burns incense and aromatic herbs; the *milluchiri*, who prepares ritual baths and uses aluminum in healing; and the *risiri*, who offers prayers on behalf of others.[20] Chiropractors are known as *thaliri* and midwives as *usuiri*.[21]

Religious Initiation

In the Andean world, certain individuals are predestined to become ritual experts. They may be seen as "children" of the lightning deity, a belief not uncommon in the case of twins' birth.[22] Or they may have their vocation manifested in dreams. However, the usual procedure of selection requires that the candidate is actually hit by lightning. The individual who has been selected by lightning cannot refuse the vocation to become a ritual expert: he or she is expected to be instructed by an experienced ritual expert, and failing to do so can carry illness or even death. Eventually, the candidate will go through a ceremony of initiation before being capable of fulfilling the social roles of healer, priest, and fortune teller.

Selection by Lightning

People hit by lightning are empowered to perform divination and healing rituals. In the Peruvian highlands, they are known as *sanduyuq*, *yachayniyuq*, *karpayoq*, or *isquinayuq*, and believed to be capable of making the mountain spirits "speak."[23] Certain mountains "have a lot of power" and they give it to people they choose with lightning. The chosen individuals acquire a godlike status since they are under the orders of the mountains to cure the sick.[24]

The individuals selected by the impact of lightning are known among the Aymara as *rayun purita*.[25] The Aymara also distinguish the *purita* who have been hit by lightning from the *axata* who have been seized by lightning and the *pantata*, who have been hit by mistake.[26] People can be repeatedly hit by lightning, particularly if they do not understand their vocation, or if they do not take it seriously. In northern Argentina, local healers or *curanderos* are

---

20. Ibid., 47–48.
21. Llanque, *Medicina aymara*, 24.
22. Vellard, *La medicina indígena sudamericana*, 7–8.
23. Carmen Escalante and Ricardo Valderrama, *La doncella sacrificada: Mitos del Valle del Colca* (Arequipa: Universidad Nacional de San Augustín/Lima: Instituto Francés de Estudios Andinos, 1997), 95–96.
24. Ibid., 147–149.
25. Huanca, "El yatiri," 25.
26. Ibid., 43.

sometimes selected by lightning[27]; some may receive their vocation after a near-death experience or when confronted with the illness of a close relative.

The selection by lightning usually occurs at puberty, when the youngsters are devoted to herding activities and thus, more exposed to the elements. It sometimes happens as a confirmation of certain physical signs identified at birth.[28] When lightning hits the chosen person, he or she is doomed to die if somebody else has witnessed the impact directly. On the other hand, if the victim is alone, he or she will likely be revived by the lightning and empowered to become a *yatiri*.[29] In those cases, the first impact of lightning "tears the body apart." A second impact almost immediately after the previous reconstructs an improved version of the candidate, who thereafter is gifted with the power of clairvoyance. It is interesting to note that symbolic dismemberment of a candidate during the ritual of initiation has been cross-culturally documented in Eliade's famous study of shamanism.[30]

Instruction Period and Ceremonial Initiation

The procedure of instruction to become a ritual expert among the Aymara is comparatively short and simple. The *yatiri* is apprenticed to a *chamakani*, leading to an initiation ceremony that allows the candidate to become a ritual expert accepted by his community.[31] At the end of the training, his ritual knowledge is examined by his master, prior to receiving a special insignia known as the *t'aqxata*. The initiation ceremony takes place on top of a sacred mountain that is home to an ancestral *achachila* spirit.[32]

The instruction period for the Quechua ritual experts among Q'ero villagers has been analyzed in detail.[33] The candidate is adopted as a son (*waway*) and stays at the service of his master, while learning the necessary skills to become a *paqo*. First, he learns how to diagnose with coca leaves, thus becoming a diviner (*watoq*). Second, he becomes familiar with the secrets of traditional medicine in order to be educated as a healer (*hampiq*). Once the candidate undertakes his first initiation (*karpay*), he becomes a ritual expert or

---

27. Maricel Pelegrin, *Cuando la salud viene de la tierra: Una visión antropológica de la medicina popular en Jujuy, República Argentina* (Buenos Aires: Editorial Del Umbral, 2005).

28. Huanca, "El yatiri," 56–57.

29. Ibid., 59–61; Vellard, *El Hombre y los Andes* (Buenos Aires: Ediciones Culturales Argentinas 1981), 109.

30. Mircea Eliade, *Shamanism: Archaic Techniques of Ecstasy* (Princeton, NJ: Princeton University Press, 1974).

31. Huanca, "El yatiri," 65–66.

32. Llanque, *Medicina aymara*, 27.

33. Washington Rozas, "Los paqo en Qero," in *Qero: El último ayllu inka*, ed. Jorge Flores Ochoa (Cuzco: Centro de Estudios Andinos, 1983).

paqo. A higher initiation (*hatun karpay*) is required to become an *altomisayoq*, who is believed to be able to converse directly with the mountain spirits.

Initiations of the *yatiris* and *altomisas* are the only Andean ritual circumstances that may be comparable to the traditional vision quests among some Native American groups in the northern hemisphere. During the quest for a vision, candidates are secluded in isolation in an undisturbed natural setting, enduring severe fasting and exposure to the elements. The vision quests are not only part of a medicine man's education, they are universally undertaken as steps in the traditional initiation process into manhood.

In the mountains east of Cuzco, the Q'ero candidates to become *paqos* are initiated in a ceremony known as *karpay*. The ritual, as described by Rozas[34] involves visiting a mountain scenario near the sacred peaks of Colque Punku and Ausangate. In preparation for the pilgrimage, the candidate is expected to "fast" by abstaining from alcohol, salt, spices, and sexual activity. The initiation empowers the candidate to develop the ability to work and heal lovingly.

The great initiation to become an *altomisayoq* takes place in connection to the mountain pilgrimage of Qoyllur Rit'i. The ritual involves bathing in the high lakes of Yanacocha en route to the Sinacara glacier basin where the Lord of the Star of Snow ceremony takes place. The lakes of Yanacocha are full of spiritual power since their waters reflect the image of Mount Ausangate in the distant horizon. The power is infused to the candidate by means of ritual immersion. Andean ritual experts continue to undertake periodic trips to distant mountains and sacred places to gain experience and wisdom, thus becoming further empowered by means of direct contact with the supernatural forces within them.[35]

Initiation rituals for the Kallawaya candidates are held at natural settings not far from their villages within the Apolobamba mountain range. They may take place alternatively on a sacred lake like Paqocha or on a sacred mountain like Sillaka.[36] The Aymara recognize a small mountain near the city of La Paz, called Cerro Wirakoni, as the place where the candidates receive the indication from the mountain spirits to become *yatiris*. It is a very "stormy" hill, which reflects the importance of lightning in selecting ritual experts.[37]

---

34. Ibid.
35. Huanca, "El yatiri," 62.
36. Rosing, *Rituales para llamar la lluvia*, 422.
37. Freddy Taboada, "Connotaciones cúltico-religiosas en el arte rupestre aymara del Departamento de La Paz" (MA thesis, La Sociedad de Investigación del Arte Rupestre de Bolivia, La Paz, 1997), 8.

Ritual Activities and Formulas

The ritual praxis of Andean religious experts is intimately rooted in their communication with the sacred landscape. Invocations to the most powerful peaks are essential before presenting offerings or sacrifices. When invoked by an *altomisayoc* of the higher rank, the mountain spirits themselves may be summoned to appear before the participants during the ceremony. Alternatively, the mountain spirits can choose at will to communicate with ritual experts and ordinary devotees by means of intuitions and dreams.

Prayers and invocations are intended to "activate" the power in the sacred entity invoked to bestow health, fertility, and prosperity.[38] In order to attain the desired results, ritual experts are expected to undertake their performance most seriously. Devotion and commitment are reaffirmed in the ritualized repetition of the Quechua expression "*tukuy sonqoywan*," which means literally "with all my heart."

Andean invocations start with requesting permission of the sacred places in the region, as well as other participants in the ceremony. The protection and symbolic participation of more experienced ritual experts among the Kallawayas is invoked with the Quechua formula "*makinmanta*," which means "from their hands."[39]

All sacred mountains in a region are traditionally invoked one by one, literally "name by name."[40] In the Aymara area, the mountains and sacred places are carefully "recalled" in the libations, and the totalizing intention in naming "as many mountains as possible" seems to be rooted in the same logic as the Inca ceremonies of *capacocha*. According to chronicler Cristobal de Molina,[41] it was expected that during the *capacocha* pilgrimages all sacred places in the landscape were to receive offerings, as any one of them when forgotten could become angry and affect Inca well-being. In modern times, Andean ritual experts fear that a particular mountain spirit may feel "insulted" when its name is omitted during ritual invocations.[42]

Andean ritual experts sometimes invoke a particular mountain in a commendatory tone. Kallawayas are known to interrogate sacred places (*lugarniyoq*) asking why they do not send rain when offerings are properly presented

---

38. Luis Fernando Botero, *Chimborazo de los indios* (Quito: Ediciones Abya-Yala, 1990), 112.

39. Rosing, *Rituales para llamar la lluvia*, 152.

40. Ibid., 441.

41. Cristobal de Molina, *Ritos y fábulas de los incas* (Buenos Aires: Futuro, 1959 [1575?]), 92.

42. Catherine Allen, *The Hold Life Has: Coca and Cultural Identity in an Andean Community* Washington, DC: Smithsonian Institution Press, 1988), 42; Vellard, *El Hombre y los Andes* (Buenos Aires: Ediciones Culturales Argentinas 1981), 140.

to them.[43] These modern interrogations seem to echo the ways in which the Inca emperor questioned the *huacas* during ancient oracular rituals, as noted in the chronicles.[44]

The sacred places "speak" through inspiration provided to their favored ritual experts.[45] However, when invoked by a powerful *altomisayoq* they may appear in a physical form. In oracular rituals that involve summoning the mountain spirits, the *apus* appear with attributes of birds and they are capable of verbally answering questions. Higher mountains will appear as condors (*kuntur mallku*) and lower mountains as falcons (*wamanis*).

The ceremonies to summon the mountain spirits usually take place indoors. Participants include a *yatiri* or *altomisayoq* who leads the ritual and a group of devoted attendants. The room is usually dark and the windows are kept closed, although they may suddenly open up at the time when the mountains spirits announce their arrival with the sound of flapping wings. The mountain spirits, *apus* or *achachilas*, are recognized and welcomed by the ritual expert before participants ask them questions to which they reply in a distinctive falsetto human voice. Although Quechua informants have gladly provided me with firsthand descriptions of these ceremonies, ethnographic accounts that have documented them systematically are rare; only a few basic descriptions have been published.[46]

Andean Magic, Sorcery, and Healing

Witchcraft is feared throughout the Andes, since Andean people feel vulnerable to the curses and spells that are cast by sorcerers. In colonial times, some of the religious chroniclers, particularly those tasked with extirpation of idolatry, noted that sorcery was widespread in the Andes.[47] However, their perception of the types of rituals that should be labeled as witchcraft varied according to their religious background and ethnocentrism.

43. Rosing, *Rituales para llamar la lluvia*, 213.

44. Guamán Felipe Poma de Ayala, *Nueva crónica y buen gobierno*, ed. Rolena Adorno, John V. Murra, and Jorge L. Urioste (Madrid: Historia 16, 1987).

45. Rosing, *Rituales para llamar la lluvia*, 185.

46. Elizabeth Jenkins, *Iniciación en el corazón de los Andes* (Bilbao: Grupo Zeta, 1998), 8; Morote Best, Espíritus de montes, 290–306; Vellard, *El Hombre y los Andes* (Buenos Aires: Ediciones Culturales Argentinas 1981), 160-162.

47. José de Arriaga, "La extirpación de las idolatrías en Perú,“ in *Programa de Investigaciones sobre Epidemiología Psiquiátrica* (CONICET), vol. 61, ed. M. I. Balducci (Buenos Aires: CONICET, 1984 [1621]); José de Acosta, *Historia natural y moral de las Indias*, ed. Edumundo O'Gorman (Mexico City: Fondo de Cultura Económica, 1962 [1590]); Cristobal de Albornoz, "La instrucción para descubrir todas las Guacas del Piru y sus camayos y haciendas," *Journal de la Societe de Americanistes* 56(1) (1967): 7–39.

Andean *yatiris* and *paqos* customarily avoid engaging in witchcraft, a ritual practice that is typical of the sorcerers known as *layka*. Among the Aymara, elements used for witchcraft include clothing of the sick and the water in which a corpse was washed. Black miniature *illas* are used to destroy the crops and livestock of the victim; cactus wood is considered an effective neutralizer of spells.[48]

Divination Rituals Using Coca Leaves

Divination rites in the Andes are customarily performed at the beginning of a sacrificial ceremony, to learn about the disposition of the mountain spirits who will be accepting the offerings. Sometimes the "sorting" of coca leaves can be performed *ad hoc* to satisfy an individual's curiosity about the future or to learn about the condition of the soul of a deceased relative or friend.

Chroniclers reveal that divination rituals based on the organs of sacrificial victims were a fairly common practice in pre-Conquest times.[49] At present, rites of divination involving animal sacrifice can help forecast the weather for the coming agricultural season, as well as diagnosis of an illness and help in finding a curative strategy for a sick patient. Guinea pigs or *cuys* reveal a broad spectrum of information, from illnesses in the body of a human patient to ongoing conflict and gossiping within the community. The organs of a sacrificed llama are used to foresee the future: plentiful fat is believed to indicate that the crops are going to be abundant.[50]

Experts in divination by sorting the coca leaves are known in Aymara as *uñiri*, and in Quechua as *coca qhawaq*, "he who sees into the coca." Sorting the coca leaves is often done at an individual's request. At the sacred outcrop of Q'enko, one of the main *huacas* near Cuzco, I have seen *misayoqs* sorting coca leaves for visitors and local villagers.

Andean devotees draw relevant inferences based on a popular rite of divination—simply observing the candles and cigarettes that are lit during ceremonial events. These rites of divination do not call for the intervention of a ritual expert, and they can easily be camouflaged as devotional activities, especially when they take place inside a church or in the context of a Catholic service. In northwestern Argentina, during the annual ceremony to feed the spirit of Pachamama, each participant lights a cigarette, which is left standing around a hole in the ground that represents the "mouth" of Mother Earth. The way in which the ashes bend reveals valuable signs about the future of

48. Vellard, *El Hombre y los Andes* (Buenos Aires: Ediciones Culturales Argentinas 1981), 151-155.

49. Molina, *Ritos y fábulas de los incas.*

50. Rosing, *Rituales para llamar la lluvia*, 339–340.

the individual who lit it, which can include the dangerous prospect of being "eaten" by Pachamama if the ashes bend and fall towards the pit.

During the festivity of Qoyllur Ritti, Quechua pilgrims sit in the snow for hours at elevations over 5,000 meters watching their candles burn, a devotional and divination rite to help them cope with the uncertainty of the future. I have noticed that great care is paid—sometimes moving the candles from their original position—to ensure that the flame actually melts the sacred ice of the glacier.[51] Candles are carefully observed for the purpose of discerning the acceptance or rejection of offerings, as well as to identify the emotional state of people who are absent or dead. The presence of a condemned soul can be suspected if the flame is suddenly blown out.[52]

Andean Views on Illness and Healing

Disease is understood by Andean people as a temporal rejection from the Earth Mother, which is caused mainly by ritual negligence.[53] Among the Kallawayas, illness in the human body is conceived as metaphorically equivalent to mountain erosion and landslides.[54] Illnesses, falls, and deaths of domestic animals are interpreted as punishment for ritual misbehavior, such as not having paid proper respect or not having visited certain pilgrimage places.[55] Those who do not believe in the power of mountain spirits may end up captured by an evil mountain (*cerro malo*) and "lose" their souls. Under those circumstances, the intervention of a ritual expert is necessary to free the patient's soul from dangerous forces in the landscape.

Andean diseases have been thoroughly studied in northern Argentina.[56] Based on vast experience derived from over two decades of field research on supernatural aspects of Andean disease etiology, Cristina Bianchetti speaks to the difference between diseases caused by "blowing" into the soul (*sopladuras*) and those caused by the capture of the soul (*pilladuras* and *aikaduras*). Interestingly, the diseases are often explained as induced by features of the landscape such as mountains, lakes, springs, and ancient burials, as well as atmospheric forces like the wind. Andean people describe patients as having been

51. Ceruti, "Qoyllur Rit'i"; and Ceruti, *Procesiones andinas en alta montaña*.

52. Aguiló, *El hombre del Chimborazo*, 172.

53. Ibid., 165.

54. Bastien, *La montaña del cóndor*, 229.

55. Botero, *Chimborazo de los indios*, 35.

56. Palma, Nestor, "La medicina popular en el Noroeste de Argentina" (Argentina: Editorial Huemul 1978); María Cristina Bianchetti, "Cosmovisión sobrenatural de la locura: Pautas populares de salud mental," in *La puna argentina* (Salta, Argentina: Editorial V. M. Hanne, 2004); Pelegrin, *Cuando la salud viene de la tierra*; Anatilde Idoyaga Molina, "Lo sagrado en las terapias de las medicinas tradicionales del NOA y Cuyo," *Scripta Ethnologica* (CAEA Centro Argentino de Etnología Americana, Buenos Aires) 23 (2001): 9–75.

"grabbed by the Earth Mother" (*pillados por Pachamama*), "blown by the whirlwind" (*soplados por el remolino*), "caught by the old ones" (*agarrados por los gentiles, aikados*), or "haunted by the mountain" (*marados por el cerro*).

The "grip of Mother Earth" explains certain traumas and accidents, as well as congenital diseases that affect the ability to walk. Skin infections are customarily attributed to the "blowing of the whirlwind." Infants with malnutrition and chronic diarrhea are diagnosed as having been "caught by the old ones" (*aikados*), especially if their mothers have broken the taboo not to visit the cemetery during pregnancy.

Those who suffer from chronic mountain sickness are likely to be described as "haunted by the mountain." Patients diagnosed as *marados por el cerro* are believed to put their lives at risk if they continue to reside close to the mountain that has fallen in love with their soul and is longing for eternal company. Interestingly, the advice of the Andean healer who tells the patient to move away from the mountain's area of influence usually involves settling at lower elevations, which happens to result in the same prescription that Western physicians give to patients who suffer from chronic mountain sickness.[57]

Andean diseases caused by supernatural agents being blown into the body of the patient (*sopladuras*) usually require a ritual cleansing or *limpieza*.[58] On the other hand, the capture of the soul (via *pilladura, aikadura*) or its accidental loss (*susto*) calls for the intervention of a qualified healer to perform a ritual to "retrieve" it.

The capture of the soul (*pilladura* or *aikadura*), as well as its accidental loss as a consequence of sudden fright (*susto*), can lead to a delicate condition known as soul loss (*perdida del animo*). Symptoms of such loss are anxiety, attempts to run away (to the wilderness), and insomnia, among others.[59] Children are especially vulnerable when they are frightened. Adults can also suffer from a partial loss of their soul, particularly if they offend (intentionally or unintentionally) a sacred feature of the landscape, or if they neglect their ritual duties.

Skilled ritual experts are needed to "call the soul back," a ceremony in which clothing and belongings of the patient are manipulated while calling his or her name, in the place of the landscape where the victim became afraid, which is usually perceived as a "dangerous place" (*lugar bravo*). The call of the soul is one of the few magical therapeutic procedures performed in the open, since the healing rituals usually takes place indoors.

Ceremonial ingredients in the Andean pharmacopeia include *coca* leaves, alcohol, sulphur, soil, hair, fat, and llama fetuses. Mountains are the source of

57. Bianchetti, "Cosmovisión sobrenatural de la locura."

58. Aguiló, *El hombre del Chimborazo*, 170–171.

59. Vellard, *El Hombre y los Andes* (Buenos Aires: Ediciones Culturales Argentinas 1981), 103.

many of the mineral and vegetal ingredients used for healing. High-altitude pilgrimages, such as the procession to Punta Corral in northern Argentina and the Qoyllur Rit'i in Peru, provide an opportunity to collect some of the herbs found in these environs that are used in native medicine.[60] In addition to obvious logistical reasons, Andean people share the belief that herbs collected during a pilgrimage are more powerful than those gathered routinely (e.g., while herding).

The fame of the Kallawayas as herbal experts goes back to the times of the Incas.[61] The first historical account that mentions the extensive itineraries covered by the Kallawayas dates to 1766.[62] Traditionally, the Kallawaya medicine men traveled to remote villages on foot, curing the sick and trading supplies of herbs with local healers along the way.[63] They were known to go as far down as northern Argentina, or at least that was the case until a few decades ago. Modern-day Kallawayas take advantage of local buses and trucks when moving around the highlands, although some villages in northern Argentina can only be accessed on foot. In a newly globalized context, it is not uncommon to learn about the visit of a famous Kallawaya healer in a TV or newspaper advertisement.

Considerations and Conclusions

The modern Andean world does not permit consecrated lifestyles that are comparable to monastic orders in Buddhism or lifelong consecration of priests and friars in Catholicism. During the time of the Incas, the religious life of the empire was commanded by a supreme priest called *vilac oma*, and the religious hierarchy included "priests" in charge of provinces, known as *vilca camayocs*, and attendants of local shrines known as *huaca camayocs*.[64]

Consecrated women, the "chosen ones" or *acllas*, were described by the Spanish missionaries as "virgins of the Sun" and compared to the Catholic nuns. They were taken from their homes at a young age and kept in seclusion under the supervision of consecrated women (*mamacuna*), who would teach them how to weave and prepare *chicha* for religious and political ceremonies.[65]

60. Ceruti, "Qoyllur Rit'i."

61. Palma, *Estudio Antropológico de la Medicina Popular de la Puna Argentina* (Argentina: Ediciones Cabargón, 1973), 27.

62. Rosing, *Rituales para llamar la lluvia*, 55.

63. Bianchetti, "Cosmovisión sobrenatural de la locura."

64. María Constanza Ceruti, "Actores, ritos y destinatarios de las ceremonias incaicas de *capacocha*: Una visión desde la arqueología y la etnohistoria," *Xama* (Mendoza) 15–18 (2002–2005): 287–299.

65. Murúa, Juan Martín de, *Historia del Origen y Genealogía Real de los Reyes Incas del Perú* (Madrid, Biblioteca Missionalia Hispánica, 1946 [1590]), 333.

At age fourteen, some of the young women were taken out of the *acllahuasi* and given as secondary wives to noblemen or were sent to be sacrificed during state *capacocha* ceremonies.[66] Frozen female mummies of young *acllas* have been found on the Inca mountaintop shrines of Chuscha, Ampato, Pichu Pichu, Sara Sara, Quehuar, and Llullaillaco.[67] The Inca priest hierarchy and the system of chosen women collapsed shortly after the Spanish conquest.

The connection with Andean peaks is fundamental since peasants believe that the sacred mountains share their power with people who have been chosen to become ritual experts. The candidates may have exhibited particular physical signs at birth, but their status is to be confirmed (or signaled) by lightning at puberty. After proper instruction and an initiation rite, the ritual experts can conduct healing ceremonies and perform rites of divination. The highest form of Andean ritual expertise involves the ability to summon the mountain spirits.

Nowadays, Andean ritual experts base their interaction with Catholic priests on reciprocal complementarity. This possibility is enhanced by the fact that Andean ritual experts are approached for activities of divination and healing, in which Catholic priests are not expected to engage. The Aymaras and Quechuas, who acknowledge the proficiency of their *yatiris* and *altomisas* in communicating with the sacred landscape, still have Catholic priests as mediators with the spiritual forces of the heavenly realms, including God, the Virgin Mary, and patron saints. Masses and prayers for souls of the dead are held in high esteem, although the direct involvement of a priest during the funerals can have a limiting effect on the ability to comply with traditional offerings and rites.[68]

The fact that Catholic priests are celibate means that they do not acquire the status of maturity associated with married people in Andean society.[69] In that sense, their celibacy contributes to the perception of priests as somewhat "pure" intercessors, a role that is usually assigned to children.[70] A good example is provided by Father Gustave le Paige, who lived among the Atacameño people in northern Chile until his death. His incursions as amateur archaeol-

---

66. Acosta, *Historia natural y moral de las Indias*, 241.

67. María Constanza Ceruti, *Embajadores del pasado: Los niños del Llullaillaco y otras momias del mundo* (Salta, Argentina: Editorial de la Universidad Católica de Salta, 2009); Reinhard and Ceruti, *Inca Rituals and Sacred Mountains.*

68. María Constanza Ceruti, "Andean mountains and funerary rituals," *Latin American Indian Literatures Journal* 28(1) (2012): 1–27.

69. Xavier Albó, "La experiencia religiosa aymara," in *Rostros Indios de Dios*, comp. M. Marzal, pp. 81–140 (La Paz: Hisbol, 1992), 103.

70. María Constanza Ceruti, "The religious role of children in the Andes, past and present," *AmS-Skrifter* (Archaeological Museum, University of Stavanger) 23 (2010): 125–133.

ogist and mountaineer—even when he was in his eighties and had recently survived heart surgery—were encouraged by the local residents of San Pedro de Atacama in the belief that the mountain spirits would be more inclined to accept him because he was a priest.[71]

During the Spanish invasion and throughout colonial times the interaction between Andean communities and Catholic missionaries was not devoid of tensions, fueled in part by the idolatry extirpation campaigns undertaken by the Augustinian, Dominican, and Mercedarian friars. The Taqui Onkoy religious movement can be understood as a reaction against the intrusion of Catholic beliefs and suppression of traditional Andean rituals.

Mestizo chronicler Felipe Guaman Poma de Ayala provides an insightful description of the questionable lifestyle led by some priests living in the Andes in the early XVII century. His extraordinary illustrated chronicle entitled *Nueva cronica y buen gobierno* (1987)—published circa 1613 CE—devotes dozens of pages to *curas doctrineros* who are accused of forcing couples into marriage, taking young girls as concubines, forcing single women and widows into weaving for them, beating the elderly, and cruelly punishing children. His unique illustrations depict priests engaging in activities such as playing cards with the *corregidores* and "drinking with the drunkards." The captions often describe those priests as self-centered and prone to lose their temper and unleash their anger.

One of Guaman Poma's drawings, which portrays a half-dozen children carried on horseback, is entitled "the sons of the priest." The text associated with the image blames the notorious decrease in the indigenous population (and simultaneous increase in the number of *mestizo* children) on the fact that "a single priest has twelve children and keeps all single women as concubines." Another depiction, entitled "the preaching of the priest," humorously reveals the undertone of Andean resistance: the illustration shows the *doctrinero* cleric preaching from the pulpit with his finger raised in admonition, while some native people in the crowd are sleeping soundly.

If some *doctrinero* priests and extirpators of idolatries caused such a pitiful impression in the minds of Andean people during the colonial times, it was the Franciscan friars who brought a measure of credibility and compassion to their world. Guaman Poma's depiction of a Franciscan friar shows him holding a cross and sharing a piece of bread with an indigenous man, while addressing him in the Quechua language. The title of the illustration describes the Franciscan friar as a holy man who shows compassion towards the poor people. The text added to the image explains that Franciscans—"all of them," accord-

71. María Constanza Ceruti, "A la sombra del volcán Licancabur: Santuarios de altura en los cerros Toco, Juriques y Laguna Verde," *Xama* (Mendoza, Argentina) 15–18 (2002–2005): 301–313.

ing to the author—are reverends and saints worthy of praise for their virtues of humility, charity, honesty, generosity, and selflessness.

Franciscan spirituality, with its emphasis in simplicity and its profound sensitivity towards nature, has a lot in common with Andean religiosity. In an active process of syncretism that has been ongoing in South America for five hundred years, the Franciscans should be acknowledged for building cultural bridges that are now available to native ritual experts and Catholic priests and missionaries, to work together for the well-being of the Quechua and Aymara peoples of the Andes.

Chapter 7
Mocama Life at Santa Cruz de Guadalquini: Persistence and Accommodation under the Mission Bell

Keith Ashley

Spanish colonization of La Florida during the late sixteenth through early eighteenth centuries was designed in part to draw indigenous populations into Spain's expanding imperial empire through the establishment of mission communities at extant Native villages. Although early attempts at religious conversion were made by Jesuits, greater success in instructing indigenous Southeast populations in the Catholic religion and introducing aspects of Hispanic culture to them was achieved by Franciscan missionaries under the protection of the colonial government.[1] From the colony's perspective, the intent of the mission system extended well beyond religious conversion. It was part of a "highly structured economic enterprise" in which mission Indians labored to outfit the La Florida colony with food and a much-needed work force for defense, construction, and other infrastructural support, thereby weaving Natives into the political and commercial fabric of the colony.[2] Under the mission bell, some Native cultural practices persisted, others were modified,

1. Michael V. Gannon, *The Cross in the Sand: The Early Catholic Church in Florida 1513–1870* (Gainesville: University Press of Florida, 1965), 20–35; Bonnie G. McEwan, "The Spiritual Conquest of La Florida," *American Anthropologist* 103 (2001); Jerald Milanich, *Laboring in the Fields of the Lord: Spanish Missions and Southeastern Indians* (Washington, DC: Smithsonian Press, 1999).

2. Kathleen A. Deagan, "Transformation of Empire: The Spanish Colonial Project in America, *Historical Archaeology* 37 (2003): 3; John E. Worth, "Spanish Missions and the Persistence of Chiefly Power," in *The Transformation of the Southeastern Indians, 1540–1760*, ed. Robbie Ethridge and Charles Hudson (Jackson: University Press of Mississippi, 2002), 54; Tamara Spike, "St. Augustine's Stomach: Corn and Indian Tribute Labor in Spanish Florida," in *Florida's Working-Class Past: Current Perspectives on Labor, Race, and Gender from Spanish Florida to the New Immigration*, eds. Robert Cassanello and Melanie Shell Weis (Gainesville: University Press of Florida, 2009).

and new ones took root, making daily life a hybrid of indigenous and Spanish practices tailored to local ecological and social conditions.[3]

This chapter discusses the Mocama mission of Santa Cruz y San Buenaventura de Guadalquini, focusing primarily on its twelve-year existence (1684–1696) as a distinct mission community in northeastern Florida. Emphasis is placed on its history and on results of archaeological excavations at the mission site, known archaeologically as the Cedar Point site, by the University of North Florida (UNF) between 2005 and 2012. I conclude with some general statements on Mocama politics and identity during the late seventeenth century.

The Mocama

Mocama was the maritime dialect of the Timucua language spoken by groups in extreme northeastern Florida and southeastern Georgia at the moment of European arrival.[4] The Mocama-speaking Timucua were among the first Native peoples of mainland North America encountered and described by sixteenth-century Europeans. In fact, the southeastern Atlantic coast was ground zero for early French and Spanish colonization efforts in North America, meaning the Mocama and other lower Atlantic tidewater groups bore the initial brunt of sustained European Contact and entanglement beginning in 1562. Franciscan missionization among the Mocama commenced in 1587 and continued in their homeland until around 1705 and after relocation in the vicinity of St. Augustine until 1763.

The founding of San Agustín (St. Augustine) in 1565 set in motion a chain of events that forever transformed the lives of southeastern Native Americans. But Spanish colonization of La Florida (1565–1763) entailed far more than the oversimplified and deterministic sequence of Contact, population loss, missionization, subjugation, and demise in which Natives are portrayed as passive pawns in an arena of world politics. To the contrary, while change was inevitable, the Mocama mediated the winds of Spanish missionization through choices and actions that redefined their culture and helped distinguish themselves from their Native neighbors as they negotiated what it meant to be Mocama in a world that was both indigenous and Spanish.

3. Milanich, *Laboring in the Fields of the Lord,* 130–156.

4. Jerald Milanich and William Sturtevant, *Francisco Pareja's 1613 Confessionario: A Documentary Source for Timucuan Ethnography* (Washington, DC: Smithsonian Press, 1972), 1; Kathleen Deagan, "Cultures in Transition: Fusion and Assimilation among the Eastern Timucua," in *Tacachale: Essays on the Indians of Florida and Southeastern Georgia during the Historic Period*, eds. Jerald T. Milanich and Samuel Proctor (Gainesville: University Press of Florida, 1978), 91; Julian Granberry, *A Grammar and Dictionary of the Timucua Language* (Gainesville: University Press of Florida, 1993), 6.

FIGURE 1. Mocama mission locations.

San Buenaventura y Santa Cruz de Guadalquini and Other Mocama Missions

Around 1607, the Franciscan order founded the Mission San Buenaventura de Guadalquini at the southern end of St. Simons Island, Georgia, making it the northernmost Mocama mission along the Atlantic coast of La Florida (Figure 1). Although southern St. Simons Island has been considered traditional Mocama territory by some mission researchers,[5] my colleagues and I contend that in pre-Columbian times the entire island was within the spatial

5. John H. Hann, *A History of the Timucua Indians and Missions* (Gainesville: University Press of Florida, 1996), 18; Jerald T. Milanich, *The Timucua* (Cambridge, MA: Blackwell Publishers, 1996), 98; Milanich, *Laboring in the Fields of the Lord*, 47; John E. Worth, *The Struggle for the Georgia Coast: An Eighteenth-Century Spanish Retrospective on Guale and Mocama* (Tuscaloosa: University of Alabama Press, 2007), 12.

domain of the Muskogee-speaking Guale Indians.[6] According to our argument, Mocama speakers from the mainland and/or barrier islands south of the Satilla River (Georgia) were relocated north to the upstart mission of San Buenaventura as part of a Spanish-led effort to reconfigure the social landscape of coastal Georgia in the years following the 1597 Guale Rebellion. In effect, an indigenous Guale island became the home of a transplanted Mocama community during the first decade of the seventeenth century. Regardless of who controlled the island prior to Europeans, the Guadalquini mission was undoubtedly a Mocama affiliate throughout its nearly century-long existence in three different locations along the Atlantic coast of Georgia and Florida.

During the early seventeenth century, three other Mocama missions existed below St. Simons Island, including San Pedro de Mocama on Cumberland Island, Georgia, San Juan del Puerto on Fort George Island, Florida, and Santa Maria de Sena on Amelia Island, Florida. These friar-occupied missions or *doctrinas* were surrounded by smaller Native communities or *visitas* under the ecclesiastical tutelage of a nearby mission priest.[7] As the seventeenth century wore on and the indigenous populations dwindled as a result of the cumulative effects of disease, changes in diet and living conditions, and out-migration, a concerted effort (*congregación*) was made to draw the once dispersed scattering of Mocama communities into the *doctrinas*. The directed aggregation (*reducción*) of Mocama missions themselves began in the mid-1650s with the abandonment of San Pedro, and the relocation of its resident population to Santa María, who in turn all moved to San Juan in 1665. By 1696, the surviving Mocama population from all missions had been moved to San Juan del Puerto.

Relocation to Florida

The retreat of Spanish mission communities from the present-day Georgia coast to northeastern Florida was less out of desire and more out of necessity. The seventeenth century was an age of rampant colonial and imperial expansion in the Americas. While Spain believed it held unassailable rights to La Florida, France and England thought otherwise. With the establishment of

---

6. A discussion on the cultural affiliation of St. Simons Island can be found in Keith H. Ashley, Vicki L. Rolland, and Robert L. Thunen, "Missions San Buenaventura and Santa Cruz de Guadalquini: Retreat from the Georgia Coast," in *Life Among the Tides: Recent Archaeology on the Georgia Bight*, Anthropological Papers of the American Museum of Natural History, no. 98 (New York: American Museum of Natural History, 2013), 397–400.

7. For more information on the Mocama mission system, see Keith Ashley, "Grafting onto the Native Landscape: The Franciscan Mission System in Northeastern Florida," in *From La Florida to La California: Franciscan Evangelization in the Spanish Borderlands*, eds. Timothy J. Johnson and Gert Melville (Berkeley, CA: The Academy of American Franciscan History, 2013), 150–158.

the English Virginia colony, Chichimeco Indian raiders in the 1660s set their sights on the inhabitants of Spanish missions along the Georgia coast for capture as slaves to be returned to Virginia for sale to the highest bidder.[8] With the founding of Charles Town in 1670, slave raiding intensified as the Carolina militia and Indian allies outfitted with flintlock rifles targeted coastal La Florida missions.

Not only were missions under threat of attack by English and Indian slavers, they also had to contend with French corsairs, who were looting Atlantic coastal missions during the early 1680s.[9] Pirates eventually robbed and burned the San Buenaventura mission church and *convento* on St. Simons Island, although villagers escaped to the adjacent mainland prior to the assault. Against this turbulent backdrop, Spanish administrators decided to accelerate their plans to close down the Georgia coastal missions and move them to safer locations in northeastern Florida. The abandonment of San Buenaventura in 1684 was an outcome of this organized and wholesale withdrawal of Spanish missions from present-day Georgia to Florida.[10]

The Florida destination for San Buenaventura was somewhat of a controversy. The Spanish governor insisted that the Guadalquini community move to and unite with the existing settlement at San Juan del Puerto, the primary and only other Mocama mission in existence at the time. Guadalquini's residents apparently balked at this idea and instead took refuge across the sound to the west on an adjacent and unoccupied barrier island one league from San Juan.[11] Once settled, documents refer to this mission as Santa Cruz y San Buenaventura de Guadalquini (or more simply Santa Cruz de Guadalquini). The name Santa Cruz is apparently a holdover reference to the earlier and long-abandoned (ca. fifty years) Mocama mission *visita* of Vera Cruz that had been on the island. The Guadalquini community, however, would remain in this location for only twelve years, as the settlement was again uprooted and moved to San Juan in 1696. Six years later (1702), San Juan and the other Guale mission in northeastern Florida were assaulted and burned by Carolina troops and Indian allies. Although most mission Indians survived the attack, the communities would be reassembled some thirty miles to the south within the protective walls of St. Augustine.

---

8. Worth, *The Struggle for the Georgia Coast*, 15–18.

9. Amy T. Bushnell, *Situado and Sabana: Spain's Support System of the Presidio and Mission Provinces of Florida*, Anthropological Papers of the American Museum of Natural History 74 (New York: American Museum of Natural History, 1994), 162; Hann, *A History of the Timucua Indians and Missions*, 269–271; Worth, *The Struggle for the Georgia Coast*, 41–42.

10. Worth, *The Struggle for the Georgia Coast.*

11. Hann, *A History of the Timucua Indians and Missions*, 271; Worth, *The Struggle for the Georgia Coast*, 198.

Archaeology of the Cedar Point Sites

The exact whereabouts of the 1684–1696 Santa Cruz mission on the modern Florida landscape was unknown prior to 2005, when large amounts of mission-era pottery were recovered from the Cedar Point site (8Du81) along the southeastern edge of Black Hammock Island. Including the 2005 field season, UNF has devoted portions of six summer archaeological field schools to investigating the southern end of the island.[12] These projects are part of a joint program between UNF and the National Park Service (Timucuan Ecological and Historic Preserve). As a result, nearly 700 shovel tests (50×50 cm) and more than 140 1×2-meter units have been excavated. At present, a small gap still exists in the distribution of our shovel tests across the southern part of the island, but the main parts of the Santa Cruz mission and probable earlier *visita* of Vera Cruz have been surveyed. The core mission area (compound) covers approximately two hectares along the southeastern edge of the island. A few localized, yet dense, late mission-period shell middens have been identified between 500 and 1000 meters to the southwest among an extensive spread of pre-Columbian and Contact-period refuse at the Cedar Point West site (Figure 2).[13] We believe that these late-seventeenth-century shell middens represent outlying households associated with the relocated Santa Cruz mission community.[14] To date, however, most excavations have focused on the core mission area.

---

12. A review of the results of the 2005, 2006, 2007, and 2009 field seasons can be found in Ashley, Rolland, and Thunen, "Missions San Buenaventura and Santa Cruz de Guadalquini: Retreat from the Georgia Coast," 406–419.

13. These household middens are situated between 500 and 900 meters southwest of the core mission area at the Cedar Point West site (8Du63). Three weeks in 2010 were spent testing one of these household middens. See Keith H. Ashley, Vicki L. Rolland, and Robert L. Thunen, "Betz-Tiger Point and Cedar Point Preserve: Survey and Field School, Phase II," report on file with the Florida Division of Historical Resource (Tallahassee: Florida Division of Historical Resources, 2010), 124–157.

14. Shovel testing suggests that the mission community was more dispersed than the two-hectare core area at the Cedar Point site, with some residents living nearly a kilometer from the mission center. This might have been the case in the early years of the relocated mission. In 1685 the Mocama who had just relocated to Santa Cruz formally requested the colonial government to allow "some Indians of Colones, Yguajas [Guale], and from Yamasee mission of Asajo [St. Simons Island, Georgia]" to move to Santa Cruz, and their petition was granted. Perhaps these refugees established scattered households on the outskirts of the Santa Cruz community, as they did on St. Simons Island, in effect forming small ethnic enclaves. In 1689 the mission was reported to house sixty families or an estimated population of 300. With a mission this large, the community very well may have been quite dispersed for agricultural purposes; see Hann, *A History of the Timucua Indians and Missions*, 271–272; Worth, *The Struggle for the Georgia Coast*, 124.

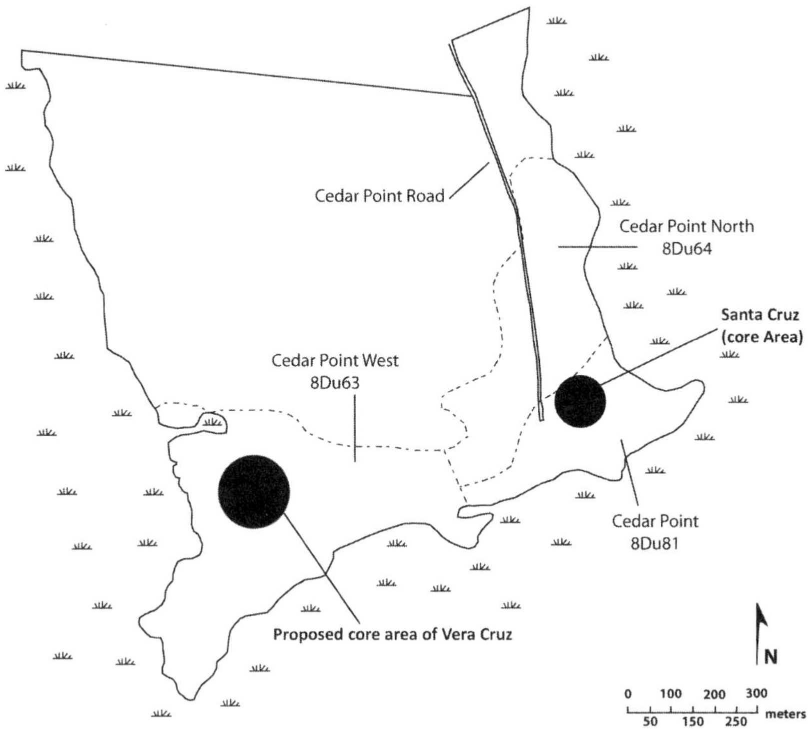

FIGURE 2. Archaeological sites at southern end of Black Hammock Island.

Mission Architecture

The architecture of mission communities in La Florida differed from that found elsewhere in the Americas. Most notably, those of southeastern North America lacked any buildings made of stone, masonry, tile, or adobe. Tabby, a concrete that includes oyster shells and lime, was used sparingly in making late sixteenth century structures in the town of St. Augustine, while the use of coquina rock was a little more common in the garrison community. Tabby, however, did not become widespread until the eighteenth and nineteenth centuries when it was employed in the construction of buildings associated with coastal plantations and mills. As for the mission frontier, all structures, from houses to churches, were made of wood (upright posts, wattle, or hewn boards) and thatch, although in some instances walls were plastered with a clay daub. These materials were for the most part perishable, and no extant ruins today mark their former existence.

The first three field seasons at Santa Cruz unearthed only a few mission-period features, including a series of shell-filled postholes in Units 28 and 30.

In 2009, eight 1×2-meter and two 1×1-meter units were excavated north and south of these two units. This expansion, designated Block C, exposed a perpendicular alignment of features representing a building corner, labeled Structure 1.[15] Not satisfied with the extent of our horizontal exposure, we returned to Block C in the summer of 2011, with the goal of exposing as much of the posthole pattern as possible within a six-week field period. As a result, thirty 1×2-meter and three 1×1-meter units were excavated. Because we had not fully exposed the outline of Structure 1 in 2011, we revisited Block C in the summer of 2012 and excavated twenty-five more units, bringing the total size of Block C to 140 m^2 (or sixty-six 1×2-meter and eight 1×1-meter units).

Forty-three subsurface features were recorded in Block C. Twenty of these were large postholes filled with shell midden that included mission-period artifacts, animal bones, and oyster, clam, and large whelk shells. In cross-section, the outline of a flat-bottomed post was clearly discernable in most postholes. Shell midden appears to have been added to postholes to stabilize the post and perhaps sweeten the soil in order to deter bug infestation. Figure 3 provides a composite view of Structure 1, which combines the 2007–2012 Block C excavations. Sixteen shell-filled posthole features outlined a rectangular structure that measured approximately 10×7 meters. Two additional shell-filled postholes were within Structure 1 and appear to represent an internal wall. Two more postholes occurred outside the building and were aligned parallel to the eastern end of the building's southern wall. The largest postholes were those forming the two interior rows along the building's long axis. These were likely load-bearing posts that supported a gabled roof.

Building materials recovered during excavations included preserved pieces of a few wooden posts in postholes, iron nail and spike fragments, and daub (hardened clay); the latter was not recovered in any significant amounts until the 2011 and 2012 field seasons.[16] The restricted distribution of daub against the background of posthole locations suggests that Structure 1 consisted of two rooms: a heavily daubed wall room measuring ca. 4×7 meters to the west and a slightly larger ca. 6×7-meter undaubed room to the east. The latter room may have had lightly thatched walls or perhaps was open, making it more like a *ramada*. The structure lacked a prepared clay floor, although the daubed room apparently possessed a dirt floor above the prehistoric shell midden. Within the eastern (undaubed) section of the structure, we encoun-

15. A review of Structure 1 as it appears after the 2009 field season can be found in Ashley, Rolland, and Thunen, "Missions San Buenaventura and Santa Cruz de Guadalquini," 408–411.

16. More architectural hardware might be expected from a building of this size, but because the abandonment of Santa Cruz was a planned move to San Juan, everything worthy of reuse may have been taken when the mission's inhabitants left for San Juan.

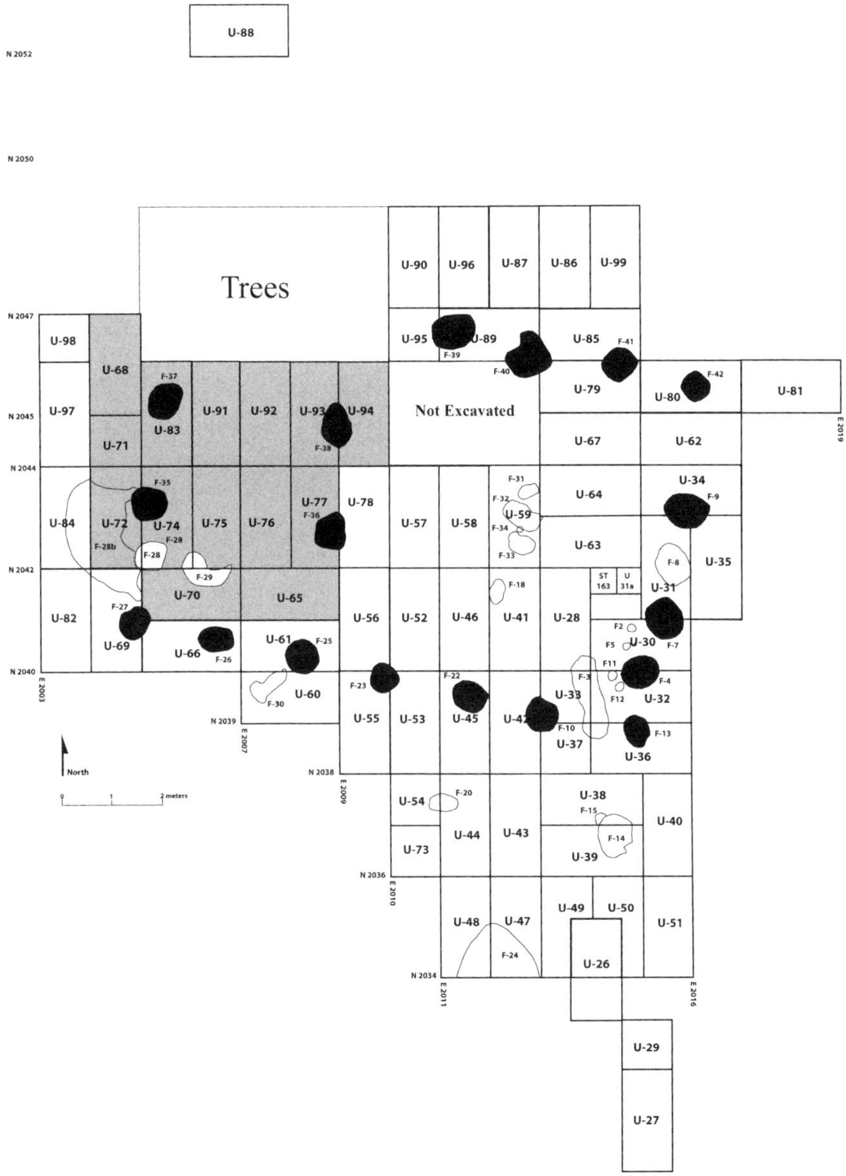

FIGURE 3. Outline of Structure 1, Cedar Point site (shaded units produced large amounts of daub).

tered a mission-period shell midden along with a series of burned (possible) posts, fire pits, and areas of dark soil, heat-altered sand, charcoal, and ash. These features combined with the open-sided nature of this portion of the structure and the composition of the midden's ceramic assemblage suggest that cooking and food processing activities took place in the undaubed section of Structure 1.

The daubed portion of the structure, separated from the open kitchen area by a daubed wall, might represent a living area or storage room. It could represent a combined *convento*-kitchen, particularly in light of the religious items recovered from Block C. The latter included two small crosses (one brass with a Latin inscription and the other a lead Greek cross), a brass necklace strand, and a brass ring fragment. In addition, a brass sacred heart of Jesus finger ring was found ten meters south of Block C in 2006. Fifteen glass beads and a few kaolin pipe fragments also were recovered. The size of Structure 1 is similar to that of *conventos* or friaries at other mission sites in La Florida. However, it is unclear whether Santa Cruz had a resident priest or shared one with San Juan during its twelve years in Florida. It is possible that the structure served multiple functions either concurrently or sequentially. At the present time, we believe the church may have existed on a slight rise sixty meters southwest of Structure 1, based on the partial exposure of burials and a possible shell footer during testing along an existing paved road.[17]

Material Culture and Subsistence

What have we learned about Mocama material culture during the late mission period based on our work at Santa Cruz? Even after more than a century of missionization, Native artifacts still dominate within refuse middens. Indigenous San Marcos pottery is the prevailing domestic ware in all contexts at Santa Cruz, as it is at other coeval Mocama, Guale, and Timucua sites along the Atlantic coast.[18] Olive jar and other European coarse earthenwares occur in moderate amounts and likely served as storage containers. Colonowares, or vessels of European form manufactured of local clays by Native potters using traditional firing techniques, also are found in low to moderate frequencies, depending on context. However, broad-scale sampling shows that colonowares and European tablewares such as majolica, while far more common in the center of the mission compound, were not the sole possessions

---

17. Ashley, Rolland, and Thunen, "Missions San Buenaventura and Santa Cruz de Guadalquini," 411–412.

18. San Marcos is also known as Altamaha series pottery. See various chapters in *From Santa Elena to St. Augustine: Indigenous Ceramic Variability (A.D. 1400–1700)*, eds. Kathleen Deagan and David Hurst Thomas, Anthropological Papers of the American Museum of Natural History, 90 (New York: American Museum of Natural History, 2009).

of resident friars and other Europeans. In fact, red-filmed, brimmed plates have a low-density and sporadic dispersal across broad village areas, both at Santa Cruz and nearby at San Juan.[19] It is unclear if these locations represent elite households, or if most villagers possessed colonowares that were used on special occasions.

Shovel testing in areas well beyond the mission core at Santa Cruz has produced small amounts of glass and metal artifacts; the same is true for testing at San Juan del Puerto. A rosary bead, a gunflint, two kaolin pipestems, and olive jar and colonoware pieces were recovered from household middens located nearly one kilometer from the mission compound at Santa Cruz. Additional pipe fragments and gunflints were found in the core area. The recovery of the latter indicates that the residents of Santa Cruz were armed to protect themselves from land and sea attacks by the English, French, or other Native groups.

Finally, an interesting aspect of the Mocama material culture is the large number of modified pieces of shell and animal bone, representing formal and informal tools, which indicates the continued production of traditional Native bone and shell tools. The frontier nature of the missions combined with infrequency and limited amount of supplies from Spain may have played a role in the lack of European material culture in Florida missions. In addition, records indicate that the most common items gifted to mission Indians were articles of clothing, blankets, cloth, or foodstuffs, all of which rarely survive on archaeological sites.[20] In terms of missions, trade goods appear most frequently at garrisoned communities such as Santa Catalina de Guale and San Luis de Talimali, positioned along the northern and western edges of La Florida, respectively.

With respect to the domestic economy, midden deposits indicate that subsistence still centered on local foods and long-held adaptations to coastal life. Although mission inhabitants were exposed to Old World domesticated plant and animal species, they maintained a dependence on estuarine resources, mostly fish and shellfish. Fishing persisted as an important subsistence pursuit, and the range of fish body sizes suggests that a variety of capture methods

19. Ashley, Rolland, and Thunen, "Betz-Tiger Point and Cedar Point Preserve: Survey and Field School, Phase II," 84, 86, report on file with the Florida Division of Historical Resource (Tallahassee: Florida Division of Historical Resources, 2010), 124–157; Keith Ashley and Rebecca Gorman, "Archaeological Survey of the Slough Sites, Fort Georgia Island Florida," report on file with the Florida Division of Historical Resources (Tallahassee: Florida Division of Historical Resources, 2010), 38; Martin F. Dickinson and Lucy B. Wayne, "Archaeological Testing of the San Juan de Puerto site (8Du53) Fort Georgia Island Florida," report on file with the Florida Division of Historical Resources (Tallahassee: Florida Division of Historical Resources, 1985), 5–8.

20. John E. Worth, *Timucuan Chiefdoms of Spanish Florida*, vol. 1, *Assimilation* (Gainesville: University Press of Florida, 1998a), 36, 135–143.

(group or single) were utilized. Among the mammal remains are deer, raccoon, opossum, rabbit, squirrel, and bear. Unlike the early California missions, those in Florida were not stocked with cattle, sheep, or horses for the friars to draw upon "in convincing natives to accept their tutelage."[21] Evidence of domesticated species includes peach pits, some pig bones, and a single cow bone, but currently there is no evidence of sheep, goat, or chicken within the analyzed samples at Santa Cruz. The specific elements recovered and their conditions suggest that body processing and preparation did not vary between native and introduced mammals. Compared to pre-Contact midden assemblages, the biggest difference in subsistence remains is an increase in the quantity of preserved corn, which is no surprise given that maize production intensified among the Mocama during missionization.[22]

Discussion and Conclusion

In the balance of this chapter I touch upon a few issues pertinent to our Mocama research. First is our approach, which is guided by the notion that all Contact situations are complex and distinctively structured by social and historical processes particular to those involved. Native reactions to European expansionist policies and imperialist strategies across the Americas were varied and rooted in divergent pre-Columbian histories and traditions. As Cobb states, "processes of colonialism and imperialism cannot be fully comprehended until complexity and diversity are projected back in time."[23] Focus must rest squarely on the historical contexts in which groups create and recreate their social relations through time. This necessitates long-term historical studies that span the artificial (and unnecessary) divide between pre-history and history.[24] Forefronting particular processes and histories do not deny a broader comparative perspective. The archaeology of colonialism lends itself

21. John H. Hann and Bonnie G. McEwan, *The Apalachee Indians and Mission San Luis* (Gainesville: University Press of Florida, 1998), 32.

22. As of October 2014, a detailed paleoethnobotanical study had yet to be undertaken of the carbonized plant remains from the site.

23. Charles R. Cobb, "Archaeology and the "Savage Slot": Displacement and Emplacement in the Premodern World," *American Anthropologist* 107 (2005): 564.

24. Kent G. Lightfoot, "Culture Contact Studies: Redefining the Relationship between Prehistoric and Historic Archaeology," *American Antiquity* 60; Laura L. Scheiber and Mark D. Mitchell eds., "*Across a Great Divide: Continuity and Change in Native North American Societies, 1400–1900* (Tucson: University of Arizona Press, Tucson, 2010); Stephen W. Silliman, "Social and Physical Landscapes of Contact," in *North American Archaeology*, eds. Timothy Pauketat and Diana DiPolo Loren (Malden, MA: Blackwell Publishing, 2005); John E. Worth, "Bridging Prehistory and History in the Southeast: Evaluating the Utility of the Acculturation Concept," in *Light on the Path: The Anthropology and History of the Southeastern Indians*, ed. Thomas J. Pluckhahn and Robbie Ethridge (Tuscaloosa: University of Alabama Press, 2006).

to a comparative approach, because cross-cultural comparisons allow us to explore some of the "real commonalities" experienced by both Natives and newcomers.[25] Moreover, such comparisons contribute to a better global understanding of the patterns and processes of culture contact and change, both past and present.

What about politics and identity as they pertain to the Mocama? Ethnohistoric information indicates that at the moment of European arrival (1560s), Mocama social organization was based on ranked clans.[26] Villages were led by a chief, who was a member of a noble lineage and assisted by a council of principal men. Some hereditary leaders not only controlled their home village but also maintained a political grip on a small group of subordinate settlements in the immediate area. Intervillage alliances were cemented through marriage, and Mocama chiefdoms often engaged in internecine raiding with other Timucua groups, making for a volatile landscape at the time of European arrival. Chiefs and their closest kin monopolized the esoteric knowledge on which society and cosmology were built and further spread an ideology that both defined and buttressed their lofty status. Such a political structure clearly falls within the anthropological definition of chiefdom, although the size and degree of ranking and stratification among the Mocama appears to have been on a smaller scale compared to that of other contemporaneous Native societies in the interior Southeast.[27]

For the Mocama, the first few decades of Contact (1560s and 1570s) witnessed the introduction of diseases and the execution of a scorched-earth strategy of compliance by the Spanish living within the Mocama territory.[28] The failure of chiefs to cease the spread of epidemics or to repel Spanish encroachment likely worked to undermine their leadership powers. Eventual acceptance of missions in 1587 appears to have been a power play by the Mocama elite to maintain chiefly control rather than surrender it, as their territory and population began to decline. In the Native political arena, St. Augustine was a paramount chiefdom vying for control, and the Mocama, as well as other Southeast Indians, followed Natives' protocol as they engaged the interlopers in diplomatic relations.[29] The military might of the Spanish combined with

25. Silliman, "Social and Physical Landscapes of Contact," 274.

26. Hann, *A History of the Timucua Indians and Missions*, 83; Milanich, *The Timucua*, 156–157.

27. Charles R. Cobb, "Mississippian Chiefdoms: How Complex?," *Annual Review of Anthropology* (2003): 66–68.

28. Hann, *A History of the Timucua Indians and Missions*, 70.

29. John E. Worth, *Timucuan Chiefdoms of Spanish Florida*, 13–18, 35–37; Rebecca Saunders, "Forced Relocation, Power Relations, and Culture Contact in the Missions of La Florida," in *Studies in Culture Contact: Interaction, Culture Change, and Archaeology*, ed. James G. Cusick, Center for Archaeological Investigations, Occasional Papers no. 25

trade goods proved a compelling incentive for chiefs to ally themselves with the newcomers. Foreign gifts doled out by colonial officials served to legitimate chiefly authority, as exotic raw materials and sumptuary goods from far-flung areas of eastern North America had done in pre-Contact times. Early in the mission period, once one chief accepted Christianity, others followed suite, fearing that those consenting to Christianity would "possibly supplant them by becoming the chiefdom's broker with the new power source."[30] This gambit was nothing new to southeastern Indian politics.

John Worth and Amy Bushnell argue convincingly that the indigenous chiefly titles and elite honors extended well into the colonial period among the missionized Timucua and Apalachee, respectively.[31] Pledging obedience to the Spanish Crown and openly accepting friars into their communities ensured the preservation of a chief's secular control over villagers. Their privileged status was recognized by colonial officials, who exempted chiefs from Indian labor requirements issued by the governor and presented them with gifts on certain occasions. In time, mission Indians became familiar enough with the colonial system to use it to their advantage.[32] Ultimately, however, chiefs were subject to the governor of St. Augustine and religion was guided broadly by the Catholic Church. But Spain needed the support and reinforcement of the Native political structure to sustain its struggling St. Augustine colony.

The layout of mission communities not only reflected but shaped this political and religious structure. From the opening decades to the waning years of missionization, churches existed alongside Native council houses in the *doctrinas* of La Florida.[33] Politics transpired in Native council houses, while worship was confined to churches. The former buildings continued to maintain a formal arrangement of assigned seats based on political rank, and meetings followed long-established rules and traditions, including consumption of the sacred black drink.[34] According to Spanish documents, a 1695 formal visitation to Santa Cruz de Guadalquini was held in the village council house

---

(Carbondale: Southern Illinois University, 1998), 413; David Hurst Thomas, "War and Peace on the Franciscan Frontier," *From La Florida to La California: Franciscan Evangelization in the Spanish Borderlands*, eds. Timothy J. Johnson and Gert Melville (Berkeley, CA; Academy of American Franciscan History, 2013), 125.

30. Hann, *A History of the Timucua Indians and Missions*, 142.

31. Worth, "Spanish Missions and the Persistence of Chiefly Power," 241; Amy T. Bushnell, "Ruling 'the Republic of the Indians' in Seventeenth Century Florida," in *Powhatan's Mantle: Indians in the Colonial Southeast*, Peter H. Wood, Gregory A. Waselkov, and M. Thomas Hatley (Lincoln: University of Nebraska Press, 1989), 139, 142–144.

32. Saunders, " Forced Relocation, Power Relations, and Culture Contact in the Missions of La Florida," 417.

33. Milanich, *Laboring in the Fields of the Lord*, 142–143.

34. John H. Hann, "1630 Memorial of Fray Francisco Alonso de Jesus on Spanish Florida's Missions and Natives," *The Americas* 50 (1993): 94–95.

and was attended by a colonial representative and a series of chiefs and other men of titled lineages,[35] suggesting the persistence of noble families, even if only in name. Until late in the mission period, Mocama missions were essentially Native communities with a lone friar as their only European resident. In fact, as mentioned previously, Santa Cruz may have shared a Franciscan missionary who resided full-time at nearby San Juan de Puerto.

Santa Cruz provides an illustrative example of the continuing influence of chiefs in village politics. Despite having lived under the mission bell for more than a century, including the previous few decades under constant threat of English raiders and French pirates, the Guadalquini chief did not comply with the governor's request in 1684 to relocate his St. Simons Island village to the San Juan mission. This act of resistance suggests that Mocama missions still exercised a degree of social and political autonomy. Even in their new location, Santa Cruz continued to drag their heels and feign compliance for another twelve years, lamenting that they had not moved yet due to "their being tied up with plantings and with other occupations that they have been called upon for in the service of his majesty . . . [and] if at the moment they are not doing so [moving to San Juan], it is because it is time already for their field preparation."[36] But when questioned as to why in the "past years they had not sown the field that is set aside [community field?]," the chief responded that it "was because of the shortage of provisions that existed, for which this year they are disposed to plant it."[37] The mission remained firmly entrenched on Black Hammock Island in 1695 despite the governor's concern for the "risks that are entailed, while they are in the said place of Santa Cruz, being overrun by the enemies by way of the mainland."[38] Although a council house for Santa Cruz had already been built at San Juan at the time of the 1695 visitation, the community did not move there until the next year (1696).[39] In the end, their move to San Juan appears tied to the death of the chief at San Juan and promotion of the Santa Cruz chief to provincial chief.

Finally, contrary to popular views, there was no such thing as a single historic Indian identity, even among the missionized Indians of La Florida. A

35. Juan de Pueyo, "General Visitation of the Provinces of Guale and Mocama Made by the Captain Don Juan de Pueyo by Title and Nomination of the Señor Don Laureano de Torres y Ayala, Knight of the Order of Santiago, Governor and Captain General of the City, Presidio and Provinces of St. Augustine of Florida for His Majesty, January 25, 1695," in Visitations and Revolts in Florida, translated by John H. Hann, *Florida Archaeology* 7 (1993): 222, 241.

36. Ibid., 243.

37. Ibid., 243–244.

38. Ibid., 243. Earlier Pueyo refers to these enemies as "bandit pagan Indians who roam about on the mainland" (235).

39. Ibid., 243.

key factor contributing to the colony's multiethnic composition was that "linguistic difference[s] remained distinct" throughout the mission period.[40] In fact, La Florida was divided into mission provinces based on the dominant Native language in the region. Even as the number of missions was reduced and communities combined, Guale always merged with Guale and Mocama with Mocama (Timucua).[41] This is not to say that Spanish missions were bounded communities—they were not. Missions Indians were actively engaged in external relations with other Indians, and some missions along the La Florida periphery were pluralistic societies, although most of their residents likely spoke dialects of the same language (e.g., Muskogean or Timucua).

As for the four Mocama missions, until the waning decades of the seventeenth century, each was composed mostly of Timucua speakers, although they may have housed speakers of different Timucuan dialects. While external relations between Guale and Mocama were peaceful throughout most of the seventeenth century, the two were traditional enemies in pre-Contact times. Moreover, tensions and outward hostilities were still apparent during the Guale Rebellion of 1597 and shortly thereafter. A shared language, sense of being, and history on the part of each group combined with their longstanding rivalry likely played a role in the maintenance of separate Mocama and Guale identities throughout the mission period. We must remember that identity is context-driven and subject to constant social negotiations that entails both culture continuity and change. Traditions of the past are not propelled into the future simply by being customary; they are actively set in motion and do not exist apart from the actions that create/re-create them.[42]

Culture contact was nothing new to America's indigenous populations, although the circumstances of European colonization were different and the pace was more accelerated and intensive than any encountered by their pre-Columbian ancestors. Throughout the mission period, the Mocama continuously mediated between old and new ways of doing and perceiving things; this mediation simultaneously entailed accommodation and resistance in the ongoing production of culture and tradition. While in the eyes of the Spanish the Mocama may have been seen as generic mission Indians or neophytes, they maintained an ongoing identity that distinguished them from the Guale and other missionized Indians of La Florida. Moreover, the mission-era Mocama should not be treated as diluted versions of what they once were, because such a portrayal renders them irrelevant in the production of their

---

40. Worth, "Spanish Missions and the Persistence of Chiefly Power," 241.

41. Worth, *The Struggle for the Georgia Coast*, 47–50.

42. Timothy R. Pauketat, "A New Tradition in Archaeology," in *The Archaeology of Traditions: Agency and History Before and After Columbus*, ed. Timothy R. Pauketat (Gainesville: University Press of Florida, 2001), 1–15.

own culture. Mocama identity was ongoing and it persisted in the Native council houses, agricultural fields, and mission churches of Spanish Florida, although it differed from what existed at the dawn of the European invasion.

In sum, excavations at Santa Cruz de Guadalquini (1684–1696) in Jacksonville, Florida have exposed refuse middens, pits, and the outline of a clay-daubed building. We have uncovered artifacts showing that coastal Mocama Indians at this time were armed with flintlock rifles and acquired goods of Spanish and British origin, yet continued to craft items of clay, bone, and shell. They grew corn and ate European peaches and pigs, but also fished, gathered shellfish, and hunted deer, as they had for millennia along the Atlantic coast. Their distinctive identity persisted, as they had yet to assimilate fully into colonial Spanish life.

Chapter 8
Fray Francisco de Pareja and the Cultures of Confession

Timothy J. Johnson

Es ciencia el confesarse, la cual con el ejercicio se aprende como las demás ciencias y artes, pues frecuentando la confesión, se ilustra el entendimento. To confess oneself is a science, which one learns like the other sciences and arts with exercise, such that by frequenting confession, understanding is illuminated.[1]

---

1. The transcription and English translation (slightly modified by author) are from George Aaron Broadwell's unpublished manuscript of Francisco Pareja, *Confessionario en lengua castellana y timuquana con algunos consejos para animar al penitente* (Mexico: Diego López Dávalos, 1613). From a technical perspective, it should be noted that Pareja's was most likely working with the Mocama dialect of Timucua, see Keith Ashley, "Grafting on to the Native Landscape: The Franciscan Mission System in Northeast Florida," in *From La Florida to La California: Franciscan Evangelization in the Spanish Borderlands*, eds. Timothy J. Johnson and Gert Melville (Berkeley: Academy of American Franciscan History, 2013), 146. I want to thanks Liza Noetzel for commenting on this essay and her insights regarding Pareja's literary corpus.

Confession may be illuminating to some, but burning a confessional manual brings light to others as demonstrated by the Augustinian friar Martin Luther in Wittenberg on the morning of December 10, 1520. Luther, in the company of fellow university theologians and students, consigned the recent bull of excommunication (*Exurge Domine*) from Pope Leo X and the *Summa Angelica* to the flames. He dismissed this widespread manual of the confessional genre, named after the Franciscan friar, Angelo Carletti di Chivasso, as diabolical, not angelic.[2] Luther's anger, which was stoked undoubtedly in no small measure by the papal edict to burn his own works, emerged again in 1521 when he condemned the Fourth Lateran Council (1215) for bewildering the consciences of Christians throughout the world by dictating, among other things, that the faithful should go to confession—the so-called Easter duty—once a year.[3] Fray Francisco de Pareja's first pre-confessional question to Timucua penitents in the *Confessionario* of 1613 is straightforward and direct: "Did you confess yourself last Lent?"[4] Although the practice of universal confession met widespread resistance in the Late Middle Ages and later, during the Reformation–Counter Reformation period among Catholics and Protestants alike, the production of confessional manuals such as Pareja's flourished on both sides of the Atlantic.[5] His opening line of inquiry presupposes an emerging culture of confession, in which the

2. Roberto Rusconi, *L'ordine dei peccati: La confessione tra Medioevo ed età moderna* (Bologna: il Mulino, 2002), 277. For Luther's rationale, see Martin Luther, "Why the Books of the Pope and His Disciples were Burned by Doctor Martin Luther," trans. Lewis W. Spitz, in *Luther's Works*, vol. 31, ed. Harold J. Grimm (Philadelphia: Muhlenbery Press, 1957), 383–395.

3. Chloë Taylor, *The Culture of Confession from Augustine to Foucault: A Genealogy of the 'Confessing Animal'* (New York: Routledge, 2009), 63.

4. Spanish: "¿Confesaste te la Cuaresma pasada?" Timucua: "Quaresma yoqua na pirama orobinicho?" Later in the *Confessionario* the question and answer are somewhat different with a difference in the Timuca that emphasizes the Lenten (Easter) dimension: "¿Confesaste el año passado? Quaresma yoquema orobinibicho?" (f. 205v). On pre-confessional questions in Nahua and Mayan Confessional Manuals, see Mark Z. Christensen, *Nahua and Maya Catholicisms: Texts and Religion in Colonial Central Mexico and Yucatan* (Stanford/Berkeley, CA: Stanford University Press/American Academy of Franciscan History, 2013), 170–178. In 1642, Juan de Palafox y Mendoza lamented that the large quantity of manuals in circulation threatened the unity and purity of the Catholic Church; see Christensen, *Nahua and Maya Catholicisms*, 259. The first general attempt to regulate publishing in the colonial territories occurred some ten years earlier; see *General Rules and Orders Taken from the New Index of Prohibited and Purged Books* (Seville: 1632) in *The Inquisition in New Spain, 1536–1820: A Documentary History*, ed. and trans. Johns F. Chuchiak IV (Baltimore: Johns Hopkins University Press, 2012), 98–104.

5. According to Patrick J. O'Banion, the production of confession manuals was something of a "cottage industry" in early modern Spain; see his *The Sacrament of Penance and Religious Life in Golden Age Spain* (University Park: University of Pennsylvania Press, 2012), 26–32.

faithful are reminded of their identity and ongoing responsibility. In Pareja's view, the Timucua textual audience, whose members included an ever-increasing number of literate men and women, are already nascent "confessing animals" in the language of Michel Foucault.[6] While the universal cross-cultural imperative of self-revelatory disclosure is disputed,[7] Pareja's reference to science and notable commitment to the literary arts leaves little doubt that he labored to construct the "Old World" culture of confession in the "New World" of the Americas. The ultimate outcome of his efforts is impossible to gauge; nevertheless, linguistic studies suggest that Pareja's own attempts in the near term were mediated, if not altered and enhanced, by Timucua authors-editors in a fashion consonant with the audience's native language and the potential pastoral reception of written and spoken texts.[8]

This exploratory essay focuses on Fray Pareja's project by examining how the production of the *Confessionario* emerges from a "confessing" textual community among the Timucua natives and their Franciscan pastors of northeastern Florida.[9] This inquiry cannot be isolated from the larger context of literary genres, performative texts, and the decisive shift in early modern European religious consciousness. Initially viewed through a canonical lens as the yearly recitation of sinful behavior followed by proscribed penitential actions, the emerging concept and practice of confession in early modern Spain emphasized a growing sense of frequent introspection, conscious interiority, and the need for accurate self-knowledge. How the native Timucua population accepted, contested, and ultimately informed the Christian worldview is difficult to discern but traces of possible answers are still visible in the *Confessionario* and other works attributed to Pareja. This evidence, among other writings, suggests the existence of a unique expression of a rich textual Timucua Christianity that resists reduction to a simple variant of Spanish religious culture.

---

6. Michel Foucault, *The History of Sexuality: An Introduction*, vol. 1, trans. R. Hurley (London: Penguin Books, 1990), 59.

7. Taylor, *The Culture of Confession from Augustine to Foucault*, 1–3.

8. George Aaron Broadwell, "Invisible Authors: Uncovering Native Identity and Intention in Timucua Religious Texts," presented at Linguistic Society of America, January 2014 (available at https://www.academia.edu/5622039/Invisible_authors_Uncovering_native_identity_and_intention_in_Timucua_religious_texts).

9. On Francisco de Pareja's life and literary works, see Luis Resines Llorente, *Catecismos americanos del siglo XVI*, vol. 1 (Salamanca: Junta de Catilla e León, 1992), 178–185. According to Resines, Pareja authored numerous works in Spanish/Timucua and one in Spanish/Mexican (Nahua). For this Spanish/Nahua text, see Francisco de Pareja, *Doctrina christiana muy útil y necesaria, México 1578*, ed. and comm. Luis Resines (Salamanca: Edíciones de la Universidad de Salamanca, 1990). See also Lisa Marie Noetzel, "Friar Francisco Pareja: Missionary and Linguist," in *From La Florida to La California*, 203–214.

Indigenous Literacy and Textual Communities

On June 12, 1614, the commissary general of the Indies, Fray Juan de Vivanco, signed a decree that sent Fray Luis Jerónimo de Oré as visitator general to the newly established province of Saint Helen (Florida and Cuba). As a Creole lector of the Franciscan order, polyglot linguist, and a prolific author in his own right, it is not surprising that the record of Oré's official visitation singled out the literary accomplishments of his confrere, Francisco Pareja.[10] What is noteworthy, in particular, are Oré's comments about the Timucua literacy and visible reception of Pareja's texts:

> One of the religious who has been most useful in the conversion of the Indians has been Fray Francisco Pareja who has dedicated himself to the ministry of teaching the Indians. And in order that he might be useful not only to those of his own mission and district but all in that province and language of Timucua in which he is skilled—since he has worked among them for more than twenty years—he has written and published several books called La Doctrina Christiana and Catecismo and Confessionario and other devotional tracts. These are always in the hands of the Indians. With ease many Indian men and women have learned to read in less than two months, and they write letters to one another in their own language.[11]

Some fifteen years later in 1630, the *custos* of Santa Helena Province, Fray Francisco Alonso de Jesús, confirmed the commitment of the friars to literacy among the Timucua, as well as the Guale and Apalachee.[12] Wherever there was a *dotrina*, his confreres had established a school for children since teaching is the most effective manner of imprinting on the lands and hearts of the people Christian discipline and doctrine. Their pedagogical approach focused on *letras*, that is, the acquisition of grammar, syntax, and vocabulary. This is far more than rote recitation by memory of religious teachings. Already, he

10. Luis Gerónimo de Oré, *Relación de los mártires que a avido en las provincias de la Florida* (Madrid?, ca. 1617). More recently, Luis Gerónimo de Oré, *Relación de los mártires que a avido en las provincias de la Florida*, ed. A. Lopez (Madrid, 1931), 108. On this text, see Raquel Chang-Rodríquez, *Relación de los mártires de la Florida del P.F. Luis Jerónimo de Oré (c. 1619): Estudio preliminar, cronología, edición modernizada y anotada, y bibliografía* (Lima: Fondo Editorial, 2014).

11. Fray Luis Jerónimo de Oré, *The Martyrs of Florida, 1513–1616*, trans. Maynard Geiger (New York: Joseph F. Wagner, 1936), 103. On Oré's own career, see Noble David Cook, "Beyond the Martyrs of Florida: The Versatile Career of Luis Gerónimo de Oré," *The Florida Historical Quarterly* 71(2) (October 1992): 169–187.

12. Archivo Gral. de Indias, Seville Mexico, Legajo 302, Fray Francisco Alonso de Jesús, Custodio de la Florida. John Hann's translation is found in The St. Augustine Foundation Center for Historical Research at Flagler College in Saint Augustine, Florida

notes, there were more than twenty thousand baptized indigenous Christians as well as fifty thousand catechumens. Among these numbers, there were, "many who know how to read and write, to which they are all inclined, men as [well as] women. And thus they learn with great ease. And some, on learning letters, learn by themselves with great ease."[13] When Gabriel Díaz Vara Calderón, the bishop of Havana, recounted his visitation in the provinces of the Guale, Timuqua, Apalache, and Apalachoooli in 1674–1675, he remarked as well that children, both male and female, went to church and school throughout the week where they were taught by an *athequi* or interpreter and, when necessary, disciplined under the watchful eye of another person delegated for this duty.[14]

Interest in *letras*, and performative texts in general, was found throughout schools as well as churches. Indeed, as Bishop Calderon notes, the New Testament, which is the primary text of Christianity, dictated congregational seating during worship as women were to be seated on the side of the church where the epistle was read (right side facing sanctuary), while the man gathered on the other side in front of the where the gospel (left side facing sanctuary) was proclaimed.[15] Here the physical placement of the Christian scriptures, which themselves served as the wellspring of knowledge and arbitrator for all other written texts, organized and defined both the physical and spiritual place of women and men within the community. Both inside and outside the schools and churches Calderon visited, the indigenous Christians displayed an intense liturgical life marked by frequent attendance on Sundays and feast days throughout the year, penitential practices, the singing of hymns, and participation in devotional activities such as the rosary and *salve regina*.

---

13. Legajo 302, 16.

14. Calderón, Visitation 1675, n.d., Havana, Bishop of Cuba to Antonio de Rozas, ST AGI 54-3-2/2 bnd 1958. I would like to thank Diana Reigelsperger at Flagler College for her photocopy of this document on microfilm in the Stetson Collection. The chronicle of Pareja's Franciscan province of Castille, *Coronica y historia de la fundacion y progresso de la provincia de Castilla de la Orden del bienauenturado padre san Francisco* (Madrid: En la Imprenta Real, 1612) reports that daily liturgical participation (boys and girls) at mass and vespers together with doctrinal instruction was to be standard practice in all *doctrinas*, 116–117.

15. Calderón, Visitation, 1675. The division of church by gender is mentioned by Fray Francisco Alonso de Jésus as well, who claims that it was the practice of the ancient church; see Legajo 302, 17. On gender division in medieval churches, see Gabriela Signori, "Links oder rechts"? Zum 'Platz der Frau' in der mittelalterlichen Kirche," in *Zwischen Gotteshaus und Taverne. Öffentliche Räume in Spätmittelalter und Früher Neuzeit*, eds. Susanne Rau and Gerd Schwerhoff (Köln/Weimar/Wien: Bohläu, 2004), 339–382. On liturgical performace in the Southwest, see Kristin Dutcher Mann, "Cycles of Celebration: High Holy Days in the Franciscan Missions of Northern New Spain,"in *From La Florida to La California*, 271–283.

As Fray Luis Jerónimo de Oré, Fray Francisco Alonso de Jesús, and Bishop Gabriel Díaz Vara Calderón all attest, the Franciscans had succeeded in establishing numerous textual communities[16] in an atmosphere of rising literary throughout La Florida. Their activities fall within the so-called *Pax Hispanum* of the seventeenth century.[17] The complexity of languages in this relatively brief historical interlude is striking given the various dialects of Timucua alone. Many indigenous Christians were no doubt introduced to Spanish in their contacts with colonial representatives. In addition, there was ongoing use of Latin within liturgical services, including participation in the eucharist and the divine office, as reported by Fray Pareja as early as 1602[18] and evidenced in the trilingual *Forme Breve de administrar los Sacramentos* of Fray Gregorio de Movilla from 1635.[19] Equally noteworthy is the native ability to read, which may be a better marker for literacy in the early modern period than writing skills. Whereas the Franciscans instructed Timucua children, at the time both male and female, in reading and writing skills, many children on the European continent in cities such as Bologna and Cremona were taught Christian doctrine through simple oral recitation and memorization without access to books.[20]

Fray Pareja and Franciscan Textual Communities

The declaration of Fray Pareja to his confrere Blas de Montes in 1602 opens a window on his work within Timucua communities that were clustered around the *dotrina* of San Juan del Porto. In addition to San Juan, Pareja names nine *visitas* within walking distance from the *dotrina* that together totaled approximately five hundred Christians. The intensity of Pareja's pastoral activities and the involvement of his indigenous fellow Chris-

---

16. On textual communities, see Brain Stock, *Listening for the Text: On the Uses of the Past* (Philadelphia: University of Pennsylvania Press, 1997).

17. John E. Worth, "Inventing Florida: Constructing a Colonial Society in an Indigenous Landscape," in *Native and Spanish New Worlds: Sixteenth-Century Entradas in the American Southwest and Southeast*, eds. Caly Mathers, Jeffrey M. Mitchem, and Charles M. Haecker (Tuscon: University of Arizona Press, 2013), 196.

18. *Declaración de P. Fr. Francisco Pareja. San Agustín, 14 septiembre de 1602*, in P. Fr. *Jerónimo de Oré, Relación histórica de la Florida escrita en el siglo xvii (II Apêndices)*, ed., prologue, and notes P. Atanasio López (Madrid: Libería General de Victoriano Suárez, 1933), 26. On the celebration of the divine office, see Mariano Errast, *El primer convento de América: Historia y forma de vida de los franciscanos en su convento de la ciudad de Santo Domingo 1516–1820* (Santo Domingo: Editora Corripio, 2006), 215–225.

19. Fray Gregorio de Movilla, *Forme Breve de Administrar los Sacramentos a los Indios, y Españoles que viven entre ellos* (Mexico: Por Iuan Ruyz, 1635).

20. Dominique Julia, "Reading and the Counter Reformation," in *A History of Reading in the West*, eds. Guglielmo Cavallo and Roger Chartier, trans. Lydia G. Cochrane (Amherst: University of Massachusetts Press, 1999), 261.

tians are impressive. "*Los naturales*" not only participated through attendance, but also officiated in some ministerial capacity at both sung masses and the evening divine office of vespers.[21] While certainly not ordained, selected members of the greater San Juan del Porto community clearly held leadership positions during public worship. Given the nature of these hierarchical liturgies, a working knowledge of selected sacred writings was necessary. The performance of these ritual texts, in the context of Pareja's efforts to preach in the vernacular over a seven-year period, reveal a nascent textual community formed around the proclamation, interpretation, and eventual production of a series of foundational writings. His efforts among the Timucua continued until his departure for Mexico in 1610. Well versed, no doubt, in the requisite steps leading to publication due to his previous experience in Mexico, Pareja witnessed the rapid publication of several texts in Spanish/Timucua. An overview of his biography and selected literary chronology demonstrates his intense efforts:

1569	Fray Francisco de Pareja (native of Auñon from the Madrid convent) arrives in Mexico.
1578	Pareja publishes *Doctrina Christiana* in Spanish (Castilian)/Mexican (Nahua).
1595	Pareja arrives in Florida.
1602	Pareja writes a declaration to Fray Blas de Montes about Timucua literacy and liturgical practice.
1610	Permission given in St. Augustine for publication of the *Confessionario*, *Arte*, and the *Cathechismo*. Texts sent to Mexico for permissions and publication.
1612/17?	*Cathecismo, y Breve Exposición de la Doctrina Christiana* published in 1612 (second edition in 1617).
1612	*Cathecismo, en lenqua Castellana y Timuquana* published.
1613	*Confessionario* published.
1614	*Arte* published in 1614.
1614	Fray Luis Jerónimo de Oré visits Florida and mentions the *Doctrina*, *Confessionario*, and *Cathecismo*
1614?/27	*Cathecismo y Examen para los que comulgan* published (second edition in 1627).
1616	Pareja elected Minister Provincial of the newly established Province of Saint Helen.
1628	Death of Fray Francisco de Pareja

21. The declaration of Pareja's confrere, Baltasar López, on the following day, confirms Timcucan involvement in the liturgy; see *Declaración de P. Fr. Baltasar López, San Agustín, 15 septiembre de 1602*, in *P. Fr. Jerónimo de Oré, Relación histórica de la Florida*, 29. The enduring impact of liturgical duty or "officium" is explored by Giorgio Agamben, *Opus Dei: An Archaeology of Duty*, trans. Adam Kotsko (Stanford, CA: Stanford University Press, 2013).

As the preceding chronology notes, Pareja published the *Doctrina Christiana* in Mexico in 1578 before his arrival in Florida in 1595.[22] This published text, and others he authored, fall under the Category One distinction, that is to say, a work approved by the requisite authorities, which assisted Spanish clergy in the performance of their duties in the appropriate native language.[23] Although a particular book might appear with the name of a certain friar or other cleric, the Native involvement in the composition of the work in question often begs the question as to authorship.[24] Indeed, the intense, multilingual pre-publication and, in some cases, post-publication composition and editing, indicates that frequently unknown indigenous authors should be recognized for their efforts. At the same time as natives were possibly co-authoring Category One texts, ecclesiastics such as the friars encouraged indigenous literacy and doctrinal education throughout Mexico and Yucatan by utilizing works in the same category as the *Doctrina Christiana*. While produced with clerical approval, these texts often had circulated among the native population and young boys—and perhaps young girls—trained under the supervision of the friars at times returned to their towns to teach and preach on their own.

Franciscan efforts to educate-evangelize the natives in the Caribbean and soon after in Mexico as well as Yucatan resulted in textual communities throughout the region. Organized around written texts often jointly authored, these communities promoted reading and writing among indigenous children, together with various levels of authoritative interpretation and liturgical performance. The native facility to engage the friars in these multilingual, cultural contexts impressed them, and Queen Isabella commended the Franciscans for their pedagogical labors.[25] This obvious Franciscan commitment to literary production may appear surprising given the prevailing image of Francis of Assisi as a mendicant dedicated to the poor; nevertheless, he is the same individual who wrote the first extant text in the Umbrian dialect, *Il Cantico del frate sole*, and authored as a layman numerous writings in Latin.[26] His delight in language expressed in his ecstatic outbursts in French

22. Resines, *Catecismos americanos del siglo XVI*, vol. 1, 178–182. For the text, see Francisco de Pareja, *Doctrina cristiana muy útil y necesaria* (Mexico, 1578) (facs.) (Salamanca: Universidad de Salamanca, 1990). The chronology of Pareja's texts is taken from Resines, *Catecismos americanos*, vol. 1, 178–185.

23. Christensen, *Nahua and Maya Catholicisms*, 70–73.

24. Ibid., 35, 55–57.

25. Ibid., 54.

26. Attilio Bartoli Langeli, "Gli scritti da Francesco: L'autografia di un illiteratus," in *Frate Franceso d'Assisi* (Spoleto, 1994), 121–122. With regard to Francis's high estimation of his literary accomplishments, see 156–159. The friars of Pareja's Castilian province also extolled their own literary prowess; see *Coronica y historia*, 127–128.

as well carried over into his fraternity, where the production and collection of books evoked such fervor that it is possible to claim that his confreres practiced a "religion of the book" that clearly distinguished them from their mendicant counterparts, the Dominicans.[27]

The Production of Knowledge and the Confessing Community

Given the longstanding Franciscan interest in books and the decades-long experience of textual communities in Mexico and Yucatan, it is not surprising that Fray Pareja focused his attention on linguistic acquisition and literary production when he arrived in Florida from Mexico in 1595. Fray Luis Jerónimo de Oré, Fray Francisco Alonso de Jesús, and Bishop Gabriel Díaz Vara Calderón are in agreement that Pareja and others dedicated themselves to following the general pattern of education and evangelization found in other provinces of New Spain. Jerónimo de Oré's testimony from 1614 is particularly significant because it mentions both Pareja's literary achievements—including the *Doctrina Christiana* published in Mexico—and the widespread distribution of his Spanish–Timucua texts among the natives of present-day northeast Florida. Appearing in 1613 in Mexico, by 1614 the *Confessionario* was already in circulation in northeast Florida.

The contents of the *Confessionario* are divided into the large confessional and small confessional as Pareja notes.[28] There is also a two-fold closing section on the question of blessings and curses and a final indulgence. With 230 folios, the *Confessionario* is one of the largest exemplars of the genre when compared to similar works from Mexico and Yucatan.[29] The basic structure is a follows:

Large Confessional
Title Page [unmarked]
Indulgences [unmarked]
Permissions [unmarked]
Table of Contents [unmarked]
Errors [unmarked]
Introduction to the Effects of the Sacrament of Confession [f. 9]
Thirteen Reasons for Going to Confession [f. 42]
Prayers before and after Confession [f. 55]

---

27. Attilio Bartoli Langeli, "La cultura scritta dell'ordine dei Minori," in *Francesco d'Assisi e il primo secolo della storia francescana*, eds. Attilio Bartoli Langeli and Emanuela Prinzivalli (Torino: Biblioteca Einaudi, 1997), 296–297.

28. "Las demás preguntas para Caciques, mandadores, y Principales, que fueren necesarias se torna del Confesionario grande," *Confessionario* (f. 217v.).

29. On this genre in Mexico and the Yucatan, see Christensen, *Nahua and Maya Catholicisms*, 159–192.

Exhortation [f. 64]
Three Dispositions of the True Penitent [f. 65]
General Confession in the Timucua Language [f. 112]
Questions before Confession [f. 117]
Questions based on the Ten Commandments [f. 121]
Questions based on the Seven Mortal Sins [f. 194]
Accusations Regarding the Fourteen Acts of Mercy [f. 200]
Exhortation [f. 202]

Small Confessional
Introduction [f. 203]
Questions before Confession [f. 204]
Questions based on the Ten Commandments [f. 205]
Summa of Fray Diego de Victoria on Swearing with the Name of God [f. 218]
Redondillas of Fray Damian de Vegas on Swearing and Blasphemy [f. 226]
Indulgences [f. 230]

Although Pareja's *Confessionario* follows the model of other similar manuals stretching back into the early medieval period, it emerges from the unique encounter of Spanish early modern spirituality within the Timucua culture of northeast Florida of the early seventeenth century. An examination of the contents offers insight into the science of confession and the knowledge friars like Pareja intended to produce in the construction of Timucua Christianity. The systematic, intentional questioning of the penitent illustrates the nature of the faith that ecclesiastical authorities sought to promote.[30] Questions posed in one culture but ignored in another suggest the knowledge the confessor has of the challenges facing the penitent's embrace of Christianity and the knowledge that must be constructed and practiced within the culture. As Michel Foucault argues, Christianity is a "confessing faith" that includes much more that a singular external act of confession; indeed, while the faith is confessed in creeds and deeds, the willingness and ability to recognize, reveal, and adjudicate interior dispositions must also be cultivated.[31] The promotion of catechisms in the wake of the Council of Trent, and the corresponding explosion of confessional manuals, fostered textual communities such as Pareja's San Juan del Porto, where "*los naturales*" and "*los españoles*" negotiated and contested what knowledge would constitute Timucua Christianity. The outlines of this distinctive expression of Christianity are reflected in the major themes Pareja explored and the Timucua authors' reworking of the material.

30. Christensen, *Nahua and Maya Catholicisms*, 168–169.
31. Michel Foucault, "About the beginning of the hermeneutics of the self (1980)" in *Religion and Culture: Michel Foucault*, selected and ed. Jeremy R. Carrette (New York: Routledge, 1999), 169–181.

Pareja, who wrote in the style of a well-versed theologian, had authored an extended reflection on the Book of Genesis and the nature of creation in his *Catecismo* of 1627[32] that is nowhere to be found in his 1612 *Catecismo*. Published perhaps first in 1614, the edition in the year preceding his death reveals Pareja's interest in theological underpinnings of the Christian discourse on the natural world is directly linked to the supposed superstitious practices that he sought to eradicate in the first edition of the *Confessionario*. The situation Pareja faced in Florida differed from what he encountered in Mexico, since the Timucua did not appear to practice a highly organized, hierarchical religion and thus did not display the telltale signs of widespread idolatry. Sinful practices are identified everywhere but no architectural structures are mentioned.[33] Furthermore, given the decentralized structure of knowledge production and dissemination, there was no priestly caste per se that could be engaged in dialogue or persecuted. Shamans and other natives who continued the native rituals of healing where influenced by demonic forces, according to Pareja, as were all those who joined them by ascribing power to the knowledge offered through ritual performances involving maize, fish, and other elements of the natural world. In this light, the ritual practice of auricular confession, together with the other literary and liturgical activities mentioned by Pareja, Bishop Calderón, and others became ever more important avenues of embodying the knowledge proper to the Christian narrative.

What stood in the way of Timucua Christian maturity, in the eyes of Fray Pareja, were the demonic forces at work in their—and his—culture. Here he joins the ranks of a growing number of Europeans in the early modern period whose experience was framed in varying degrees by the "great demonological fair" of the late fifteenth and early sixteenth centuries.[34] Although the emphasis on the demonic in his writings may rile contemporary sensitivities, it pales in comparison to the drama that was played out later in Loudon, France in 1632 and in Salem, Massachusetts in 1692. Pareja attested that the Timucua were Christian. When queried by Fray Luis Jerónimo de Oré in 1614 as to whether the Natives were true Christians, he replied, "What pertains to faith and belief, God is the One who can judge. We can judge only by a persons's

32. Mauricio Damian Rivero, *The Worlds of God: Religious Texts and the Counter-Reformation in the Spanish World* (Florida International University: Ph. D. Dissertation 2000), 206.

33. On the religious practices of the Timucua, see John H. Hahn, *A History of the Timucua Indians and Missions* (Gainesville: The University Press of Florida, 1996), 114–121. Hahn notes at least one instance where idols were destroyed by a Timucua chief, 115.

34. Michel de Certeau, *The Possession of Loudon*, trans. Michael B. Smith (Chicago: University of Chicago Press, 2000), 2–6. On the demonic in the "New World," see *Angels, Demons and the New World*, eds. Fernando Cervantes and Andrew Redden (Cambridge: Cambridge University Press, 2013).

exterior manifestations, who by the actions he performs, presumably shows forth the workings of faith."[35] With this measurement, Pareja asserted that the Natives often displayed a better knowledge when confessing the doctrines of the faith than the Spaniards. Furthermore, both the indigenous men and women played an active role in evangelizing their counterparts, assisted in various liturgical functions, formed confraternities, and taught each other how to sing and read in their community houses. When it came to confession of sin, Pareja claimed they readily sought out priests, and, despite the repeated reference in the *Confessionario* to demonic influences in Native rituals, he denied the existence of any trace of idolatry, witchcraft, or superstition among them that might impede their reception of holy communion.[36]

Conclusion

The science of confession, according to the *Confessionario*, required frequent practice in much the same manner as the other arts and sciences and leads to illumination. The writings of Fray Francisco de Pareja, together with those of his confreres and other ecclesiastical figures, demonstrate the lengths the Franciscans went in order to create a textual community of confessional practice through fostering literacy and liturgy. Reminiscent of the first decades of Christianity, Timucua men and women engaged their counterparts and shared in the dissemination of the Gospel teachings. Their confession of the faith, be it spoken, recited, written, or prayed, marked a unique expression of Christianity that has long since all but disappeared.

Martin Luther claimed that the practice of confession could foster irreparable harm, and that manuals like the *Confessionario* should be condemned to the flames. That Pareja's text, which reveals the forgotten voices of his Timucua co-authors, escaped intentional destruction or careless neglect is most fortunate. Nevertheless, two stories or *exempla* offer a cautionary note as to how to proceed in the study of the *Confessionario*. In the first story, a priest noted for his holiness fell into the sin of fornication due to the cunning of the Devil. Taking human form, the Devil accused the cleric before the local bishop. To strengthen his claim, the Devil wrote down the place, person, time, and witness. In the meantime, the priest begged for God's mercy, and confessed his sin with sincere contrition and humility. When asked to produce evidence to the judge, the Devil handed over the text, but to his surprise, neither he nor the judge found any words. The notes implicating

35. Oré, *The Martyrs of Florida*, 104–105.

36. Ibid., 106. Fray Francisco Alonso de Jesús also claims that the indigenous people were eager to confess even if it was difficult for them to do so; see in Legajo 302, 16–17.

the priest had been erased. As the Devil disappeared, he said he had no knowledge of the priest.[37]

Another story confirms the connection between erasure or disappearance and confession. Once the Devil's attempts to drown a sinful woman crossing a bridge were foiled because she made a thorough accounting of her sins to a priest. While the Devil waited, she crossed over the bridge without incident because the Devil had no knowledge of her, and thus could not recognize her.[38] The knowledge gained through the science of confession stole away the knowledge the Devil possessed.

In the case of the Timucua people, many believed the process of confession and the acquisition of knowledge erased their sins, but their confession of Christianity, and the cultural-social dynamics unleashed by their contact with the Spanish certainly were major factors in their erasure as a people. As their disappearance is mourned, it is also important to mourn the loss of their dynamic expression of Christianity. Not simply a silent subset of colonial Spanish Catholicism, Timucua Christians were active agents in the adaptation and negotiation of the faith so many of them embraced, died for, and at times resisted. Their textual communities, where they studied *letras*, preformed and presided at multilingual liturgies, translated various languages, interpreted texts, and engaged their counterparts in the work of evangelization, are manifest in numerous Spanish sources. Once thought to be almost unrecognizable as a people, a return to the writings of Fray Pareja and the examination of the Timucua contribution found within the pages of the *Confessionario* and other texts cannot raise the dead, but it can help the living gain a glimpse of these people from afar and honor those who have preceded us.

37. Pareja, *Confesionario en lengua castellana y timuquana*, fol. 26v. See also fol. 25v-26r. On the use of exempla in the medieval tradition and their later adaptation in Mexico, see Danièle Dehouve, *L'évangélisation des Aztèques ou le pécheur universel* (Paris: Maisonneuve & Larose, 2004).

38. Pareja, *Confesionario en lengua castellana y timuquana*, fol. 28r. See also fol. 34r.

Chapter 9
Shadow Authors: The Texts of the Earliest Indigenous Florida Writers

George Aaron Broadwell

Timucua is an extinct language of northern Florida. Its relationship with other languages is unclear. Two Franciscan priests, Francisco Pareja and Gregorio de Movilla produced an *arte*, four catechisms, confessional, and *doctrina*. Other materials, including perhaps a dictionary, have been lost. Their dates of production were approximately 1603 through 1627. There are also two letters written in the language, probably by native speakers. In total there are about two thousand pages of bilingual Timucua–Spanish text.

Methods for Studying the Timucua Language

Our knowledge of Timucua comes almost entirely from seventeenth-century Spanish colonial documents. The most important of these fall into two categories: a Latinate grammar by Pareja (1614) (hereafter the *Arte*), giving a treatment of some aspects of Timucua grammar, and several long volumes of parallel Spanish–Timucua religious materials, including a confessional, three catechisms, and a *doctrina* (explication of Christian doctrine).[1] There are explorations of a few areas of Timucua grammar in Gatschet and in Adams

*An expanded version of this chapter has been published as Alejandra Dubcovsky and George Aaron Broadwell, "Writing Timucua: Recovering and Interrogating Indigenous Authorship," *Early American Studies*, Volume 15, Number 3, 2017, 409–441.

1. Francisco Pareja, *Catecismo en lengua castellana, y Timuquana. En el qual se contiene lo que se les puede enseñara los adultos que an de ser baptizados* (Mexico City: Impresa dela Viuda de Pedro Balli, 1612); ibid., *Catecismo y breve exposición de la doctrina christiana* (Mexico City: Casa de la viuda de Pedro Balli, 1612), ibid., *Confessionario en lengua castellana y timuquana con unos consejos para animar al penitente* (Mexico City: Emprenta de la viuda de Diego Lopez Daualos, 1613), ibid., *Arte y pronunciacion de la lengua timucuana y castellana* (Mexico City: Emprenta de Ioan Ruyz, 1614), ibid., *Catecismo en lengua timuquana y castellana* (Mexico City: Emprenta de Ioan Ruyz, 1627).

and Vinson.[2] The only modern account of Timucua grammar is Granberry, but there are large gaps in his account of the language.[3]

In order to get a better understanding of Timucua grammar, I have developed a corpus of the extant Timucua texts, along with their parallel Spanish translations. The corpus is still in development, and new material is being added, with an eventual aim of including all Timucua text. The current corpus is about 72,000 orthographic words of Timucua, and was designed to include a range of styles and authors. It is composed of the following materials:

- four-fifths of Pareja's 1613 *Confessionario*
- two-thirds of Pareja's large 1612 *Catecismo* (1612a)
- one-fourth of Pareja's small 1612 *Catecismo* (1612b)
- all of Pareja's large 1627 *Catecismo*
- two-thirds of Movilla's 1635 *Doctrina*
- two-thirds of Pareja's 1614 *Arte*

The corpus has been analyzed with FieldWorks Language Explorer (FLEx), a tool designed by SIL International. Because Timucua is an extinct language, with no reliable dictionary, the meanings of most words and morphemes in the texts are deduced by examining multiple contexts of use. The powerful concordance functions of FLEx and its abilities to ensure consistency in interlinear glossing were extremely helpful in deciding on likely glosses for the material.

Through this corpus-based approach to the Timucua language, it is now possible to read many Timucua texts for the first time and to compare them to the Spanish texts with which they stand in parallel. As might be expected, there are often discrepancies between the two. I argue in subsequent sections that some discrepancies are particularly revealing.

Authorship of the Timucua Materials

If we ask who authored the Timucua books, the answer may seem obvious at first. The authors were Francisco Pareja and Gregorio de Movilla. When we think more carefully about how the books were written and the role that

---

2. Albert Gatschet, "The Timucua language," *Proceedings of the American Philosophical Society* 16 (1877): 1–17; ibid., "The Timucua language," *Proceedings of the American Philosophical Society* 17 (1878): 490–504; ibid., "The Timucua language," *Proceedings of the American Philosophical Society* 18 (1880): 465–502 and Lucien Adams and Julien Vinson, eds. *Arte de la lengua timuquana, compuesto en 1614 por el padre Francisco Pareja, y publicado conforme al ejemplar original único* (Paris: Maisonneuve Frères et Ch. Leclerc, 1886).

3. Julian Granberry, *A Grammar and Dictionary of the Timucua Language* (Tuscaloosa: University of Alabama Press, 1993).

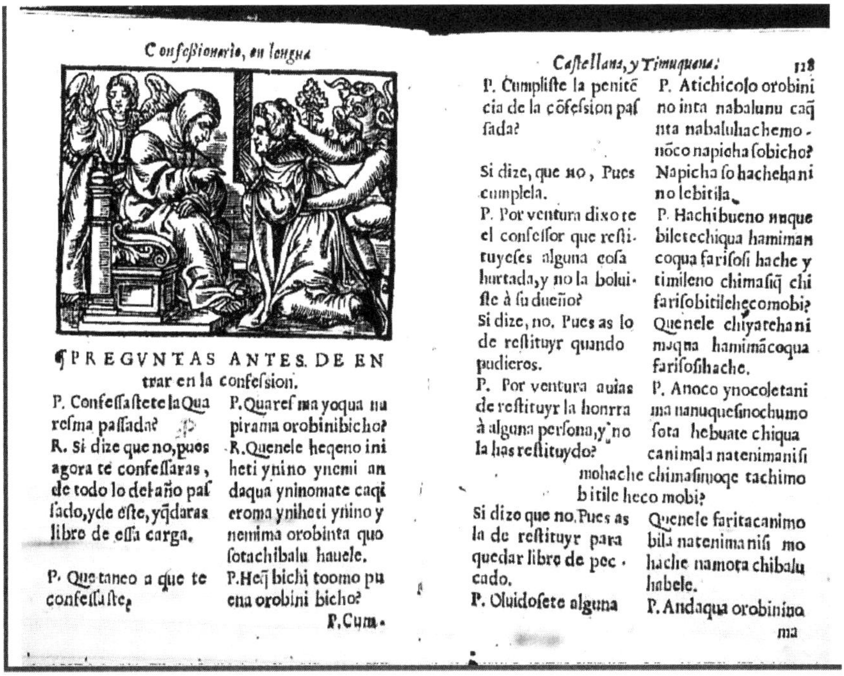

Confeſsionario, en lengua

¶ PREGVNTAS ANTES DE ENtrar en la confeſsion.

P. Confeſſaſtete la Quareſma paſſada?	P. Quareſma yoqua na pirama orobinibicho?
R. Si dize que no, pues agora te confeſſaras, de todo lo del año paſſado, y de éſte, y q̃daras libre de eſſa carga.	R. Quenele heqeno iniheti ynino yncmi andaqua yninomate caqieroma yniheti ynino ynemima orobinta quoſotachibalu hauele.
P. Que tanto a que te confeſſaſte?	P. Heq̃ bichi toomo puena orobini bicho?
	P. Cum-

Caſtellana, y Timuquana. 118

P. Cumpliſte la penitẽcia de la cõfeſsion paſſada?	P. Atichicolo orobinino inta nabalunu caq̃nta nabaluhachemo-nõco napicha ſobicho?
Si dize, que no, Pues cumplela.	Napicha ſo hachehani no lebitila.
P. Por ventura dixo te el confeſſor que reſtituyeſes alguna coſa hurtada, y no la boluiſte à ſu dueño?	P. Hachibueno nuque biletechiqua hamiman coqua fariſoſi hache y timileno chimaſiq̃ chi fariſobitilehecomobi?
Si dize, no. Pues as lo de reſtituyr quando pudieros.	Quenele chiyatchani maqua hamimãcoqua fariſoſihache.
P. Por ventura auias de reſtituyr la honrra à alguna perſona, y no la has reſtituydo?	P. Anoco ynocoletanima nanuqueſinochumo ſota hebuate chiqua canimala natenimaniſi mohache chimaſinoqe tachimobitile heco mobi?
Si dizo que no. Pues as la de reſtituyr para quedar libre de peccado.	Quenele faritacanimobila natenimaniſi mohache namota chibalu habele.
P. Oluidoſete alguna	P. Andaqua orobinino ma

Timucua speakers played in writing these books, there is good evidence that one or more unnamed Timucua people are the unnamed co-authors of these texts. Thus some Timucua people used their literacy skills in the early seventeenth century to express their own perspectives as they worked alongside Catholic priests in the task of translating doctrinal material.

Among the parallel Timucua-Spanish documents, the most significant are two catechisms and a confessional.[4] Francisco Pareja was not the author of any of these works in the way we usually understand authorship. Let us consider a sample page of the Confessional to better understand this claim.

The text is in two columns, with the Spanish on the left and the Timucua on the right. Pareja edited the Spanish, that is, he selected and sometimes modified standard questions found in any Spanish-language confessional of the period.

But what about the Timucua-language column on the right? Did Pareja speak and write Timucua well enough to compose this version himself? Did Pareja explain the meaning to a bilingual Timucua, who translated the sentence verbally, after which Pareja wrote the Timucua? Or did the Timucua speaker write the Timucua unassisted by Pareja? Was Pareja present at the time of the

4. See note 1.

composition of the Timucua version, or did he give a Spanish confessional to a trusted Timucua convert and ask him or her to produce a translation?

In this chapter I would like to present two arguments that Pareja is not the sole author of these texts, based on two main arguments. First, that there are multiple dialects present in the text. And second, that a close reading of the Timucua texts shows many divergences from the Spanish which Pareja is unlikely to have intended.

Linguistic and Orthographic Diversity in the *Confessionario* versus the *Short Catechism*

Some of the texts seem to have had multiple Timucua co-authors. This is clearest in Pareja's short catechism (*Catecismo breve*), which I will compare with the *Confessionario*, a text that appears to have a single Timucua co-author.

Evidence for multiple co-authors comes from some slight dialect diversity among Timucua speakers. The linguistic evidence seems to show that speakers differed in the pronunciation of the plural argument suffix /-bo/. For one group of Timucuas (BO dialect), the pronunciation was consistently [bo], while for another group of Timucuas (BUO dialect), the pronunciation varied between [bo] and [b^{w}o].

Because the writing of Timucua in the early texts was not standardized, the spelling of this suffix can offer a clue as to the dialect of the writer. Texts that consistently spell the plural argument suffix <bo> are likely to be from a speaker of the BO dialect, while texts that alternate between the <bo> and <buo> spellings are likely to be from the BUO dialect.

The *Catecismo breve* appears to come from a speaker of the BUO dialect, with a fairly smooth distribution that averages about 48% <bo> to 52% <buo> throughout the text. Consider the following table and figures.[5]

Folio range	bo	buo	Total	% bo	% buo
6–26	10	21	31	32	68
27–46	10	12	22	45	55
47–66	10	11	21	48	52
67–86	7	5	12	58	42
127–146	7	4	11	64	36
147–166	7	4	11	64	36
	51	57	108		
Mean	8.5	9.5	18		

5. The count begins with folio 6 because that is where the Timucua text begins, the previous pages being Spanish introductions. Folia are grouped into bins of 9 to 10 pages for the purpose of this count. The number of instances of /bo/ between bins ranged from a high of 24 to a low of 2, with a mean of 4.75 instances.

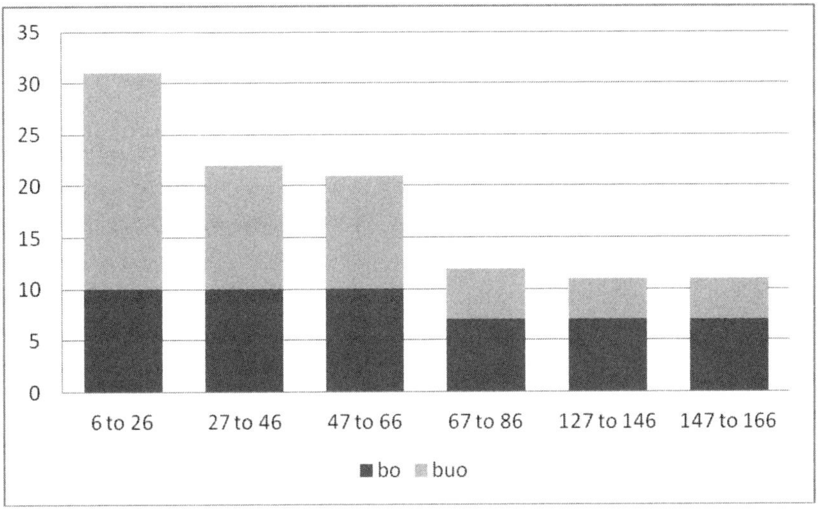

In contrast, the distribution in the *Confessionario* is very different. The beginning of the text is almost entirely in the BO dialect—the first 119 folia have one instance of <buo>. But something very unusual happens at folio 120—the pattern begins to change, and now <bo> and <buo> begin to alternate in the pattern that is characteristic of the BUO dialect of Timucua. This pattern continues until roughly folio 159, when the text reverts to the uniform BO dialect, which it continues to the end of the text.[6] The following chart and graph show the pattern in more detail:

Folio range	**bo**	**buo**	**Total**	**% bo**	**% buo**
9–29	15	0	15	100	0
30–49	3	1	4	75	25
50–69	4	0	4	100	0
70–89	2	0	2	100	0
90–119	7	0	7	100	0
120–139	12	3	15	80	20
140–159	8	4	12	67	33
160–179	6	0	6	100	0
180–199	2	0	2	100	0
200–219	4	0	4	100	0
Total	63	8	71		
Mean	6.3	0.8	7.1		

6. It is difficult to determine the end of the BUO co-author's portion. There are no instances of <buo> after f159, but a speaker of the BUO dialect might very well write several pages with only <bo>. So perhaps some pages in the f160s also belong to this section.

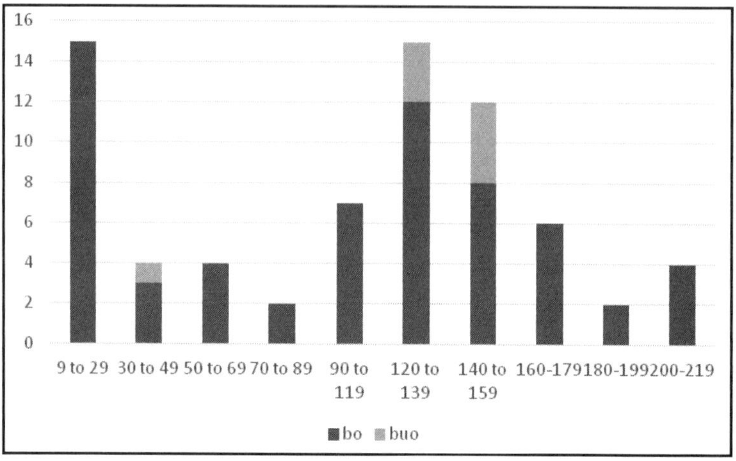

I believe the simplest way to explain this strange distribution of the spellings in the document is to posit at least two Timucua co-authors in the *Confessionario*. The first co-author spoke the BO dialect of Timucua and wrote the first 119 folia of the document. The first co-author also probably wrote the last forty or fifty folia (roughly f160–219 or f170–219) of the *Confessionario*.[7]

The second co-author spoke a BUO dialect of Timucua and wrote the middle section of the *Confessionario*, folia 120 to 159. This co-author is probably not the same Timucua person who authored the *Catecismo breve*, because <bo> and <buo> spellings appear in approximately equal frequency in the *Catecismo breve*. The co-author of the middle section of the *Confessionario*, in contrast, spoke a BUO dialect, but spelled <buo> at a much lower rate. As the chart shows, there are twenty-seven instances of the /bo/ morpheme in folia 120–159 of the *Confessionario*, and the author spells it as <bo> twenty times, and as <buo> seven times. That is a roughly 3:4 to 1:4 ratio.

The folia 120–159 section also coincides with a significant thematic boundary in the text, sometimes called the "Superstitions" section. The preceding folia (f117v–119v) are the questions prior to confession, and the introduction and explanation of the first commandment begins on folio 119v and continues to f121, followed by questions on the first commandment. These end, and then on folio 123, we encounter a section labeled:

> *Ceremonias, agueros y supersticiones que aun usan algunos* (Ceremonies, auguries, and superstitions that some still follow)[8]

7. I will not attach too much significance to the single instance of a <buo> spelling in this passage.
8. Pareja, *Confessionario,* f123.

This section is made up of a set of questions about traditional Timucua beliefs that are fascinating for their ethnographic content, as discussed in Milanich and Sturtevant (1972).[9] Confessants were asked questions such as "Are you a healer?" "Have you placed a new candle or fire to cure someone?" "Have you cured someone by calling the Devil?" "When it thundered, did you whistle to the sky to have clouds or rain via [in response to] your evil prayers?" "Have you taken the skin of the poisonous snake or of the black snake and with black guano and other herbs have you tried to bewitch someone or have you bewitched them or wished to do so?" and "In order to begin to take food out of the storehouse, have you prayed?"

The questions fit awkwardly within the context of confessional questions about the ten commandments, which resume at folio 133 with the second commandment. The third, fourth, and fifth commandments follow in a fairly conventional way. But after the fifth commandment, there is another ethnographically specific set of questions about healing/curing, pregnancy, abortion, traditional healers, the use of herbs, and witches. Like the previous set, it refers to traditional Timucua practices and asks the confessants whether they persist in non-Christian practices. Thus this middle section is not only different linguistically from the rest of the text, it has different content as well.

Clearly the evidence of linguistic diversity within the Timucua text seems fatal for the hypothesis that Pareja learned Timucua well enough to write these texts himself. If he had done so, he surely would not have switched dialects halfway through the book. But the orthographic diversity also seems very problematic vis-à-vis the idea that Timucua assistants translated the Spanish verbally and Pareja wrote down their translations. For if Pareja were writing down the Timucua himself, it is likely he would have used a standard way of writing the verbal suffixes after scores of pages of text.

I believe the orthographic diversity shows that Timucuas themselves were writing their language in the early seventeenth century. The unnamed Timucua co-authors here tried to write texts that matched their own pronunciations of the language, and thus when they differed in dialect, their texts show those differences. The orthographic differences in the *Confessionario* also suggest that for a large text, various sections might be assigned to different native co-authors who would work to produce Timucua versions. Pareja's role, I suggest, might be more like that of an editor, taking existing Spanish language devotional material, assigning various sections of it to trusted Timucua converts for translation, and then assembling, copying, and preparing the finished products for printing.

---

9. Jerald Milanich and William Sturtevant, *Francisco Pareja 1613 Confessionario: A Documentary Source for Timucuan Ethnography* (Tallahassee: Division of Archives, History, and Records Management, Florida Department of State, 1972).

Of course, one of the clear dangers of such an enterprise is that the priest running the operation does not truly understand all the subtleties of the language under translation. That introduces the possibility of texts that begin to diverge from their sources; a possibility I discuss in more detail in the next section.

Co-author out of control: Textual divergence in Timucua translation

The Timucua co-author of the middle section seems to have been assigned the task of producing the questions about native practices and superstitions. But it is in close reading of the "Superstitions" portion of the *Confessionario* that one begins to notice suspicious divergence between the Timucua text and the Spanish text. Consider the following passage.[10]

Nia	chipacanoleta				etamina hinayelaha					
nia	chi -	pacano	le	-ta	eta	-mi	nahi	-naye	la	-ha
woman	2B	single	cop	part	pregnant	3poss	exist	2sA	cop	irrealis

iniheti inino acoma chinecoco lahacu yunchi
iniheti ini -no acoma chi- ine -coco -la -hacu yunchi
sin commit nmzr great 2B commit emphatic vsuff comparative shame

nomabetaleqe aruquima iqueninaye qere nabueta nebeleca
-no ma beta -leqe aruqui -ma iqueni -naye -qere na- bueta nebeleca
nmzr art to,for focus baby art kill 2sA comp instr from (comparison big

acola inecalua iquoma nantela niapacanoleta ciyuchita
acola inecalua iquoba -ma nante -la nia pacano -leta ci- yuchi -ta
very grave sin large art called affirm woman single if 2B shame part

hanimate iquenetiqua nihache
-hanima -te iquene -tiqua -ni –hache
although ConFoc kill must not must not –imper

Si fuere soltera y se sabe que esta preñada, por que no aborte o achocandolo como suelen se le dira. Hija aunque yncurriste en peccado mortal, mira

10. Passages from the Timucua corpus are presented in three lines of analysis. The first line is the original spelling and punctuation, while the second is a morphological analysis. The third line shows the gloss (posited meaning) of each morpheme. The passages are followed by the corresponding Spanish from the text, a translation of the Spanish, and a literal translation of the Timucua.

Morphological glosses use the following abbreviations: 1, 2, 3 = 1st, 2nd, 3rd person, A, B = agreement from the A (actor) or B (patient) paradigm, affirm = affirmative, art = article, benef = benefactive, caus = causative, comp = complementizer, ConFoc = contrastive focus, cop = copula, desir = desiderative complement, imper = imperative, indef = indefinite, instr = instrumental, neg = negative, nmzr = nominalizer, part = participle, poss = possessor, q = question, recip = reciprocal, s = singular, vsuff = verbal suffix of uncertain meaning que caeras en otro mas grave si mal pares no hagas tan grave peccado aunque passes verguença llevala a Dios.

If she were single and it is known that she is pregnant, it is to be said to her that she is not to abort or choke the unborn child as they are accustomed to do. My daughter, although you have fallen into mortal sin, beware that you will fall into an even more serious one if you have brought about a miscarriage. don't commit such a grave sin even if it means shame, bear the sin in God's name.

(Lit. If you are a single woman and are pregnant you have committed a great sin, but it is more shame when you kill the child. This is the greater sin, called mortal sin. If you are a single woman and are ashamed, you must not kill.)[11] [*Confessionario*, f147]

There are other passages as well that seem to show different Timucua and Spanish attitudes towards sex and shame. The following two passages come from the *Confessionario* folio 164 (and are thus possibly by the BUO co-author)

Inihiminco anoeyo napatabo hero maninoma
inihi -mi -nco ano eyo na- patabo -he -ro mani -no -ma
spouse 3poss indef person other instr have sex future desir want nmzr art

nate quenta haue manibicho ?
nate quen -ta -haue mani -bi -ch -o
pardon be (emphatic) part irrealis pardon past 2A q

Haz consentido que alguno ande con tu consorte?

Have you consented that someone walk with your spouse?

(Lit. Have you pardoned your wife when she wanted to have sex with another person?)[12] [*Confessionario* f164]

Anopira comeleta niamate nata hibuasi mota
anopira comele -ta nia -mate nata hibua -sI mo -ta
Indian act voluntarily part woman and consent say benef say part

viroma nacunata hibuasomata mosobi cho ?
viro -ma nacu nata hibua -so mo -ta moso -bi chi- -o
male,husband art and then consent say caus say part advise/say past 2A q

As concertado que algunos se casan a uso de indios sin dar parte al paracho?

Have you arranged that someone be married according to the Indian way without giving notice to the parish priest?

---

11. Pareja, *Confessionario*, f147.
12. Ibid., f164.

(Lit. Did you advise that ceremonies should be voluntary and that the woman should speak (her consent) and then that the man should speak (his consent)?)[13] [*Confessionario* f184]

Here the emphasis of the Spanish text is that permission of the priest is required before two people can marry. Surely there is nothing amiss in arranging weddings where both parties consent; it is just that such consent is not sufficient for a marriage unless a priest also gives permission.

Our Timucua co-author chooses to translate the passage in a way that just focuses on the couple and edits the priest out of the question altogether. It is hard to imagine that a priest translating the passage would make the same choice!

The Timucua is also sometimes more direct in its language about sexuality, while the Spanish uses euphemisms and circumlocutions. Consider the following two examples:

Inihiminco patabosintanaqeno ysono lebitima
inihi -mi -nco patabo sin -ta naqeno yso -no -lebi ti -ma
spouse 3poss indef have sex recip part if use nmzr must neg art

ysobicho yanacu quososiro manibicho ?
yso -bi -ch -o yanacu quoso -siro mani -bi -ch -o
use past 2B q and then,thus make desir want past 2A q

Usando del matrimonio a sido por la via ordinaria o has desseado que sea de otro modo?

Making use of marriage, has it been in the ordinary way or have you desired that it be in a different way?

(Lit. If you were having sex with your wife, did you use that which must not be used and did you intend to do it?)[14] [*Confessionario* f164]

Aanoco nahebuastechiqua huema hibita
ano -co na- hebua -s -te -chi -qua hue -ma hibi -ta
person indef instr speak benef part 2A if hand art take the hand part

cumechipaliqe vna oquoye biturumota yribobi ?
cume chi- pali -qe vna oquo -ye bituru mo -ta yribo -bi
heart 2B excite and then body body 2sPoss get aroused? caus part stand past

Hablando con alguna persona o tomandote la mano vinote alguna alteración de la carne?

Speaking with some person or taking your hand, did some change in the flesh come to you?

13. Ibid., f184.
14. Ibid., f164.

When you spoke to a person and took the hand, did you get excited and did your flesh get hard and stand?[15] [*Confessionario* f158]

Some Timucua customs are ascribed to the devil in the Spanish version, but not in the Timucua version. In the following passage, the Timucua version only mentions *ituhu*, "to pray," but the Spanish refers to *la ceremonia de el Demonio*, "the Devil's ceremony."[16]

Nimota uquata ituhuta honosoma enesota onaquosta
nimota uqua -ta ituhu -ta honoso -ma ene -so -ta ona quos -ta
antlers? take part pray part deer art see caus part affirm make part

ituhuta iquenihale manda bohobi cho ?
ituhu -ta iqueni -ha -le man -da boho -bi chi- -o
pray part kill irrealis affirm:1sgA want part believe past 2A q

Para cazar algun venado as tomado las hastas de otro venado, as le rezado la ceremonia de el Demonio.

In order to hunt some deer did you take the antlers of another deer and pray over them the Demon's ceremony?

(Lit. Did you believe "Taking horns and praying, I will see the deer and by doing this, I will pray and kill it"?)[17] [*Confessionario* f130]

Similarly, in the following example, the Spanish describes the practice of blowing at the wind as *tus malos rezos* ("your evil prayers"), but the Timucua contains no corresponding evaluation.

Numa hebuama bimetaqe ituhuta iposibicho ?
numa hebua bime -ta -qe ituhu -ta ipo -sI -bi chi- -o
sky/heaven speak blow? part if pray part extinguish benef past 2A q

Tronando, as soplado asta el Cielo para detener el nublado o agua con tus rezos malos?

Thundering, have you blown toward the heavens in order to stop the clouds or water with your evil prayers?

(Lit. When the heavens spoke, did you blow and pray to extinguish it?)[18] [*Confessionario* f150]

In other cases, the Timucua text adds or omits cultural details not found in the Spanish translation. Consider the following examples.

---

15. Ibid., f158.

16. The word *nimota* in the following passage is a hapax legomenon in the current Timucua corpus. From context, it appears to mean 'antlers', but this reading is not completely certain.

17. Ibid., f130.

18. Ibid., f150.

Hachipile uquestanaye yabima ichuquinetiqua nimaca
hachipile uques -ta -naye yabi -ma ichuquine -tiqua -ni –maca
animal kill part 2sA bone art throw:down must not must no –prohibit

uquesinoma ubua-hauetila mota bohota mobi cho
uquesi -no -ma ubua -haue -ti -la mo -ta boho -ta mo -bi chi- -o
kill nmzr art enter irrealis neg affirm say part believe part say past 2A q

As dicho los guesos de lo caçado no los arrogeys, que no entrara mas en el laço y parãça, sino colgados o poneldos en las palmas de la casa?

Did you order that the bones of the game must not be thrown away, lest the game would no longer enter into the snare or trap, but that they (the bones) must be hung up or placed on the roof of the house?

(Lit. Did you say and believe that when animals are killed, the bones must not be thrown away lest the animals not enter the place of killing?)[19] [*Confessionario* f130]

Abo pahama honote coso habeleta ituhubicho ?
abo paha -ma hono -te coso -habe -leta ituhu -bi chi- -o
tall,giant house art food ConFoc do irrealis purpose pray past 2A q

Para comenzar a sacar la comida de la garrita, has rezado?

In order to begin to take food out of the storehouse, have you prayed?

(Lit. Did you pray in order to do the food in the high house?)[20] [*Confessionario* f150][21]

The cumulative effect of all these discrepancies makes it very unlikely that the same person wrote both the Spanish and Timucua. If Pareja is the author of the Spanish text, other unnamed native writers composed the Timucua.

Literacy, Letters, and the Timucua

The Spanish intention in translating these documents in Timucua was to have native people read them in their own language. Thus Spanish mission education included training Timucuas to read and write. We do not know how extensive Timucua literacy was, but Native people wrote letters to each other and to Spanish authorities (two have survived). Many other Timucua literacy materials existed (e.g., spellers, readers) but have been lost. (These materials are mentioned in a 1630 letter by Fr. Alonso de Jesus.[22] Timucua

---

19. Ibid., f130.

20. Ibid., f150.

21. The Timucua merely says 'do' the food, presumably referring to an action that was obvious to a native reader, while the Spanish appears to explain the action in more detail for a non-native author.

22. John H. Hann, "1630 Memorial of Fray Alonso de Jesus on Spanish Florida's Missions and Natives," *The Americas* 50 (1993): 99.

converts learned to recite catechismal responses, prayers, the Credo, and so on in Timucua.

Literacy, protest, and rebellion

Worth cites the 1660 testimony of Clemente Bernal, that the interception of a Spanish letter was one of the sparks for the Timucua Rebellion.

> . . . the cacique of San Martín, named Lúcas Menéndez, had made a meeting of caciques in the said village of San Pedro de Potoxiriba, the cause which moved him, according to what he said , was a letter that he said he had intercepted from the said Governor/ [–] he said he wrote it, and that in it, the sending to call upon the principals and the rest of the people of the said provinces of Apalachee and Timucua for the aid of this city was in order to make them slaves, and not because there was news of enemies, and that an Indian who knew Spanish had read the said letter.[23]

The cacique Lúcas Menéndez mentioned in this testimony subsequently sent a letter in Timucua to the Spanish authorities in St Augustine, warning them not to come to his hacienda Worth. (This letter has not survived.)[24] Native letters thus seem to have been the one of the means by which a rebellion against the Spanish was planned.

In his 1660 testimony after the Timucua Rebellion, the adjutant Pedro de la Puerta said that

> Governor Don Diego de Rebolledo asked him what motive had the said Indians for this, and the said Don Juan responded that before, the said cacique of San Martín had written him a letter, being on horseback from this city in order to go to his said hacienda, though [the letter] being in the language of Indians which he did not understand, he had not opened it. He had proceeded with his journey, and having arrived at the said hacienda of La Chua, he gave the letter to an Indian who he had in his service who spoke Spanish. . . .[25]

A lesson from this testimony is that literacy is a powerful tool. Once native people become literate, they can use their literacy as a means to promote Christianity or to promote rebellion.

The 17th century Timucua authors discussed here were part of a larger literate population of Timucua people. We do not know how widely dispersed

---

23. John Worth, "The Timucuan Missions of Spanish Florida and the Rebellion of 1656" (PhD diss., University of Florida, 1992), 228.

24. Ibid., 228

25. Ibid., 372.

Timucua literacy was, but the existence of monolingual books in Timucua Movilla (1635) and Timucua letters show that there were certainly many people who could read and write their language.[26]

Conclusions: Agency, Authorship, and History

The linguistic evidence shows us that there are at least two Timucua co-authors in the *Confessionario*, as shown by their different dialects. The primary Timucua co-author of the 1612 short catechism is different than the primary co-author of the *Confessionario*. Although Pareja is listed as the "author" of both, the distinct language and content in the two raises a number of issues that make it very unlikely he wrote the Timucua portions. These texts then are the work of unnamed Timucua co-authors whose work was made possibly by the flowering of literacy among Timucua Christian converts in the seventeenth century.

Although the Timucua are a vanished people, we can gain insight into their perspectives from Timucua authors' writings four hundred years ago. These texts (Pareja 1612a, 1612b, and 1613) are the oldest writings in a North American indigenous language outside Mexico. The unnamed authors are thus the earliest Native writers in this country. In summary, the Franciscans of Florida created not only converts, but also bilingual co-authors among the Timucua.

---

26. Gregorio de Movilla, *Explicacion de la Doctrina que compuso el cardenal Belarmino, por mandado del Señor Papa Clemente 8.* Traducida en Lengua Floridana: por el Padre Fr. Gregorio de Movilla (Mexico City: Imprenta de Iuan Ruyz, 1635).

Chapter 10
Beyond Reducción *and Coalescence: Population Aggregation and the Spanish Missions of La Florida*

Elliot H. Blair

In recent years there has been a trend towards archaeological approaches to the study of colonialism that strongly engage in cross-cultural comparisons.[1] Such comparisons have often proceeded along several distinct dimensions, such as comparisons between types of colonial enterprises (e.g., mission, mercantile, and settler),[2] comparisons that consider national origin of the colonizers (e.g., British, French, Spanish), and comparisons based on subsistence strategies and sociopolitical complexity of Native peoples.[3] For the Spanish Borderlands, and mission enterprises in particular, comparative analyses have also often focused on differences between missionary orders (e.g., Franciscan, Jesuit, and Dominican).

Recently Lightfoot et al. argued for "a more comprehensive, comparative approach to archaeological studies of colonialism that considers how indigenous societies with varied political economies may have instigated and experienced very different processes and outcomes in their encounters with European colonists."[4] Presenting a case study from Alta California, we contrasted the

---

1. Gil J. Stein, "Introduction: The Comparative Archaeology of Colonial Encounters," in *The Archaeology of Colonial Encounters: Comparative Perspectives*, ed. Gil J. Stein (Santa Fe: School of American Research, 2005); Claire L. Lyons and John K. Papadopoulos, "Archaeology and Colonialism," in *The Archaeology of Colonialism*, eds. Claire L. Lyons and John K. Papadopoulos (Los Angeles: Getty Research Institute, 2002); Chris Gosden, *Archaeology and Colonialism: Cultural Contact from 5000 BC to the Present* (Cambridge: Cambridge University Press, 2004); Kent G. Lightfoot, "Culture Contact Studies: Redefining the Relationship between Prehistoric and Historical Archaeology," *American Antiquity* 60(2) (1995): 89–103.

2. Kent G. Lightfoot, *Indians, Missionaries, and Merchants: The Legacy of Colonial Encounters on the California Frontiers* (Berkeley: University of California Press, 2005).

3. Mariah F. Wade, *Missions, Missionaries, and Native Americans: Long-term Processes and Daily Practices* (Gainesville: University Press of Florida, 2008).

4. Kent G. Lightfoot, et al., "The Study of Indigenous Political Economies and Colonialism in Native California: Implications for Contemporary Tribal Groups and Federal Recognition," *American Antiquity* 78(1) (2013): 90.

types of encounters that hunter-gatherers in that region had with Franciscan missionaries with those experienced by the more sedentary, agricultural chiefdoms of the American Southeast. While cautioning that a simple contrast between hunter-gatherers and agrarian peoples was too "coarse-grained" to have much analytic utility, we argued that the timing and magnitude of *reducción* policies that were implemented among hunter-gatherer populations in California resulted in severe social transformations from the onset of missionization, which varied greatly in rate and magnitude from those transformations experienced by agrarian populations in the Southeast and Southwest. While being careful to note that this contrast was not to suggest that the peoples of La Florida did not experience population relocations, political reconfigurations, and disruptions in social networks, this comparison highlights a tension that exists in the literature on the missions of La Florida, regarding the scale, meaning, and even existence of Spanish *reducción* in the region (discussed below).

Another comparative framework that has been employed specifically in the Southeast, and that I would argue runs somewhat parallel to the *reducción* question in that it too revolves around questions of population relocation and aggregation, is the juxtaposition of "coalescent" societies with "traditionalist" societies.[5] The former refers to those societies that were formed and reconfigured in the aftermath of the disease and slave raiding that created what Ethridge has termed the Mississippian "shatter-zone."[6] These include groups such as the Cherokees, Creeks, and Catawbas, who mostly avoided early and sustained colonial encounters with the Spanish, but were later drawn into the British colonial economy. The latter, the "traditionalist" societies, were those that largely maintained pre-Contact political structures throughout sustained colonial encounters with the Spanish (e.g., Guale, Apalachee) and the French (e.g., Natchez).[7]

---

5. Robbie Ethridge and Charles Hudson, "The Early Historic Transformation of the Southeastern Indians," in *Cultural Diversity in the U.S. South: Anthropological Contributions to a Region in Transition*, eds. Carole E. Hill and Patricia D. Beaver, 34–50 (Athens: The University of Georgia Press, 1998); Robbie Ethridge and Sheri M. Shuck-Hall, eds. *Mapping the Mississippian Shatter Zone* (Lincoln: University of Nebraska Press, 2009); Robbie Ethridge, *From Chicaza to Chickasaw: The European Invasion and the Transformation of the Mississippian World, 1540–1715* (Chapel Hill: University of North Carolina Press, 2010).

6. Ethridge and Shuck-Hall, *Mapping the Mississippian Shatter Zone*; Robbie Ethridge, "Introduction: Mapping the Mississippian Shatter Zone," in *Mapping the Mississippian Shatter Zone*, eds. Robbie Ethridge and Sheri M. Shuck-Hall, pp. 1–62 (Lincoln: University of Nebraska Press, 2009); Ethridge, "Creating the Shatter Zone: Indian Slave Traders and the Collapse of the Southeastern Chiefdoms," in *Light on the Path: The Anthropology and History of the Southeastern Indians*, eds. Thomas J. Pluckhahn and Robbie Ethridge, 207–218 (Tuscaloosa: University of Alabama Press, 2006).

7. For a detailed discussion and a different comparative vocabulary see Eric E. Bowne, "Southeastern Indian Polities of the Seventeenth Century: Suggestions toward an Analytical Vocabulary," in *Native American Adoption, Captivity, and Slavery in Changing Contexts*, ed. Max Carocci and Stephanie Pratt (New York: Palgrave Macmillan, 2012).

My argument here is that these two parallel, comparative approaches highlight a distinct tension in how we conceptualize the colonial interactions of the Native peoples involved in the Spanish mission system of La Florida. First, by emphasizing an absence of Spanish *reducción* policies, there is a distinct, though largely unintentional, hint that the population relocations that occurred in Spanish Florida—generally being instigated by the Native peoples themselves—lacked the degree of trauma and disruptiveness that occurred elsewhere in the Spanish Borderlands. Second, I would argue that the contrast between coalescent and traditionalist communities—while accurately descriptive—also serves to unintentionally minimize the trauma and disruptiveness of the mission system, by emphasizing the persistence of traditional structures among missionized peoples. As Robbie Ethridge has argued, "Scholars are beginning to understand that the collapse and transformation of Southern Native societies were not uniform across space and time. If we are to comprehensively understand the full transformation of the Mississippian world, we need an interpretive framework against which each instance of collapse and reformation can be placed."[8] Along these lines, in the rest of this paper, rather than proceeding from a broad-scale, comparative position, I take a more "granular" look[9] at the Guale missions of coastal Georgia, considering how population movements and "types" of aggregation played out during the seventeenth and early eighteenth centuries.

I begin by discussing the diversity of perspectives that scholars have employed while speaking about "*reducción*" in Spanish Florida. I continue by reviewing John Worth's detailed documentation of the population movements and aggregations that occurred along the Atlantic coast of La Florida in the seventeenth and eighteenth centuries, primarily focusing on episodes involving Mission Santa Catalina de Guale and highlighting details that provide evidence for the social and political difficulties inherent to such relocations.

Following this, I consider such evidence and compare it with how other researchers have contextualized it—both when specifically discussing the missions of La Florida and also when engaging in cross-cultural comparisons. Finally, while noting a disconnect between the evidence and the scholarly contextualization of the region, I conclude with a broader discussion of *reducción* and coalescence, considering how these and related concepts articulate with the documentary and archaeological evidence.

8. "Introduction: Mapping the Mississippian Shatter Zone," 2.

9. Maria Ximena Senatore and Pedro Paulo A. Funari, "Introduction: Disrupting the Grand Narrative of Spanish and Portuguese Colonialism," in *Archaeology of Culture Contact and Colonialism in Spanish and Portuguese America*, eds. Pedro Paulo A. Funari and Maria Ximena Senatore (Springer, 2015).

Reducción in Spanish Florida: Population Movement, La Florida, and Mission Santa Catalina de Guale

In the fall of 1662, Westo slave-raiders, recently relocated to the middle Savannah River, attacked the town of Huyache on the northern frontier of the Spanish Mission province of Guale, located along the Atlantic coast of Georgia.[10] This attack, though only briefly mentioned in the documentary record, was a transformative event in the province of Guale and precipitated the relocation of the northernmost Spanish mission—San Diego de Satuache—from the vicinity of the mouth of the Ogeechee River to St. Catherines Island, where it aggregated with Mission Santa Catalina de Guale sometime between 1663 and 1666. This event was neither the first nor the only episode of population relocation to occur among the Spanish missions of the Georgia and Florida coasts (see Figure 1).

John Worth[11] has documented and described this process of population movements—of contraction and retreat—in great detail for the Guale and Mocama mission provinces. Additionally, the implications of these relocations for transformations in ceramic production in the Mocama mission province, and in St. Augustine, have also been considerably explored.[12] Less considered,

10. John E. Worth, *The Struggle for the Georgia Coast: An Eighteenth-Century Spanish Retrospective on Guale and Mocama* (Tuscaloosa: University of Alabama Press, 2007), 19; Eric E. Bowne, *The Westo Indians: Slave Traders of the Early Colonial South* (Tuscaloosa: University of Alabama Press, 2005), 78.

11. John E. Worth, "Ethnicity and Ceramics on the Southeastern Atlantic Coast: An Ethnohistorical Analysis," in *From Santa Elena to St. Augustine: Indigenous Ceramic Variability (A.D. 1400–1700)*, eds. Kathleen Deagan and D. H. Thomas, Anthropological Papers of the American Museum of Natural History (New York: American Museum of Natural History, 2009), 179–207; Worth, "Razing Florida: The Indian Slave Trade and the Devastation of Spanish Florida, 1659–1715," in *Mapping the Mississippian Shatter Zone*, ed. Robbie Ethridge and Sheri M. Shuck-Hall (Lincoln: University of Nebraska Press, 2009), 295–311; Worth, *The Struggle for the Georgia Coast* (2007); Worth, "Guale," in *Handbook of North American Indians*, vol. 14, *Southeast*, ed. Raymond D. Fogelson (Washington, DC: Smithsonian Institution, 2004), 238–244; Worth, *The Struggle for the Georgia Coast: An Eighteenth-Century Spanish Retrospective on Guale and Mocama*, Anthropological Papers of the American Museum of Natural History (New York: American Museum of Natural History, 1995).

12. Worth, "Ethnicity and Ceramics on the Southeastern Atlantic Coast"; Keith H. Ashley, "Grafting onto the Native Landscape: The Franciscan Mission System in Northeastern Florida," in *From La Florida to La California: Franciscan Evangelization in the Spanish Borderlands*, eds. Timothy J. Johnson and Gert Melville (Berkeley, CA: Academy of American Franciscan History, 2013), 143–164; Rebecca A. Gorman, "The Last Mission: San Juan del Puerto and Its Role in the Aggregation and Demise of the Mocama Missions (1587–1702)," in ibid., 165–186; Gifford J. Waters, "Maintenance and Change of 18th-Century Mission Indian Identity: A Multi-Ethnic Contact Situation" (Ph.D. diss., University of Florida, 2005); Waters, "Aboriginal Ceramics at Three 18th-Century Mission Sites in St. Augustine, Florida," in *From Santa Elena to St. Augustine: Indigenous Ceramic Vari-*

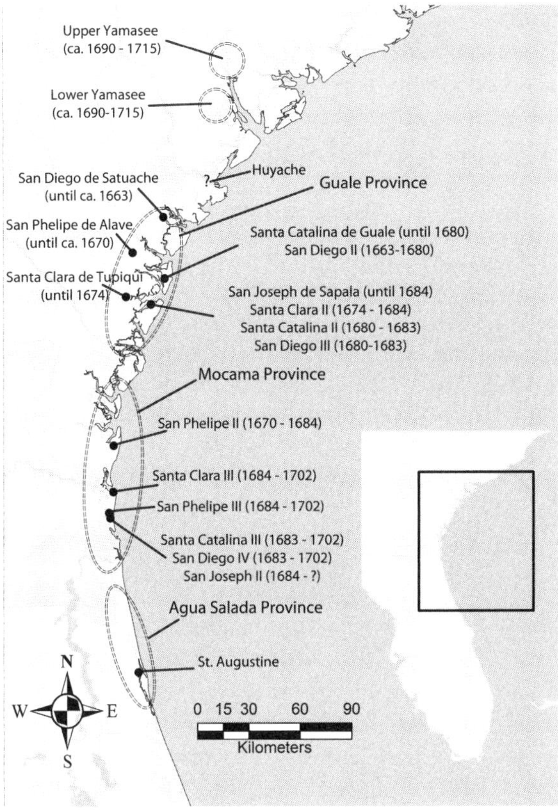

FIGURE 1. Location of 17th and 18th century towns, missions, and provinces of *La Florida* mentioned in the text.

however, are the numerous social factors—the turbulence and turmoil—that would certainly have accompanied such population aggregation and created uneasy communities throughout Spanish Florida.[13] Moreover, despite Worth's detailed documentation of this process, one of the fundamental assumptions

ability (A.D. 1400–1700), eds. Kathleen Deagan and David Hurst Thomas, pp. 165–176 (New York: American Museum of Natural History, 2009), 165–186.

13. Elliot H. Blair and David Hurst Thomas, "The Guale Uprising of 1597: An Archaeological Perspective from Mission Santa Catalina de Guale (Georgia)," in *Indigenous Landscapes and Spanish Missions: New Perspectives from Archaeology and Ethnohistory*, eds. Lee M. Panich and Tsim D. Schneider (Tucson: University of Arizona Press, 2014), 35–37; Elliot H. Blair, "The Guale Landscape of Santa Catalina de Guale: 30 Years of Geophysics at a Spanish Colonial Mission," in *Life among the Tides: Recent Archaeology on the Georgia Bight*, eds. Victor D. Thompson and David Hurst Thomas (New York: Anthropological Papers of the American Museum of Natural History, 2013), 385–388.

made to differentiate the mission enterprises of Florida from those elsewhere in the Spanish Borderlands, was that the Native Floridians—as members of sedentary agricultural chiefdoms—did not undergo the difficult, traumatic, and disruptive processes of *reducción* and *congregación* that occurred elsewhere, such as in Texas, Alta California, and South America.

> The spiritual success of missions required that Indians live in towns, within the sound of the mission bell and the reach of the sacraments, and the "civilization" of Indians required that they follow the Spanish ideal of urban life. In Florida and New Mexico, missionaries found ample Indians already living in towns. On occasion, the friars tried to relocate sedentary natives in order to increase the size of towns, make them more defensible, and minimize travel to distant *visitas*. In general, however, the Franciscans in Florida and New Mexico did not need to devote energy and resources to congregating or "reducing" dispersed natives into towns, or *reducciones*, as they had done earlier in the Caribbean and in central New Spain, and as they would do again in eighteenth-century Texas or California.[14]

The above passage written by David Weber, one of the foremost historians of the Spanish Borderlands, reflects a common opinion regarding missionization in La Florida: *reducción* did not occur in the region. Other scholars have expressed similar sentiments, though often with subtle caveats. For instance, Hann[15] has argued that formal policies of *reducción* did not occur in La Florida, with the sedentary agricultural communities of the region not requiring population relocation in order to facilitate conversion. He suggested that when relocation was required, later in the mission era, it was at the instigation of secular—not religious—authorities. He wrote: "As far as is known, Florida's friars did not follow a policy of forceful reduction or *congregación* in establishing their first missions among Timucua-speakers. . . . The only phenomenon resembling *congregación* involved migrants from the hinterland who came to coastal villages so that they might become Christians. But this was a spontaneous voluntary phenomenon, distinct from the more or less coerced migrations that constituted *congregación* in places such as California."[16] Similarly, Saunders[17] has noted that

---

14. David J. Weber, *The Spanish Frontier in North America* (New Haven, CT: Yale University Press, 1992), 107–108.

15. John H. Hann, "Demographic Patterns and Changes in Mid-Seventeenth Century Timucua and Apalachee," *The Florida Historical Quarterly* 64(4) (1986): 371–372.

16. Hann, *A History of the Timucua Indians and Missions* (Gainesville: University Press of Florida, 1996), 168.

17. Rebecca Saunders, "Forced Relocation, Poor Relations, and Culture Contacts in the Missions of La Florida," in *Studies in Culture Contact: Interaction, Culture Change, and Archaeology*, ed. J.G. Cusick (Carbondale: Center for Archaeological Investigations, Southern Illinois University, 1998), 405.

reducción was "not systematically implemented" and Milanich[18] considered reduction to have only occurred as an outcome of population loss, with consolidation occurring as communities succumbed to disease. Deagan observed that *reducción* policies were only employed "under circumstances of population decline and social upheaval, such as that seen in seventeenth- and eighteenth-century Florida."[19]

Several key threads run through these positions. First, there is the question of timing. How critical, analytically, is it when *reducción* occurred in the mission era? Second, how important is the directionality of *reducción*? Does variation of the push/pull factors and who elected to instigate population relocations (e.g., Native peoples, missionaries, or secular authorities) matter? Finally, what is the role of motives? Does it truly matter if the goals are economic, religious, or demographic?

I return to these questions later, but regardless of caveats about motives, timing, and the instigation of reductions, there is ample documentary evidence that relocation and aggregation were extensive and continual processes in Spanish Florida. While Hann[20] suggested that population relocations in La Florida—when they occurred—were at the behest of secular authorities, Bushnell has documented a number of instances in which Franciscans directly suggested that population aggregations be undertaken. For example, she noted that Fray Pedro Bermejo, in 1602, "suggested that the ones living in 'hamlets of three and four and five houses' be reduced to the head towns, to 'help one another in their labors,' and to 'be better indoctrinated,' and to make it easier for their friars to 'visit them in their necessities and infirmities.'"[21] Worth has also documented accounts of Franciscans advocating for *reducción*, including one by Fray Luís Gerónimo de Oré, and he presented extensive details of the actual implementation of such relocations.[22] Despite the friars' requests for relocations in order to help them in their ministries, however, the two primary

---

18. Jerald T. Milanich, *Laboring in the Fields of the Lord: Spanish Missions and Southeastern Indians* (Washington, DC: Smithsonian Institution Press, 2006), 111.

19. Kathleen Deagan, "St. Augustine and the Mission Frontier," in *The Spanish Missions of La Florida*, ed. Bonnie G. McEwan (Gainesville: University Press of Florida, 1993), 89.

20. Hann, "Demographic Patterns and Changes in Mid-Seventeenth Century Timucua and Apalachee," 371–372.

21. Amy Turner Bushnell, "The Sacramental Imperative: Catholic Ritual and Indian Sedentism in the Provinces of Florida," in *Columbia Consequence*, vol. 2, *Archaeological and Historical Perspectives on the Spanish Borderlands East*, ed. David Hurst Thomas (Washington, DC: Smithsonian Institution Press, 1990), 479.

22. John E. Worth, *Timucuan Chiefdoms of Spanish Florida*, vol. 2, *Resistance and Destruction*, The Ripley P. Bullen Series (Gainesville: University Press of Florida, 1998), 27–32; Luís Gerónimo de Oré, *The Martyrs of Florida (1513–1616)*, trans. Maynard J. Geiger, vol. 18, *Franciscan Studies* (New York: Joseph F. Wagner, 1936), 118.

factors driving population relocations within the provinces of Guale and Mocama were population loss and flight from predatory slave raids.

Writing in 1617, a number of friars specifically requested that the Native communities be aggregated:

> We request that Your Majesty would be served to command that, whenever these necessities occur, as long as the governors are advised by the [Franciscan] prelate, these disordered [settlements] should be drawn together since there is not one inconvenience, *through those that have to join together not being from different families or languages, but rather friends of friends, brothers of brothers, and relatives of relatives beforehand.*[23]

The explicit implication of this passage is that such population aggregation would have few social repercussions. As relocations were carried out, however, specific choices appear to have been made in order to avoid social and political complications. For example, Worth suggests that perhaps Mission San Phelipe de Alave, originally located on the Georgia mainland, was relocated to Cumberland Island, in Mocama territory, in 1670 rather than aggregating with the nearby, and politically associated, Mission Santa Catalina due to political disputes.[24]

Worth also provides numerous examples that hint at the difficult and complex social entanglements that actually emerged during the process of aggregation.[25] For example, during the 1677 official *visitación* of Antonio de Argüelles, the Native leaders residing on St. Catherines Island "complained that the Indians of this place were passing from one Council House (*Bujio*) to another with slight cause."[26] Worth has suggested that this passage might indicate that two council houses were present within the aggregated communities of Mission Santa Catalina y San Diego, evidence of an architectural reification of distinct social identities.[27] Indeed, earlier in this same account, Hann translates: "Argüelles . . . caused to be assembled in the principal council houses [sic] of the said village the caciques, heirs, *mandadores,* and the rest of the leading men (*principales*) of the said village."[28] Perhaps the plural form of "council houses," that Hann suggests is an error, is actually further confirmation of Worth's supposition.

---

23. Worth, *Timucuan Chiefdoms of Spanish Florida*, 2: 28; emphasis added by Christopher M. Stojanowski, *Biocultural Histories in La Florida: A Bioarchaeological Perspective* (Tuscaloosa: University of Alabama Press, 2005), 40, citing Pareja et al. (1617).

24. Worth, *The Struggle for the Georgia Coast* (2007), 23, 193.

25. Ibid.

26. John H. Hann, "Visitations and Revolts in Florida, 1656–1695," *Florida Archaeology* 7 (1993): 89.

27. Worth, *The Struggle for the Georgia Coast* (2007), 30; see Fred Lamar Pearson, "The Arguelles Inspection of Guale: December 21, 1677–January 10, 1678," *The Georgia Historical Quarterly* 59 (1975): 210–222 for an alternative interpretation of this passage.

28. Hann, "Visitations and Revolts in Florida, 1656–1695."

Also in 1677, during the same visitation at the combined community of San Joseph de Sapala and Santa Clara de Tupiqui on Sapelo Island, the *mica* Ana Estasia of Tupiqui told Argüelles that tribute due to her by the leaders of San Joseph was not being provided, despite their obligations.[29] This complaint, and the negative response from Felipe, the cacique of Sapala, highlight, as noted by Worth, that aggregation resulted in difficult social and political "stresses,"[30] particularly in a context in which the immigrant community was politically dominant, forcing the local community to somewhat unwillingly assume a subordinate position within their own town.

In 1680 Mission Santa Catalina and San Diego, following another Westo attack, relocated southward to Sapelo Island, aggregating with the previously combined missions of San Joseph de Sapala and Santa Clara de Tupiqui. Three years later, following an attack by the pirate Grammont, Governor Barbosa proposed further southward retreat, with the four mission communities aggregated on Sapelo Island to resettle on the former location of Santa Maria de Sena on Amelia Island. But, despite Barbosa's observation on both the desirability and feasibility for all four communities to relocate together to Santa Maria, the move did not occur en masse, nor did all four communities ultimately move to the same town. Santa Catalina and San Diego did relocate together in 1683, while San Joseph and Santa Clara delayed until the following year after yet another pirate raid. Following this raid some members of the Sapala and Tupiqui communities fled northward and joined the emerging Yamasee confederacy in South Carolina. The remaining members of the San Joseph community joined Santa Catalina and San Diego at the former location of Santa Maria, while the remaining members of Santa Clara moved to the northern tip of Amelia Island, occupying an abandoned former Yamasee town.[31] As Worth has pointed out, the separation of Sapala and Tupiqui, after fusing ten years earlier, is another indicator of the tensions and difficulties of the aggregation process.[32] However, Worth noted that the split between Tupiqui and Sapala was relatively short-lived, with Sapala rejoining Tupiqui on the northern end of Amelia Island sometime between 1685 and 1695.[33] It is unclear whether the re-aggregation of the communities was related to a reconciliation or to new political difficulties between Sapala and the communities residing at Santa Maria.

This configuration of Guale communities located on Amelia Island—with Santa Clara y San Joseph located on the northern end, Santa Catalina y San

29. Ibid., 90.
30. Worth, *The Struggle for the Georgia Coast* (2007), 30.
31. Ibid., 38–45; Worth, "Ethnicity and Ceramics on the Southeastern Atlantic Coast."
32. Worth, *The Struggle for the Georgia Coast*(2007), 45.
33. Ibid., 54, n. 43.

Diego located at Santa Maria, and San Phelipe located between the two—persisted until 1702 when a combined British and Indian force led by Colonel James Moore marched down the coast, destroying all of the mission towns on Amelia Island and ultimately laying siege to St. Augustine.[34] Following this attack the Guale communities from Amelia Island relocated to the vicinity of St. Augustine, aggregating into continually fewer *doctrinas* during the first half of the eighteenth century before the final retreat from Florida to Cuba in 1763.[35]

Not all of the Guale residing on Amelia Island in 1702, however, retreated towards St. Augustine following Colonel Moore's attack. Some instead fled northward, joining the Yamasee confederacy in South Carolina. Many of the constituent towns of the Upper Yamasee first appeared in the documentary record in the early eighteenth century, almost simultaneously with the Moore's attack on La Florida.[36] These towns were almost all of Guale origin, and almost certainly appear to be refugees from the attacks on the coastal mission communities. Indeed, Kelton specifically notes that during the 1702 raid two Christian Guale communities were persuaded to "flee Florida and to incorporate" with the Yamasee.[37] Particularly important here is the appearance of the Upper Yamasee town of Sadkeche, and possibly the town of Tulafina in the early eighteenth century. Most scholars of the Yamasee identify Sadkeche with the Salchiches/Satuache.[38] While it is uncertain whether

34. Amy Turner Bushnell, *Situado and Sabana: Spain's Support System for the Presidio and Mission Provinces of Florida* (New York: American Museum of Natural History, 1994), 190–192; John H. Hann, "St. Augustine's Fallout from the Yamasee War," *The Florida Historical Quarterly* 68(2) (1989): 180–200.

35. Worth, *Timucuan Chiefdoms of Spanish Florida*, 2: 147–158.

36. Worth, "Yamasee," in *Handbook of North American Indians*, vol. 14, *Southeast*, ed. Raymond D Fogelson (Washington, DC: Smithsonian Institution, 2004), 248.

37. Paul Kelton, "Shattered and Infected: Epidemics and the Origins of the Yamasee War, 1696–1715," in *Mapping the Mississippian Shatter Zone: The Colonial Indian Slave Trade and Regional Instability in the American South*, eds. Robbie Ethridge and Sheri M. Shuck-Hall, pp. 312–332 (Lincoln: University of Nebraska Press, 2009), 324.

38. Worth, "Yamasee"; William Green, Chester B. DePratter, and Bobby Southerlin, "The Yamasee in South Carolina: Native American Adaptation and Interaction along the Carolina Frontier," in *Another's Country: Archaeological and Historical Perspectives on Cultural Interactions in the Southern Colonies*, eds. J. W. Joseph and Martha Zierden (Tuscaloosa: University of Alabama Press, 2002), 13–29; Verner W. Crane, *The Southern Frontier, 1670–1732* (Tuscaloosa: University of Alabama Press, 2004 [1929]); William G. Green, "The Search for Altamaha: The Archaeology of an Early Eighteenth-Century Yamasee Town" (MA thesis, University of South Carolina, 1991); Alex Y. Sweeney, "Investigating Yamasee Identity: Archaeological Research at Pocotaligo" (MA thesis, University of South Carolina, 2003); David A. McKivergan, "Migration and Settlement among the Yamasee in South Carolina" (MA thesis, University of South Carolina, 1991); Denise I. Bossy, "Spiritual Diplomacy, the Yamasees, and the Society for the Propagation of the Gospel: Reinterpreting Prince George's Eighteenth-Century Voyage to England," *Early American Studies: An Interdisciplinary Journal* 12(2) (2014); Blair and Thomas, "The Guale Uprising of 1597."

Tulafina was a separate Yamasee town or simply associated with Sadkeche, in either case both names were linked with Santa Catalina from 1666 through 1702 through a series of three distinct relocations, before disappearing from the mission censuses in Spanish Florida after Moore's raid and appearing among the Yamasee in South Carolina at roughly the same time.[39] The historical evidence clearly suggests that after aggregating in the 1660s, thirty-five years later Satuache/Tulafina split with the Santa Catalina community. Again, like much of the evidence already presented, this highlights the difficulties, and ultimately impermanence of the aggregation process in La Florida. One final intriguing possibility pertains to the documentation of a San Diego mission, populated by Yamasee, identified in the vicinity of St. Augustine in 1726.[40] Could this San Diego represent the return of the Satuache/Sadkeche community in the aftermath of the 1715 Yamasee war? While probably a remote possibility, this would again highlight the tensions and difficulties of aggregation. If this does represent the same community, it is highly significant that rather than re-aggregating with Santa Catalina this community settled separately and identified as Yamasee, rather than Guale.

A Tension of Terminology

Fundamental to this difference in perspectives on population movement and *reducción* is a central issue of terminology. While minor debates regarding terminology and competing metaphors can be an unproductive exercise in splitting hairs, in this instance I feel that a brief review will be helpful. Indeed, as has been explored by Amy Turner Bushnell, the specific terms of how scholars understand the missions of La Florida has been structured by the terminologies, typologies, and "emphasis on institutions" originating from Borderlands historians primarily focusing on regions other than the American Southeast.[41] These terminologies, for both types of spiritual conquest and directed settlement, are often limiting, contradictory, and easily conflated. Referring to types of directed settlement, Bushnell defines the *población*—"the process of populating new territory" with Christian Indians; the *congregación*—"collecting the inhabitants of remote or depopulated settlements into fewer, more accessible, aggregate settlements"; and *reducción*—the congregation of mobile peoples into sedentary settlements. However, she notes that in practice, particularly in contexts of population loss, all three terms were often used interchangeably, referring to the "consolidating of two or more small towns of Indians."[42]

39. "The Guale Uprising of 1597," 39.

40. Worth, *Timucuan Chiefdoms of Spanish Florida*, 2: 151, table 9-3; Hann, "St. Augustine's Fallout from the Yamasee War," 193.

41. Bushnell, *Situado and Sabana*; Bushnell, "The Sacramental Imperative."

42. Bushnell, *Situado and Sabana*, 23; Bushnell, "The Sacramental Imperative," 47

This imprecision in how the terms were used in the past underscores two important points: first, historical imprecision would suggest that we should not retroactively apply an unwarranted, falsely rigid precision to the historical terminology, and second, a new vocabulary, containing analytical precision that is independent of historical terminology is both necessary and warranted. Two such vocabularies have already been constructed specifically for the Spanish missions of La Florida—one by John Worth and the other by Christopher Stojanowski.[43] Here I briefly review both, as well as consider other typologies of population aggregation in the Southeast, summarized in Table 1.

Worth's typology is particularly useful as an analytic tool in that it is completely divorced from historical terminology. He identifies four[44] distinct types of population relocations and responses to colonial pressures: contraction, relocation, aggregation, and confederation.[45] The first of these, contraction, involves the consolidation of smaller, subordinate communities into larger towns. Relocation involves the movement of a community into a currently unoccupied area. Aggregation consists of the movement of one independent community into the village of another, with the immigrant community assuming a subordinate position within the preexisting political structure. Confederation is defined as the same as aggregation, but rather than perpetuating a preexisting political organization, a new political relationship is formed.

Applying this typology to the discussion above, examples of each type can clearly be identified. First, contraction, though not documented with many specifics, is advocated, encouraged, and actualized by the Franciscans,[46] and the process is clearly observable archaeologically. Thompson et al.'s analysis of regional settlement patterns on the Georgia coast during the contact era document a considerable reduction in the number of sites compared to the Late Mississippian period.[47] Second, Worth's relocation category is exemplified by

---

43. John E. Worth, "Spanish Missions and the Persistence of Chiefly Power," in *The Transformation of the Southeastern Indians, 1540–1760*, eds. Robbie Ethridge and Charles Hudson (Jackson: University Press of Mississippi, 2002), 39–64; Stojanowski, *Biocultural Histories in La Florida*.

44. In "Spanish Missions and the Persistence of Chiefly Power," Worth actually identifies five distinct responses in his discussion. The fifth of these is what he calls assimilation, whereby Southeastern chiefdoms became fully incorporated into the Spanish colonial hierarchy. However, because assimilation is not specifically about population relocation, but rather more of a macro-description of the broader Spanish colonial enterprise, I am not including it in this discussion.

45. Ibid., 50–52.

46. Worth, *Timucuan Chiefdoms of Spanish Florida*, 2: 27–29.

47. Victor D. Thompson, et al., "Entangling Events: The Guale Coastal Landscape and the Spanish Missions," in *Life among the Tides: Recent Archaeology on the Georgia Bight*, eds. Victor D. Thompson and David Hurst Thomas (New York: Anthropological Papers of the American Museum of Natural History, 2013), 423–437.

TABLE 1. Models of Population Aggregation in Spanish Florida

	Aggregation Process	Definition	Example
Worth (2002: 50–52)	Contraction	Aggregation of local villages	Largely undocumented aggregation of subordinate communities
	Relocation	Relocation of a community to an unoccupied location	Relocation of Mission San Diego de Satuache and Mission Santa Catalina de Guale to the former Santa Maria on Amelia
	Aggregation	Movement of one community into the village of another, immigrant community geneally assumes a subordinate political status	Relocation of Mission San Diego to Satuache to Mission Santa Catalina de Guale ca. 1663–1666
	Confederation	Identical to aggregation, except a new political organization is formed	Guale communities joining the Yamassee confederacy (ca. 1684–1702)
Stojanowski (2006:40–42)	Stage 1 Congregación	Aggregation of local villages	Largely undocumented aggregation of subordinate communities of the Guale-Tolomato chiefdom aggregating at Mission Santa Catalina
	Stage 2 Congregación	Intraprovincial consolidation of doctrinas	Relocation of Mission San Diego de Satuache to Mission Santa Catalina de Guale (ca. 1663–1666)
	Type 1 Reducción	Interprovincial consolidation of doctrina	Relocation of Mission San Diego de Satuache and Mission Santa Catalina de Guale to the former Santa Maria on Amelia Island (1683)
	Type 2 Reducción	In-migration of nonmissionized groups	Yamassee community established at Santa Maria on Amelia Island (1667–1683)
Beck (2013:158, 195–196, 210, 244)	Regional Consolidation (contraction/ formation)	Aggregation of local villages	Largely undocumented aggregation of subordinate communities of the Guale-Tolomato chiefdom aggregating at Mission Santa Catalina
	Regional Integration (chieftaincy formation)	Rearticulation of multicommunity structures disjoined by the commodification of traditional political economies	Guale communities joining the Yamassee confederacy (ca. 1684–1702)
	Coalescence	Nation building, or the joining of chieftaincies	Formation of the Creek Confederacy

the 1683 move of Mission Santa Catalina y San Diego from Sapelo Island to Amelia Island and the abandoned former location of the Mocama mission Santa Maria.[48] Multiple episodes of aggregation are also evident in the documentary record (e.g., Satuache aggregating with Santa Catalina on St. Catherines in 1663). While many examples of aggregation closely conform to Worth's definition—with the immigrant community adopting a subordinate position—examples of the inverse also occurred. For example, as discussed above, when Santa Clara de Tupiqui aggregated with San Joseph on Sapelo Island, the *mica* of Santa Clara and her lineage assumed the preeminent position, however uneasily. Worth's final category, confederation, is exemplified by the relocation of Guale communities from Spanish Florida in the late seventeenth and early eighteenth centuries to South Carolina where they joined Yamasees.

Somewhat similar to Worth's formulation, Stojanowski has defined four different varieties of population aggregation specific to the missions of Spanish Florida: stage 1 and 2 *congregación* and types 1 and 2 *reducción*.[49] Stage 1 *congregación* refers to the aggregation of local villages into a single *doctrina*. This is identical to what Worth identifies as contraction.[50] Stage 2 *congregación* is the aggregation of different *doctrinas* of the same province to a single location. Depending on numerous sociopolitical and historical factors, this type of relocation could either proceed similarly to Worth's contraction or aggregation. Type 1 *reducción* is the complete replacement and relocation of populations across provincial boundaries and type 2 *reducción* refers to the in-migration of non-missionized Native groups from outside Spanish Florida. Both of these could operate similarly to Worth's relocation and aggregation, depending on whether the incoming community was moving into an occupied or unoccupied location.

One term that is absent from both typologies but which has seen increasing usage in the colonial Southeast and is clearly related to this discussion is "coalescence." While Ethridge identifies Worth's "confederation" as analogous to coalescence, more precise definitions have been offered.[51] Kowalewski has reviewed the use of the term coalescence across regions and states that the coalescent society is not a social type, but rather one of several possible outcomes due to specific social responses that occur during times of social

48. Rebecca Saunders, *Stability and Change in Guale Indian pottery, A.D. 1300–1702* (Tuscaloosa: University of Alabama Press, 2000); Saunders, "Stability and Ubiquity: Irene, Altamaha, and San Marcos Pottery in Time and Space," in *From Santa Elena to St. Augustine: Indigenous Ceramic Variability (A.D. 1400–1700)*, eds. David Hurst Thomas and Kathleen Deagan (New York: Anthropological Papers of the American Museum of Natural History, 2009), 83–111; Worth, *The Struggle for the Georgia Coast* (2007); Worth, "Ethnicity and Ceramics on the Southeastern Atlantic Coast."

49. Stojanowski, *Biocultural Histories in La Florida*, 29.

50. Worth, "Spanish Missions and the Persistence of Chiefly Power."

51. Ethridge, "Introduction: Mapping the Mississippian Shatter Zone," 61, n. 127.

stress, such as during warfare, population decline, and population movement.[52] Other outcomes he identifies include surrender and flight. Notably, Kowalewski—citing Worth—points out that the Southeastern missions did not result in coalescence, though it is unclear from his discussion how population aggregations within the mission system would be categorized or described. Partially relying on Kowalewski's model, in several recent publications Birch has also discussed the process of coalescence, though often situating it quite broadly and equating it with other terms such as agglomeration, aggregation, convergence, fusion, and nucleation.[53] Additionally, she specifically defines it as "small village communities [coming] together to form larger and more complex social aggregates."[54] Such a definition, however, effectively excludes many of the Southeastern coalescent communities. Indeed, few would describe the transition from Mississippian chiefdom to confederacies such as the Creek and the Choctaw as either beginning with small, independent, communities or resulting in a "more complex" social form.

Also discussing coalescence, Beck has recently proposed a model of aggregation that includes three distinct components: regional consolidation, regional integration, and coalescence.[55] In his model, regional consolidation is equated with Worth's process of contraction and describes what occurred among the Spanish mission populations.[56] He suggests that coalescence should be considered a process of nation building, and, in the Southeast specifically, one that arises through the aggregation and integration of chieftaincies, which he defines, following Redmond, as "loosely organized, regional polities" that operate periodically among "autonomous village societies."[57] He distinguishes coalescence from a process he calls regional integration, or chieftaincy formation.[58] According to this formulation, he considers the formation of the

52. Stephen A. Kowalewski, "Coalescent Societies," in *Light on the Path: Essays in the Anthropology and History of the Southeastern Indians*, eds. Thomas J. Pluckhahn and Robbie Ethridge (Tuscaloosa: University of Alabama Press, 2006), 94–122.

53. Jennifer Birch, "Coalescence and Conflict in Iroquoian Ontario," *Archaeological Review from Cambridge* 25(1) (2010): 29–48; "Coalescent Communities: Settlement Aggregation and Social Integration in Iroquoian Ontario," *American Antiquity* 77(4) (2012): 646–670; "Between Villages and Cities: Settlement Aggregation in Cross-Cultural Perspective," in *From Prehistoric Villages to Cities: Settlement Aggregation and Community Transformation*, ed. Jennifer Birch (New York: Routledge, 2014), 1–22.

54. Birch, "Coalescent Communities," 646.

55. Robin Beck, *Chiefdoms, Collapse, and Coalescence in the Early American South* (Cambridge: Cambridge University Press, 2013).

56. Ibid., 158; Worth, "Spanish Missions and the Persistence of Chiefly Power," 50–51.

57. Beck, *Chiefdoms, Collapse, and Coalescence in the Early American South*, 195, 244; Elsa M. Redmond, "The Dynamics of Chieftaincy and the Development of Chiefdoms," in *Chiefdoms and Chieftaincy in the Americas*, ed. Elsa M. Redmond (Gainesville: University Press of Florida, 1998), 3.

58. Beck, *Chiefdoms, Collapse, and Coalescence in the Early American South*, 210.

Yamasee confederacy—including the integration of the Guale communities fleeing Spanish Florida—to be an act of regional integration, not coalescence.

Discussion

I began this paper by noting the position of Southeastern mission communities vis-à-vis comparative analyses that often situate these communities as being traditionalist ones that did not undergo the tumultuous process of *reducción*. After a brief survey of the literature that presented this position, I posed several questions: How critical, analytically, is when *reducción* occurred in the mission era? Second, how important is the directionality of *reducción*? Does variation of the push/pull factors and who elected to instigate population relocations (e.g., Native peoples, missionaries, or secular authorities) matter? Finally, what is the role of motives? Does it truly matter if the goals are economic, religious, or demographic? Of course, these are interrelated questions.

The episodes of population relocation and aggregation that occurred in Spanish Florida occurred throughout the mission period, instigated by multiple actors, for multiple reasons. At times the Franciscans, secular authorities, and the Native people themselves all instigated episodes of aggregation and relocation. While early episodes often revolved around access to trade goods and efforts by the Franciscans to facilitate conversion, later episodes often occurred in response to catastrophic population loss due to epidemic diseases and flight from predatory slave raiders. This variety is highlighted by the diversity of aggregation models I reviewed. While Beck's model had only one category that directly applied to the Southeastern missions—regional consolidation—both Worth and Stojanowski defined three types of aggregation specific to the mission communities. Indeed, I would suggest that combining each of these models—Worth and Stojanowski's that specifically consider aggregation within the Spanish missions and Beck's that examines coalescence in a broader southeastern context—would help provide a more nuanced and specific comparative framework, such as called for by Ethridge,[59] that would facilitate both detailed "granular" analyses of the specifics of population relocations and robust comparative analyses across the Southeast. At the same time, far more detailed—and useful—cross-cultural comparisons between the missions of the Southeast and elsewhere could be facilitated by the increased use of terminology that goes beyond coalescence and *reducción*.

---

59. Ethridge, "Introduction: Mapping the Mississippian Shatter Zone," 2.

Chapter 11
Mission San Joseph de Sapala: Seventeenth-Century Franciscan Mission Efforts on Sapelo Island, Georgia

Richard W. Jefferies and Christopher R. Moore

Introduction

Starting in the late sixteenth century, the Kingdom of Spain established a series of missions throughout La Florida whose primary purpose was to convert the resident Indians to Christianity. In 1573, the governor of La Florida dispatched Franciscan friars to St. Augustine and Santa Elena to minister to the coastal peoples of modern northern Florida and southeastern South Carolina. These efforts expanded during the first part of the seventeenth century, leading to the establishment of Franciscan missions among the Timucua, Apalachee, Mocama and Guale Indians who occupied much of what is today southern Georgia and northern Florida.[1]

In addition to imposing a new spiritual orientation, the missions provided the Spanish with some degree of administrative control over the provinces and helped discourage colonization by other European powers, particularly France and England. The strategic position of the Guale homeland between the capital of Spanish La Florida in St. Augustine and the increasingly important British settlement of Charles Town to the north placed the Guale in a seventeenth-century geopolitical hotspot.[2]

At the time of Spanish contact, the Guale occupied a relatively narrow strip of coastal Georgia extending from the Ogeechee River in the north to

---

1. Grant D. Jones, "The Ethnography of the Guale Coast through 1684," in *The Anthropology of St. Catherines Island*, eds. D. H. Thomas, G. D. Jones, R. S. Durham, and C. S. Larsen, vol. 1, *Natural and Cultural History* (New York: American Museum of Natural History, 1978), 178–179; Michael V. Gannon, *The Cross in the Sand: The Early Catholic Church in Florida, 1513–1870* (Gainesville: University Press of Florida, 1983).

2. John E. Worth, *The Struggle for the Georgia Coast* (Tuscaloosa: University of Alabama Press, 2007), 23.

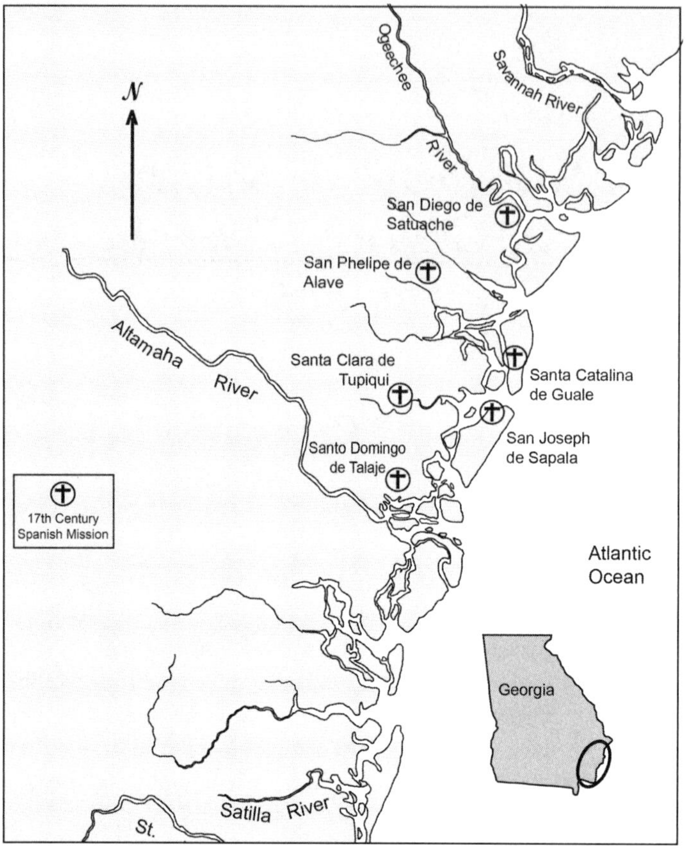

FIGURE 1. Seventeenth-Century Spanish Missions in the Guale region of *La Florida*.

the Altamaha River in the south.[3] The Guale regional chiefdom included at least five distinct local chiefdoms, each comprised of related towns and kin groups. One of these, the Espogache-Tupiqui chiefdom, was positioned near the mouth of the Sapelo River. Two of the chiefdom's principal towns, Tupiqui and Sapala (Figure 1), were historically linked twin political centers situated across Sapelo Sound from one another.[4]

A small group of Spanish shipwreck survivors who passed through the Guale province in 1595 observed very few signs of a Spanish presence, specif-

3. John E. Worth, "Guale," in *The Handbook of North American Indians*, ed. Raymond D. Fogelson, vol. 14, *Southeast* (Washington, D.C.: Smithsonian Institute Press, 2004), 238–244.

4. Ibid., 240.

ically noting the absence of any church or convent. Most of the Guale lived on the mainland, leaving the barrier islands to the feral pigs.[5]

The beginning of the seventeenth century marked a major demographic shift for the Guale that resulted in their gradual movement from the mainland to the "barrier" islands, like Sapelo and St. Catherines. The sounds, rivers, and marshes that surrounded the islands offered more protection from enemy raids than the mainland, provided good observation points for detecting the movement of foreign intruders along the coast, and served as efficient lines of transportation and communication between mission towns. Perhaps most importantly, the islands limited Guale movement, making it easier for the Spanish to watch over them and extract tribute and labor.[6]

By the early 1600s, the Franciscan friars had established six missions in Guale towns (Figure 1). The provincial capital, Santa Catalina de Guale, was on St. Catherines Island, with other missions on Sapelo Island; along the Ogeechee, Newport, and Altamaha rivers; and on the mainland west of Sapelo.[7] The Georgia missions were expressly established for converting the Guale to the Catholic faith and integrating them into the economic and political structure of La Florida's colonial system.

Missions were usually established in towns where the Guale chiefs lived and where the council houses stood. The mission, consisting of a small compound in the much larger Guale town, usually consisted of a church and a convent where a single friar lived. Although the Franciscans ran the towns' religious activities, they were politically subordinate to the traditional Guale chiefs and their counselors. Interaction between the towns and the Spanish military in St. Augustine was conducted by the hereditary chiefs, although resident friars often served as agents for the chiefs when disputes arose between the Guale and the Spanish military or government.

The incorporation of the Spanish mission system into the Guale world also brought the *repartimiento*, a labor relationship that required a specified number of unmarried male Guale to go to St. Augustine each year to build fortifications or work in the maize fields. These visits exposed the Guale men to diseases for which they had no immunity, often contributing to or causing their deaths.[8]

---

5. Fray Andrés de San Miguel, "An Early Florida Adventure Story," trans. John H. Hann (Gainesville: University Press of Florida, 2001), quoted in Amy T. Bushnell, "Situado and Sabana: Spain's Support System for the Presidio and Mission Provinces of Florida" *Anthropological Papers of the American Museum of Natural History*, no. 74 (New York: American Museum of Natural History, 1994), 64.

6. Amy T. Bushnell, "Situado and Sabana," 65.

7. Worth, *Struggle for the Georgia Coast*, 10.

8. John E. Worth, "Spanish Missions," New Georgia Encyclopedia, June 5, 2014, accessed September 17, 2014, http://www. georgiaencyclopedia.org/articles/history-archaeology/spanish- missions.

By the early seventeenth century, Sapala (Figure 1), and the associated Mission San Joseph de Sapala, had emerged as a regional center and was the only Guale town on Sapelo Island.[9] In the 1660s, a fifty-year period of relative peace was shattered when Chichimeco (known to the English as Westo) raiding parties armed with British guns descended the Altamaha River and began attacking Guale communities and mission towns.[10] Chichimeco losses during the attack on the Guale and a Spanish counterattack provided time for waves of unconverted refugees, who would eventually coalesce to become the Yamasee, to make their way to the coast where they came under Spanish protection. The threat of continued harassment by their enemies led Guale leaders to request that the provincial governor establish an infantry garrison at Santa Catalina to defend them from future attacks. In return, the Guale promised to help support the garrison by supplying deer, fish, firewood, and cassina, along with Guale-manufactured jars, bowls, and pitchers.[11]

The Santa Catalina garrison, established in 1673, consisted of only a few soldiers in 1680.[12] For a short time, the garrison provided some protection for Santa Catalina's residents, along with refugees from the mainland mission of San Diego de Satuache, who had moved to St. Catherines when their town was threatened by the Chichimeco.[13]

The increasing frequency and intensity of Chichimeco attacks on Guale towns spurred the further contraction of Guale settlements into ever more crowded communities and their migration from the mainland to the barrier islands. Sometime between 1673 and 1675, Mission Santa Clara de Tupiqui, the last remaining mainland Guale mission, moved to the seemingly more secure Sapelo Island, joining Mission San Joseph de Sapala. Pedro de Arcos's 1675 census reported that fifty "persons" resided in Sapala at that time.[14] In 1680, another Chichimeco attack, this time on the provincial capital at Santa Catalina de Guale on St. Catherines Island, destroyed that town and the mission. Feeling extremely vulnerable to additional raids, the people of Satuache and Santa Catalina, along with the Spanish garrison, retreated a short distance south to Sapelo Island where they joined the combined populations of Tupiqui and Sapala.

Although the four towns were aggregated on Sapelo Island, Worth suggests that they maintained politically and likely spatially discrete populations.

---

9. Worth, "Guale," 240.

10. Worth, *The Struggle for Georgia Coast*, 15–16.

11. Ibid., 53, 114.

12. David H. Thomas, "The Archaeology of Mission Santa Catalina de Guale, vol. 1, Search and Discovery," *Anthropological Papers of the American Museum of Natural History* 63, no. 2 (New York: American Museum of Natural History, 1987), 56.

13. Worth, *The Struggle for Georgia Coast*, 32.

14. Ibid., 15–18, 23. John Worth, "Sapelo Island during the Spanish Colonial Era." Paper presented at the Society for Historical Archaeology. Conference on Historical and Underwater Archaeology. Albuquerque, New Mexico, 2008.

The aggregation of Guale towns on Sapelo Island is reflected by a significant population increase. Worth's interpretation of the 1681 census figures reported by Captain Fuentes indicates that Sapelo Island's total adult native population was about 186 Guale and 67 Yamasee. Sapala's adult Guale population consisted of 15 males and 19 females; Tupiqui's adult Guale population was slightly greater at 23 males and 25 females.[15] The adult population of the two aggregated towns would have approached 85 adults, plus an unknown number of subadults.

Two years later in 1683, Lieutenant Captain Francisco de Barbosa's (1683) census reported 86 adult males on Sapelo, almost the same number as before the Chichimeco raid (n=87). Although the total population of the four towns remained fairly constant, that of Sapala and Tupiqui increased, while Santa Catalina and Satuache declined.[16]

Two Franciscan friars were reported at Sapala in 1680, but only one, Fray Simón de Salas, remained after the attack on Santa Catalina. This single friar was left to service the populations of all four towns from 1680 until the final retreat from Guale province in 1684. What became of the other missionary at Sapala and the one reported at Santa Catalina in 1680 is unknown.[17]

The consolidation of the Guale refugees put Sapala on the northern frontier of Spanish Florida.[18] Captain Francisco de Fuentes, the *teniente* of Guale province, recommended that Sapala be fortified because he considered it to be the "heart of the said province, and it ought to be garrisoned with all care for the security and consolation of everyone. . . ."[19] The Spanish governor wanted to increase the size of the garrison from eight to twenty men, but in the end he sent only four additional soldiers. The garrison continued to protect Sapala and its residents through late 1684, when the news of nearby pirates led the garrison's captain to order the priest to gather the mission furnishings and to retreat to the mainland. Viewing discretion as the better part of valor, the soldiers and their Guale allies withdrew to the mainland in short order.[20]

The end of Mission San Joseph de Sapala came in 1686 when the Spanish returned to Sapelo to attack the Yamasee who had occupied the mission.[21] During this raid, the Spanish burned the priest's house, along with the mission and several other houses.[22] The remains of this mission church and its associ-

15. Ibid., 12, and table 5.
16. Ibid., Table 1 and 34.
17. Ibid., 54.
18. Ibid., 105.
19. Ibid., 33. Francisco de Fuentes, "Testimony Concerning the Resettlement of Santa Catalina, 10-27-1680" (1680), quoted in ibid.
20. Ibid., 40–41.
21. Ibid., 194.
22. William Dunlop, "Captain Dunlop's Voyage to the Southward, 1687." *South Carolina Historical and Genealogical Magazine* 30 (1929):131–132.

ated friary, cemetery, and other buildings lie undiscovered somewhere among the scattered Guale shell midden piles at the north end of Sapelo Island.

Mission San Joseph de Sapala played a critical role in the lives of the Guale and the history of the Spanish mission effort in La Florida for nearly one hundred years. It served as the aggregation point for several dislocated Guale towns, including the provincial capital of Santa Catalina de Guale. The coalescence of these formerly independent chiefdoms on Sapelo Island created new challenges for maintaining social order and structuring intergroup relationships. Also, the Spanish garrison charged with protecting the Guale town and mission from attack was stationed at Sapala for more than four years.

Searching for Sapala and Mission San Joseph de Sapala

Archaeologists and historians have devoted considerable effort to relocating the sites of Guale towns and their associated missions.[23] Archaeological investigations at St. Catherines Island, Darien Bluff, Harris Neck, and Thomas Landing have identified the probable locations of several.[24]

Twentieth-century efforts to locate the site of Mission San Joseph de Sapala on Sapelo Island yielded inconclusive evidence. Excavations and surveys at Bourbon Field, Kenan Field, and High Point have yielded Altamaha ceramics,[25] and Spanish coarse earthenware and majolica have been recovered from

23. John T. Lanning, *The Spanish Missions of Georgia* (Chapel Hill: University of North Carolina Press, 1935); Lewis H. Larson, "1952 Season," Georgia Historical Commission Archaeological Survey of the Georgia Coast, University of Georgia, Athens, GA (1952); Buddy Sullivan, *Early Days on the Georgia Tidewater: The Story of McIntosh County and Sapelo: Being a Documented Narrative Account, with Particular Attention to the County's Waterway and Maritime Heritage; Plantation Culture and Uses of the Land in the 19th Century; and a Detailed Analysis of the History of Sapelo Island*, 6th ed. (Darien, GA: McIntosh County Board of Commissioners, 2001).

24. David Hurst Thomas, "Native American Landscapes of St. Catherines Island, Georgia," *Anthropological Papers of the American Museum of Natural History* 88 (New York: American Museum of Natural History, 2008); Joseph R. Caldwell, "Cultural Relations of Four Indian Sites on the Georgia Coast" (MA thesis, University of Chicago, 1943); Sheila K. Caldwell, "A Spanish Mission Site near Darien," *Early Georgia* 1, no. 3 (Fall 1954): 13–17: Sheila K. Caldwell, *Archaeological Excavations at the Darien Bluff Site, 9MC10, 1952–1953*, eds. Mark Williams, Richard W. Jefferies, and Mary C. Scales. Laboratory of Archaeology Series Report 81 (Athens, GA: University of Georgia, 2014): US Department of the Interior Fish and Wildlife Service, *Archaeological Investigations at 9McI41, Harris Neck National Wildlife Refuge, McIntosh County, Georgia*, by Chad O. Braley, Lisa D. O'Steen, and I. R. Quitmeyer. Contract no. 14-16-004-84-019, 1986. Lewis H. Larson, "Cultural Relationships between the Northern St. Johns Area and the Georgia Coast," *Florida Anthropologist* 11, no.1 (February 1958): 11–22.

25. Morgan R. Crook, "Evolving Community Organization on the Georgia Coast," *Journal of Field Archaeology* 11, no. 3 (1984): 247–263; Lewis H. Larson, "The Spanish

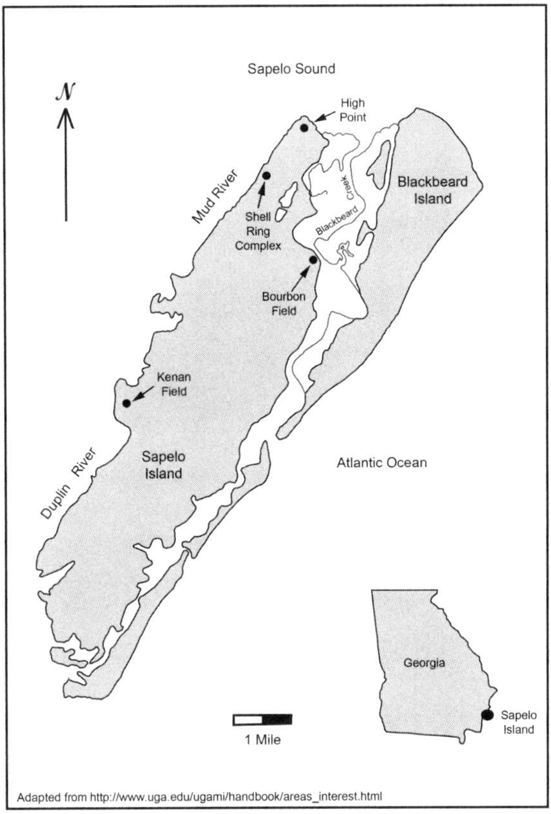

FIGURE 2. Selected Sapelo Island sites that have yielded seventeenth-century European manufactured artifacts.

several non-mission sites on Sapelo Island (Figure 2). For many years, researchers thought that Bourbon Field, located in the northeastern part of the island, was the best candidate for the mission site.[26] However, intensive testing by University of West Florida archaeologists yielded only limited evidence of a Spanish presence.[27]

on Sapelo," in *Sapelo Papers: Researches in the History and Prehistory of Sapelo Island, Georgia*, ed. Daniel P. Juengst. West Georgia College Studies in the Social Sciences 19 (Carrollton, GA: West Georgia College, 1980), 35–45; Nicholas Honerkamp and Jeffrey L. Brown, *Archaeological Survey and Testing at High Point Plantation (Mc66), Sapelo Island, Georgia* (report to the Georgia Department of Natural Resources, Univeristy of Tennessee, Chattanooga, August 2008).

26. Larson, "The Spanish on Sapelo"; Worth, *The Struggle for Georgia Coast*, 194.

27. Victor Thompson, personal communication, 2008.

John Worth's examination of the 1683 Alonso Solana map suggests that Sapala may have been on the northwestern corner of Sapelo Island.[28] This location appears to be very near the famous Sapelo Island shell rings where University of West Georgia archaeologists found Mission period artifacts in the 1970s. This location (Figure 2) is slightly farther southwest of Santa Catalina de Guale than the two leagues reported in 1680 when Santa Catalina and Satuache moved to Sapelo.

Statements regarding the "aggregation" of Tupiqui and Sapala suggest that they were in close proximity to one other on the northern end of Sapelo Island.[29] The locations of Satuache and Santa Catalina following the 1680 Westo raid are more problematic. Bushnell reports that the Santa Catalina refugees "established themselves on Sapelo at a place six leagues away from the deserted town. . . ." She suggests that the relocated Santa Catalina could have been located up to four leagues south of Sapala.

Creating a Vision of Sapala and Mission San Joseph

Although limited archaeological investigations near the location of Sapala marked on the Solona map had yielded Mission period ceramics,[30] prior to the advent of the Sapelo Island Mission Period Archaeological Project (SIMPAP) in 2003, little was known about their context or association. If this was the site of Sapala, how large was the town? How was it organized? What kinds of architecture were present? Where was the mission complex? What kinds of material remains should be expected? Following the example set by David Hurst Thomas with his Mission period research program on St. Catherines Island, we scoured compilations of recently translated and/or interpreted sixteenth- and seventeenth-century Spanish clerical, military, and government documents to help answer these questions.[31]

---

28. John E. Worth, "Sapelo Island During the Spanish Colonial Era" (paper presented at the Society for Historical Archaeology 2008 Conference on Historical and Underwater Archaeology, Albuquerque, NM, 2008); Daniel L. Simpkins, "A Preliminary Report on Test Excavations at the Sapelo Island Shell Ring, 1975," in *Sapelo Papers: Researches in the History and Prehistory of Sapelo Island, Georgia*, ed. Daniel P. Juengst. West Georgia College Studies in the Social Sciences 19 (Carrollton, GA: West Georgia College, 1980), 68; Worth, *The Struggle for Georgia Coast*, 32.

29. Worth, *The Struggle for Georgia Coast*, 22–23; Bushnell, "*Situado and Sabana,*" 149.

30. Simpkins, "A Preliminary Report. . . ," 68; Richard W. Jefferies and Victor D. Thompson, "Mission Period Native American Settlement and Interaction on Sapelo Island, Georgia" (paper presented at the 62nd Annual Meeting of the Southeastern Archaeological Conference, Columbia, South Carolina, November 2005).

31. Jones, "The Ethnohistory of the Guale Coast"; Bushnell, "*Situado and Sabana,*" San Miguel, *An Early Florida Adventure Story;* Worth, *"Guale"*; Worth, *The Struggle for Georgia Coast.*

A typical seventeenth-cenury Guale town consisted of subrectangular houses and associated outbuildings scattered around a central plaza or public space,[32] along with outlying houses and agricultural fields. Andrés de San Miguel, a shipwrecked Spaniard who spent several days in 1595 at the mainland Guale town of Asao described a typical Guale house as having walls made of unfinished logs and covered with palm foliage. He reported that all of the houses, including the chief's, were small and built "simply for their shelter" because "they have little to keep in them." The residence of the senior cacique had several small rooms and contained more "provisions" (primarily maize and chickens) than the other houses.[33]

Major Guale towns had a large, circular council house and other types of public buildings.[34] Council houses were the political centers of Guale towns; they were where dances and other rituals took place, where political deliberations (including plans for war) occurred and also where travelers and visitors were lodged.[35] For many groups, probably including the Guale, the council house provided an architectural and material link to place and was an important focus of community identity.[36]

San Miguel described a council house in Asao as a large round building constructed from pine trees stripped of their branches and bark. The base of each tree was set into the ground and their tops were joined together, creating an umbrella-like framework. The building was large enough to provide sleeping space for three hundred men. In a nearby village, San Miguel observed the head chief and his leading men in a large, clean plaza near the council house.[37]

A recent survey of architectural remains from ancestral Guale sites along the Georgia coast by Keene and Garrison indicated that Guale construction techniques could be quite variable. Guale domestic structures reported from archaeological investigations at several sites dated between C.E.1300 and 1450 include both square and rectangular buildings and rectangular buildings with rounded corners. Guale houses from this period were single-post structures constructed with wattle-and-daub or wattle-and-thatch, and some included clay-plastered interiors. Walls of Guale structures were sometimes decorated with incised curvilinear designs like those found on Guale pottery,

32. Jones, The Ethnohistory of the Guale Coast,"192; Worth, "Guale," 241.

33. San Miguel, *An Early Florida Adventure Story*, 65.

34. Worth, "Guale," 241.

35. Gary Shapiro and John Hann, *Documentary Image of the Council Houses of Spanish Florida Tested by Excavations at the San Luis de Talimali Mission*, in *Columbian Consequences: Archaeological and Historical Perspectives on the Spanish Borderlands East,* ed. David Hurst Thomas (Washington DC: Smithsonian Institution Press, 1990), 477–491.

36. Christopher B. Rodning, "Mounds, Myths, and Cherokee Townhouses in Southwestern North Carolina," *American Antiquity* 74 (July 2009).

37. San Miguel, *An Early Florida Adventure Story*, 66–67.

and some had prepared clay floors, central hearths, and associated trash and/or smudge pits.[38]

The town of Sapala probably contained similar architectural features as those described above. For example, in 1681 Captain Fuentes was observed leaning against the council house wall talking to some soldiers and two Guale leaders.[39] This structure was probably constructed adjacent to the plaza in a style similar to that of the Asao council house. Guale wattle-and-thatch or wattle-and-daub domestic structures and their associated activity areas would have been scattered in and around the town.

In addition to Guale structures, Sapala contained Spanish-constructed buildings that were components of the mission complex. Archaeological investigations at Mission Santa Catalina de Guale and other mission sites revealed several types of mission buildings, including a church, friary, kitchen, and possibly a garrison if soldiers were present.[40] The church and associated buildings were often constructed near the council house and plaza. Since officials of the church and military often disagreed, the soldier's barracks were usually built away from the mission complex.[41]

Spanish construction techniques were quite distinct from those that the Guale used to build their wattle-and-thatch structures. However, most mission buildings in La Florida were wattle-and-daub structures likely built by the Guale largely using traditional Guale techniques and construction materials. Vertical planking or wall boarding more typical of Spanish architectural styles was used to cover the exteriors of some mission churches, indicating that mission architecture represented a compromise between imported Iberian and local traditions.[42] For the Franciscans living at Sapala, the arrangement of space within

38. Deborah Keene and Ervan Garrison, "A Survey of Irene Phase Architecture on the Georgia Coast," in *Life among the Tides: Recent Archaeology on the Georgia Bight*, eds. Victor D. Thompson and David Hurst Thomas, *Anthropological Papers of the American Museum of Natural History*, 98 (New York: American Museum of Natural History, 2013), 289–316.

39. Bushnell, "*Situado and Sabana,*" 150.

40. Thomas, *Archaeology of Mission Santa Catalina de Guale*, 76–80.; Jerald T. Milanich and Rebecca Saunders, *The Spanish Castillo and the Franciscan Doctrina of Santa Catalina, at Santa Maria, Amelia Island, Forida (8Na41)* (Gainesville, FL: Florida Museum of Natural History Dept. of Anthropology, 1986); Rebecca Saunders, "Architecture of the Missions Santa Maria and Santa Catalina de Amelia," *Florida Anthropologist* 44 (1991): 126–138. Rebecca Saunders, "Continuity and Change in Guale Indian Pottery: A.D. 1350–1702" (Ph.D. diss., University of Florida, 1992). Rebecca Suanders, *Excavations at 8Na41: Two Mission Period Sites on Amelia Island, Florida* (Miscellaneous Project Report 35) (Gainesville: Florida Museum of Natural History, Department of Anthropology, 1988).

41. Thomas, *Archaeology of Mission Santa Catalina de Guale*, 79.

42. Ibid., 77; Saunders, "Architecture of the Missions. . ."; Bushnell, "Situado and Sabana," 76; Thomas, *Archaeology of Mission Santa Catalina de Guale*, 75; Barbara L. Voss, "Gender, Race, and Labor in the Archaeology of the Spanish Colonial Americas," *Current Anthropology* 49, no. 5 (October 2008).

the mission complex and the church's furnishings were likely much more important than the materials from which the church buildings were constructed.

Captain William Dunlop, a Scotsman who visited the abandoned site of Sapala in 1687, reported the burned remains of a fort and the "brick" or "mud-packed" walls of the mission's convent and church.[43] However, the exact nature of the "brick" to which he refers remains uncertain; that is, was it high-fired bricks like those used in modern construction or, more likely, burned clay from a wattle and daub structure? Interestingly, the University of West Georgia excavations near the Sapelo shell rings[44] reported fragments of low-fired brick. If this "brick" is attributable to Mission period activity, it provides strong support for the proximity of the actual Spanish mission and its associated structures.

Archaeological Findings—Survey

We have been investigating the previously identified Mission period component near the Sapelo Shell Ring complex since 2003.[45] This river-edge location is characterized by relatively level terrain, except for the large Late Archaic shell rings and more than twenty shell midden piles that dot the landscape.

Our approach has employed a diversified data collection strategy incorporating topographic mapping, systematic shovel testing, geophysical survey, metal detector survey, and unit excavation to assess cultural deposits found in this roughly 60,000 m^2 area. The detailed topographic map derived from the survey data clearly shows the large Late Archaic shell ring (Shell Ring II) and the smaller shell middens to the north (Figure 3, A). Recently acquired LIDAR images are providing additional insights on the site's topographic variability and the positions of its cultural and natural features.

Shovel probes and unit excavations have yielded numerous Mission period artifacts. These items include Guale-manufactured Altamaha pottery (Figure 4), fragments of majolica and coarse earthenware vessels; glass beads;

43. William Dunlop, "Captain Dunlop's Voyage to the Southward, 1687," *South Carolina Historical and Genealogical Magazine* 30, no. 3 (July 1929): 131–132; Worth, *The Struggle for Georgia Coast*, 54.

44. Simpkins, "A Preliminary Report. . . ,"68.

45. Jefferies and Thompson, Mission Period Native American Settlement; Richard W. Jefferies and Christopher R. Moore, *In Search of Mission San Joseph de Sapala: Mission Period Archaeological Investigations on Sapelo Island, Georgia—2003–2007* (submitted to the Georgia Department of Natural Resrouces, Atlanta, GA, 2009); Richard W. Jefferies and Christopher R. Moore, "Mission San Joseph de Sapala: Mission Period Archaeological Research on Sapelo Island," in *Life among the Tides: Recent Archaeology on the Georgia Bight*, eds. Victor D. Thompson and David Hurst Thomas, *Anthropological Papers of the American Museum of Natural History*, 98 (New York: American Museum of Natural History, 2013), 345–374.

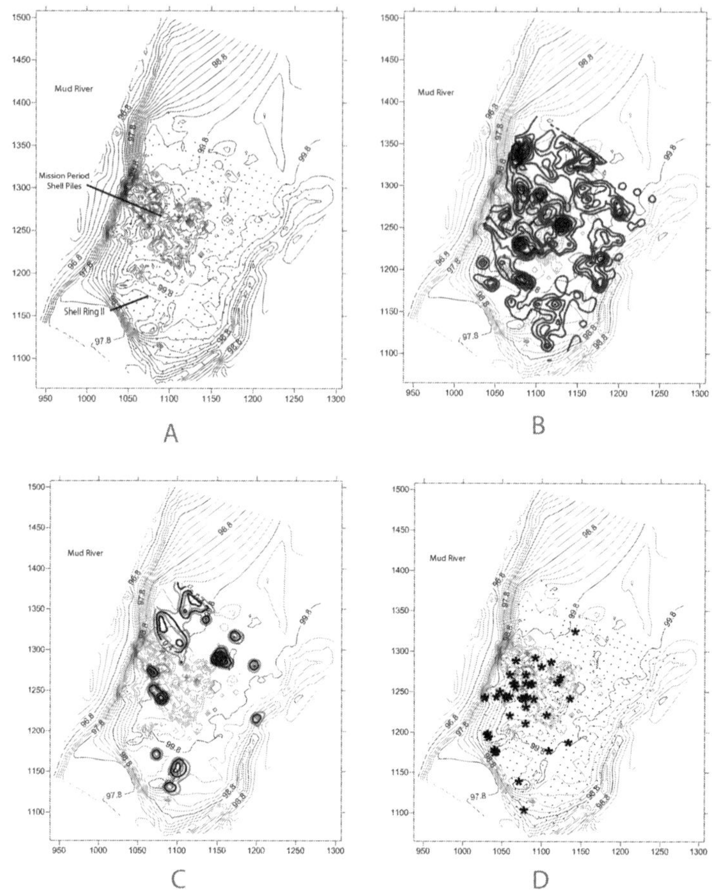

FIGURE 3. Maps of Site 9Mc23 north of Shell Ring II showing site topography and distribution of shovel probes (A) and distributions of all Altamaha sherds (B), Altamaha Red Filmed sherds (C), and Spanish/European-derived ceramics (D). All distributions are based on shovel probe data.

wrought iron nails and spikes; pieces of cast iron cauldrons and an iron pail; and a variety of military items, such as musket balls, shot, sprue, and part of a matchlock gun.

Analyses of probe contents are providing important insights on site stratigraphy, the history of site occupation, and the organization of the Mission period community. Ceramic data have proven particularly useful for investigating the Mission period occupation. Most shovel probes and excavation units have yielded Altamaha pottery manufactured by the Guale and other Mission period coastal groups (Figure 3, B). The highest density occurred

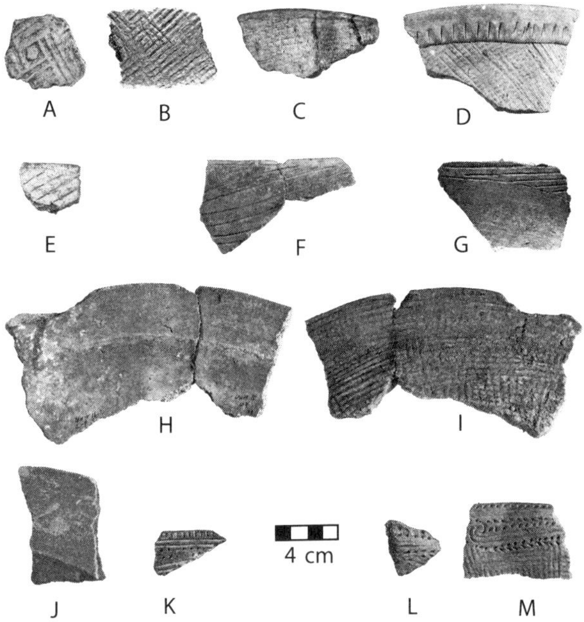

FIGURE 4. Altamaha series ceramics from north of Shell Ring II: Altamaha Complicated Stamped (A and B); Altamaha Overstamped (C and D); Altamaha Incised (E–G); interior of Altamaha Red Filmed Bowl (H); exterior of H showing overstamped surface (I); Altamaha Red Filmed (J); Unidentified Altamaha with Paired Hemiconical Punctate motif (K and L); Altamaha Overstamped with Paired Hemiconical Punctate motif (M).

immediately north of Shell Ring II in the vicinity of the circular shell middens, suggesting that they mark an area of intensive Guale activity. Subsequent testing of some of these shell piles confirms that many are associated with the Mission period occupation.[46]

Shovel probes also yielded European ceramics (Figure 3, D) and Altamaha Red Filmed colonoware pottery (Figure 3, C) commonly associated with Georgia Spanish missions.[47] Most of the European ceramics, including examples of blue-on-white majolica pottery, came from shovel probes placed among the shell midden piles (Figure 5, A–M). Sherds from olive jars or other

46. Richard W. Jefferies, *Archaeological Investigations of a Mission Period Shell Midden at 9Mc23, Sapelo Island, Georgia* (report submitted to the Georgia Department of Natural Resrouces, Atlanta, GA, 2010).

47. Saunders, "Continuity and Change in Guale Indian Pottery," and Rebecca Saunders, *Stability and Change in Guale Indian Pottery: A.D. 1300–1702* (Tuscaloosa: University of Alabama Press, 2000).

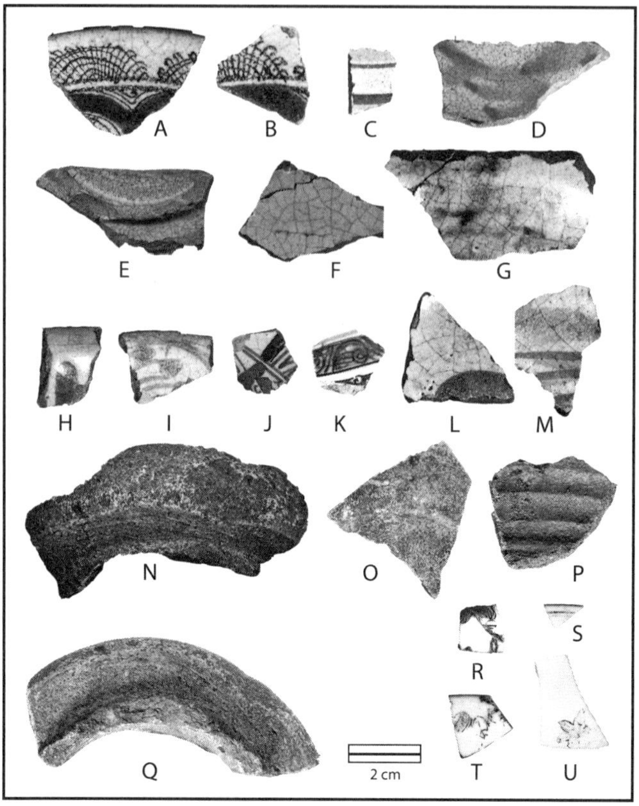

FIGURE 5. Majolica (A–M), other coarse earthenware (N–Q), and porcelain (R–U) from shovel probe and excavation unit contexts. Images D and E show the exterior and interior, respectively, of majolica bowl; images N and Q show side and bottom of "middle style" olive jar rim.

similar kinds of coarse earthenware vessels are more widely distributed but still concentrated among the shell piles (Figure 5, N–Q). Additional European artifacts found among the shell piles include fragments of porcelain serving vessels (Figure 5, R–U), building hardware such as wrought iron nails, spikes, and tacks, and military hardware such as lead shot, a cannonball and part of a matchlock musket.

While the shovel probe data are useful for examining the general distribution of Mission period artifacts, we have been unable to locate any structural evidence of the mission church or its associated buildings. However, several excavation units placed near shovel probes that yielded Mission period artifacts revealed scattered post molds, clay concentrations that may have once supported structure posts, and several large shell-filled pits.

Archaeological Investigations—Excavation

In spring 2010, we conducted a geophysical survey of the southern part of the project area where many shovel probes had yielded Mission period artifacts. Our resistance survey identified a particularly interesting anomaly in the western-most survey grid. The square feature measured approximately 7 × 7 m, suggesting that it could represent a structure. The recovery of wrought iron nails from shovel probes in this area indicated that it might be a Mission period building.

Excavation of the area containing the geophysical anomaly revealed an intact Mission period midden. Removal of the midden exposed an assortment of features and post molds, many of which contained Mission period artifacts. Post molds occurred throughout the excavated area, but their arrangement did not define an obvious structure. Two parallel trenches, located along the exposed area's northern and southern margins, respectively, likely represent components of a structure that, based on its contents, had a military function. Four unfired clay features also may be structural components,[48] as may several areas of compacted sand. Parts of at least three Altamaha vessels, a conch shell cup, a cannon ball, and several other items found in the same level where many of the posts originate suggest that this level represents a floor, providing additional support for the presence of a structure in this area.

Excavation units placed a short distance east of our main block also have exposed Mission period post molds and features, including four large shell-filled pits that contained numerous Mission period items and well-preserved faunal and botanical remains. The presence of wrought iron nails and spikes, including one from a post mold, serves as additional evidence for nearby Mission period structures.

Spanish pottery, represented by a variety of coarse earthenware, majolica, and porcelain sherds, occurred throughout the excavated area. Fragments of Spanish earthenware storage vessels, including many olive jar sherds, were distributed across the units. Temporally diagnostic sherds indicate that they are examples of the "middle style" olive jars manufactured from 1560 to 1800.[49] Majolica ceramics also were widely distributed, but in lower frequencies than the coarse earthenware sherds. The majolica sherds, many exhibiting blue-on-white or polychrome decorations, represent fragments of serving vessels such as plates, cups, or bowls. Most of these sherds came from vessels manu-

---

48. See Brent R. Weisman, *Excavations on the Franciscan Frontier: Archaeology at the Fig Springs Mission* (Gainesville: University Press of Florida, 1992), 57.

49. Kathleen Deagan, *Artifacts of the Spanish Colonies of Florida and the Caribbean, 1500–1800,* vol. 1, *Ceramics, Glassware, and Beads* (Washington, D.C.: Smithsonian Institution Press, 1987), 35.

factured in either Puebla or Mexico City, Mexico between about C.E. 1650 and the Spanish abandonment of Sapala in 1684. Types recovered to date include Aucilla Polychrome, San Luis Blue on White, and Puebla Polychrome.[50]

Building hardware, consisting of wrought iron nails and spikes, has a much more restricted distribution compared to other artifact types. Our investigation of the geophysical anomaly yielded no building hardware despite their presence in nearby shovel probes. The absence of these items suggests that the anomaly interpreted to be a structure was built using traditional Guale construction techniques that did not require nails. Alternatively, nails may have been removed from the structure after its abandonment and recycled elsewhere. In contrast, units placed just to the east of the anomaly yielded a variety of nails and spikes, perhaps reflecting the remnants of a Spanish-constructed building.

This area also yielded objects and by-products resulting from the use, maintenance, and repair of weapons. Ammunition ranged from very small lead shot to large musket balls that could have been fired from Spanish matchlock muskets. A section of an iron cannonball, probably fired from a six-pounder cannon, indicates either that the Spanish garrison had such a weapon or that it was a piece of "incoming" ordinance fired from a ship.

Several of our excavation units yielded small pieces of lead "sprue," the byproducts of casting musket balls. Analysis of sprue from Santa Elena and Fort San Felipe in South Carolina revealed that more lead shot casting occurred inside the fort than in the town of Santa Elena, demonstrating the close association of this material with military activity.[51] Our unit excavations also yielded a small cast brass button that may have come from a doublet, a snug-fitting buttoned jacket. Fancy versions of this garment were commonly worn by members of the seventeenth-century Spanish infantry.[52] Collectively, these artifacts support a Spanish military presence in this part of the site. Given that the Spanish military and friars were often at odds,[53] it is likely that the church complex was located elsewhere.

---

50. Jefferies and Moore, "In Search of Mission San Joseph de Sapala"; Jefferies and Moore, "Mission San Joseph de Sapala."

51. Carl Steen, "Lead Shot from Santa Elena and Ft. San Felipe," in *Spanish Artifacts from Santa Elena*, eds. Stanley South, Russell K. Shrowronek, and Richard E. Johnson, Occasional Papers of the South Carolina Institute of Archaeology and Anthropology, Anthropological Studies 7 (Columbia: University of South Carolina, 1988), 87.

52. George Gush, "Spanish Infantry," *Renaissance Warfare*, accessed August 20, 2014, http://greatestbattles.iblogger.org/Renaissance/14&15_Spanish.htm; Kathleen Deagan, *Artifiacts of the Spanish Colonies of Florida and the Caribbean, 1500–1800,* vol. 2, *Portable, Personal Possessioins* (Washington, D.C.: Smithsonian Institution Press, 2002), 162–163.

53. Thomas, *Archaeology of Mission Santa Catalina de Guale*, 79.

Spanish and Guale Foodways on Sapelo

Our Sapelo Island research is also providing new insights on Mission period subsistence practices in Spanish Georgia. The majority of the faunal remains recovered from features, post molds, and unit column samples reflect a traditional Guale diet of white-tailed deer and marsh-estuarine resources. Old World domesticates such as chickens, pigs, and cows occur, but in low frequencies. Interestingly, cottontail rabbit was the most heavily exploited wild mammal other than deer,[54] which may indicate the Guale were raising rabbits alongside small numbers of domestic chickens and pigs. The beef was likely imported from the Timucua or Apalachee provinces.[55] A recent study of vertebrate faunal remains from St. Catherines Island also indicates that domestic animals made up a relatively low percentage of foodstuffs. Based on these findings, the Spanish, as well as the Guale, appear to have consumed many more Guale foods than traditional Spanish foods.[56] This pattern of meat procurement and consumption conforms to one in which the diets of both the Guale and the Spanish were based on traditional Guale foods.[57]

Botanical samples from the same proveniences confirm the indigenous orientation of foodways at San Joseph de Sapala. The most abundant food item was maize, although we recovered nearly 150 fragments of carbonized fungi from one context. Other seeds and fruits occurred in limited quantities, including boneset, chenopod, poor man's pepper, three-seeded mercury, undifferentiated grasses, dock, and wild grape. The only non-Native plant specimens recovered were several peach seed fragments.[58] Analysis of four of the peach pits yielded calibrated, Bayesian modelled AMS dates ranging from 1635 to 1685 at the 95 percent confidence level.

Ethnohistoric evidence helps further elucidate the nature of Eurasian imports to Sapelo Island during the Mission period. A 1595 account by a Span-

---

54. Carol E. Colaninno, "Animal Remains from Mission Period Deposits at the Sapelo Island Shell Ring Complex (9MC23)," manuscript on file, Zooarchaeology Laboratory, Georgia Museum of Natural History, University of Georgia, Athens.

55. Kathleen Deagan, "St. Augustine and the Mission Frontier," in *The Spanish Missions of Florida*, ed. Bonnie G. McEwan (Gainesville: University Press of Florida, 1993), 87–110.

56. Elizabeth J. Reitz, Barnet Pavao-Zuckerman, Daniel C. Weinand, and Gwyneth A. Duncan, *Mission and Pueblo Santa Catalina de Guale, St. Catherines Island, Georgia: A Comparative Zooarchaeological Analysis*, Anthropological Papers of the American Museum of Natural History 91 (New York: American Musuem of Natural History, 2010), 1–275.

57. Christopher R. Moore and Richard W. Jefferies, "Who Were the Guale? Reevaluating Interaction in the Mission Town of San Joseph de Sapala," in *Indigenous Landscapes and Spanish Missions: New Perspectives from Archaeology and Ethnohistory*, eds. Lee M. Panish and Tsim D. Schneider (Tucson: University of Arizona Press, 2014), 79–92.

58. Renee Bonzani, personal communication, 2012.

ish shipwreck survivor, Fray Andrés de San Miguel, reported wild pigs present on an island near Sapelo Island,[59] and William Dunlop made reference to figs, peaches, artichokes, and onions growing in the priest's garden on Sapelo in a 1687 account.[60] Whether the "priest's garden" referred to by Dunlop was maintained by the Spanish or the Guale is unknown. It is likely that indigenous peoples throughout the Southeast rapidly incorporated introduced foodstuffs into their mixed hunting, gathering, and gardening economies.[61]

Upon arriving in La Florida, the Franciscans who serviced the various mission communities would have experienced a diet very different from the typical Iberian diet consisting of cuts of meat from domesticated animals, bread, and various Eurasian fruits and vegetables. While pigs and chickens were raised on Sapelo, most meat consumed by the Franciscans was from wild sources, primarily white-tailed deer and seafood. Rather than traditional Spanish meals made with Spanish recipes, local Guale cuisine, seasoned with local spices and whichever Old World fruits and vegetables could be grown in sandy coastal soils, would have been the standard fare. Beef and cheese would have been rare, arriving only on occasion from ranches to the south. Maize replaced wheat and barley as the staple grain, and what wheat was imported to the region was likely closely guarded and rationed for the Eucharist host.

Interpreting Sapala

Variation in the distribution of Mission period artifacts across the project area may reflect different activity areas within the community. The distribution of Altamaha sherds and Spanish artifacts recovered during systematic shovel probing indicates that the Guale occupation (presumably the town of Sapala) clusters around an area of low artifact density surrounded by several shell midden piles. We are currently interpreting this low-density area as the site's plaza. The shell midden piles consist of domestic refuse associated with Guale households and/or the Spanish mission. Dispersed midden piles located north of the plaza likely represent outlying households interspersed among Guale agricultural fields. This settlement pattern, if confirmed by testing, is highly reminiscent of the pre-mission Guale settlement pattern described by Jones and is very different from the Spanish settlement pattern evident at St. Augustine and San Luis in Apalachee Province.[62]

---

59. San Miguel, *An Early Florida Adventure Story,* 57–58.

60. Dunlop, "Captain Dunlop's Voyage to the Southward."

61. Julia E. Hammett, "Interregional Patterns of Land Use and Plant Management in Native North America," in *People, Plants and Landscapes,* ed. Kris Gremillion (Tuscaloosa: University of Alabama Press, 1997), 195–216.

62. Jones, "The Ethnohistory of the Guale Coast,"179; Deagan, "St. Augustine and the Mission Frontier"; Willet A. Boyer III, "Nuestra Senora del Rosario de La Punta: Life-

The Eurocentric focus of Mission period research leaves one with the distinct impression that the mission church was the focus of mission towns. However, the arrangement of buildings around a hypothetical central plaza at Sapala removes any structure from the center. If the mission church was located on the plaza, it was likely one of several administrative/public buildings that shared this space. Included among these was the council house, the presence of which is confirmed by an ethnohistoric account of a meeting held at the Sapala council house between Arguelles, the *mica* of Tupiqui, and several leading men of Sapala.[63] Interestingly, our recent excavations have uncovered the remains of a structure that we interpret to be the location of a military support structure (perhaps a barracks) present at Sapala between the abandonment of Santa Catalina in 1680 and the retreat from Sapelo in 1684. If this structure is a Spanish building, a hypothesis supported by the concentration of military hardware in this area, then it is a Spanish structure that was southwest of and possibly peripheral to the activities that took place around the plaza. This pattern conforms to seventeenth-century accounts of soldiers being housed away from the church and other mission buildings.

Although preliminary, our survey data from the location of the Mission San Joseph and the Guale town of Sapala indicate that Sapala was organized in a manner reminiscent of pre-Contact Guale communities. Sapala appears to have been a Guale, not a Spanish town. A mission is located somewhere within the confines of the greater Sapala community, but all evidence currently indicates that the mission was incorporated into a preexisting settlement plan and not necessarily the focus of community life. Furthermore, if the Santa Catalina mission buildings can be cited as analogues, then the Sapala mission and any other Spanish structures would have been made, at least partly, from traditional Guale construction materials,[64] lending further support to the contention that the Spanish friars and soldiers were living in a Guale world.

Future research on Sapelo Island's Mission period cultural heritage will focus on locating and investigating cultural features attributable to both the island's Guale and Spanish residents. In doing this, we hope to learn more about the people of these two distinct cultures and how, in the face of a rapidly changing sociopolitical landscape, their lives were changed by each other's presence and the events of the world that surrounded them. Of particular

---

ways of an Eighteenth-Century Colonial Refugee Mission Community, St. Augustine, Florida" (MA thesis, University of Florida, 2005); Bonnie G. McEwan, "Hispanic Life on the Seventeenth-Century Florida Frontier," in *The Spanish Missions of La Florida*, ed. Bonnie G. McEwan (Gainesville: University Press of Florida, 1993), 295–321.

63. Fred Lamar Pearson, *Spanish-Indian Relations in Florida: A Study of Two Vistas, 1657–1678* (New York: Garland Publishing, 1990), 211–212; Bushnell, "Situado and Sabana,"150.

64. Thomas, *The Archaeology of Mission Santa Catalina de Guale*, 77.

interest is how the Guale dealt with the increasingly heterogeneous population of Sapala created by the aggregation of formerly independent Guale towns and how the residents handled the many anomalous relationships that aggregation created among the Guale inhabitants and between the Guale and their Franciscan priests.

Chapter 12
Spiritual Diplomacy—The Tama Yamasees and La Florida's Franciscan Missions

Denise I. Bossy

In 1619 La Florida's governor, Juan de Salinas, reported to King Felipe III the promising news that the Indian *cacique* (chief) of Tama (Altamaha) had requested that the Spanish send a Franciscan missionary to his chiefdom.[1] For several decades the Spanish had been interested in exploring Tama, located in the interior of Georgia. As one of Salinas's predecessors explained, such exploration "mattered for attracting souls for heaven and for the growth of Your Royal patrimony that a settlement be made in . . . La Tama."[2] In La Florida, as elsewhere in the Spanish Americas, church and state ambitions were deeply intertwined. Believing that Tama teemed with potential converts, as well as food supplies and natural minerals (particularly silver, gold, and diamonds), the Spanish had already attempted several expeditions into the region. Their ambitions to convert Tama Indians and to establish a Spanish foothold in the region were further intensified by rumors of English encroachment south of Virginia both before and after the founding of Jamestown in 1607.[3]

Despite their promising overture, however, the Tamas rejected Spanish missionary and colonization efforts. During their early interactions with the Spanish they had entertained the notion of diplomacy, but the unfolding of Spanish ambitions soon put an end to that: the Tamas were by no means interested in becoming subjects of the fragile Spanish empire in the Southeast. It would take a series

1. Juan de Salinas to His Majesty, May 24, 1619, AGI SD 255, Stetson Collection, St. Augustine Historical Library.

2. Governor Gonzalo Méndez de Canço to His Majesty, February 28, 1600, trans. by John Hann, "Tama and the Hinterland behind Santa Elena," mss on file at P.K. Yonge Library of Florida History (University of Florida, Gainesville), 1.

3. For the best summary of Spanish expeditions into the interior, see John E. Worth, "Late Spanish Military Expeditions in the Interior Southeast, 1597–1628," in *The Forgotten Centuries: Indians and Europeans in the American South, 1521–1704* (Athens: University of Georgia Press, 1994), 104–124.

of devastating slave raids by Westo Indians in the mid-seventeenth century to create the conditions under which even a small segment of the Tama population might consider the potential advantages of a spiritual and political relationship with the Spanish. Forced to abandon their homeland, the Tamas moved east to the coast and joined with other refugees in creating a new community that soon became known as the Yamasees, taking the root of their name "Yama" from the "Tama" chiefdom. Borne out of the chaos wrought by slave raids and colonialism, the Yamasees exhibited a remarkable willingness to periodically splinter, migrate, and strategically ally with Indian and European communities when it benefited them. During the long period of Franciscan missionary activity in the southeast (1572–1763), Tamas and other Yamasee Indians moved into, through, and out of the missions. Some stayed for a few years, others stayed for decades, and still others rejected the Franciscans altogether.

The group of Yamasees who most meaningfully engaged with the Spanish Franciscans was a splinter of the Tamas who moved into the mission province of Apalachee in the 1670s. There they established a town that the Spanish called Nuestra Señora de la Candelaria de la Tama.[4] Scholars have paid little attention to the Yamasees in Apalachee, focusing instead on those who lived in the Guale-Mocama missions for less than twenty years and overtly rejected conversion to Catholicism. The Tama Yamasees of Candelaria, on the other hand, meaningfully engaged in what I call "spiritual diplomacy" with the Spanish for several decades: participating in practices and ceremonies that were understood by both parties as religious as well as political. Spiritual diplomacy had deep indigenous roots. Southeastern Indians understood spiritual and political power as symbiotic; caciques and cacicas were considered to be spiritual as well as political leaders with special access to sacred and political knowledge, connections, and technology. The Tama cacique who invited Spanish missionaries to his chiefdom in 1619 hoped to build not just a new political connection but one that was grounded in spiritual power and knowledge. As a sixteenth-century Calusa paramount chief explained to a Spanish missionary, his people expected that he "know what kings are obliged to know."[5] This

---

4. Most important in the study of the Tamas in Guale-Mocama is John E. Worth, *The Struggle for the Georgia Coast* (Tuscaloosa: University of Alabama Press, 2007). Hann recounts the establishment of Candelaria in Apalachee and its later reconstitution in St. Augustine in John H. Hann, *Apalachee: The Land between the Rivers* (Gainesville: University Press of Florida, 1988). While scholars implicitly draw a distinction between the Tamas and the Yamasees, noting that there were both Tamas and Yamasees in Apalachee, I believe that this is a false distinction. The Tamas played a central role in the ethnogenesis of the Yamasees, and were both Tama and Yamasee. To indicate my recognition of the mutivalent quality of their identity, I will use the term Tama Yamasee to denote the people of Candelaria.

5. Father Juan Rogel to Father Jerónimo Ruiz del Portillo, April 25, 1568, in John H. Hann, ed. and trans., *Missions to the Calusa* (Gainesville: University Press of Florida, 1991), 248.

helps to explain why some Southeastern Indians in La Florida (and beyond) sought out or welcomed Franciscan missionaries and expressed interest in Catholic rituals, stories, songs, and theological principles.

While indigenous in origin, spiritual diplomacy worked especially well in La Florida because Franciscan missionaries played a particularly prominent role in Indian diplomacy and because Spanish diplomatic practices included rituals that Southeastern Indians (and the Spanish) recognized as spiritually significant. Diplomatic gift giving, for instance, was a cornerstone of spiritual diplomacy in La Florida. From elites to commoners, Southeastern Indians sought access to goods that were not locally made or available because such goods were potent symbols of the receiver's connections. Goods given by Spanish missionaries and officials to Indian caciques were especially powerful signifiers of not just earthly connections but also supernatural ones. The great distance that the goods traveled across the Atlantic (their regional rarity) augmented their spiritual power. Though the Spanish hoped and even expected that Indian allies and converts would fully embrace Roman Catholicism and renounce their own beliefs, they were often disappointed. In their spiritual encounters with the Spanish, Yamasee and other Southeastern Indians read Franciscan rituals, symbols, and words through their own cultural frameworks, and for their own spiritual and political reasons.[6] Yamasees adopted and shed their Catholicism to fit their own political and spiritual needs.

This essay focuses on the Tama Yamasees who lived in Apalachee (and later St. Augustine), tracing their movements in and out of Franciscan missions from the 1670s to the 1710s to explain why some Tama Yamasees chose to engage in spiritual diplomacy with the Spanish even while the majority did not. The first section examines the coalescence of the Yamasees, arguing that the movement of several hundred Tama Yamasees into Apalachee was reflective of a larger strategy by the nascent Yamasees who splintered and lived in dispersed, though interconnected, towns. Drawing on older practices of migration and older diplomatic networks with Indians who lived in La Florida, the Yamasees created a web of communities that spread across the Southeast. Each Yamasee community made strategic alliances with outsiders, reviving or developing relationships that could help to sustain and protect their discrete clans and towns while creating new opportunities for the Yamasees as a whole. In this way the Tama Yamasees of Apalachee were quite typical of other Yamasee communities.

However, the Tama Yamasees were unusual in the degree to which they engaged in spiritual diplomacy with the Spanish. The second section of the

---

6. Denise I. Bossy, "The Yamasees, the Society for the Propagation of the Gospel, and Spiritual Diplomacy: Reinterpreting Prince George's Voyage to England, 1713–5." *Early American Studies* (Spring 2014): 366–401.

essay analyzes Tama Yamasee relationships with the Spanish, arguing that the Tama Yamasees saw decided spiritual, political, and practical advantages in allying with the Spanish and were willing to nominally convert to Catholicism as part of this alliance. Nonetheless, the Spanish and Tama Yamasees often had divergent expectations for what conversion and alliance entailed. When the Spanish attempted to assert spiritual and political dominion over the Tama Yamasees, many left their mission (as did other Yamasees across La Florida). They used the Yamasee network to relocate north. But they did not sever their ties with the Spanish irrevocably, and some Tamas returned to La Florida when their alliance with the British of South Carolina fell apart in 1715. In many ways the Tama Yamasees' interactions with the Spanish fit a more general pattern of Yamasee dispersal, migration, and alliance.

The Tama Yamasees

The Yamasees first came together as a people in the mid-seventeenth century, pulled together by a shattering series of slave raids that forced them to leave their homelands. Movement was at the heart of Yamasee ethnogenesis and the Yamasees continued to use regional movement as a core strategy to survive the chaos wrought by colonialism. The Tamas played a primary role in these migrations and in the effort to reconstruct and extend Yamasee networks with other Indian (and European) communities across the region. Yamasee interactions with the Guales and Apalachees, in particular, predated European colonization and many Yamasees who traveled to or moved into these regions in the second half of the seventeenth century sought to renew their connections with these Indian peoples. They might also consider creating new connections with the Spanish who lived in these places, but they knew the Spanish decidedly less well.

In the 1650s the Tamas assumed a leadership role in the first phase of Yamasee ethnogenesis when several Indian chiefdoms relocated from the Oconee-Ocmulgee river region in interior Georgia to the coast. These chiefdoms—Altamaha (La Tama), Ocute, and Ichisi (and perhaps Toa)—were pushed out of interior Georgia by slave raids led by Westo Indians (the Spanish referred to them as the Chichimecos). Fleeing to the coast, the Oconee-Ocmulgee refugees initially sought an alliance with Indians in the Santa Elena region. When the Westos began to attack their new settlements in the 1660s, the Oconee-Ocmulgee Indians (now joined by Indians from Santa Elena) looked to the Indian missions in La Florida as a potential answer to their renewed problems. Led by the Tamas, the Oconee-Ocmulgee Indians moved near and then into missions in the Guale-Mocama region in the 1660s. The Oconee-Ocmulgee and Guale Indians had a long history of trade and diplomacy that predated Spanish colonization and shaped events in the sixteenth and seventeenth centuries.[7]

The Spanish were well aware of the relationship and actively sought to capitalize on it. When Governor Gonzalo Méndez de Canzo sent a Franciscan-led expedition into the interior of Georgia in 1597 he requested that the paramount cacique of Guale provide an Indian entourage to guide the Spanish. The first objective of the Spanish friars leading the expedition—Fray Pedro Fernández de Chozas and Fray Francisco de Beráscola—was to visit the Tama chiefdom. The Guale paramount cacique consented and put at the head of the Guale entourage his own heir, Don Juan, and "thirty Christian and non-Christian Indians."[8] Don Juan's presence was critically important to the potential success of the Spanish expedition because it would indicate to the Tamas that the Spanish were worth listening to. Indeed, Spanish descriptions of this first encounter confirm that the Tamas welcomed the Spanish into their council house and that Fray Chozas followed the protocols of Indian diplomacy. Don Juan had undoubtedly educated Chozas in these critically important formalities. And so Fray Chozas knew to enter Tama with fanfare—the Spanish friars carried the cross and rang their bell—and to demonstrate respect by listening to the hosts—Chozas described himself as "quiet for a long time." Last but not least, he knew what *not* to ask for. Instead of demanding that the Tamas convert or ally with the Spanish, Chozas had his interpreter, the Spanish soldier Gaspar de Salas, explain to the Tamas that the Spanish had come for "protection and lodging."[9] This was but the first stage of their spiritual diplomacy, and it was important not to rush things. The Tamas expected foreign dignitaries to present themselves as potential friends and to acknowledge Tama power.

While the Guale entourage was critical to the success of the Franciscan party, Don Juan and the paramount cacique had their own reasons for leading the Spanish expedition. This was an opportunity for Don Juan (and by exten-

---

7. Rodrigo Rangel, "Account of the Northern Conquest and Discovery of Hernando de Soto," trans. by John E. Worth, in *The De Soto Chronicles: The Expedition of Hernando de Soto to North America in 1539–1543,* vol. I, eds. Lawrence A. Clayton, Vernon James Knight Jr., and Edward C. Moore (Tuscaloosa: University of Alabama Press, 1993), 273. In the 1540s Ocute was the paramount chiefdom in the Oconee-Ocmulgee region and had a number of tributaries perhaps including the Guale chiefdom. Charles Hudson, "The Social Context of the Chiefdom of Ichisi," in David J. Hally, ed. *Ocmulgee Archaeology, 1936–1986* (Athens: University of Georgia Press, 1994), 179.

8. Fray Alonso de Escobedo, "La Florida," in *Pirates, Indians and Spaniards: Father Escobedo's "La Florida,"* ed. James W. Covington (St. Petersburg: Great Outdoors Publishing Co., 1963), 22–24. For a full transcription of Escobedo's epic poem see Alexandra Elizabeth Sununu, "Estudio y edición anotado de 'La Florida' de Alonso Gregorio de Escobedo O.F.M. (Ph.D. diss.: City University of New York, 1993), especially 451–458.

9. Ibid.

sion his chiefdom of Tolomato) to exert some influence over this emerging new political network, and remain as much as possible at its center. Such connections with outsiders were essential to the influence that the paramount chiefdom was able to exert within Guale itself.[10] The initial stage of spiritual diplomacy went well and the Franciscans reported that the Tamas seemed likely to convert. Then a side trip to Ocute precipitated a marked deterioration in the political atmosphere. The cacique of Ocute welcomed the Spanish but then warned them not to proceed: the Indians beyond Ocute still harbored ill will against the Spanish (a legacy of Hernando de Soto's violent 1540 entrada in the region) and were likely to oppose a new Spanish intrusion. It is not clear whether the cacique of Ocute was telling the truth. Perhaps he simply wished to prevent the Spanish from allying with Indians beyond his control. Still, such suspicions about the Spanish were widespread. When Chozas and the rest of his entourage backtracked to Tama, they found a war rather than a welcoming party. Not yet convinced that the Spanish were ready allies and following Ocute's lead in rejecting the Spanish, the Tama cacique very nearly had his men scalp Fray Chozas.[11]

Even in this rejection we can see evidence that the Tamas were making decisions that were far more influenced by their networks with other Indian chiefdoms than with the Spanish. Shortly after Chozas returned from Tama, the Guale Indians instigated what scholars have traditionally understood as a revolt against the Franciscans. While the newer interpretation is that this revolt was in large part an internal civil war led by Asao to displace Tolomato as the paramount chiefdom in Guale, there is evidence of an even broader Indian context to consider in order to unravel the catalysts and implications of the revolt. The timing of Altamahas's rejection of the Franciscans and the subsequent Guale Revolt point to this: the Spanish traveled to Tama in July and by October the Guale Revolt was underway. Five Spanish Franciscans were killed in the Guale Revolt including Fray Beráscola, one of the two Franciscans who had originally traveled to Tama and Ocute. The other Franciscan was the first to report news of the revolt; Fray Chozas was stationed at San Pedro in Mocama, very near to the revolt's epicenter. Moreover, when the new paramount of the Guales, Asao's cacique Don Domingo, assembled an army of Indians to hunt down and kill Don Francisco and Don Juan he requested and received military assistance from Tama. The Tamas adjusted to the internal changes in Guale by reaffirming their

---

10. John Worth, "Spanish Missions and the Persistence of Chiefly Power," in Robbie Ethridge and Charles Hudson, eds. *The Transformation of the Southeastern Indians, 1540–1760* (Jackson: University Press of Mississippi, 2002), 39–64.

11. The paramount chief of Ocute had a particularly nasty encounter with Soto, and was ultimately forced to display his submission to the Spanish by gifting Soto food and laborers and genuflecting before the Cross. See Rangel, "Account of the Northern Conquest," 270–273.

alliance to the new paramount chief through the participation in this patently political act. The relationship between Guale and Tama was pivotal to the Guale Revolt both in its origins and conclusion, shaping external relations with the Franciscans and the Spanish more generally.[12]

Thus, when the Tamas and other associated Oconee-Ocmulgee peoples moved into Guale in the 1660s to escape Westo slave raids they were relocating to a world they already knew, a world that was marked by old political alliances and kinship ties. Observing this coalescence in their midst, the Spanish called the reorganized Oconee-Ocmulgee people the "Yamasis."[13] Following diplomatic paths and relationships, the Yamasees dispersed into several major settlement zones in the 1660s and 1670s. By 1667 there were at least six Yamasees settlements in the Franciscan mission province of Guale-Mocama; by 1680 the Yamasee population in La Florida had grown to between seven hundred and eight hundred people. The majority of Yamasee settlements were established in the Guale-Mocama region (nine in all); another two were along the Upper St. Johns in the Timucua province. A single Yamasee site was located in Apalachee. It was the largest Yamasee settlement in La Florida with a population of at least three hundred in 1675.[14]

There is some speculation that the Tama Yamasees might have begun to move into Apalachee as early as the 1660s, instead of accompanying other Tamas and Oconee-Ocmuglee peoples in their moves first to Santa Elena and then Guale.[15] But it is also possible that they did accompany the larger group to the coast and later relocated to Apalachee. In either case, there are a

12. Only one friar then in Guale was spared. For this new interpretation of the Guale Revolt, see J. Michael Francis and Kathleen M. Kole, *Murder and Martyrdom in Spanish Florida: Don Juan and the Guale Uprising of 1597*, Anthropological Papers of the American Museum of Natural History, no. 95 (New York: American Museum of Natural History, 2011). Chozas was the first to inform the governor of the revolt; see "A Letter from Fray Pedro Fernández de Chozas, October 4, 1597," in Francis and Kole, *Murder and Martyrdom*, 69–70. On don Diego contacting Tama to request men to accompany him on the expedition to Yfusinique to kill don Francisco and don Juan, see "Investigation into the death of don Juanillo, Indian from Guale and his vassals, November 27, 1601," in Francis and Kole, *Murder and Martyrdom*, 136–138.

13. Fray Carlos de Anguiano, April 6, 1663, quoted in John E. Worth, *The Struggle for the Georgia Coast: An 18th-Century Retrospective on Guale and Mocama* (New York: American Museum of Natural History, 1995), 92; William Green, Chester B. DePratter, and Bobby Southerlin, "The Yamasee in South Carolina: Native American Adaptation and Interaction along the Carolina Frontier," in J. W. Joseph and Martha Zierden, eds. *Another's Country: Archaeological and Historical Perspectives on Cultural Interactions in the Southern Colonies* (Tuscaloosa: University of Alabama Press, 2002), 16; William Green, *The Search for Altamaha: The Archaeology and Ethnohistory of an Early 18th Century Indian Town* (Columbia: South Carolina Institute of Archaeology and Anthropology, 1992), 13–14.

14. Worth, "Yamasee," 247; Hann, *Apalachee*, 360.

15. Hann, *Apalachee*, 35.

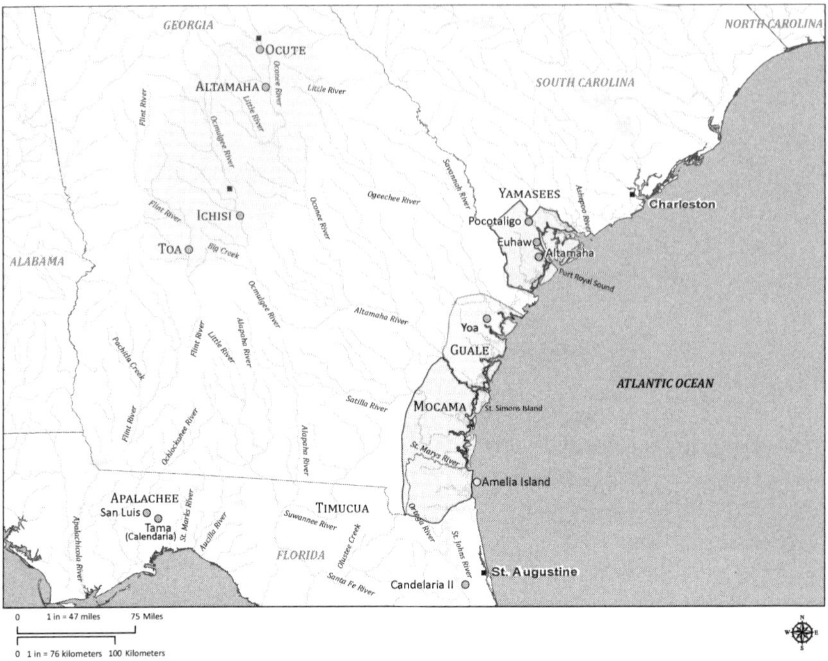

FIGURE 1. Map of Yamasee homelands. Map by David W. Wilson and Donatella Schianomoriello, Center for Instruction and Research Technology, University of North Florida.

number of reasons that explain why a group of Tamas splintered and migrated separately to Apalachee. Given inter-town politics and migration practices within the Mississippian world to which the Tamas belonged, the most likely explanation is that the Tamas who moved to Apalachee came from a distinct lineage or town within the Altamaha (Tama) chiefdom. Mississippian chiefdoms like Altamaha consisted of at least four to seven distinct towns under the leadership of the head chief, but power often shifted between elite lineages over generations.[16] Perhaps a particular family lineage left Altamaha for Apalachee as part of a regular process of fissioning, liable to occur when chiefdoms became unstable and lineages or towns looked for more secure regions. Fissioning could also occur when chiefdoms that had grown in size and power gave rise to "daughter towns," which relocated yet maintained connections

16. Robbie Ethridge, *From Chicaza to Chickasaw: The European Invasion and the Transformation of the Mississippian World, 1540–1715* (Chapel Hill: University of North Carolina Press, 2010), 48–49.

to their mother town.[17] From Apalachee the Tama Yamasees certainly maintained their connections with other Yamasees.

There were decided political advantages for a lineage to establish its own Tama town in Apalachee; there a new or displaced chief and his lineage might enjoy an opportunity to rise to power. Besides, Apalachee was probably a familiar trekking region. There is some evidence that paths connected Apalachee and Oconee communities. For example, in 1540 an Indian youth and trader named Perico guided Hernando de Soto from Apalachee to Altamaha and Ocute along paths with which he seemed quite familiar. Perhaps Tamas relocated to Apalachee in the mid-seventeenth century along the same route.[18] Cultural similarities doubtless facilitated this move. The Tamas and Apalachees likely spoke Muskogean languages that were mutually intelligible. Since both peoples were part of the Mississippian world, they had similar cultural expressions, political structures, technology, and religious beliefs.[19] While there were important distinctions between them, they had enough in common for the Tamas to make a life near the Apalachees.

The Tamas who moved to Apalachee sometime before 1674 were very clearly interested in positioning themselves close to the core of Apalachee power and yet they also maintained their sovereignty in the province. As Spanish records and Figure 2 indicate, the Tama Yamasees were careful when deciding where to settle within Apalachee. Rather than establishing their town on the outskirts of the province, the Tamas built their new town close to Mission San Luis the largest Indian town in Apalachee and the center of both the Apalachee and Spanish spheres in the region. San Luis was both the central governing town of the Apalachees and the second seat of government for the Spanish, and the mission at San Luis was the head of the Franciscan province.

---

17. Archaeological research on the Oconee region suggests that from 1450 to 1600 C.E. a lengthy phase of peace promoted population growth and the proliferation of small settlements within and beyond the Altamaha chiefdom as family lineages established their own homesteads. The Tamas thus had much experience with fissioning when they moved into Apalachee. Mark Williams, "Indian Ceramics of the Spanish Atlantic Coast: The View from the Interior of Georgia and South Carolina," in *From Santa Elena to St. Augustine: Indigenous Ceramic Variability (A.D. 1400-1700)*, eds. Kathleen Deagan and David Hurst Thomas, Anthropological Papers of the American Museum of Natural History No. 90 (New York: American Museum of Natural History, 2009), 113–121; Stephen A. Kowalewski and James W. Hatch, "The Sixteenth-Century Expansion of Settlement in the Upper Oconee Watershed, Georgia," *Southeastern Archaeology* 10 (Summer 1991): 1–17.

18. Rangel, "Account of the Northern Conquest," 273..

19. On the question of language, see Bonnie G. McEwan, "Apalachee and Neighboring Groups," in *Handbook of North American Indians*, vol. 14: *Southeast*, 669. For example, when Domingo de Leturiondo made an official visitation of Apalachee in 1677–1678, he was able to use the same interpreter for the Yamasees at Candelaria and the Apalachees. John H. Hann, *Visitations and Revolts in Florida, 1656–1695* (Tallahassee: Florida Bureau of Archaeological Research, 1993), 80.

In short, the mission at San Luis was a potent spiritual and political place, at the heart of the region's network.[20]

Candelaria stood on the *camino real*, the road that connected Apalachee and St. Augustine. It was situated roughly one league from Mission San Luis, in the center of the province.[21] The proximity to San Luis ensured that the Tama Yamasees were kept apprised of news and were included in diplomatic events. For example, when Domingo de Leturiondo conducted an official visitation of Apalachee in 1677, he started at San Luis and his next stop was Candelaria.[22] In 1675 the Spanish sent Lieutenant Governor Claudio Luis de Florencia to live in Mission San Luis and the Spanish population grew to include not only soldiers and officials but also Spanish ranchers and their families. Mission San Luis, and Apalachee more generally, became increasingly crucial to the Spanish colony supplying most of the colony's Indian labor (and corn) and serving as a bulwark against the English and later the French. Both the Apalachee and Spanish of San Luis welcomed the relocated Tama Yamasees, expecting that that they would contribute to the protection and well-being of the region. Candelaria remained in Apalachee until attacks by Creek and other Indians and British soldiers forced the community to leave in 1704.

Spiritual Diplomacy

Understanding how the Tama Yamasees who lived in Apalachee thought about their relationship with the Spanish requires a reconceptualization of Franciscan missions. For most Yamasees these were not spaces defined by reli-

20. Hann, *Apalachee*, 2.

21. Constructed in 1656, Mission San Luis was home to the chief of Anhaica who had relocated his community to the new site and built a large council house able to accommodate over two thousand people. Traditionally, Anhaica was the head war town of the Apalachees and in the 1650s the Spanish constructed a blockhouse and stationed their garrison at Mission San Luis. Anhaica had been an early object of Franciscan missions, and was probably included in the first wave of permanent missions established among the Apalachees by the Spanish in 1633. Hann, *Apalachee*, 35–37 and 150. To date there has been no archaeological work focusing on the Yamasee occupation at the Candelaria site. Archaeologist John Hann believed it was near Lake Ella. John H. Hann, "Summary Guide to Spanish Florida Missions and *Visitas* with Churches in the Sixteenth and Seventeenth Centuries," *The Americas* 46 (April 1990): 490. More recently, scholars have suggested that Candelaria was probably at or near the site of San Luis de Xinayca (1633–1656). Some mission period artifacts were collected during excavations of the Martin site bordering on Xinayca, but the excavation and analysis focused on the sixteenth century component. This was the site of Hernando De Soto's winter encampment (1539–1540). Personal communication with Bonnie McEwan, February 5, 2015. Also see Charles R. Ewen and John H. Hann, *Hernando de Soto among the Apalachee: The Archaeology of the First Winter Encampment* (Gainesville: University Press of Florida, 1998).

22. Visitation and Auto for Tama, December 25, 1677, in Hann, *Visitations and Revolts*, 105.

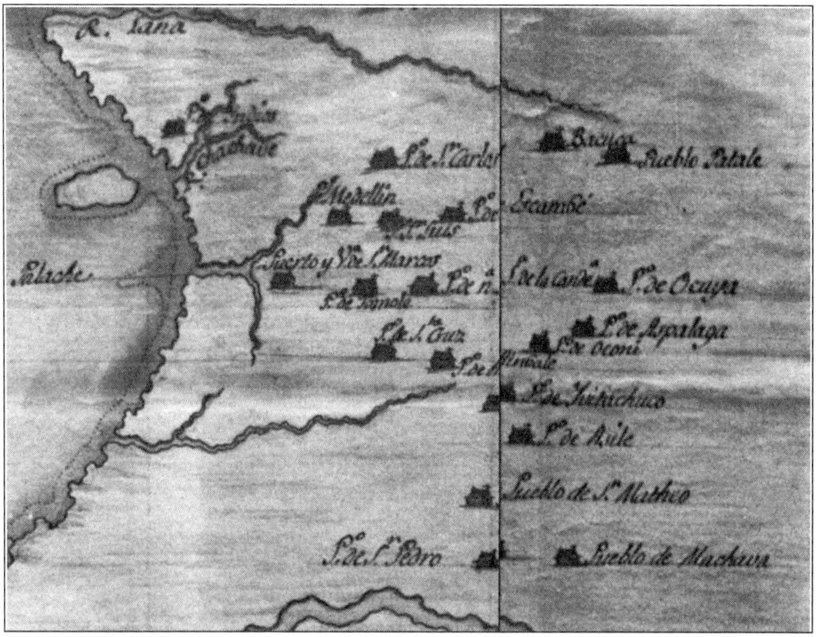

FIGURE 2. Close-up of Apalachee from 1683 map of Florida showing the location of Candelaria.[23]

giosity. Rather, missions were important hubs in their expansive networks. This is not to say that the decided spirituality of these locales was unimportant to the Yamasees. To the contrary, the Yamasees saw great advantages in moving into spiritually powerful spaces, particularly during what was an especially chaotic period for them. All the same, many of the Yamasees who moved into Spanish missions found their experiences alienating and decided to leave. That Candelaria did not completely collapse under these internal strains speaks to the importance that some Tama Yamasees placed on spiritual diplomacy with the Spanish and with the Apalachees.

In these migrations and alliances we can see a strategy developed by the Yamasees in response to the potentially shattering effects of Westo slave raids, Franciscan conversion demands, the Spanish *repartimiento* labor draft, and British trade abuses. Given these pressures, the Yamasees chose to move closer to (and away from) Indian allies and, occasionally, to the Spanish and English colonies. Through their seventeenth and eighteenth-century migrations the

23. Mapa de la Ysla de la Florida remitido el Gobernador Márquez de la Cabrera, 28 de Junio de 1683. http://rla.unc.edu/Mapfiles/CU-2/Ultramar2-048.jpg (accessed March 1, 2015). Hann attributes this map to Alonso Solana. Hann, *Apalachee,* 45–46.

Yamasees established ties—confirmed by kinship alliances—with the Guales, Mocamas, Apalachees, Timucuas, and Apalachicolas. Some Yamasees also created ties with the Spanish, confirmed by their decision to live in Franciscan mission provinces and sometimes by their decision to convert to Catholicism. Their conversions must be seen as strategic. This is not to suggest that they could not also be sincere. Still, for the majority of Yamasees, Catholicism amounted to a ritual that, although they recognized it as sacred, did not displace their own traditions or faith. Moving away from the Franciscans was always a viable option and one that the Tama Yamasees exercised. The Yamasees' readiness to migrate helps to explain both the initial establishment of Nuestra Señora de la Candelaria de la Tama in Apalachee and also the later sporadic departures of small groups and individuals from the Yamasee town that neighbored Mission San Luis.

In the first years of Candelaria's history, apparently few Tamas converted to Catholicism and perhaps they were not unduly pressured to do so by the Spanish. By practice Franciscans in La Florida tried to persuade rather than force Indians to convert, engaging in a multi-step process to attract and keep converts. Initially they focused on converting Indian caciques, other elites, and their children, hoping that the baptism and conversion of such leaders would promote the widespread conversion of the populace. Caciques were the spiritual and political leaders of their communities and an essential component of their power rested on their access to spiritually potent rituals, objects, ceremonies, and stories. Indian leaders who chose to nominally convert to Catholicism did so in order to access new sources of spiritual and political power. There is good evidence that many Indian caciques capitalized on their spiritual alliances with the Spanish to preserve or even augment the authority of their family lineages, often for generations. Only once Indians had become part of the Church did the Franciscans generally use more coercive and punitive measures to keep them in line. Prior to the time of conversion the friars often had to allow Indians to set the pace and terms of interaction.[24] This ongoing friction and violence reveal a fundamental conflict over spiritual beliefs and practices. Though the Spanish wanted and expected to progressively baptize and catechize whole towns, and indeed all of indigenous La Florida, Indians appropriated, negotiated, and rejected Catholic tenets and practices to fit their own needs, beliefs, and agendas.[25]

---

24. John E. Worth, *Timucuan Chiefdoms of Spanish Florida*, vol. 1, *Assimilation* (Gainesville: University Press of Florida, 1998), 35–43.

25. Willet A. Boyer, "Missionization, Negotiation, and Belief: The Role of the Acuera Chiefdom in Colonial Seventeenth-Century Florida," in *Indigenous Landscapes and Spanish Missions: New Perspectives from Archaeology and Ethnohistory*, eds. Lee M. Panich and Tsim D. Schneider (Tucson: The Unviersity of Arizona Press, 2014), 41–56.

The first known instance of Catholic religious activity among the Tama Yamasees was in 1675 when Bishop Gabriel Díaz Vara Calderón made an official visitation of the province and bestowed on Tama its first Catholic name: Purificación de Tama. The mission town would more commonly be called Nuestra Señora de la Candelaria de la Tama.[26] Calderón described Candelaria as one of two villages of "heathens" in Apalachee. While he noted that the Indians living in the other heathen town were "gradually being instructed and baptized," he did not say the same of Candelaria, which implies that the Tama Yamasees had accepted little religious instruction.[27] As late as 1699 the *mico* (cacique or chief) of La Tama was described as "new in the faith." The use of the Muskogean title *mico* reinforces the idea that the Tama Yamasees were slow to adopt Spanish titles and to fully embrace spiritual diplomacy with the Spanish.[28]

In the 1670s and 1680s the Spanish faced two challenges in La Florida that made them particularly eager to do what they could to encourage the new Tama Yamasees to stay in Apalachee. The first challenge was demographic. Over the preceding century the Indian mission populations across La Florida had dramatically declined as a result of emigration, disease, and direct attacks on the missions by slave raiders (and pirates). In the early seventeenth century when the first Franciscans arrived in Apalachee, the population had been approximately 30,000. By the 1670s it had declined by over 60 percent down to 11,000.[29] The second challenge was the colony of Carolina, established by the English in 1670 in the northern borderlands of La Florida as an overt challenge to Spanish sovereignty. The English quickly made their presence felt across the region, creating trade alliances with Indian communities both on the coast and inland—including the Yamasees—and developing an expansive trade in enslaved Indians that sparked a devastating series of slave raids on the Franciscan missions between the 1680s and 1710s.[30] In

26. Lucy L. Wenhold, trans. and ed., "A 17th Century Letter of Gabriel Díaz Vara Calderón, Bishop of Cuba, Describing the Indians and Indian Missions of Florida," *Smithsonian Miscellaneous Collections*, vol. 95, no. 16(1936): 9. On the movement of Tamas into Apalachee before 1675, see Hann, *Apalachee*, 35. Calderón named this new town Purificación de Tama to mark the date of the consecration, February 2, which was a Catholic holiday that celebrated the completion of the Virgin Mary's purification following the birth of Jesus. The mission, however, would more commonly be called Nuestra Señora de la Candelaria de la Tama because February 2 is also Candelaria, a celebration that marks the presentation of Jesus in the temple. Hann, *Apalachee*, 36.

27. Wenhold, "Calderón," 9.

28. Don Patricio, Cacique of Ivitachuco, and Don Andrés, Cacique of San Luis, to the King, February 12, 1699, in *Here They Once Stood: The Tragic End of the Apalachee Missions*, eds. Mark F. Boyd, Hale G. Smith, and John W. Griffin (Gainesville: University Press of Florida, 1951), 24–25.

29. Hann, *Apalachee*, 164–167.

30. Alan Gallay, *The Indian Slave Trade: The Rise of the English Empire in the American South, 1670–1717* (New Haven, Connecticut: Yale University Press, 2002); John E. Worth,

light of these twin challenges the Spanish were surprised and pleased to discover in the 1670s that the Tama Yamasees had established a town in Apalachee and they were eager to make them allies. Governor Hita Salazar described the Yamasees as a "foreign tribe" that had "planted its seat" in Apalachee. Most promisingly, he characterized the Candelaria Yamasees as "a docile people and of very good character in everything alluded to."[31]

Though the Spanish tried to incorporate the Tama Yamasees into the Apalachee mission system, they nonetheless had to recognize the sovereignty of Candelaria apart from Apalachee. In 1677 Governor Salazar sent Domingo de Leturiondo on an official visitation of Apalachee and Timucua. His tour began with a large assembly meeting of the head caciques of Apalachee. Next, in keeping with Salazar's orders, Leturiondo called together all of the "Yamasee caciques and Indians" then living "in the place of San Luis of the Provinces of Apalachee" for their own visitation.[32] Salazar recognized that, while the Yamasees lived near San Luis, they were not subjects of Apalachee. They were, however, significant enough in number and status to warrant a separate meeting. Instead of calling the Yamasees to Tomole (where the general assembly was held) or to San Luis, Leturiondo went to Candelaria. That he went there directly after the general assembly signals the importance that the Spanish saw in promoting a good initial alliance with this new group so close to San Luis. The meeting in Candelaria on December 24, 1677 was uneventful. When Leturiondo assembled "the caciques and leading men and the rest of the people" in the "principal council house" to formally ask if they had anything to report or request, or any grievances to enter they simply replied "that they had nothing to ask for or to state."[33] These were early days.

Tama Yamasees lived in the Apalachee province until 1704 but, while the Spanish tried to integrate Candelaria into their colony, for the Yamasees both in and beyond La Florida Candelaria was a node in their own network that stretched across the southeast. Yamasees moved into and out of Candelaria as it suited them. In 1675, for example, one unnamed Tama Yamasee man expressed his intentions to quit Candelaria and rejoin those Yamasees who

---

"Razing Florida: The Indian Slave Trade and the Devastation of Spanish Florida, 1659–1715," in *Mapping the Mississippian Shatter Zone: The Colonial Indian Slave Trade and Regional Instability in the American South* (Lincoln: University of Nebraska Press, 2009), 295–311.

31. Governor Hita Salazar to the Queen, August 24, 1675, in Hann, *Visitations and Revolts in Florida, 1656–1695*, 43.

32. Appointment of Domingo de Leturiondo as Visitor, November 6, 1676, in Hann, *Visitations and Revolts*, 97.

33. After Candelaria, Leturiondo visited San Luis and another ten Indian towns within the province. (Tellingly, he visited the "heathen nation" of the Tocopacas on the southern portion of the province last of all.) Visitation and Auto for Tama, December 25, 1677, in Hann, *Visitations and Revolts*, 105.

were actively involved in slave raiding against the Spanish missions. The Yamasee had been traveling to a big chunkey match at Ivitachuco with a friend from San Luis (Alonso).[34] As the two men made their way southwest along the *camino real*, they met up with an old friend of Alonso's: Atanacio from Tomole.[35] Initially Atanacio was very hospitable, offering his old friend and the Yamasee a place to rest. But as the three men began to smoke tobacco, the Yamasee "told them how he had spent some time wandering in the company of the Yamasees." For decades the Apalachees had experienced nighttime attacks by Indians whom they believed to be Chiscas living to the west. While Chiscas had led many of these attacks, the Yamasees had also begun to attack the missions in the 1670s. Atanacio's own uncle had been killed in this recent attack. When the Tama man bragged that it was the Yamasees, not the Chiscas, "who had killed the people of Machava (Machaba) and Patali (Patale)," Atanacio came to the horrifying realization that he had just shared a smoke with one of his uncle's murderers. Atanacio became enraged. While his old friend wandered off to find firewood, Atanacio killed the "heathen Indian of the Tama nation," using the Tama Yamasee's own hatchet when his back was turned. Atanacio then tried to cover up the murder by disemboweling his victim and sinking the body in a small pond nearby.

Atanacio murdered the Tama Yamasee for reasons both traditional and new. In Atanacio's matrilineal society, a nephew was expected to avenge the murder of his uncle in order to fulfill clan justice and quiet his uncle's spirit. His murder of the Yamasee was, in this sense, part of traditional Southeastern Indian blood revenge. But he claimed to have murdered the Yamasee because the man intended to deliberately reject conversion and not only forsake his own salvation but join a people who had admittedly killed and enslaved Catholic Indians.[36] When called in for questioning by the Spanish authorities,

---

34. Chunkey was a common game among Southeastern Indians, and involved throwing a spear as close as possible to a round flat chunkey stone as it moved across a field. Chunkey (*quicio*) and the ball game (*el juego de pelota*) were an opportunity for men to socialize, express their town pride, and display their martial skills. The ball game, in particular, became a source of concern for Franciscan missionaries in Apalachee in the mid-1670s who objected to the overt Indigenous spirituality and perceived physical brutality of the game. By the 1650s, friars had briefly banned the game, but in 1657 the governor forced them to relent on this prohibition. Hann, *Apalachee*, 73. When Bishop Calderón visited Apalachee in 1674, he, too, tried to ban the *pelota*, but was forced to rescind his order, in no small part because Father Juan de Paiva objected to the bishop's ban. Amy Turner Bushnell, "'That Demonic Game': The Campaign to Stop Indian Pelota Playing in Florida, 1675–1684," *The Americas* 35 (July 1978): 6–7.

35. Also called San Martín de Apalachee.

36. Auto and Atanacio's Confession, June 25 1675, in Hann, "San Pedro y San Pablo de Patale: A Seventeenth-Century Spanish Mission in Leon County, Florida," *Florida Archaeology* no. 5 (1991): 154–156.

Atanacio deliberately crafted his explanation for the crime in terms that he knew would resonate with his audience. In his confession Atanacio contended that his rage had turned murderous "because of the said Tama Indian's having said that . . . he was not going to come back among Christians because he did not wish to become one." Having experienced life with both the Catholic Indians of Apalachee and those Yamasees to the north of Apalachee who had rejected a spiritual alliance with the Spanish, the Tama had made the choice to leave Candelaria for the so-called wandering Yamasee community "because of having enjoyed a good life, he wished to go back with them." In justifying his murder of the Yamasee man, Atanacio reminded the Spanish that "heathen Indians" had long been a threat to the Spanish mission system.[37]

Since the sixteenth century the Spanish had linked settlement with conversion, believing that in order for Indians to convert they would also have to be rooted to a single place. When Governor Salazar described the Yamasees of Candelaria as "a docile people," his implicit hope was that these particular Yamasees would prove to be less wild and wandering than so many of their kin and therefore easier to convert into Spanish Catholics and subjects.[38] Indian migratory practices were the greatest impediment to Spanish expansion in the Southeast. Settling Indians within fixed towns was part of a larger project to convert Indians into tax-paying Catholics and tribute-generating farmers. And Franciscans and royal officials largely agreed on these goals: Indian sedentism was necessary for promoting Spanish colonization in the Southeast.[39]

For the Yamasees, wandering and settling down were both effective tactics: the choice of one over the other hinged on circumstances. At the same time, the ability to reach their own decisions about when to stay in place and when to move elsewhere was essential to their sovereignty. As the Spanish increasingly tried to control which Indians lived where in La Florida, the Yamasees found these aspects of their sovereignty challenged. In 1681, for instance, Yamasees south of St. Augustine at the mission of Mayaca brought a suit against their former friar who had taken the town's ornaments and bells and abandoned the mission because the caciques had permitted "the Infidels to associate with the

---

37. "Fray Miguel de Valverde and Fray Rodrigo de la Barrera, 1674," in Hann, *Visitations and Revolts*, 35.

38. Governor Hita Salazar to the Queen, August 24, 1675, in Hann, *Visitations and Revolts*, 43.

39. Amy Bushnell, "The Sacramental Imperative: Catholic Ritual and Indian Sedentism in the Provinces of Florida," in *Columbian Consequences*, vol. 2: *Archaeological and Historical Perspectives on the Spanish Borderlands East* (Washington, D.C.: Smithsonian Institution Press, 1990), ed. David Hurst Thomas, 475–490; Bushnell, "'None of these Wandering Nations Has Ever Been Reduced to the Faith': Missions and Mobility on the Spanish-American Frontier," in *The Spiritual Conversion of the Americas*, ed. James Muldoon (Gainesville: University Press of Florida, 2004), 142–167.

Christians."[40] A number of Yamasees had already left Mayaca, moving north to Yamasee mission towns on Amelia Island (San Pedro and Santa Maria) where they would be among kin. Their decision to leave Mayaca also seems to have been an overt rejection of Christianity. Defending the Mayaca's friar some years later, a fellow friar described the Yamasees of Mayaca as a people who "regularly are in the woods in order not to be forced to farm or to settle a town" and who had not accepted a missionary because of "the reluctance on the part of the natives to live like Christians."[41] For the Mayaca Yamasees, like many other Yamasees, determining who could live in their towns and where those towns were located was essential to their sovereignty.

During the 1680s the Yamasees left the Guale-Mocama missions en masse after nearly two decades of largely refusing to convert to Catholicism. There had been some small-scale emigrations prior to 1683, as some Yamasees left Guale-Mocama much as they did Apalachee in order to cultivate alliances with other Indian communities away from La Florida. During the 1670s, for instance, some Yamasees relocated to Apalachicola, another coalescent Indian community north of Apalachee that would come to be known as the Lower Creeks.[42] Then, a series of slave raids by the Westos and their allies in 1680 and a pirate attack in 1683 convinced most Yamasees in Guale-Mocama to leave La Florida.[43] Led by the *mico* Altamaha, the Yamasees from Guale-Mocama moved back to Santa Elena (renamed Port Royal by the English), where there was soon a new Scottish settlement associated with South Carolina. Altamaha's people were quickly joined there by a thousand other Yamasees from Apalachicola and other settlements, including some Yamasees from Candelaria in Apalachee.[44]

---

40. Domingo de Leturiondo, Petition on behalf of Francisco and Matheo, caciques of Mayaca, 1682 [?], Mary Ross Papers, Georgia Department of Archives and History, folder 59, item 65.

41. Report of Fray Martín Lasso, March 15, 1682, folder 59, item 65, and Fray Juan Miguel de Villaroel to the Governor, June 21, 1681, folder 59, item 65, Mary Ross Papers, Georgia Department of Archives and History. Six Yamasees had made this move to Santa Maria and San Pedro: Pacauqui (man), Micayoga (man), Tupadque (man), Hultaapale (woman), Muscha (boy), Tasigaia (man). Another two Yamasees had gone to live with the Salchiches near San Felipe in Guale: Quiypa (woman) and Saquila (boy). Governor Don Juan Márquez Cabrera to Fray Juan Miguel de Villaroel, June 22, 1681, Mary Ross Papers, folder 59, item 65.

42. Joseph Hall, "Anxious Alliances," in Alan Gallay, ed., *Indian Slavery in Colonial America* (Lincoln: University of Nebraska Press, 2009), 163.

43. The Westo-allied group attacked at least one Yamasee town on St. Simons Island: Colon, originally from Escamacu (Santa Elena). Worth, *Struggle for the Georgia Coast*, 35, 27–28.

44. They were also joined by Guale Indians who increasingly abandoned the Spanish missions. The Guales had lived in Spanish missions and had converted in large numbers since the late sixteenth century but at that point severed their ties with the Spanish and

By the 1680s and 1690s two sources of tension were evident between the Yamasees of Candelaria and the Spanish in the region: Yamasees had increasingly come under pressure to convert to Catholicism and increasingly experienced exploitation by Spanish Franciscans and laypeople. While Spanish lay and clerical officials encouraged missionaries to tread carefully when establishing a spiritual and political alliance with new Indian communities, some Franciscans used violent methods to keep converts in line once Indians had accepted a resident friar and a portion of the population had converted to Catholicism.[45] This was certainly the case in Candelaria, and the unnamed Yamasee man who was murdered along the *camino real* was not alone in deciding to rejoin the Yamasees to the north in order to escape the pressures of conversion. Reflecting on fifteen years of missionary activity among the Yamasees of Candelaria, Governor Diego de Quiroga observed that several hundred Yamasees had left Candelaria in the 1680s and 1690s because of the ineptitude and brutality of their missionaries. The first resident friar of Candelaria, Juan Ángel, was grossly negligent and many Yamasees had either lapsed into idolatry or left the mission for South Carolina as a result. There were so few converts left in Candelaria by 1688 that the Franciscan provincial was willing to send Fray Ángel to Rome, thus leaving the town for a time without a friar. The next friar, Domingo Santos, actively drove away many Yamasees because of his liberal use of whipping to keep converts in line. Together, Quiroga claimed, they were directly responsible for the departure of several hundred Yamasees from Candelaria.[46]

Despite Quiroga's attempt to lay all of the blame at the friars' feet, in fact Indians across Apalachee had levied serious charges of abuse against not just Franciscans but also Spanish officials for some time. Quiroga's precedessor, Juan Márquez Cabrera, appointed and protected a lieutenant governor of Apalachee who was particularly abusive in the 1680s, and frequently physically and verbally accosted Apalachee caciques, leaders, and common people.[47] During the last several decades of the seventeenth century, Franciscan friars, royal officials, and Spanish ranchers increasingly fought over Indian souls and labor in Apalachee

---

established the upper towns in the Yamasee community. Green, DePratter, and Southerlin, "The Yamasee in South Carolina," in J. W. Joseph and Martha Zierden, eds., *Another's Country: Archaeological and Historical Perspectives on Cultural Interactions in the Southern Colonies* (Tuscaloosa: University of Alabama Press, 2002), 17.

45. Bushnell, "The Sacramental Imperative," 485.

46. John Tate Lanning, *The Spanish Missions of Georgia* (Chapel Hill: University of North Carolina Press, 1935), 195–199; Maynard Geiger, *Biographical Dictionary of the Franciscans in Spanish Florida and Cuba, 1528–1841* (Paterson, NJ: St. Anthony Guild Press, 1940), 25, 106. It should be noted that these accusations were part of a larger political power struggle between the governor and Franciscan officials.

47. See, for example, Testimony by Don Matheo Chuba, May 29, 1687, "Matheos Documents, Phases I and II," John H. Hann Collection, University of Florida.

as the two other major mission provinces (Timucua and Guale-Mocama) also experienced dramatic population collapses.[48] The Spanish relied on Indian labor to support their households, churches, ranches, and a growing export economy out of San Marcos. In 1694 the cacique of Candelaria registered two formal complaints during the official visitation of the region. Both complaints indicate that Spanish ranchers were exploiting Yamasee women. As the cacique reported to the governor's visitor, Joaquín de Florencia, three Yamasee women had been kidnapped from Candelaria by a Spanish rancher, Marcos Delgado, who refused to return them claiming that "he has permission from the señor visitor to have them."[49] Another Spanish rancher (Diego Jiménez) refused to pay a Candelaria woman, Chugutta Francisca, for the domestic work she performed on his hacienda. In both cases the Spaniards were not only ranchers but also military men who drew on their political power to exploit Yamasee women; Delgado had led a Spanish military expedition in 1683 and Jiménez was the adjutant. The Candelaria cacique noted that two of the three Yamasee women whom Delgado had kidnapped were "young," suggesting that Indian women were also being sexually exploited.[50] Joaquín de Florencia tried to address Yamasee (and Apalachee) complaints, issuing an order that only Indian women accompanied by their husbands could be employed on Spanish ranches.

But the abuses continued. In 1699 the principal cacique of Apalachee town and the cacique of San Luis wrote to the King to complain about conditions at San Luis. Members of the former deputy governor's family, the Florencias, were once again causing trouble. Their cattle damaged San Luis's cornfields, they disrespected caciques, and forced Indian women to work without payment. But the problems did not end there. Spaniards had forcibly occupied several Indian homes, driving many Indians from San Luis to the "woods" or to the Province of Guale. One of the major complaints was that the Florencias had "compelled the *mico* of la Tama . . . who is skilled in tan-

---

48. For example, in 1681 Governor Márquez de Cabrera wrote to Juan Florencia to ensure that the Indians of Apalachee focused on growing and harvesting "the King's" corn and beans rather than hunting or fishing or working for anyone else, and mandated that Florencia read these orders "[i]f any priest tries to meddle in this." Governor Márquez de Cabrera to Captain Juan Fernández de Florencia, January 20, 1681, Mary Ross Papers, folder 56, item 50.

49. Visitation of Our Lady of Candelaria, December 7, 1694, in Hann, *Visitations and Revolts*, 176. Delgado's ranch, Our Lady of the Rosary, was to the east of Candelaria between Patale and Bacuqua. Hann, *Apalachee*, 60. Delgado was not only a rancher but also a soldier in the presidio, and had led a Spanish expedition to gather information about French incursions in Mobile Bay. Mark F. Boyd, trans., "The Expedition of Marcos Delgado from Apalachee to the Upper Creek Country in 1686," *The Florida Historical Quarterly* 16 (July 1937): 2. Also see Hall, *Zamumo's Gifts*, 89–94.

50. Visitation of Our Lady of Candelaria, December 7, 1694, in Hann, *Visitations and Revolts*, 176.

ning, to prepare skins for them without pay for his work." As a result, the Tama mico "went to the place of Saint George" (Charleston) and the caciques of Apalachee town and San Luis expressed their "fear" that "others may follow him."[51] Fleeing abusive Franciscan missionaries, exploitative Spanish ranchers, and the Florencias, hundreds of Tama Yamasees left Candelaria to rejoin their Yamasee kin in South Carolina.[52]

While the population of Candelaria dwindled because of Spanish conversion demands and exploitative labor practices, the missions of Apalachee also suffered intensified slave raids. Between 1703 and 1704 a combined series of attacks by the British and Southeastern Indians, including some Apalachees and Yamasees, resulted in the destruction of many Apalachee towns and the virtual abandonment of the province. The Yamasees of Candelaria seem to have escaped enslavement, likely moving to Savanno Town in South Carolina and perhaps then joining the Yamasees in Port Royal. Select Yamasees and Creeks continued to raid Indian communities in La Florida into the 1710s, expanding their targets to include Indians who were not living in missions like the Calusas.[53] These attacks resulted in a massive depopulation of Florida Indian mission and non-mission communities.

As they migrated to Port Royal, Yamasees who had engaged in spiritual diplomacy with the Franciscans now tried to apply their practices to their new encounters with the English. The most detailed example of this is provided by the narrative of a Yamasee "Prince" whose name is lost to us. Born in 1696 in a Spanish mission community in the Guale-Mocama province, the Prince was the son (or nephew) of the cacique of the Yoas, a community that may have originated in the same Oconee-Ocmulgee region as Tama or in Guale, and that had embraced spiritual diplomacy earlier and more fully than the Tamas.[54] Because of his elite status, the Prince was undoubtedly baptized as

51. Don Patricio, Cacique of Ivitachuco, and Don Andrés, Cacique of San Luis, to the King, February 12, 1699, in *Here They Once Stood: The Tragic End of the Apalachee Missions*, eds. Mark F. Boyd, Hale G. Smith, and John W. Griffin (Gainesville: University Press of Florida, 1951), 24–25.

52. Spanish exploitation of Indian labor was well known throughout the region, and the Spanish had to promise the Apalachicolas that they would not suffer from the same exploitation if they admitted Franciscan missionaries. Report of Fray Rodrigo de la Barrera, December 8, 1681, Mary Ross Papers, folder 59, item 65.

53. By 1710 the Yamasees were raiding into Calusa territory, prompting the Calusas to reach out to the Spanish for assistance. A significant number of Calusas, 270 in all, fled to Cuba in 1711. Hann, *Missions to the Calusa*, 325–327.

54. Letter from Gonzalo Méndez de Canzo, February 23, 1598, in Francis and Kole, eds., *Murder and Martyrdom*, 98; "Relacion del Viage que Hizo el Senor Pedro de Ibarra, Gobernadors y Capitan General de Florida, a Visitar los Pueblos Indios de las Provincias de San Pedro y Guale, Noviembre y Diciembre de 1604," in Manuel Serrano y Sanz, ed., *Documentos Históricos de la Florida y la Luisiana, siglos XVI al XVIII* (Madrid: Biblioteca de los Americanistas, 1912), 187.

a young child and educated in a Spanish school before his community was forced to flee in 1702 as an invading force of English, Yamasee, and Lower Creeks destroyed their mission on Amelia Island.[55] The Yoas made their way to South Carolina just a bit before the Tamas of Candelaria, where they joined the growing Yamasee confederacy near Port Royal.

Though welcomed by their kin, the Yoas—or Euhaws, as the English called them—nonetheless had to negotiate their position in the Yamasee geopolitical world. To do so, the Yoas drew on the spiritual diplomacy that their chiefly lineage had practiced with the Spanish for over a hundred years in La Florida. The British missionary society active in South Carolina, the Society for the Propagation of the Gospel (SPG), had tried with little success to persuade Indians to convert to Anglicanism ever since first sending missionaries to the colony in 1702. The SPG's underlying hope was that the Yamasees' prior exposure to Roman Catholicism might render them more receptive to Anglicanism and better prepared to understand it. British colonial trader Thomas Nairne remarked that "it [is] easier for us to undertake propagating the Christian faith among them, than tis for the Northern Colonies besides that their Language is micht with abundance of Spannish words perticularly those pertaining to Religion."[56]

In 1713 the Prince's father, clan, and the *mico* of Altamaha agreed to send the Prince to England where he would be instructed by Anglican schoolteachers and tutors. By traveling to London the Prince would have direct access to the epicenter of British political and spiritual power, a claim that no other Yamasee or Southeastern Indian could make. He would also gain skills that were vital to his future career in Yamasee politics, including sacred Anglican rituals and stories, and fluency in English language, culture, and mathematics. This daring voyage could elevate the position of Euhaw within the Yamasee confederacy and the regional power of the Yamasees more generally. After twenty-one months in England, the Prince was baptized in the Royal Chapel at Somerset House and presented to King George I.[57]

But in most other ways the Prince's trip was an abject failure. While the Prince had proven a promising student, the Yamasees and the SPG had divergent and mutually exclusive objectives. The SPG wanted to transform the

55. Jerald Milanich, "Gone but Never Forgotten: Mission Santa Catalina on Amelia Island and the 1702 Raid," *El Escribano* 39 (2002): 1–15. For the several hundred Yamasee participants, see Steven J. Oatis, *A Colonial Complex: South Carolina's Frontiers in the Era of the Yamasee War, 1680–1730* (Lincoln: University of Nebraska Press, 2004), 47–48.

56. Thomas Nairne to Doctor Marston, St. Helena, August 20, 1705, SPG Papers in Lambeth Palace Library, England, 17:89–90.

57. This section on the Yamasee Prince is drawn from my article on his voyage. Bossy, "Spiritual Diplomacy, the Yamasees, and the Society for the Propagation of the Gospel: Reinterpreting Prince George's Eighteenth-Century Voyage to England," *Early American Studies* 12 (Spring 2014): 366–401.

young man into a missionary who would promote the submission of the Yamasees to the British empire. In keeping with this goal, they repeatedly impeded his efforts to engage in spiritual diplomacy. Instead of looking upon him as a foreign diplomat, they treated the eighteen-year-old as a child who should conform to the demands of a culturally foreign educational system. The voyage was a failure on a larger geopolitical scale, too. By the time the Prince finally returned to South Carolina in September 1715, his family had been forced to flee the colony and had decided to move near St. Augustine.

Five months earlier, in April, a large-scale pan-Indian war against South Carolina had started in the Yamasee town of Pocotaligo. Many Yamasees had suffered a litany of abuses at the hands of the British. British traders enslaved Yamasee family members, stole Yamasee lands and property, and abused Yamasee women and even political leaders. Faced with mounting debts and increasing colonial violence, a council of Yamasees and Lower Creeks decided that the best course of action was war against the British colony of South Carolina. They would soon be joined by many other Southeastern Indian communities who shared their concerns and grievances.[58] Hoping to keep the peace with the South Carolinians, the Prince's father had resisted joining in this retributive war against colonists who increasingly enslaved and exploited Southeastern Indians. When he learned of his son's return, the Euhaw *mico* looked for a way to get back to Charleston without being killed and made the decision to move his community from their sanctuary in St. Augustine northwards to "an Island between Port Royal and St Augustines" in the hope of reuniting with his son. But in the spring the *mico* and his family were captured by British colonists and sold into slavery, sharing the same fate as tens of thousands of other Southeastern Indians before and during the Yamasee War.[59]

As the Euhaws, Tamas, and other Yamasees evacuated from South Carolina they relied on their networks to find safety in the midst of violence. Some of the Tama Yamasees returned to La Florida where the Spanish were once again eager for an alliance. The Franciscan mission system had all but collapsed across La Florida under the weight of slave raids, disease, and emigration.[60] In 1717 the Spanish happily noted that the Yamasees had three new settlements in St. Augustine, now the only area of significant missionary activity. Among them was Our Lady of Candelaria de la Tamaja, a community of

---

58. For the most comprehensive study of the Yamasee War, see William L. Ramsey, *The Yamasee War: A Study of Culture, Economy, and Conflict in the Colonial South* (Lincoln: University of Nebraska Press, 2008).

59. Francis le Jau to Secretary, March 19, 1716, Letterbook B4, #58, United Society for the Propagation of the Gospel (USPG) Archives, Rhodes House, Oxford University, England; Johnston to Secretary, April 4, 1716, Letterbook B4, #62, UPSG Archives.

60. John H. Hann, "St. Augustine's Fallout from the Yamasee War," *The Florida Historical Quarterly* 68 (October 1989): 182.

163 Yamasees whose principal cacique, Don Antonio de Ayala, and the majority of the population was Tama (55%). Attached to the Tama community were two other Yamasee communities with their own caciques who were subordinate to Don Ayala. This Candelaria II, as I refer to it, also had one of the only two garrisoned forts among the ten Indian towns in 1717, a clear sign of the town's importance to the Spanish and the vulnerability of the Yamasees who were now the targets of attacks from the British and some Creek Indians in part because of their renewed alliance with the Spanish.

Missionary records demonstrate that the Tamas in Candelaria II had the highest rate of conversion to Catholicism among the Yamasees of St. Augustine in the first years of their settlement. In his 1728 report Fray Joseph de Bullones (the Franciscan provincial) gave a brief history of the Tama who did return to St. Augustine: "Thama was a village of heathen Indians who came from San Jorge, after being with the English." Bullones reported that "through the mediation of the will of God and the zeal of the ministers they reduced and converted the cacique, and many others were baptized following his example."[61] Or perhaps we should frame this as a *re*-conversion. Given both this high rate of conversion and the recycling of the name Candelaria, it is likely that some (if not all) of the Tama Yamasees who lived in Candelaria II had also lived in the earlier Candelaria in the Apalachee province. Although there had been pressure to accept Catholic baptism in Apalachee, there the Tama Yamasees had been a fairly small community in Spanish eyes. Now, they became the focus of Franciscans who were clinging to the last vestiges of the mission system. Moreover the Tama Yamasees needed to make a strong show of their allegiance to the Spanish, having been allied with the British over the previously thirty years and having engaged in a number of slave raids and attacks against Indian missions and even St. Augustine itself.

Candelaria II had a church "of palm" where Fray Marcos de Ita Salazar celebrated mass and "where the Christian doctrine was taught."[62] In 1717 only 18 percent of the Yamasees in the three mission towns near St. Augustine were Christian, but at Candelaria II, 36.7 percent of the Tamas (thirty-three of ninety people) were Christian. This included Don Ayala, five of his eight leading men (62.5%), ten of his twenty warriors (50%), nine of the twenty-five women (36%), three of the eighteen boys (16.7%), and five of the eighteen girls (27.8%). In contrast, in the two communities attached to Candelaria only one of the sixty Yamasees under cacique Tospe (Huspah) were counted as Christian and it seems Tospe himself had not yet converted, and while cacique Ocute was Christian only one of his twelve people had converted (a man). The

61. Fray Joseph de Bullones to the King, October 5, 1728, in *Missions to the Calusa* (Gainesville: University Press of Florida, 1991), ed. and trans. John H. Hann, 376–377.

62. Ibid.

conversion rate at Candelaria II continued to be high: another eighty-two adults and twenty-three children were baptized between 1718 and 1723.[63] In 1725 the mission town was attacked by "the Uchise Indians" (Lower Creeks Indians) during mass. The priest fled, taking the church chalice with him, and many of the Tama Yamasees were killed or taken captive. The survivors moved near the presidio and briefly settled on the site of old Tolomato, but they then relocated to the prior site of Mose with the Apalachees. The population dwindled so that by 1728 there were only six Indians left at Mose.[64]

It is worth noting that less than half of the Yamasees went to La Florida after the Yamasee War. A significant number went instead with the Lower Creeks to the Chattahoochee River.[65] Among them was at least one band of Tama Yamasees. As Diego Peña traveled through Lower Creek towns in 1717 he came to a "little place" governed by a "Christian Indian called Augustín, from Apalache, belonging to the Tama nation."[66] Despite identifying himself through name and spiritual affiliation with the Spanish, mico Augustín had made the decision not the return to La Florida. Perhaps he realized all too well what Spanish alliance would cost in this new era.

The Yamasees were a young coalescent community in the 1670s with a remarkable—though not unique—practice of maintaining separate settlements in different locations simultaneously across the Southeast. The experiences of the Tama Yamasees, in particular, reveal how many Yamasees got through the seventeenth and eighteenth centuries by means of selective and strategic migrations and alliances with Indians and Europeans. More specifically their experiences disclose how spiritual diplomacy and geopolitics operated at a local level. As they purposefully moved across the Southeast, the Yamasees lived near and sometimes within Indian and European communities to foster their political networks. Even as the majority of the Yamasees rejected Franciscan missionaries, there was a distinct community of Tama Yamasees who lived near the Spanish and actively engaged with Catholicism. While some of the people of Candelaria pursued spiritual diplomacy through conversion to Catholicism, individuals (or perhaps clans?) made their own choices about conversion. The Yamasee network provided options to those who wanted to leave Candelaria. Through their seventeenth- and eighteenth-century migrations and their selective engagement in spiritual diplomacy with the Spanish the Yamasees of Candelaria fostered their connections while creating new links with Europeans and gaining new access to spiritual knowledge and cultural skills.

---

63. Hann, "St. Augustine's Fallout," 192.

64. Ibid., 193.

65. Ramsey, *The Yamasee War*, 117-8.

66. Diego Peña, Diary of a trip that he made to Apalachicola, Sabacola, September 20, 1717, "Spanish Contact with Florida's Neighboring Indians, 1717–1718," Hann Collection, 28.

Chapter 13
At the Mouth of the Wolf: The Archaeology of Seventeenth-Century Franciscans in the Jemez Valley of New Mexico

Matthew Liebmann

On March 19, 1696, Fray Francisco de Jesús María Casañas wrote with a quivering hand to his superior in Santa Fe. Stationed at a remote Pueblo Indian mission village the Spaniards called San Diego del Monte y Nuestra Señora de Remedios, Fray Francisco had heard the rumblings of rebellion. Talk of Native insurgency was burning through the Pueblos of northern New Mexico, and in those early spring days the friar noted that recently "from what the wind brings it appears to be burning even hotter." He had already appealed for military reinforcements from the governor of New Mexico, Don Diego de Vargas. But Vargas rebuffed Fray Francisco's request for additional soldiers, claiming that he "did not have enough bread for that big a wedding" (*No tenía tanta pan por tanta boda*). Frustrated but stoic, Fray Francisco accepted his fate. He wrote to his *custodio* that he did not wish to suffer the same demise as the twenty-one Franciscan brethren famously martyred en masse in the Pueblo Revolt of 1680. "To place myself at the mouth of the wolf, so that he may swallow me and drink my blood, my mother did not bear me . . . for that purpose. For I did not come to seek death but rather the lives" of Native American converts, wrote Fray Francisco. Yet if his congregants presented him with "the prize" of martyrdom, the friar stood ready to receive their gift. "If they do not revolt today," he predicted, "they will tomorrow."[1]

Unfortunately for Fray Francisco, tomorrow arrived in the early Monday morning hours of June 4, 1696, when the Jemez residents of San Diego del Monte joined forces with their Tewa, Keres, northern Tiwa, and Tano neigh-

1. J. Manuel Espinosa, ed. *The Pueblo Revolt of 1696 and the Franciscan Missions in New Mexico: Letters of the Missionaries and Related Documents* (Chicago: Institute of Jesuit History, 1988), 200, 299.

bors in the lesser-known "Second Pueblo Revolt" of 1696. Like they had sixteen years earlier, the Puebloans rose up against the Spaniards in their midst, killing five Franciscan priests and twenty-one colonial settlers throughout New Mexico. At San Diego del Monte the Jemez residents lured Fray Francisco from his mission church under the pretense that a sick woman needed him to hear her confession. Once outside the chapel door, two warriors clubbed the friar to death, leaving his corpse to rot at the foot of a cross Fray Francisco had erected in the cemetery.[2] Following the disposition of the friar's body, the people of San Diego del Monte ripped the mission bell from its moorings, smashed statues of the saints, and shattered crosses in harmony with their Pueblo brothers-in-arms at other missions throughout northern New Mexico.[3]

Just one year earlier Fray Francisco had overseen construction of the mission church at San Diego del Monte. He designed a modest, one-room structure that blended almost seamlessly with the adjacent Pueblo architecture. About the same size as a large Pueblo kiva (the traditional ritual chamber favored by the Jemez and other Puebloans), the humble structure huddled in the corner of the village, wedged between the apartment-style rooms. In this way, the San Diego del Monte mission contrasted starkly with its precursor, San José de los Jemez, a giant fortress of a church that stood thirteen kilometers (eight miles) to the north at the ancestral Jemez village of Giusewa. Built seventy-five years earlier during one of the initial large-scale campaigns to convert the Pueblo peoples to Christianity, San José loomed over the surrounding landscape, a monument to the power and authority of the Spaniards' god.[4]

With stone walls tall enough to grasp the sky, San José de los Jemez evoked permanence and stability. Its cavernous nave held hundreds of proselytes in rapt attention, and a fifteen-meter (fifty foot) tall octagonal belfry ensured that its clanging mission bells would be heard far and wide. San José was an architectural marvel, built to awe and inspire. Constructed in 1621 at the behest of an enterprising friar named Fray Gerónimo de Zárate Salmerón, the mission church was praised as "*un templo grandioso*" by the custodial head

2. Espinosa, *The Pueblo Revolt of 1696*, 250. John L. Kessell, Rick Hendricks, and Meredith Dodge, eds. *Blood on the Boulders: The Journals of Don Diego de Vargas, New Mexico 1694–1697*, 2 vols. (Albuquerque: University of New Mexico Press, 1998), 750.

3. Matthew J. Liebmann, *Revolt: An Archaeological History of Pueblo Resistance and Revitalization in 17th Century New Mexico* (Tucson: University of Arizona Press, 2012), 216–219.

4. Robin E. Farwell, "An Architectural History of San Jose de Giusewa, Jemez National Monument, New Mexico" (MA thesis, University of New Mexico, 1991); James E. Ivey, *Una Muy Suntuosa y Curiosa Yglesia: A Structural Assessment of the Mission Church of San Jose de Giusewa, Jemez State Monument, New Mexico*, 1991, Manuscript on File, National Park Service, Southwest Regional Office, Santa Fe; George Kubler, *The Religious Architecture of New Mexico in the Colonial Period and Since the American Occupation* (Albuquerque: University of New Mexico Press, 1940), 82–84.

of the Franciscans in New Mexico.[5,6] San José's architectural grandeur was no accident. Fray Zárate Salmerón had cut his architectural teeth overseeing the construction of causeways in Mexico City, and the engineering skills he learned on the shores of Lake Texcoco served him well when he traveled north to New Mexico.[7]

Considering the fact that both of these churches were constructed under similar circumstances, among the same ethnic group, separated by less than eight decades and eight miles, it is hard to imagine two seventeenth-century Spanish colonial churches more dissimilar in appearance. The pueblo of the latter housed the children of those who constructed the former. In each case just one solitary Franciscan priest oversaw the design of the building, with construction performed by the native Jemez residents of the two villages. But San José de los Jemez and San Diego del Monte differ radically in terms of scale, plan, architectural elaboration, and placement in the landscape. The seminal event separating the construction of these two churches was the Pueblo Revolt of 1680, when the Native peoples of New Mexico banded together to expel their Spanish colonizers in the most renowned Indigenous uprising in the history of the American Southwest.[8] The Revolt of 1680 forced the Franciscans to radically revise their evangelical policies and strategies among the Pueblos, changes that are reflected in the architectural differences between these two missions. Ultimately, the Franciscan churches of the Jemez Valley exemplify larger patterns of Spanish–Pueblo relations in seventeenth-century New Mexico. They represent not merely a pair of isolated, centuries-old archaeological ruins, but open a window into the tenuous and shifting world of Puebloans and Franciscans at the edge of the Spanish American empire in the 1600s.

Franciscan Missions in the Jemez Valley

For the Spanish colonizers of New Mexico, the Pueblo villages along the northern Rio Grande and its tributaries were a land of margins and peripheries.[9] As one disconsolate colonial governor put it, this territory was "at the ends of

---

5. Frederick Webb Hodge, *Fray Alonso de Benavides' Revised Memorial of 1634*, eds. George P. Hammond and Agapito Rey (Albuquerque: University of New Mexico Press, 1945), 69.

6. France V. Scholes, "Notes on the Jemez Missions in the Seventeenth Century," *El Palacio* 44 (1938): 67–68.

7. Farwell, "An Architectural History of San Jose de Giusewa," 26.

8. Liebmann, *Revolt.*

9. Mark T. Lycett, "On the Margins of Peripheries: The Consequences of Differential Incorporation in the Colonial Southwest," in *The Postclassic to Spanish-Era Transition in Mesoamerica*, eds. S. Kepecs and R. T. Alexander (Albuquerque: University of New Mexico Press, 2005).

the earth and remote beyond compare."[10] To the Spaniards, the Pueblos of New Mexico were perched on the periphery three times over: in relation to Iberia, the entire colonial project in the Americas was peripheral; as the northernmost outpost of New Spain, La Nueva Mexico was peripheral to its namesake city 1000 miles to the south; and as the villages defining the outer boundaries of this region, the Pueblos were peripheral to the Spanish capital of Santa Fe. Nearly a century ago, historian Herbert Eugene Bolton labeled this region "the Spanish borderlands" (as an antidote to Frederick Jackson Turner's American *frontier*).[11] But seventeenth-century New Mexicans did not etch their borders clearly in the sand. Rather, these were largely *borderless* lands, an area characterized by shifting alliances, miscegenation, and contested occupation.[12] In an attempt to impose order upon this seeming chaos, the Spaniards quickly dubbed the sedentary maize farmers of the northern Rio Grande "Pueblo Indians" (*indios de pueblos*) to distinguish their civilized nature from that of the "savage" *indios bárbaros* who roamed the outskirts of the region, the ancestors of modern-day Diné (Navajo), Apache, and Ute peoples.

On the eve of their discovery of Europeans, Pueblo peoples lived in an estimated seventy-five to one hundred different villages located throughout modern-day New Mexico and northeastern Arizona.[13] These settlements generally consisted of multistoried masonry or adobe dwellings bordering on central plazas, varying in size from just a few rooms to numbers in the thousands, with multiple plazas and kivas.[14] The peoples shared broad similarities in material culture, subsistence strategies, religious practices, and political organization, yet the Pueblos differed in significant ways as well. At the time of first contact with Europeans, they spoke seven separate mutually unintelligible languages, each with multiple dialects. As a result, the Pueblos of the northern

---

10. John L. Kessell, *Remote Beyond Compare: Letters of Don Diego de Vargas to His Family from New Spain and New Mexico, 1675–1706* (Albuquerque: University of New Mexico Press, 1989), 168.

11. Herbert E. Bolton, *The Spanish Borderlands: A Chronicle of Old Florida and the Southwest* (New Haven, Connecticut: Yale University Press, 1921).

12. Jeremy Adelman and Stephen Aron, "From Borderlands to Borders: Empires, Nation-States, and the Peoples in Between in North American History," in *American Historical Review* 104 (1999): 814–841.

13. Albert H. Schroeder, "Pueblos Abandoned in Historic Times," in *Handbook of North American Indians*, vol. 9, ed. A. Ortiz (Washington, D.C.: Smithsonian Institution, 1979), 236–254: Boyd Pratt and David Snow, *The North Central Regional Overview: Strategies for the Comprehensive Survey of the Architectural and Historic Archaeological Resources of North Central New Mexico, Vol. 1: Historic Overview of North Central New Mexico* (Santa Fe: New Mexico State Historic Preservation Division, 1988).

14. Jonathan Haas and Winnifred Creamer, "Demography of the Protohistoric Pueblos of the Northern Rio Grande, A.D. 1450–1680," in *Current Research of the Late Prehistory and Early History of New Mexico*, Vol. 1 of Special Publication, ed. B. J. Vierra (Albuquerque: New Mexico Archaeological Council, 1992), 21–27.

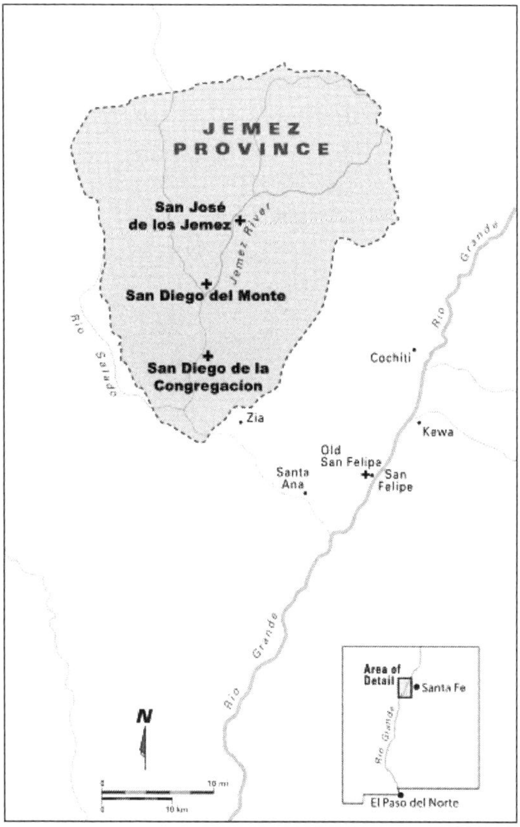

FIGURE 1. Seventeenth-century Franciscan missions of ancestral Jemez Province, New Mexico.

Rio Grande did not think of themselves as a unitary ethnic group prior to Spanish colonization. Rather, the sedentary villages of sixteenth-century maize farmers were dispersed across the region into a series of scattered settlement clusters, each with broadly defined, separate ethnolinguistic identities.[15]

One of those settlement clusters gathered together the Towa-speaking people west of the Rio Grande, an ethnic group that self-identified as *Hemish*, later transliterated as "Jemez" by the Spaniards (see Figure 1). The Jemez people lived in ten (or more) large villages in and around the Jemez Valley, a

15. E. Charles Adams and Andrew I. Duff, ed., *The Protohistoric Pueblo World, A.D. 1275–1600* (Tucson: University of Arizona Press, 2004); James E. Snead, Winifred Creamer, and Tineke Van Zandt, "Ruins of Our Forefathers: Large Sites and Site Clusters in the Northern Rio Grande," in *The Protohistoric Pueblo World, 1275–1600*, ed. E. C. Adams and A. I. Duff (Tucson: University of Arizona Press, 2004), 26–34.

steep canyon that cuts a swath through the northern New Mexico mountains seventy-five kilometers (about forty-five miles) west of Santa Fe.[16] For more than two and a half centuries prior to the Spaniards' arrival, the Jemez farmed the flat mesa tops and hunted in the shadows of the valley's deep canyons. Sometime in the late 1400s, a group of Jemez people founded a village in the valley bottom, nestled into a hillside adjacent to a series of hot springs. They called their village Giusewa, meaning "pueblo at the hot place."[17]

The Jemez first encountered Europeans in 1541, but witnessed the foreigners only sporadically for the next six decades. Not until 1598 did the Spaniards establish a permanent presence in the region. That year Don Juan de Oñate led a colonizing expedition of 570 settlers up the Rio Grande, seeking untold riches.[18] The Crown's "Royal Orders for New Discoveries" left no doubt that Oñate's primary responsibility, if not his principal ambition, was the salvation of Indigenous souls. As such, he brought along eight priests and two lay brothers to minister to his new Native subjects.[19] Among this number was Fray Alonso de Lugo, a priest assigned to the remote Jemez Province. Fray De Lugo chose Giusewa as the base for his missionary activities, and there he and his *donado* oversaw the construction of a small temporary mission in September of 1598. This first church in the Jemez Province was a decidedly modest structure, reflecting the priorities of the colony at the time. It featured a simple rectangular nave about five meters (sixteen feet) long and four and a half (fourteen feet) meters wide. (Similarly humble mission structures arose at Awatovi, Pecos, and Quarai during the initial phase of Franciscan settlement at those pueblos as well.) Apparently Fray De Lugo's efforts among the Jemez were less-than-well received, however, and he left New Mexico in 1601.[20]

---

16. Jeremy Kulisheck, "Settlement Patterns, Population, and Congregacion on the 17th Century Jemez Plateau," in *Following Through: Papers in Honor of Phyllis S. Davis*, vol. 27, eds. R. N. Wiseman, T. C. O'Laughlin, and C. T. Snow (Archaeological Society of New Mexico, 2001), 83; Matthew Liebmann, "Burn the Churches, Break Up the Bells: The Archaeology of the Pueblo Revolt Revitalization Movement in New Mexico, A.D. 1680–1696" (Ph.D. diss., University of Pennsylvania, 2006), 144.

17. John P. Harrington, "The Ethnogeography of the Tewa Indians," in *Twenty-ninth Annual Report of the Bureau of American Ethnology for the years 1907–1908* (Washington, D.C.: Government Printing Office, 1916), 393.

18. Carroll L. Riley, *The Kachina and the Cross: Indians and Spaniards in the Early Southwest* (Salt Lake City: University of Utah Press, 1999), 44.

19. Marc Simmons, "History of Pueblo–Spanish Relations to 1821," in *Handbook of North American Indians: Southwest*, vol. 9, ed. A. Ortiz (Washington, D.C.: Smithsonian Institution, 1979), 181; Jim Norris, *After "The Year Eighty": The Demise of Franciscan Power in Spanish New Mexico* (Albuquerque: University of New Mexico Press, 2000), 8; David J. Weber, "Pueblos, Spaniards, and History," in *What Caused the Pueblo Revolt of 1680?*, ed. J. W. David (Boston: Bedford/St. Martins, 1999), 4.

20. Scholes, "Notes on the Jemez Missions in the Seventeenth Century": 62; Ivey, *"Una Muy Suntuosa y Curiosa Yglesia."*

By 1605 it became abundantly clear to both the governor and his superiors that the Kingdom of New Mexico did not contain the riches for which Oñate yearned. The viceroy recommended that the Spaniards withdraw from New Mexico completely. Its isolation and distance from Mexico City made the colony too difficult to sustain. The Franciscans protested. What the territory lacked in mineral wealth, they argued, it made up for in souls. How could the Crown turn its back on its newest citizens? The friars claimed to have baptized over seven thousand Indians already, and now the Crown had a moral responsibility to minister to these new converts. They appealed to the King to fund the colony out of the royal coffers. Accordingly, in 1609 King Phillip III transformed New Mexico from a proprietary venture into a royal colony whose primary role both in word and deed was to proselytize to the Native peoples. The missionary effort in New Mexico exploded. Over the next two decades, more than thirty new missions sprouted in Pueblo villages across the colony.

Una Muy Suntuosa y Curiosa Yglesia: San José de los Jemez

The New Mexican churches raised between 1610 and 1640 tended to be far grander affairs than the simple chapels founded under the Oñate regime. Many of them still stand nearly four centuries later at places like Abó, Quarai, and Acoma—a testament not only to the friars' architectural design skills, but to the thousands of hours of labor invested by Pueblo hands. At Giusewa, Fray Zárate Salmerón re-established the mission, vacant since De Lugo's departure twenty years prior.[21] Dubbed San José de los Jemez, Zárate Salmerón's church was more grandiose than any other erected in the Jemez Valley, before or since (see Figure 2).

The Mexican-born friar-engineer employed a standard unit of measurement throughout the construction of San José (a *vara* of eighty-four centimeters/thirty-three inches), belying the careful plans he drafted beforehand. Its footprint was huge, enclosing an interior space of 335 square meters. The exterior walls stretched to a height of nearly twelve meters (thirty-nine feet). Without the use of supporting arches, their loftiness required a thickness of two meters (six feet) or more. With its colossal walls and rooftop parapets, San José de los Jemez looked as much like a fortress as it did a church. Pueblo builders quarried the stone from a nearby limestone outcrop, breaking off pieces with stone tools and wedges. This ledge stone technique allowed them to use harder

21. Ivey, "*Una Muy Suntuosa y Curiosa Yglesia*," 13–14; Michael L. Elliott, *Pueblo at the Hot Place: Archaeological Excavations at Giusewa Pueblo and San Jose de los Jemez Mission, Jemez State Monument, Jemez Springs, New Mexico* (Sante Fe: New Mexico State Monuments, 1991), 8.

FIGURE 2. Early twentieth-century photo of San José de los Jemez at Giusewa.

limestone masonry rather than the softer volcanic tuff blocks employed by the Jemez to build their homes at Giusewa.[22] From the back of the church the massive, three-story octagonal bell tower stood sentinel over the mission, rising to a height of fifteen meters (fifty feet) above the church floor.

Fray Zárate Salmerón selected the location of his new church carefully. He placed the mission on high ground, looking down into the plazas of the nearby Pueblo village. But because the site did not harbor a flat area large enough to accommodate his planned structure, its Jemez builders were forced to gauge a notch out of the hillside, making room for the head of the church by carving into the bedrock. Like the mission churches built at the pueblos of Pecos, Abó, Quarai, Gran Quivira, Acoma, Hawikuh, and Awatovi during this period, the church at Giusewa was built to astound and to dominate the local landscape.[23]

22. Gloria Fraser Giffords, *Sanctuaries of Earth, Stone, and Light: The Churches of Northern New Spain, 1530–1821* (Tucson: University of Arizona Press, 2007), 81.

23. Hodge, *Explorations and Field Work*, 61–72; ibid., Frederick Webb Hodge, *History of Hawikuh, New Mexico: One of the So-called Cities of Cibola*. Frederick Webb Hodge Anniversary Publication Fund 1, Southwest Museum (Los Angeles: Ward Ritchie Press, 1937); Ross Gordon Montgomery, Watson Smith, and John Otis Brew, 1949, "*Franciscan Awatovi: The Excavation and Conjectural Reconstruction of a 17th-Century Spanish Mis-*

Only when visitors entered the front doors would San José reveal its most magnificent and ingenious qualities, however. Inside, the nave stretched forty *varas* (33.5 meters/110 feet) into the distance. Light poured into the sanctuary through six massive, gypsum-glazed windows lining the sanctuary. (We know the materials used in their construction because archaeologists uncovered large quantities of gypsum beneath these windowsills in 1922.)[24] Massive trees, fourteen meters (forty-six feet) long, served as vigas, bearing the roof on their backs. Murals draped the walls in red and yellow ochre, blue and green malachite, and white gypsum. Checkerboard and fleur-de-lis motifs dazzled the eyes, bordered by intertwined vines and leaves. In other parts of the church traditional Puebloan icons of clouds, maize plants, flowers, and wild game embellished the walls.[25] San José probably even sported a raised wooden floor—a rare luxury in seventeenth-century New Mexico. Archaeologists uncovered a series of joist support stones and plinths running down the central and outer aisles of the nave, suggestive of a timber floor that once lay on top.[26]

Regardless of how brilliant the murals or how resplendent the light spilling in through the windows, though, visitors' eyes inevitably fixated on the altar above all else. Fray Zárate Salmerón employed several cunning architectural techniques to focus the congregation's attention.[27] The walls of the nave converge slightly as they approach the sanctuary, bowing inward toward the altar. The wooden floor sloped gradually upward from the back of the nave to the front. The sanctuary sat elevated above a series of eight steps hewn out of bedrock, with the altar sitting on a *banco* three steps higher. And the three windows on each side of the church decreased in length as they approached the sanctuary (originally measuring six, five, and four varas, respectively; see Figure 3).[28] This regular diminishing created an optical illusion that appeared to lengthen the nave, stretching the lanky torso of the church to a vanishing point at the altar. Zárate Salmerón's clever tricks prompted the head of the Franciscan order in New Mexico to describe San

---

sionary Establishment at a Hopi Indian Town in Northeastern Arizona," Papers of the Peabody Museum 36, Reports of the Awatovi Expedition 3, Peabody Museum, Cambridge; Kubler, *The Religious Architecture of New Mexico*; Alden C. Hayes, *The Four Churches of Pecos* (Albuquerque: University of New Mexico Press, 1974).

24. Lansing B. Bloom, "The Jemez Expedition of the School," in *El Palacio* 14 (1923): 14–20.

25. Marjorie F. Lambert, "Mural Decorations in the San José de los Jemez Mission Church," in *Papers of the Archaeological Society of New Mexico 4: Collected Papers in Honor of Bertha Pauline Dutton*, ed. A. H. Schroeder (Albuquerque: Albuquerque Archaeological Society, 1979), 185–192.

26. Ivey, *"Una Muy Suntuosa y Curiosa Yglesia,"* 3, 7.

27. Kubler, *The Religious Architecture of New Mexico*, 68; Farwell, "An Architectural History of San Jose de Giusewa," 107; Ivey, *"Una Muy Suntuosa y Curiosa Yglesia."*

28. Ivey, *"Una Muy Suntuosa y Curiosa Yglesia,"* 11.

FIGURE 3. Nave of San José de los Jemez.

José in its heyday as *una muy suntuosa y curiosa yglesia* ("a breathtaking, sumptuous and distinguished church."[29]

Archaeologists have conducted extensive excavations at Giusewa over the past century, including nine field seasons between 1910 and 1978.[30] Curiously, despite recovering more than 100,000 potsherds and countless lithic and bone artifacts, archaeology has revealed almost no artifacts that can be traced directly to Fray Zárate Salmerón or his Franciscan successors. Marjorie Lambert surveyed a sample of the ceramics excavated from Giusewa, but found "an almost total lack of European artifacts and/or pottery."[31] Just one sherd of San Luis Blue-on-cream majolica and two plain white tin-glazed sherds appear in the Giusewa collections, the only artifacts with a confirmed Iberian biography yet found at San José de los Jemez.[32] Even so, the friars did leave their mark on the production of local Jemez pottery. Among the

29. Baker H. Morrow, ed. *A Harvest of Reluctant Souls: The Memorial of Fray Alonso de Benavides, 1630* (Niwot: University Press of Colorado, 1996), 29.

30. Elliott, *Pueblo at the Hot Place.*

31. Marjorie F. Lambert, "Spanish Influences on the Pottery of San Jose de los Jemez and Giusewa, Jemez State Monument (LA 679), Jemez Springs, New Mexico," in *Collected Papers in Honor of Erik Kellerman Reed*, ed. A. H. Schroeder, Archaeological Society of New Mexico Papers 6 (Albuquerque: Albuquerque Archaeological Society Press, 1981), 215.

32. Elliott, *Pueblo at the Hot Place,* 66.

remains of tens of thousands of traditional Puebloan vessels unearthed at Giusewa excavators have found numerous items exhibiting Spanish forms and influences manufactured in the style of the local ware, Jemez Black-on-white pottery. The shattered remains of multiple Jemez Black-on-white "soup plates" (small, shallow bowls with flaring, everted rims), Spanish-style cups, a sconce, a candelabra, a cross, and a chalice all came to light in excavations in the 1920s and 1930s.[33] The fact that the women of Giusewa manufactured these "Spanish" artifacts in the local style is not entirely surprising, as Jemez Black-on-white pottery dominates the ceramic assemblage of the Jemez region. In fact, Jemez Black-on-white comprises 94 percent of the decorated pottery at Giusewa, spanning both the pre-Hispanic and mission periods.[34]

The proportions of these hybrid Jemez-Spanish ecclesiastical artifacts correspond remarkably with the standard size and shape of typical Christian accouterment of the period, suggesting that either their creators were personally familiar with these types of vessels, or—more likely—that someone intimately acquainted with chalices and sconces oversaw the manufacturing process. Possibly the potters copied the forms of other chalices and sconces that the priest brought with him to Giusewa. The mixing of the two traditions is further evident in the decoration of the chalice, which combines the Jemez convention of concentric lines encircling the upper register of the inside of the bowl with the Christian crosses that adorn the bottom of the bowl interior and the underside of the base.

The Passion of San José: Death and Resurrection in the Jemez Valley

San José's bells and whistles may well have proven effective in aiding conversions during these early days of Franciscan activity among the Jemez. Fray Zárate Salmerón bragged of baptizing 6,566 souls during his time there. Certainly his successes were aided by the fact that he spoke the Jemez language, Towa. Franciscan missionaries rarely bothered to learn Native tongues in seventeenth-century New Mexico. Yet in his 1627 *Relaciones,* Zárate Salmerón wrote that he not only spoke the Jemez language but had penned a Christian *doctrina* in Towa.[35]

Even with this linguistic dexterity, Zárate Salmerón found the craggy landscape of the Jemez Province—what another Franciscan called "terribly rugged and inhospitable" (*asperessimas y inhabitables*)—an impediment to his

33. Bloom, *The Jemez Expedition*, 20; Lambert, *Spanish Influences*, 224–228.

34. Elliott, *Pueblo at the Hot Place*, 80.

35. Alicia Ronstadt Milich, *Relaciones: An Account of Things Seen and Heard by Father Jerónimo de Zárate Salmerón from the Year 1538 to Year 1626* (Albuquerque: Horn and Wallace, 1966), 26.

evangelical progress. As a remedy to this challenging terrain Zárate Salmerón instituted a policy of *congregación* in the province, attempting to collect the Jemez people scattered throughout the mesa top villages into a central place to facilitate proselytization. As the *custos* put it: "recognizing the impossibility of administering well those Indian mountaineers," the friar "induced them to live in a pueblo, which with their help he founded in a very suitable place."[36] Thus it came to pass that only a year after establishing San José, Fray Zárate Salmerón oversaw the construction of a new mission among the Jemez, probably located twenty-one kilometers (thirteen miles) to the south. There, in a wide, flat floodplain at the southern end of the Jemez Valley, the friar founded a second church.

Whatever gains Fray Zárate Salmerón thought he made in the initial years of his ministry among the Pueblos were repudiated in 1623, when the Jemez people revolted for the first time. The parishioners of the two missions rose up, destroying their villages before fleeing them entirely. While traces of the destruction of the southern village have yet to be discovered—excepting historical references that it was "burned down" and "totally abandoned"—the archaeology of Giusewa provides some useful clues regarding what happened in the 1623 uprising.[37] Excavators discovered a telltale layer of charred wood and ash when they removed the fill from San José's nave, testifying to the destruction of the church.[38] Apparently the Jemez residents of Giusewa set fire to Zárate Salmerón's celebrated temple in an apparent protest against the Franciscan's presence. Flames spilled across the ceiling toward the entrance of the church, engulfing the giant wooden doorway. When the lintel beam burned through and finally gave way, the balcony above it crashed to the ground. The choir loft crumpled too, further fueling the immolation. The windowsills turned to ash, collapsing the giant lateral clerestory windows in on themselves. Finally, the fire gnawed its way through the tree-trunk vigas one by one. The roof caved, bringing down the parapets with it. With its scalp smoldering on the floor, blue sky poured into the church to illuminate the charred murals. A uniform dusty black replaced their formerly dazzling colors. Architectural historian Jake Ivey notes that when the flames finally died out, the building probably looked very much like it did in the early twentieth century (see Fig. 2).[39]

Following the destruction of San José and her sister church to the south, the missions' neophytes scattered to the winds, returning to the ancestral villages that dotted the mesas and canyons surrounding Giusewa. Try as they

36. Frederick Webb Hodge, *Fray Alonso de Benavides' Revised Memorial of 1634*, eds. George P. Hammond and Agapito Rey (Albuquerque: University of New Mexico Press, 1945), 69.

37. Hodge, *Fray Alonso de Benavides*, 70.

38. Bloom, *The Jemez Expedition*, 17.

39. Ivey, *"Una Muy Suntuosa y Curiosa Yglesia,"* 9.

might to put their colonizers at their backs, however, the wraiths of mission life stalked them with no mercy. Two waves of epidemic diseases ravaged the Jemez between 1623 and 1626, no doubt sicknesses from the Old World introduced by the Spaniards. When the spirits known as *Kliwah* ("refuse winds") finally left their villages, only half the Jemez people remained breathing.[40] With the survivors in an unending state of mourning and the Jemez world collapsing around them, opportunity once again rapped on the doors of the Franciscans. Into the plague-ridden vacuum swept the friars, rebuilding the missions at Giusewa and Walatowa in 1626.

San José reclaimed most of its former glory, but the remnants of the fire necessitated a few architectural modifications. Workers enlarged the windows, enclosed a doorway, and built a new choir loft, though they couldn't salvage the balcony. Gone too was the luxurious wooden floor, replaced by one of puddled adobe. Artists reanimated the walls with bright frescoes, covering the soot with leaflets and fleur-de-lis of blue, green, yellow, and white.[41] At San José's sister village in the southern end of the valley the Franciscans apparently decided to wipe the slate clean, starting anew. They christened this new village San Diego de la Congregación. According to the *custodio* this congregación village rivaled the planned communities of today, containing a church, friary, "houses already built" for Jemez neophytes, and schools to teach them trades.[42] Scholars debate the location of San Diego de la Congregación,[43] but Mike Elliott's calculations using Geographic Information Systems software convincingly situate the 1626 mission in the area of the modern village of Walatowa (also known today as Jemez Pueblo).[44] While the plan and exact location of the church remain unknown—it may be buried under the present pueblo—San Diego de la Congregación reportedly boasted "a high tower," suggesting that it bore more than a passing similarity to San José.[45]

---

40. Elsie Clews Parsons, "*Pueblo Indian Religion*," Vol. 2 (Chicago: University of Chicago Press, 1939), 938; Morrow, *A Harvest of Reluctant Souls*, 29; Matthew J. Liebmann et al., "Native American depopulation, reforestation, and fire regimes in the Southwest United States, 1492–1900 CE," *Proceedings of the National Academy of Sciences* 113 (6) doi:10.1073/pnas.1521744113.

41. Ivey, *"Una Muy Suntuosa y Curiosa Yglesia,"* 11–12.

42. Morrow, *A Harvest of Reluctant Souls*, 29.

43. Scholes, "Notes on the Jemez Missions in the Seventeenth Century," Lansing B. Bloom and Lynn Mitchell, "The Chapter Elections in 1672," *New Mexico Historical Review* 13 (1938): 85–119; Farwell, "An Architectural History of San Jose de Giusewa"; Ivey, *"Una Muy Suntuosa y Curiosa Yglesia."*

44. Michael L. Elliott, *Mission and Mesa: Some Thoughts on the Archaeology of Pueblo Revolt Era Sites in the Jemez Region, New Mexico,* ed. R. Preucel (Albuquerque: University of New Mexico Press, 2002).

45. John L. Kessell, Rick Hendricks, and Meredith Dodge, eds. *To the Royal Crown Restored: The Journals of Don Diego De Vargas, New Mexico 1692–1694* (Albuquerque: University of New Mexico Press, 1995), 203.

The Gathering Storm: 1630–1680 in New Mexico

For the next five decades the Franciscan fathers and their Pueblo parishioners danced a delicate minuet. The priests labored to boost their numbers of converts while simultaneously attempting to eradicate traditional Pueblo religion. Complicating this relationship even further was the colonial government in Santa Fe. Although the missions and the secular colonial administration existed in a symbiotic relationship, friction and mistrust characterized the church–state relationship in New Mexico for much of the seventeenth century.[46] Franciscans, colonial officials, and *encomenderos* battled repeatedly during this period, with the Pueblos often caught in the middle. The friars and governors frequently fought over control of the Native labor pool, leaving the Pueblo people in a precarious position—forced to choose between being good Christians in the service of God or loyal vassals in service of the Crown. Pleasing the governor might earn the friars' reprobation. At other times, secular officials punished the Pueblos for serving the Franciscans. In seventeenth-century New Mexico, there was often no way to be a "good Indian." Obeying one branch of the colonial system frequently meant defying the other.

Tensions simmered as the friars grew increasingly intolerant of the masked kachinas dancing in the plazas and the smoky late-night gatherings in the wombs of the kivas. Throughout the custody of New Mexico, Franciscans attempted to drive the devil from the pueblos through the destruction of kivas; confiscation of kachina masks and ritual paraphernalia; prohibition of ritual dances; and periodic arrests, whippings, and executions of Pueblo religious leaders (who they referred to as *hechiceros*, or "sorcerers"). In the 1630s, for example, the *custos* boasted that he had burned "more than a thousand idols of wood" in a single blaze while their shocked Pueblo wardens looked on in dismay. In 1660, the Franciscan leadership decreed an unconditional prohibition of kachina dances, and missionaries were instructed to collect and destroy all materials of "idolatry." Shortly thereafter, priests reportedly incinerated sixteen hundred kachina masks.[47]

What happened at Giusewa during the fifty years following 1630 is shrouded by the mists of time. Church records for this period were destroyed, and the few documentary sources that survive make no mention of missionary activities at San José during this interval. By 1628 the Franciscans considered

---

46. France V. Scholes, "*Troublous Times in New Mexico, 1659–1670*," Historical Society of New Mexico, Publications in History, vol. 11 (Albuquerque: University of New Mexico Press, 1942): 55–57.

47. Scholes, "*Troublous Times in New Mexico, 1659–1670*," 59; Hodge, *Fray Alonso de Benavides*, 43; Edward H. Spicer, *Cycles of Conquest: The Impact of Spain, Mexico, and the United States on the Indians of the Southwest, 1533–1960* (Tucson: University of Arizona Press, 1962), 160–161.

San Diego de la Congregación the primary center of missionary activity among the Jemez, leading France Scholes, the dean of New Mexican colonial history, to conclude that the friars abandoned San José sometime during the 1630s.[48] Yet the archaeology of Giusewa hints that Jemez people continued living at the site even after the priests were long gone. The presence of Kotyiti Glaze polychrome pottery (i.e., "Glaze F," produced between 1625 and 1700) in greater quantities than other Rio Grande glazewares may be an artifact of continued occupation of the site following the Spaniards' departure.[49] More convincing is the fact that Jemez people converted one of the rooms of the *convento* into a kiva, an act that almost surely occurred without a friar in residence.[50] With the priests gone, the Jemez installed a ventilator shaft, a hearth-and-deflector, and a sipapu in the floor. Nonetheless, this post-Franciscan occupation at Giusewa was probably brief, lasting no more than a decade or two at most. By the late 1650s, the Jemez no longer lived at Giusewa. When the Governor of New Mexico visited "the baths of San José de los Jemez" in 1658, he reported the area to be *despoblado* (uninhabited).[51]

While Giusewa was in decline, its sister site of Walatowa rose phoenix-like from its ashes. The mission of San Diego de la Congregación flourished during the 1630–1680 period. In 1642 the *custos* reported that "the pueblo of Jemez has a splendid church, a good convent, a choir and organ, and 1800 souls under its administration." By 1661 friars were raving about the mission, calling it "*la mayor administración*" in New Mexico. If there were any doubts regarding San Diego de la Congregación's earlier status, by this time it indubitably served as the principal mission among the Jemez. Six years later the provincial of the Franciscan Order in Mexico City noted that the two priests who served the Jemez at San Diego de la Congregación were not enough, decreeing that a third would be added. And in August 1672 the chapter meetings of the Holy Custody of the Conversion of St. Paul and the provinces of New Mexico took place in the convent of "San Diego de los Jemez," indicating the status that this church and pueblo had attained as a center of missionary activity in New Mexico.[52]

While Franciscan records depict the Jemez Valley as a lively center of Christian conversion and worship prior to 1680, it is difficult to reconcile this rosy assessment with documents produced by the colonial government during this period. Between 1644 and 1647, the Jemez allied with neighboring "Apaches" (probably ancestral Navajos) in an attempt to overthrow the

48. Scholes, "Notes on the Jemez Missions in the Seventeenth Century," 93–94.

49. Elliott, *Pueblo at the Hot Place*, 80.

50. James E. Ivey, Personal Communication, 2014.

51. Scholes, "Notes on the Jemez Missions in the Seventeenth Century," 93–94, 96.

52. Scholes, "Notes on the Jemez Missions in the Seventeenth Century," 95–97; Bloom and Mitchell, *The Chapter Elections*.

Spaniards, killing one colonist. For this plot the Jemez were punished "with just severity" when the governor of New Mexico hanged twenty-nine of their leaders, whipping others and sending some into forced servitude. A few years later the Jemez were again implicated in planning a rebellion in league with their Keres, southern Tiwa, and Apache neighbors, for which nine of the conspirators were hanged.[53] Then in 1675, forty-seven religious leaders from Pueblos throughout the province were arrested, publicly whipped, and imprisoned. One of these *hechiceros* was hanged in the plaza at San Diego de la Congregación as an example to those Jemez persons who harbored any lingering sympathies for their traditional religion.[54]

With the hindsight typically borne of traumatic episodes, Franciscans later recalled the ominous forebodings that surfaced among the Pueblos during the 1670s. In 1675, an apparition of the Virgin reportedly visited a New Mexican girl, ordering her to "arise and announce to this custody that it will soon be destroyed for the lack of reverence it shows its priests." This miraculous revelation prompted Fray Juan de Jesús, a priest stationed at San Diego de los Congregación, to urge his Franciscan brother to cease construction on the collaterals being added to the church's nave at that time. Renowned for his gift of prophecy, Fray Juan purportedly felt that their efforts were better spent "uniting ourselves with God and preparing to die for our Holy Faith." He allegedly went on to predict "the collaterals will soon end in ashes and many of us in death."[55]

Fray Juan de Jesús's prophecy was realized on August 10, 1680, when he was martyred along with twenty of his Brothers of St. Francis during the opening days of the infamous Pueblo Revolt of 1680. After eight decades of missionary activity and Spanish rule, the enraged Pueblos threw off the yokes of their colonial masters. Together with their Navajo and Apache allies, the Pueblos banded together in a coordinated attack that succeeded in driving the Spaniards from their lands. In the process, they killed 380 colonial settlers

53. Scholes, "Notes on the Jemez Missions in the Seventeenth Century," 63, 68–69, 95–96; Charles Wilson Hackett and Charmion Clair Shelby, "Revolt of the Pueblo Indians of New Mexico and Otermin's Attempted Reconquest, 1680–1682," *Coronado Cuarto Centennial Publications, 1540–1940*, 2 Vols (Albuquerque: University of New Mexico Press, 1942), 2:299; Joe S. Sando, *Nee Hemish: A History of Jemez Pueblo* (Albuquerque: University of New Mexico Press, 1982), 118; Ivey, *"Una Muy Suntuosa y Curiosa Yglesia,"* 10; John L. Kessell and Rick Hendricks, eds. *By Force of Arms: The Journals of Don Diego de Vargas, New Mexico 1691–1693* (Albuquerque: University of New Mexico Press, 1992), 42, n.9; Riley, *The Kachina and the Cross*, 21.

54. Hackett and Shelby, "Revolt of the Pueblo Indians of New Mexico ," 2:289–290, 300–301.

55. Ramón A. Gutiérrez, *When Jesus Came, the Corn Mothers Went Away: Marriage, Sexuality, and Power in New Mexico, 1500–1846* (Stanford, CA: Stanford University Press, 1991), 131; Kessell, Hendricks, and Dodge, *Blood on the Boulders,* 371.

and two-thirds of the Franciscans stationed among them. With the priests gone, the Pueblos turned their fury on the mission churches, ripping their doors from the hinges, smashing the mission bells, desecrating the altars, and burning Catholic icons and statuary. For the next twelve years independence was returned to the Pueblo world, and the Spaniards remained in exile south of the Rio Grande.[56]

The Short Saga of San Diego del Monte and San Felipe-on-the-Mesa

With the Spaniards gone, the Jemez burned San Diego de la Congregación to the ground and migrated seven kilometers (4.4 miles) up the valley, following the winding course of the Jemez River to the north. There they settled on a mesa above the confluence of two streams, where they built a new village. Contemporary Jemez oral traditions, Spanish historical documents, and the archaeological record all confirm that this new village is the one known as Patokwa ("pueblo of the turquoise moiety."[57] It was here that a large group of Jemez people were living when the exiled Spaniards made their first foray back to the Jemez Valley under the command of Don Diego de Vargas in 1692.[58]

The seventeenth-century component of Patokwa sported two large rectangular plazas that mirrored one another, each with a kiva sunk into their southern half. Blocks of two- and three-story, apartment-style pueblo rooms surrounded the plazas in the four cardinal directions, with a fifth room block bisecting the two open areas. The four corners of the pueblo remained open, providing gateway entrances to the northeast, northwest, southeast, and southwest. It was in the southeast corner gateway that General Vargas ominously appeared in late October 1692, a harbinger of the bad times to come. Over the next two years the Jemez people fought a series of bloody battles with the Spanish colonizers and their allies.

When the dust finally settled in 1694, Vargas installed a new missionary at Patokwa, a friar named Francisco de Jesús María Casañas. Fray Francisco de Jesús established a new church, christened San Diego del Monte y Nuestra Señora de Remedios.[59] But this new structure was a far cry from the grandiosity of its predecessors. San Diego del Monte was significantly smaller—just a third of size of San José, with a nave thirteen meters long (forty-two feet).[60]

---

56. Liebmann, *Revolt.*
57. Ibid., 85.
58. Kessell, Hendricks, and Dodge, *By Force of Arms*, 520–523.
59. Kessell, Hendricks, and Dodge, *Blood on the Boulders*, 405–406.
60. Liebmann, *Revolt*, 215.

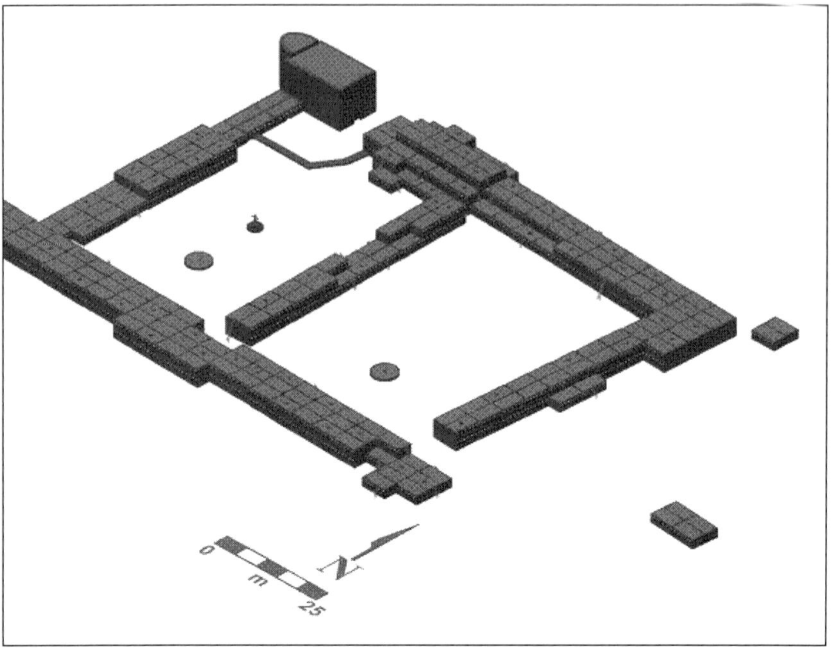

FIGURE 4. San Diego del Monte mission complex at Patokwa, circa 1695.

Unlike the looming fortress constructed at Giusewa three-quarters of a century earlier, San Diego del Monte blended almost seamlessly with the pueblo architecture surrounding it. Tucked into the northwest corner of Patokwa, the church was nestled between two adjacent pueblo room blocks (Figure 4). Its flat roof peered just over the tops of the three-story pueblo rooms surrounding it. Rather than using fortress-like walls two meters thick, San Diego del Monte was clad in masonry of identical size and material as the nearby pueblo architecture. The floor area was far smaller as well (just under 140 m^2), akin to that of a large kiva.

San Diego del Monte is not the only church built during the Spanish *reconquista* of New Mexico to exhibit these characteristics. The post-Revolt pueblo of Old San Felipe contains a similarly modest church.[61] The Spaniards neglected to record its name for posterity, but it too was located at a mesa-top pueblo founded in the tumultuous years following the Pueblo Revolt, probably in late 1693 or 1694. Like San Diego del Monte, the church at Old San Felipe was wedged into the corner of a rectangular pueblo, bordering on the plaza. It abutted the surrounding village architecture, with one side cling-

61. Kubler, *The Religious Architecture of New Mexico*, 106.

ing to the edge of a precipice. And with a petite footprint of just 100 m^2, it was even smaller than San Diego del Monte.[62]

Some of the unique characteristics of the church at Old San Felipe can be ascribed to its unique biography. In fact, this church began its unusual life as a kiva. When Vargas visited the mesa-top pueblo on September 26, 1694, he installed "the reverend missionary father and apostolic preacher, Fray Antonio Carbonel" as the minister there. Vargas recorded that the residents of San Felipe:

> showed me a tall, spacious kiva they were currently using as a chapel. I allowed this, telling them it would serve for now since this location was to the father's liking. I, the governor and captain general, told him I would order what was appropriate in the coming year.[63]

Apparently Fray Carbonel or his successor followed through with Vargas's plan, and "what was appropriate" included the replacement of the stone-walled kiva with an adobe-walled church.[64] (In 1706 the resident friar and his flock left the site, moving down from the mesa top to a settlement on the banks of the Rio Grande below.)

The churches of San Diego del Monte and San Felipe on the Mesa stand out as unique among the religious architecture of New Mexico. As the only mission churches constructed at post-Revolt refugee pueblos, these structures allow a glimpse into Franciscan-Pueblo relations in the brief, two-year period between the *reconquista* of New Mexico (1692–1694) and the Second Pueblo Revolt (1696).[65] As Kubler notes, these churches were contemporaries, and "represent a significant phase of post-Rebellion construction, characterized by small buildings, erected of adobe or stone, located among the pueblo buildings, constituting an integral part of the settlement."[66] Less ambitious in design and execution, these churches suggest that Franciscan power in New Mexico waned during this period, and hints at the new evangelical policies implemented by the friars after the Pueblo Revolt.[67] No longer did they attempt to dominate the Pueblos by ruthlessly suppressing traditional Native

---

62. Marc Treib, *Sanctuaries of Spanish New Mexico* (Berkeley: University of California Press, 1993), 232.

63. Kessell, Hendricks, and Dodge, *Blood on the Boulders*, 400.

64. Kubler, *The Religious Architecture of New Mexico*, 106–107, pl. 56.

65. Matthew Liebmann, T. J. Ferguson, and Robert Preucel, "Pueblo Settlement, Architecture, and Social Change in the Pueblo Revolt Era, A.D. 1680 to 1696." *Journal of Field Archaeology* 30 (2005): 45–60.

66. Kubler, *The Religious Architecture of New Mexico*, 107.

67. Farwell, "An Architectural History of San Jose de Giusewa," 116; John L. Kessel, The Missions of New Mexico since 1776 (Albuquerque: University of New Mexico, 1980), 11–12; George Kubler, The Rebuilding of San Miguel at Santa Fe in 1710 (Colorado Springs; The Taylor Museum, 1939).

religious practices. After 1692, the Franciscans adopted what might accurately be described as a kinder, gentler missionary strategy in New Mexico.[68] While they did not approve of the Pueblos' paganism, after 1692 the friars did tolerate its existence. Following the Pueblo Revolt, the Brothers of St. Francis were forced to adopt strategies of accommodation rather than domination in their interactions with Pueblo communities.

Interpretations

Comparing the seventeenth-century mission churches of the Jemez Valley to one another, some clear patterns emerge (Figure 5). At the most basic level, we can read this architecture as a simple reflection of Franciscan power. The early seventeenth-century mission architecture of New Mexico, exemplified by the San José de los Jemez church at Giusewa, reflects the ideology of the Franciscans during the pre-Revolt era. They saw themselves as superior to and distinct from the Puebloans, in a relationship analogous to that of stern fathers to their children. These churches and their associated mission complexes were built to distinguish themselves as separate from the existing Pueblo architecture. At Giusewa, Zárate Salmerón took considerable pains to construct San José on the highest point in the area, overlooking the pueblo room blocks. Moreover, the sheer size of these early churches relayed a message of dominion over the landscape. Their hulking forms loomed over the existing pueblo architecture. The walls of San José were six to seven times wider than those of the pueblo architecture at Giusewa. Even the materials from which they were constructed were different—at Giusewa, the pueblo rooms were constructed of volcanic tuff masonry, while the walls of San José were made of limestone. (Both materials were acquired locally.) The friars used this architecture not only to express, but to naturalize Franciscan distinction, superiority, and dominion over the Pueblos.

After the Pueblo Revolt, however, these patterns changed dramatically. When the friars returned to New Mexico with the 1680 martyrdom of their brothers fresh in their minds, they no longer attempted to emphasize their difference and dominion through architecture. The new churches they constructed were no longer designed to dominate the pueblo architecture. Now the Franciscans built their houses of worship among the existing pueblo architecture, and at a much more modest scale. Rather than using fortress-like walls two meters thick, these new churches used masonry of identical size and material as the nearby pueblo architecture. The floor area was far smaller as well, akin to that of a large kiva (quite literally at San Felipe on the Mesa). In this architecture, we can see the changes to Franciscan missionary policy that occurred in the

68. Norris, *After "The Year Eighty."*

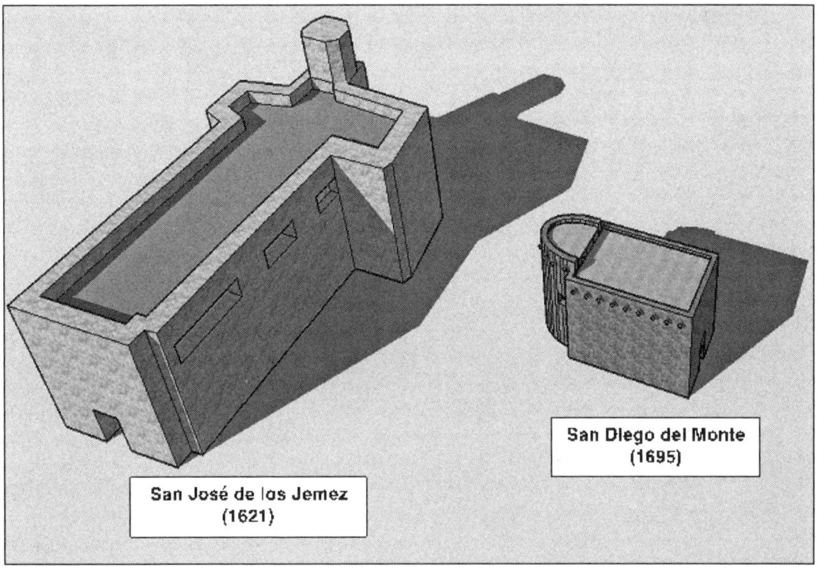

Figure 5. Churches of San José de los Jemez and San Diego del Monte.

1690s.[69] No longer did the priests separate themselves. After 1694 the friars attempted to ingratiate themselves, moving their churches directly adjacent to the pueblo plazas and living cheek-to-cheek with their congregants.

It would be a mistake, however, to end our interpretation there. To merely see these churches as a straightforward reflection of Franciscan domination and its decline is to overlook the subtleties of power that contributed to their construction, maintenance, and destruction. After all, the Franciscans did not build these churches alone. They were primarily put up by Pueblo hands. And there is good reason to believe that the Pueblos' participation in this process was not entirely coerced. While violence and intimidation were common tools of the Spanish colonial effort, there is no clear evidence to suggest that the Franciscans employed any military support in their construction efforts. Thus the size and complexity that characterized the churches built between 1610 and 1640 attests to the early successes that the friars enjoyed in their evangelical efforts among the Pueblos. Judging from the massive church structures that appeared on the New Mexico landscape in the early to mid-seventeenth century, of which San José at Giusewa is an exemplar, there had to be a significant amount of Native "buy-in" in order to raise the walls.[70]

69. Norris, *After "The Year Eighty."*

70. James F. Brooks, "Women, Men, and Cycles of Evangelism in the Southwest Borderlands, AD 750–1750," *American Historical Review* 118 (2013): 761–763.

In examining the architecture of San José and its sister churches, we can see that Franciscan brothers often succeeded in their early efforts to establish themselves in local Pueblo communities. These early successes contrast markedly with the churches built between 1694 and 1696, which show far less overall effort in their construction, but also far less differentiation from the Pueblo architecture.

James Brooks notes that the successes of the Franciscans among the seventeenth-century Pueblos broke along gendered lines.[71] Franciscans targeted women (and sometimes younger men) precisely because they tended to be marginalized in Pueblo society and excluded from traditional chambers of power. As a result, conversions likely soared among the women of villages like Giusewa in the early 1600s. It comes as no surprise, then, to see Franciscan influences disproportionately reflected in classes of material culture traditionally associated with Pueblo women: architecture and pottery. Women traditionally laid up the walls among the Pueblos, and it was probably the women who primarily stacked the masonry of San José de los Jemez. As the Franciscan *custos* noted in 1630, churches among the Pueblos were "built by the women and by boys and girls taking Christian doctrine, although this may seem an exaggeration since these structures are sumptuous and ornate. It is the custom among these nations for the women to build the houses," he continued, noting that "if we compel any man to work on building a house, he runs away and the women laugh at him. In this way, there have been erected more than fifty churches, whose ceilings are attractively carved with interlaced flowers, and whose walls are very well painted."[72]

Conclusion

In thinking about the Franciscan churches of seventeenth-century New Mexico, the patterns that emerge out of the Jemez Valley appear at first glance relatively straightforward and matter of fact. The physical structures seem to mirror the rise and decline of Franciscan power and influence. Early on the explicit policy of the Order of Friars Minor was one of domination and control, and this is reflected in the architectural elements that mark these churches as different, ascendant, and authoritative. Following their widespread martyrdom and expulsion in the Pueblo Revolt of 1680 the Franciscans changed their policies to become more tolerant, assimilative, and less obtrusive. These changes are reflected in architecture that is more similar to the surrounding pueblo buildings than it is different.

---

71. Ibid.

72. E.E. Ayer, trans., *The Memorial of Fray Alonso Benavides* (Chicago: R.R. Donnelley and Sons Co., 1916), 36.

Yet viewed from another perspective, the patterns exhibited by these churches seem counterintuitive as well. At the times when Franciscan power, influence, and authority was at its greatest, their architecture was highly militaristic and defensive. The churches of the early period, when the priests were experiencing their greatest successes, were built like medieval castles, with thick walls and soaring towers. Later, when tensions between the priests and their Pueblo congregants were at their highest, their structures become less defensive and more integrated into the surrounding community. In the absence of the historical texts, it would be easy to mistake this pattern for one of early hostility towards the priests followed by increasing acceptance by the Pueblos—the opposite of what seems to have been the case.

In their construction of militaristic churches in the early seventeenth century, the Franciscans protested too much. And by attempting to dominate the Pueblos the priests created the conditions that ultimately brought about their downfall. These churches shaped the events of the latter seventeenth century as much as they were shaped by the Pueblo people who built them.

Chapter 14
Beyond Slavery: The Institutional Status of Mission Indians

Marie Christine Duggan

> While the institution of slavery is generally associated with African Americans and with the antebellum South, it was in fact present in other regions and at other times in American history. Lorenzo Asisara's story is an example of the enslavement of Native Americans in the American Southwest.[1]

The above citation from a website for teachers reveals the extent to which in the popular mind mission Indians were slaves, and gives us some indication as to why. Lorenzo Asisara was an Indian at Mission Santa Cruz who related in 1877 how his father retaliated against a whipping in 1813 by participating in a group decision to kill a Franciscan missionary. The American Indian scholar Edward Castillo published Asisara's story in 1979.[2] The 1970s were a potent moment of self-reflection in the United States. School desegregation took place in Berkeley in 1969, and Indians occupied Alcatraz from 1969 to 1971. It would be rare to find an American of that time whose image of slavery was not cemented by the *Roots* mini-series in 1977. On the television screen, we watched Kunta Kinte's resistance as he was whipped to force him to give up his African name. For many of us, Lorenzo Asisara's story of his father's whipping at a mission did call to mind that specific image of humiliation and cultural resistance of a slave.

By the 1990s, few argued any more that mission Indian status was fundamentally distinct from slavery. Those who did sounded like relics of an outdated worldview that saw Europeans as inherently superior to Indians and Africans. Unfortunately, the very success of this anti-imperialist revision had the unantic-

---

1. Annenberg Learner: Teacher Resources and Professional Development across the Curriculum, http://www.learner.org/amerpass/unit07/authors-1.html (accessed July 5, 2014).

2. Edward Castillo, "The Assassination of Padre Andrés Quintana by the Indians of Mission Santa Cruz in 1812: The Narrative of Lorenzo Asisara," *California History* 68 (1989).

ipated result of silencing the questions that might have helped us define mission Indian status more precisely. If we squeeze our conception of missions and mission Indians into slavery, we lose sight of the social relations specific to Latin American colonialism, and thereby miss the influence of those Latin American roots on the one-third of the United States that shares the Spanish colonial past.

This essay concentrates on the 1769–1810 period, when California was part of the Spanish empire. Missions and presidios were utterly transformed around 1810 when Spain's empire collapsed. The French had invaded Spain and imprisoned the Spanish king in 1808, and by 1810 Spain's political and economic control of Spanish America was falling apart. From Buenos Aires to Lima, San Blas, and San Francisco, a decade of lawlessness and institutional change inaugurated a new period that resolved into British commercial interests dominating the Pacific littoral. Between 1769 and 1810, the Spanish Crown had tended toward suspicion of the profit motive, preferring to rely upon state-funded military and religious institutions. By the 1820s, the profit motive would take on more importance in California, when newly independent Mexico sent a governor to Alta California. The discussion here is limited to 1769–1809, when missions in California operated on a blueprint created and funded by Bourbon Spain.[3] Understanding Bourbon missions in California can provide insight into contemporaneous missions in other parts of the Spanish empire in a way that study of the diverging post-1810 structures cannot. One cannot help but wonder if the conflict betweenAsisara's father and the missionary at Santa Cruz in 1813 might have been a result of this institutional change given its timing, when the collapse of the old structure had begun and the transition to something new was not yet complete.

Economic Incentives

Whatever mission Indians were, they were not slaves—if only because Indians were not property and African slaves were. Slaves had a price, businessmen invested in them as assets as well as laborers. Like land, capital equipment, or government bonds, investments in slaves were made in the expectation of yielding a profit and perhaps capital gains. In contrast, missions in Spanish California brought no economic benefits to Spain. Under the Spanish Crown, missions were losing propositions financially, and the Bourbon government turned down opportunities to make them profitable.

Typically, California literature has focused on the political dimension of missions in colonial California, that is, the measures taken to keep Indians

3. For a discussion that includes post-1810 political economy of missions, see M.C. Duggan, "With and Without an Empire: Financing for California Missions Before and After 1810," *Pacific Historical Review* 85:1, 23–71 (2016).

from resisting or rebelling against Spanish control. In contrast, this essay begins by exploring the incentive structure of mission Indian status and the implications for Spanish California's economic evolution. A few unexpected and interesting dimensions emerge. At the conclusion, more familiar debates about political control by the Spanish of mission Indians will be addressed via a new interpretation. Modern Americans tend to view peoples as either free or enslaved, but such a dichotomy suppresses multiple ways that societies channel human behavior.

While markets typically provide incentive to increase productivity (output per person per day), the low productivity of mission Indians was marked. For example, the French visitor Captain La Perouse witnessed in 1786 the laborious method of grinding corn at Mission Carmel, and wrote, "[Indians] have no other method of breaking the grain than with a roller upon a stone." One of La Perouse's crew "made a present of his mill to the missionaries. It was difficult to have rendered them a greater service, since four women will now do the work of a hundred. . . . But the missionaries have hitherto been more attentive to their heavenly than their earthly concerns."[4] Yet by 1806, a second foreign visitor would comment that the hand mill had not been adopted, nor had any larger mills been constructed, though he had seen many in contemporaneous Spain.[5] He must not have seen the five mills that had been constructed by 1806; the Spaniards in California did know how to build them.[6] Yet with eighteen missions built by that time, the visitor was correct in so far as mills were far from the norm.

In contrast, slaves in the eighteenth century had a reputation of being highly productive. Cristina Mazzeo studied the business of an eighteenth-century slave trader in Peru, and she concluded, "In Spanish America, [African] slaves were preferred to Indians for certain tasks, especially for plantation work. It was generally considered that the output of a slave was four times that of an Indian."[7] A Bourbon advisor to the Spanish Crown acknowledged in 1762 the prevailing wisdom that labor of Africans enslaved was more

4. Jean Francois de la Perouse, *Life in a California Mission: Monterey in 1786* (Berkeley: Heydey Books, 1989 [1786]), 86–87.

5. Georg H. Von Langsdorff, cited in Robert Archibald, *Economic Aspects of the California Missions* (Washington, DC: American Academy of Franciscan History, 1978), 182.

6. The missions with mills by 1806 were Santa Cruz, San Luis Obispo, Santa Clara, San Francisco, and San Antonio. See Edith Webb, *Indian Life at the Old Missions* (Los Angeles: W.F. Lewis, 1952), 153–54 and Mardith Schuetz-Miller, *Building and Builders in Hispanic California* 1769–1850 (Santa Barbara: Santa Barbara Trust for Historic Preservation, 1994), 171, 179.

7. Cristina Mazzeo, "Vivir y morir en alta mar: La comercialización del esclavo en Hispanoamérica a fines del siglo XVIII," in *Sobre el Peru: Homenaje al doctor Agustin de La Puente Candamo* (Lima: Pontificia Universidad La Católica del Perú and Instituto Riva-Agüero, 2002).

productive: "the Indian is cheap to maintain, even if he works less than the Negro."[8] In the U.S. South and the Caribbean, plantation managers also showed a preference for slaves, though the comparison was typically to the labor of white indentured servants, whereby immigrants would sell themselves into a short-term period of service such as two to seven years in return for financing of passage to the New World and subsistence while under contract.

Whether the labor of slaves was actually higher in productivity than that of white indentured servants or Indians is a disputed question; managers might have preferred slaves for other reasons. For example, because slaves were movable property, they could be transported to the location where the labor would produce the greatest profit. This was in contrast to Indians (see below) or indentured servants, who could turn down a contract for a destination rumored to be deadly. An example of this explanation in practice was sugar plantations in Barbados. Sugar was back-breaking work under humid conditions. Even indentured servants insisted on shorter contracts for Barbados. Because slaves were property, they could be shipped to any location that the owner deemed profitable. As Gavin Wright notes, "The right of a slave owner to employ the slave in a location and at an activity of the owner's choosing, ignoring any preferences on the part of the slave" made it possible for slave owners to assign slaves to tasks that were lucrative.[9]

In contrast to slaves who were movable property, Indians throughout Spanish America were rooted to ancestral homelands (*arraigados* in Spanish). In a larger sense, being "rooted" to land was a trait that late eighteenth-century Spaniards considered desirable for content subjects. For example, Pedro de Campomanes (economic advisor to Carlos III) wrote in 1765, "in the partition of an inheritance among a group of heirs, one attempts to distribute real estate equally to each one for his greater permanence, and so that they can live rooted [*arraigados*] in their homes."[10] In contrast, growing numbers of rootless malcontents were moving to urban areas of Spain and Mexico in the late eighteenth century. The rooted nature of Indian communities stands in contrast to the situation of slaves, for whom "to the pain of being captured and sold was added the experience of being uprooted [*desarraigado*] and transported to the new world."[11] Having kin at the mission is not antithetical to also melding with new people. The development of cohesion of such a

---

8. Quoted in Luis Perdices de Blas and José-Luis Ramos Gorostiza, ""Slavery and the Slave Trade in Spanish Economic Thought, Sixteenth to Eighteenth Centuries" in *History of Economic Ideas*, 23(2) (2015): 32.

9. *Slavery and American Economic Development* (Baton Rouge: University of Louisiana, 2006), 21–26.

10. Pedro de Campomanes, *Tratado de la Regalía de Amortización* (Madrid: Artes Gráficas Ibarra, 1975 [1765]), 2.

11. Mazzeo, *Vivir y morir*, 5.

multiethnic community made up of Indian villages within a certain radius of a mission was quite distinct from the initial total lack of social ties among Africans brought thousands of miles to markets where they were sold as slaves.

Indian roots to ancestral territory were a tie that the mission structure was designed to transform, but also to sustain—perhaps because keeping Indians from becoming malcontents was their purpose in the government's eyes. Indians were indeed congregated, that is, pressured to move from their ancestral communities of fifty to one hundred people to a larger mission village of perhaps one or two thousand. A community that had lived next to the beach for hundreds of generations could find themselves moved miles inland, and hence unable to fish or perhaps even to see the ocean on a daily basis. But aspects of the landscape (such as mountains) would still have been identifiable in the community's age-old cosmology, in a way that would never be true for an African slave. When two hundred Huchiun Indians from the East Bay left Mission San Francisco in 1795, and killed the pro-Spanish Indians sent to bring them back, the Spanish responded by founding a new mission (San José) in the East Bay in 1797. Unwilling to abandon their ancestral territory, the Huchiun eventually complied. The Spanish used the Huchiun rootedness as a means to leverage Spanish social control.

Another example of Indian "rootedness" comes from Baja California in 1767, two years before Spain's political control of Alta California. King Charles III of Spain expelled the Jesuits, and when his representative José de Gálvez arrived in 1767 to turn the Baja missions over to the Franciscans, he attempted to consolidate missions with smaller populations. Although Gálvez was successful in consolidating missions that were located close together in Baja Sur, he met resistance when he ordered that Indians be moved about five hundred miles from Northern Baja to San José del Cabo at the tip of Southern Baja California. The missionary at Santa Borja, Fermín Francisco de Lasuén, successfully resisted this order on the grounds that "merely to propose it will greatly disturb the converts and frighten the gentiles away."[12] The episode reveals limits to the Spaniards' ability to relocate Indian populations. Indeed, exile was considered the near equivalent of execution. If an Indian were convicted of murder or inciting major rebellion, he or she might be banished from San Francisco to San Diego, or vice versa.[13]

Lasuén refers explicitly to missionary utilization of Indian rootedness as a method of inducing social control in Alta California in the following passage from 1790: "[The Indian] is always drawn back to the place of his birth, or to

12. Lasuén to Gálvez, December 20, 1768, in Kenneally, *Writings of Lasuén*, I: 18.

13. On exile as penalty for murder, see Causa contra Silverio y Rossa por la muerte alevosa que dio el primero a su mujer, Mission San Luis Obispo, 1796, AGN, Ramo Californias, vol. 65, expediente 6, 214–301.

the place where most of his people are. We the missionaries pay very close attention to this in the transfers which take place when new missions are founded. We send to them Indians who were baptized in those already founded, but who are native of the region or neighborhood where the new mission is established. It has been found by experience that they like this; and in no other way can they be kept quiet and induced to continue their education."[14]

The distinction between rooted Indians and slaves who could be moved to any productive task does not seem quite adequate to explain the particularly low productivity of Indians in California missions described by La Perouse and Langsdorff. Two additional factors may have held back productivity: the limited market for the produce of Indians on California missions, and the time limits placed on mission existence. The extent of the market limiting productivity is stressed by Adam Smith. His classic example was the pin factory: one man could make ten pins in a day by hand, yet ten men working together and specializing in different part of the labor (straightening the wire, cutting the pins, applying the tops, painting the tops white) could make upwards of 240 pins per man per day. Why had human beings waited until the eighteenth century to adopt the more efficient method of making pins? Smith pointed out that when a pin-maker sold only to a small village, there would have been no customer base for 240 pins per worker per day. It was only when pins could be sold all over the world by the British mercantile fleet that there was incentive to raise productivity.[15]

In terms of markets, there was little incentive for missionaries or mission Indians to come up with ways to produce more than needed for the consumption of, say, one thousand Indians if missions could not sell products to anyone. The first potential increase in a market for mission Indian produce came with the otter fur trade between 1786 and 1789. Otter hides were selling in China for three hundred pesos per hide. However, the government was not willing to offer missions more than seven pesos per hide. The head missionary, Lasuén, pointed out that the compensation was not enough to stimulate anyone to do the work. The government apparently viewed mission Indians as labor for which it should not have to pay, and never relented, so the missions did not embrace otter trade with the government.[16]

A second potential market was presidio demand for fresh foods produced by Indians or outright mission Indian labor (e.g., for building or repairing presidio structures, watching sheep, making tortillas). Early on, the military

---

14. Lasuén to Jacobo Ugarte y Loyola, Nov. 19, 1790 in Finbar Kenneally, ed. *Writings of Fermín Francisco de Lasuén* (Washington, DC: American Academy of Franciscan History, 1965), 2 vols., I: 217–218.

15. Adam Smith, *The Wealth of Nations* (New York: Random House, 1937 [1776]), 6.

16. Adele Ogden, *The California Sea Otter Trade, 1784–1848* (Berkeley: University of California Press, 1941), 22.

attempted to obtain produce and labor of mission Indians for free, but friars such as Lasuén at San Diego and Peña at Santa Clara made it clear that they expected payment.[17] By 1793, the military was regularly paying for mission produce, as revealed by the account book between the presidio and Mission Santa Barbara, which starts in that year.[18] Yet the prices were set by the government below cost. For example, from San Buenaventura, Señan wrote in 1800: "[T]he price of beef cattle is not fair. The most recent experience we had was not long ago with a cow. . . . This cow, if sold alive, or whole, was worth 4 pesos according to the government price list." Señan went on to point out that once slaughtered, the cow produced meat, lard, tallow, hide, and suet worth a combined total of twelve and a half pesos, or three times as much. He concluded: "Certainly it is not easy to swallow that this piece, whole, is worth four pesos, and when cut up, and measured, with the values of the government price list itself, is worth twelve pesos, six reales."[19]

At such prices, there was little incentive for missions to produce large amounts for trade with soldiers. Although more tools such as forges and looms were installed at missions in the 1800–1809 decade,[20] it was not until the military stopped receiving any imported goods after 1810 that missions began to install grist mills and fulling mills—standard eighteenth-century technology. One might conclude then that incentives to invest in tools to raise Indian productivity were held down by the limited price incentives offered.

There is a third explanation for the failure of missions to invest in equipment. Slave owners had incentives to raise the skill level of slaves because if slaves produced more output per hour, then the plantation owner would reap greater profits. There was no need to fear that a skilled slave might set up his own shop, because he was not free to leave. However, in contrast, while mission Indians were also not free to set up shops, the status of mission Indians was not permanent. Religious control over Indians could only persist so long as Indians were considered "uncivilized." This gave missionaries incentives to slow down the process of assimilating Indians into Spanish culture. Obviously, this incentive is perverse, given that missions were ostensibly meant to be institutions of acculturation. The way to reconcile the perverse incentive to keep Indians uncivilized with the overt goal of missions to bring Indians into the Spanish way of life, was for missionaries to bring Indians into Spanish culture, but at a slow pace. Missionaries in Mexico prolonged use of native language

---

17. Marie Christine Duggan, "Laws of the Market vs. Laws of God," *History of Political Economy* 37(2), (2005): 358.

18. Santa Barbara Mission-Presidio Account Book, Santa Barbara Mission Archive Library, Santa Barbara, California.

19. José Señan, Response to Commander Goycoechea's Accusations, October 21, 1800, Mission San Buenaventura, transcript, Santa Barbara Mission Archive Library.

20. Duggan, *With and Without an Empire*, 34.

over Spanish for reasons that could equally well have applied to eighteenth-century missionaries in California: "So long as the linguistic barrier remained [missionaries] were the indispensable intermediaries between the Indians and the civil officers. . . . [T]hey were the lords and masters of their parishioners. . . . They did not relish the prospect of giving it all up."[21] Perhaps the relative political power that speaking the native language gave missionaries is the reason that presidio commanders in California complained that Indians were not being taught Spanish more quickly.[22]

Missionaries may have been reluctant to enhance Indian abilities in various Spanish crafts for the same reason that they had some hesitancy in pushing fluency in Spanish. The end result of Indians skilled in Spanish crafts would only be to hasten interaction with non-religious Spaniards, and to bring on the time when Indians would leave mission congregations to become employees of the military personnel and other settlers. Already by 1797 there is evidence that Commander Goycoechea of Presidio Santa Barbara was paying a weaver from Mission Santa Barbara to weave cloth that Goycoechea presumably intended to sell to his men at a profit.[23] By 1825, Mexico would approve the emancipation of Indians from missions, but only for those skilled in areas that the Mexican settlers appreciated.[24]

There is a fourth reason that missions may have invested little in tools to upgrade productive capacity. An examination of missionary account books demonstrates that missionaries tended to invest any extra funds into statues, paintings, vestments, chalices, candelabra, and musical instruments. This suggests that the emotional power of religious ceremony over Indian congregations was more important to the Spanish in California than was raising productivity. The implication is that social control rather than economic extraction was the goal.

To sum up, Indians at California missions did not produce much beyond their own subsistence during the period of Spanish control (1769–1809) because the Spanish did not invest in equipment capable of raising productivity or move Indians to the location of profitable tasks. A search for an expla-

---

21. Robert Ricard, *The Spiritual Conquest of Mexico: An Essay on the Apostolate and Evangelizing Methods of the Mendicant Orders in New Spain, 1523–1572*, trans. by Lesley Byrd Simpson (Berkeley: University of California Press, 1966 [1933]), 52.

22. Señan, Response to Commander Goycoechea's Accusations. On catechism in Indians' languages, see Norval S.H. Smith and John R. Johnson, "Lengua de los Llanos," *STUF* [Language Typology and Universals, Akademie Verlag], 66(3), (2013), 299–313.

23. Marie Christine Duggan, The Chumash and the Presidio: Evolution of a Relationship, 1782–1823 (Santa Barbara, CA: Santa Barbara Trust for Historic Preservation, 2004), 23.

24. Lisbeth Haas, *Saints and Citizens* (Berkeley: University of California Press, 2014), 141.

nation revealed three possibilities. First, although the Spanish desired that Indians move a few miles away from traditional villages to mission compounds, they did not expect Indians to relocate long distances in the way that slaves were expected to go wherever profits were to be had. Eighteenth-century Spanish writing reveals that uprooted people were seen as a potential social threat, so keeping Indians "rooted" at a compound that the Spanish controlled in their ancestral territory may have been valued more than relocating Indians to locations where profitable activity could be undertaken. Second, the government refused to offer prices high enough to provide incentive for missions to produce beyond their own subsistence, for which processes such as grinding corn by hand sufficed. Third, by pledging to secularize missions as soon as Indians were "civilized," the Crown unwittingly provided missionaries with incentives to slow down the rate at which Indians attained craftsmanship in activities the Spanish valued.

Political Control

If Indians did not produce much beyond subsistence, and if Spain actually lost money on missions, why do we persist in viewing mission Indians as slaves? This temptation arises from the sense that Indians would not have built missions if left to their own devices. In this respect, Indians were not free. The crux of the matter is that being 'not free' is not the same as being 'enslaved.' There are in fact different methods of co-opting people into carrying out work that benefits others more than it benefits themselves. Paying a wage is one, physical coercion is another; exhortations based on emotion (such as patriotism or filial devotion) can also play a role. The three are not mutually exclusive, as when wages are paid to men patriotically exhorted to comply with a draft during wartime; if wages and patriotic exhortation are not enough, the threat of a prison sentence hangs in the background. It seems likely that our understanding of how missions acted to co-opt Indians should be expanded to include other methods besides brutality, without overlooking the violence that did exist.

Given our preconceptions, it is surprising to find that between 1769 and 1809, the people who went after fugitive Indians from missions were rarely Spanish soldiers. Instead, the norm was for other mission Indians to be sent after runaways. If mission Indians were ineffective and if the situation actually posed a threat to the ability of a mission to expand its influence, then the military might be brought in. The role of Indians with subordinate political power inside the mission hierarchy merits more study than it has received since Steven Hackel paved the way in 1997.[25] One example of mission Indians

25. Steven Hackel, "The Staff of Leadership: Indian Authority in the Missions of Alta California," *The William and Mary Quarterly*, 54(2), (1997): 347–376.

on the front lines of conflict with anti-mission Indians comes from Mission San Diego in 1775, when Carlos Chisli and a handful of other Kumeyaay opposed to the mission, left it in September, to prepare an attack carried out in November. During the attack Carlos Chisli led between six hundred and a thousand people to kill the missionary and burn the mission down. The next morning, the first line of defense was Indians loyal to the missionary. Diego had been the missionary's page and also the first convert to San Diego, and the godson of the military commander. At dawn, Diego led a party of mission Indian loyalists to the coast, where he fought with Carlos Chisli and shot with his bow two of Chisli's men. Diego's group then took back some of the sacred objects the rebels had taken from the mission and returned them to the Spaniards.[26]

Another example of Indians allied with the mission system as the front-line control over resistance comes from San Francisco in 1795. Baptized Saclan from Mission San Francisco received permission to leave in April, but they did not return. Two Indian *alcaldes*[27] of the mission, Pasqual Baylon (of the Peninsula Yelamu) and Rogerio (of the East Bay Huchiun) led a posse of fourteen mission Indians. They went by tule raft to the Carquinez Straight and located the resisting Saclan. However, the Saclan were numerous and angry. The resisters killed both *alcaldes* and five other posse members.[28]

The San Diego and San Francisco episodes referred to above were among the most violent conflicts between the Spanish and Indians in the pre-1809 period. In more day-to-day circumstances, Indians requested and received permission to leave the missions regularly, and often overstayed. Commander Goycoechea complained in 1800 to Fray Señan at San Buenaventura that the friar was not doing enough to keep Indians at the mission. Señan admitted that, "Some are absent for a good long time," but assured the commander, "that is always without the consent of the missionaries."[29] One is left with the sense that Mission San Buenaventura was porous. At Mission Santa Barbara in 1800, "[O]ne quarter of the Neophytes are regularly absent, some with permission, others that we baptized on their death beds who did not recover from their illness, others children who still live with their pagan parents, and some runaways."[30] At San Luis Obispo in 1796, it did not seem difficult for

26. Ernest J. Burrus, ed. *Diario del Capitán Comandante Fernando de Rivera y Moncada* (Madrid: Ediciones José Porrua Turanzas, 1967), 452, 459.

27. "*Alcalde*" is typically translated as mayor; for the California mission context, see Hackel, *Staff of Leadership*.

28. Randall Milliken, *Time of Little Choice: The Disintegration of Tribal Culture in the San Francisco Bay Area 1769–1810* (Menlo Park, CA: Ballena Press,1995), 138–141.

29. Señan, Response to Commander Goycoechea's Accusations.

30. Friars Tapis and Cortés, Response to Commander Goycoechea's Accusations, October 30, 1800, transcript, Santa Barbara Mission Archive Library.

a mission Indian to get permission to leave: "Silberio requested permission to go to the mountains for a while [*a pasear*], and after he got permission from the Father Minister to go, he advised his wife Rebeca, that they had to go to the mountains . . . to wherever they might find seeds to harvest."[31]

These statements provide a useful way to disentangle the definitions of slave and mission Indian. Indians had a significant role in protection of the mission system, which slaves did not. That in itself implies a certain amount of physical movement by mission Indians back and forth between Spanish and indigenous space in the political geography of eighteenth-century California.

The question arises as to why the mission relied on its own Indians as the first line of defense. At San Diego, the panicked, violent, and ill-informed methods of the military commander in the weeks after the 1775 attack may provide part of the answer.[32] Indians loyal to the mission may have been better suited for tracking down and recovering the specific Indians who led resistance to the mission. Because they could apprehend specific people, they were less apt to spread rebellion than the military, whose blind, large-scale arrests only served to fan the flames of resistance at San Diego.[33]

At San Francisco in 1795, the fugitives had left by boat for the Carquinez Strait. Mission Indians had tule rafts and the knowledge of currents necessary to use them. As a result, they were more effective than the Spanish military at retrieving fugitives from across the Bay, because the Spanish would have taken much longer to get from San Francisco to Napa on horseback. It is not clear *a priori* how eight unarmed men were to retrieve two hundred fugitives, unless negotiations were anticipated rather than conflict. There is a hint that the friar sent mission Indian subordinates precisely because he wished to avoid military meddling in his political management. When informed of the *alcaldes'* deaths by a mission Indian who survived the conflict, Fr. Dante stated, "Be careful what you say to any soldier, or the commander will find out."[34]

Milliken and La Perouse both concluded that Indians, once baptized, could not leave missions because military force would be used to return them. The evidence supports a slightly different interpretation. Fugitives were a common occurrence as evidenced by the stories from San Diego, San Buenaventura, Santa Barbara, San Luis Obispo, and San Francisco. When time and resources permitted, missionaries would attempt to get Indians to return to the mission by sending Indians loyal to the mission after them. For non-

31. "Causa contra Silverio y Rossa por la muerte alevosa que dio el primero a su mujer," Mission San Luis Obispo, 1796. Archivo General de la Nación (México): Ramo Californias, Volume 65, Expediente 6, Fojas 214–301.

32. Claudio Saunt, "'My Medicine Is Punishment'" *Ethnohistory* 57 (4): 679–708, (2010).

33. Burrus, *Diario.*

34. Milliken, *Time of Little Choice*, 141.

Christian villages to harbor fugitives from the mission might also instigate a posse of mission Indians sent to pressure the non-Christian village to yield the fugitives.

The Spanish military itself would only go after Indians if they actively resisted the mission system. Anti-mission Indian resistance sufficient to instigate a military response could take the form of physically harming baptized Indians, physical attacks on the mission Indian leadership, or physical attack on a missionary or a mission. After the *alcaldes* Pacual and Rogerio of Mission San Francisco were killed by Saclan at the Carquinez Strait, the Spanish military did get involved. When Diego and his band did not manage to kill or apprehend Carlos Chisli, the San Diego military commander instigated surprise nighttime raids in the villages surrounding Mission San Diego. In 1793 at Santa Cruz, two baptized Quiroste couples visited their natal village on a pass. The anti-mission leader of the village was Charquín; he had opposed the Spanish presence for years. However, it was only after he threatened to kill the mission Indians on pass in his village and took their wives that the Spanish military went after him.[35] This concept is related to, but subtly different than, that of Randy Milliken, who argued that if an Indian tried to leave the mission, the Spanish would go after him. People could and did leave missions regularly. Only organized resistance to missions brought serious pursuit. Even then, Diego's role at San Diego suggests that mission Indian loyalists might be more effective at subduing revolt because they understood the politics of the situation better than a military commander. The stories from San Diego and San Francisco leave no doubt that being a mission Indian leader was dangerous.

If military force was only a last resort, and if missions were porous, how else did the Spanish keep Indians attached to missions? Part of the answer is that the Spanish manipulated the Indians' desire to stay in their ancestral territory. Missions were built in that territory and occupied by two religious and a handful of soldiers. The military prevented Indians who resisted the mission from harming the missionaries or harming the subset of Indians who cooperated with the mission. In that way the mission could not be removed from ancestral territory. Given this persistence of a mission in their space, the local people would be pressured by their own tie to the land and to their kin to make some sort of peace with it. Missionaries had a long-term perspective and were willing to wait fifteen or twenty years until the baptism of growing numbers of kin would act as a weight pulling the rest of a community in.

There is one disconcerting implication of the distinction between the profit-motivated nature of a slave plantation and the not-for-profit status of Spanish missions. Ironically, precisely because those who invested in slaves had

35. Milliken, *Time of Little Choice*, 115–120.

to invest their own fortunes, and precisely because slaves were a source of profit, plantation owners acted in ways to protect slaves from dangerous occupations and ensured that slave diets were adequate. Because industrial work was dangerous, employers in the US south shied away from using expensive slave labor for that work, preferring to pay wages to immigrants. The short-term nature of wage labor contracts permitted the employer to escape loss in case the worker suffered injury. Because of the incentive owners of slaves had to protect their investment, they took out life insurance on slaves. Thus it might come as no surprise that there was "a strong positive rate of natural increase in the slave population.[36]" In contrast, Indian deaths outnumbered births at most missions for most years of Spain's control of California.

The way that incentives were aligned to produce that outcome comes through from an incident at San Diego in 1774. When the military commander received 800 Fanegas of wheat from Mexico to supplement the diet of his soldiers, he declined to share any of it with the Indians newly baptized at Mission San Diego, where the harvest had failed.[37] At that time, a working Spaniard living in poverty consumed about four fanegas of wheat per year, so the commander could have shared something without endangering the lives of his twenty-five men. But he did not apparently believe that he had been charged with protecting the lives of Indians in his jurisdiction, rather his job was to protect the lives of his men. It was the missionaries' role to keep Indians from rebelling. The only peso-income friars had for that purpose was the half of their stipends that they could part with, if they lived up to their ascetic ideal. Relying upon ascetic idealists to establish social control was a cheap way for Spain to control the frontier, while slaves were an expensive form of labor. Precisely because Indians were not slaves, no money had been invested by Spain in them and little profit was extracted. That combination provided little incentive to Spaniards on the frontier to ensure that Indian births exceeded deaths. Ironically, Spaniards who owned sugar plantations in the Caribbean may have had greater incentive and ability to ensure a positive natural rate of increase among African slaves, than did ascetic missionaries who volunteered to manage Indian congregations on the frontier.

This essay has clarified for California educators that slavery did not exist in Spanish California. California's early American institution of the mission was distinct from the slave plantation because it was designed for social control rather than profit. Furthermore, mission Indians were never property, as slaves

---

36. Wright, op. cit., 2. Discussion of life insurance and escaping liability by avoiding industrial employment on 73.

37. Marie Christine Duggan, *From Piety to Profits in Alta California: Institutional Change and Crisis in California, 1769 to 1834,* 91. Unpublished manuscript based on Burrus and Herr.

were. Politically, mission Indians shared with slaves the vulnerability to violent punishment with no effective recourse to the law. Yet unlike slaves, Indians were incorporated into the mission hierarchy and mission Indians were the first line of defense to retrieve fugitives, if retrieval was judged appropriate. The military tended to be sent only after fugitives who actively fomented resistance. While African slaves were movable property to be allocated to the most profitable location, the Spaniards did not want to break the Indians' tie to their geography or kin; rather, they wanted to manipulate it. Rootedness to people and place is precisely what the eighteenth-century Spanish used to pressure Indian people to enter the Spanish way of life through the invisible "gates" of the mission.

The limited life span of a mission provided missionaries with a perverse incentive not to change Indian life-ways too quickly. So long as Indian productivity at Spanish crafts was low and age-old economic practices (such as the acorn harvest) coexisted with mission agriculture, the civilizing role of missions could reasonably be said to be incomplete. The perverse incentive not to change Indian life-ways too quickly was reinforced by the low prices offered by the government for mission products. It also dovetailed with the missionaries' own desire to invest in objects for religious ceremony instead of equipment that could have raised the output and quality of Spanish products made by Indians at missions. The overall conclusion is that the Spanish designed missions for social control, in contrast to plantations designed for profit.

By projecting assumptions made in modern times onto the past, we can wind up inadvertently blinding ourselves from seeing most of the stories. The examples provided come from research into archives where the motives of the actors from the past are less hidden. Indians and missionaries become three dimensional, and emerge as more active in making the socio-economic history of California than the ill-fitting slavery paradigm permitted. One essay can only be a first step. Further research into these unexpected aspects of the social relations and institutional framework of the Spanish period of California is overdue.

Chapter 15
Death, Mourning, and Accommodation in the Missions of Alta California

Lee M. Panich

Spanish missions are seen by many indigenous people and scholars alike as sites of profound loss. Across the Borderlands of North America, the native individuals and families who entered mission establishments faced terrible and often lethal challenges posed by introduced diseases, strict labor demands, corporal punishment, and unsanitary conditions. In California, as elsewhere, death was part and parcel of the mission experience for many indigenous neophytes as well as the resident Franciscan missionaries. This chapter explores how native people and Franciscans in Alta California negotiated their divergent but deeply held views about what constituted proper death, burial, and mourning practices. These issues are examined using evidence drawn from pre-Contact archaeological sites, ethnographic information collected by early anthropologists, mission-era archaeological deposits, and from the writings of the Franciscans and other contemporary observers. I argue that native neophytes in Alta California persisted in honoring their dead in culturally appropriate ways while the Franciscans varied in their attitudes toward indigenous mortuary practices.

Mortuary Practices in Native California

California was one of the most densely populated and diverse regions of North America prior to European colonization, with hundreds of independent polities speaking dozens of different languages.[1] Although such a wide spectrum of indigenous societies makes generalization difficult, the following summary presents key aspects of Native Californian mortuary practices in the missionized area between San Diego and the San Francisco Bay.

---

1. Kent G. Lightfoot and Otis Parrish, *California Indians and Their Environment: An Introduction* (Berkeley: University of California Press, 2009).

Pre-Contact archaeological evidence offers a wealth of information concerning the diversity of indigenous mortuary practices prior to the onset of European colonialism. Archaeologically, it appears that most Native Californian groups maintained formal cemeteries, often on the margins of village settlements. A variety of methods were used to dispose of the bodies of the deceased, although most groups favored either burial or cremation; some employed both methods, reserving one or the other for particular purposes. Secondary burials and secondary cremations are occasionally noted in the archaeological record. Among those groups who buried their dead, flexed burials were most common in pre-Contact times, but burials in the extended position were not unknown. Throughout the state, large proportions of the population were interred or cremated with grave goods, which likely served as markers of the deceased's social or political status. Important categories of grave goods included *Olivella* shell beads or clamshell beads (depending on the region), bone tools, chipped stone tools, and ground-stone implements.[2] One notable regional pattern is the occurrence of banjo-shaped *Haliotis* (abalone) pendants interred with certain individuals in the greater San Francisco Bay area. These distinctive pendants appear to be associated with the spread of the Kuksu ceremonial cult.[3] Archaeologists have additionally noted the material correlates of annual mourning ceremonies, which are particularly well documented in the archaeological record of the Los Angeles Basin.[4]

Ethnographic information collected by early anthropologists also reveals important information about mortuary practices before and after colonization. Mourning ceremonies are one of the most well-known practices documented in Native California. These rituals typically commemorated all of the previous year's dead and could attract dozens or even hundreds of individuals who brought with them offerings such as baskets, beads, and ornaments. With some local differences, the annual mourning ceremony seems to have been practiced throughout nearly all of the coastal strip and inland valleys affected

2. Regionally specific archaeological overviews can be found in Jon M. Erlandson and Terry L. Jones, eds. *Catalysts to Complexity: Late Holocene Societies on the California Coast* (Los Angeles: Cotsen Institute of Archaeology, University of California, 2002); and Terry L. Jones and Kathryn A. Klar, eds. *California Prehistory: Colonization, Culture, and Complexity* (Lanham, MD: AltaMira Press, 2007).

3. Mark G. Hylkema, "Tidal Marsh, Oak Woodlands, and Cultural Florescence in the Southern San Francisco Bay Region," in *Catalysts to Complexity: Late Holocene Societies of the California Coast*, eds. Jon M. Erlandson and Terry L. Jones (Los Angeles: Cotsen Institute of Archaeology, University of California, 2002), 233–262.

4. Kathleen L. Hull, John G. Douglass, and Andrew L. York, "Recognizing Ritual Action and Intent in Communal Mourning Features on the Southern California Coast," *American Antiquity* 78 (2013): 24–47.

by Franciscan missionization in Alta California.[5] Ethnographic information additionally illuminates how Native Californians honored the deceased at the time of death. As supported by archaeological data, native informants interviewed by anthropologists reported wide variation across the state in the use of burial, cremation, or both. Though the details differed throughout the region, native mourners often participated in ritual wailing, hair cutting, body painting in particular colors, and the burning of the property of the deceased.[6]

Death and Mourning in Colonial California

With the onset of missionization in Alta California in 1769, many indigenous groups were forced to negotiate the social world of the Franciscan missions. The development of the mission system and the implications for native people is an important topic of current scholarly research.[7] Of primary consideration is how native groups and individuals continued, reinterpreted, or modified their traditional practices within the twenty-one colonial missions of Alta California where Franciscan padres instituted a program of enculturation intended to convert Native Californians to Catholicism and Euroamerican life-ways. One aspect of this intercultural negotiation that has received only slight attention is the manner in which native people accommodated or resisted Franciscan teachings about proper ways to dispose of and honor the deceased. In the following sections, I offer a synthesis of the archaeological and documentary evidence for how native people and Franciscan missionaries negotiated this aspect of missionization in Alta California.

Documentary Evidence

Due largely to the meticulous record keeping of the Franciscans, documentary evidence from colonial California contains a wealth of information regarding indigenous life at the missions, including insight into how native people buried and mourned their dead. The most comprehensive overview of indige-

---

5. Alfred L. Kroeber, *Handbook of the Indians of California*, Bureau of American Ethnology Bulletin, no. 78 (Washington, DC: Smithsonian Institution, 1925), Stephen Powers, *Tribes of California* (Berkeley: University of California Press, 1976).

6. Kroeber, *Handbook of the Indians of California*; Richard A. Gould, *Aboriginal California Burial and Cremation Practices*, University of California Archaeological Survey Reports, no. 60 (Berkeley, 1963), 149–168.

7. Lisbeth Haas, *Saints and Citizens: Indigenous Histories of Colonial Missions and Mexican California* (Berkeley: University of California Press, 2014); Steven W. Hackel, *Children of Coyote, Missionaries of Saint Francis: Indian Spanish Relations in Colonial California, 1769–1850* (Chapel Hill: University of North Carolina Press, 2005); Kent G. Lightfoot, *Indians, Missionaries, and Merchants: The Legacy of Colonial Encounters on the California Frontiers* (Berkeley: University of California Press, 2005).

nous burial and mourning practices, as well as Franciscan attitudes toward them, are found in the answers to the Interrogatorio of 1813–1815.[8] This document queried the Franciscans on several aspects of indigenous life. Question 21 explicitly asks, "Do they use any strange ceremonial at the time of burial or mourning?" Responses to other questions also contain relevant information, including prompts regarding superstitions (question 10) as well as human sacrifice,[9] idolatry, and other ceremonies (questions 28 and 29). The Franciscans' responses fall into four general categories: those that reference Catholic doctrine, those that describe indigenous practices outside of the missions, those that describe native practices in mission settings, and those that describe native practices without geographic context (Table 1). For example, the response to question 21 regarding burial and mourning customs from missionaries at Mission San Carlos includes statements relating to the first three categories:

> As pagans, their method of burial was to dig a large hole in which they placed the corpse. . . . All the relatives throw beads and seeds upon the dead in token of their love for the deceased. As Christians they are buried according to the ritual of the Church. Nevertheless, in secret they cling to their pagan practice. As a sign of mourning the father, mother, child, husband or wife or brother or sister cut off their hair. . . . Moreover they throw ashes over their entire bodies, weep bitterly, abstain from food, and the old women smear their faces with pitch. . . .[10]

As Table 1 suggests, there is no strong patterning in the responses given to the questions about burial and mourning, and some variation may result from how individual missionaries interpreted the question. However, when supplementary information from other questions is included, Franciscans at a minimum of ten missions noted the continuity of native practices at their establishments, with another three describing native practices with little contextual information. Franciscans at all missions, moreover, described indigenous practices in some form, whether they were carried out in their "pagan state" or at the mission itself. Missionaries in Alta California were thus very familiar with native burial and mourning practices. The attitudes captured by their answers include some that are particularly unfavorable—for example, the missionaries at San Juan Capistrano referred to indigenous mourning practices as "superstitious and savage customs"[11]—while others appear to have simply stated what they knew of local traditions.

---

8. Maynard J. Geiger and Clement W. Meighan, *As the Padres Saw Them: California Indian Life and Customs as Reported by the Franciscan Missionaries, 1813–1815* (Santa Barbara, CA: Santa Barbara Mission Archive Library, 1976).

9. Human sacrifice was not practiced in Native California.

10. Geiger and Meighan, *As the Padres Saw Them*, 99.

11. Ibid., 97.

TABLE 1. Summary of Franciscan Responses to Questions about Native Californian Burial and Mourning Practices from Interrogatorio of 1813–1815

Mission	Catholic Practices	Native Practices in "Pagan" State	Native Practices in Mission	Native Practices (No Location)
San Diego		(X)	X	
San Luís Rey			(X)	X
San Juan Capistrano				X
San Gabriel		X	X	
San Fernando		X	(X)	
San Buenaventura	X	X		
Santa Barbara	X	(X)	X	
Santa Inés	X		X	
San Luís Obispo		X		
San Miguel		X		
San Antonio		X	(X)	
Soledad		X	X	
San Carlos	X	X	X	
San Juan Bautista	X	X		
Santa Cruz		X	X	
Santa Clara				X
San José		X		
San Francisco		(X)		X

Notes: X = information present in response to Question 21. (X) = supplemental information from responses to other questions.

It is not clear whether indigenous mortuary practices were explicitly forbidden or simply discouraged,[12] and responses to the questionnaires of 1813–1815 suggest that some Franciscans accommodated native mortuary practices that did not directly contradict Church doctrine regarding the sacraments and proper burial. These may have included hair cutting, painting of the face or body, and crying, all of which correspond to ethnographically known mourning rituals. Yet many responses mention the offering of grave goods, a practice not in keeping with contemporary Catholic doctrine, and it may be that individual missionaries strategically ignored native mortuary traditions that they could not eliminate. The padres at Mission San Diego, for example, remarked that native practices continued when the missionaries were "careless," and missionaries at San Luis Rey stated that neophytes there placed "seeds, beads,

12. Quincy D. Newell, *Constructing Lives at Mission San Francisco: Native Californians and Hispanic Colonists, 1776–1821* (Albuquerque: University of New Mexico Press, 2009), 154–155.

and other trifles" during "burials in the mission cemetery when the missionary fathers are not looking."[13]

Beyond the Interrogatorio of 1813–1815, some additional accounts indicate that the Franciscans may have reluctantly allowed native people to mourn their dead in ways consistent with pre-Contact cultural traditions. Comte de La Pérouse, who visited the Monterey region in 1786, stated that missionaries compromised with native people and allowed modified versions of traditional bodily decoration associated with mourning.[14] Farther south, Father Gerónimo Boscana related that neophytes at Mission San Juan Capistrano disposed of "bead money" and other items belonging to deceased individuals by placing them in the grave.[15] Not all missionaries, however, tolerated native mourning practices—an account from Mission San Francisco suggests that two neophytes were whipped for loudly mourning their deceased relatives.[16]

The documentary record for Alta California also contains information indicating both accommodation and resistance on the part of native people. In her research on the experiences of Native Americans at Mission San Francisco, Quincy Newell (2009) demonstrates that neophytes there held a range of attitudes toward Catholicism. While many outwardly embraced the new religion, a significant number appear to have timed important life events such as birth and death to occur away from the mission proper. For example, more than six hundred neophytes died outside of Mission San Francisco, and roughly half of those (or approximately three hundred individuals) died in the indigenous hinterlands. Of those, Newell argues that some two hundred neophytes "elected to die among family and friends" in their natal villages.[17] Newell provides detailed descriptions of native people from Mission San Francisco who actively manipulated the policy of *paseo* (approved leaves from missions) to die on their own terms, although she notes that some individuals also made confession or received sacraments prior to departing the mission. Lastly, Newell describes several instances in which parents removed children who had fallen ill from the mission so that they could die and be mourned in culturally appropriate ways.

As part of my ongoing research at Mission Santa Clara, I examined neophyte death records available through the Huntington Library's Early Cali-

---

13. Geiger and Meighan, *As the Padres Saw Them*, 97, 119.

14. Russell K. Skowronek, "Sifting the Evidence: Perceptions of Life at the Ohlone (Costanoan) Missions of Alta California," *Ethnohistory* 45 (1998): 685.

15. John R. Johnson, "The Various Chinigchinich Manuscripts of Father Gerónimo Boscana," in *San Diego, Alta California, and the Borderlands: Proceedings of the 23rd Annual Conference of the California Mission Studies Association*, eds. R. M. Beebe and R. M. Senkewicz (Santa Clara: California Mission Studies Association, 2006), 1–19.

16. Newell, *Constructing Lives at Mission San Francisco*, 155.

17. Ibid., 152–167.

fornia Population Project (ECPP) database for similar patterns that might shed light on how native people and Spanish missionaries negotiated death and its attendant rituals.[18] Out of roughly 7,700 native neophytes recorded in the mission's death records, my analysis revealed 668 individuals who died away from Santa Clara. Seventy-eight individuals died and were buried at other missions, while 157 died outside of the mission but were eventually buried in the *campo santo* at Mission Santa Clara. The other 433 individuals appear to have died and been buried away from the mission, including many who were buried in their natal villages. Combined, these three groups represent 8.7 percent of the indigenous deaths recorded for Santa Clara. The Franciscans were likely troubled by the many neophyte deaths that occurred outside of the mission, particularly if the death occurred among unmissionized native people. In such instances, the padres often noted the possibility that the individuals in question had been cremated by their kin, a violation of Catholic doctrine.[19]

Of course, some of the neophytes who perished outside of the California missions did so accidentally. Hackel examines data on the causes of death among neophytes across Alta California, including information regarding Indians who died away from the missions.[20] He lists dozens of individuals who died of exposure, drowned, or were killed by wild animals while outside of their home missions. Violence also claimed the lives of 146 neophytes during conflicts with unbaptized Indians and 26 more at the hands of colonial soldiers.[21] He notes that these unusual and noteworthy incidents may be overrepresented in the death records, which typically do not include cause of death. It is therefore likely that many of the other deaths recorded as occurring in the hinterlands represent the intentions of certain neophytes to die in their ancestral homelands, either as fugitives or through the manipulation of mission policies like *paseo*.

The documentary record also provides details regarding the treatment of native individuals who died in residence at Alta California missions. In the case of adult neophytes, the death records typically indicate whether the deceased had received the last rites (penance, extreme unction, and/or

---

18. Huntington Library, *Early California Population Project Database* (2006), http://www.huntington.org/information/ECPPmain.htm.

19. Lee M. Panich, "'Sometimes They Bury the Deceased's Clothes and Trinkets': Indigenous Mortuary Practices at Mission Santa Clara de Asís," *Historical Archaeology* 49(4) (2015): 110–129.

20. Steven W. Hackel, "From *Ahogado* to *Zorrillo*: External Causes of Mortality in the California Missions," in *From La Florida to La California: Franciscan Evangelization in the Spanish Borderlands*, eds. Timothy J. Johnson and Gert Melville (Berkeley: Academy of American Franciscan History, 2013), 353–388.

21. Ibid., 369.

viaticum). Hackel states that 30 percent of adult neophytes died without having received penance or extreme unction, and 92 percent died without having received viaticum, or final communion.[22] Yet there appears to have been some variation among the Alta California missions regarding the administration of viaticum to adult neophytes. The records that Mariano Payeras kept during his years as the president of the Alta California missions (1816–1819) reveal that most missions administered at least some viaticums to dying neophytes, and certain missions, such as San Gabriel, performed several dozen per year. Other missions, however, reported very few; Santa Clara, for example, reported no viaticums administered to dying adult neophytes in those years.[23] My analysis of the Santa Clara death records, spanning from 1777 into the late 1840s, reveals that only about 130 neophytes received final communion during the entirety of the mission period.

These patterns may represent an area of negotiation by both the Franciscans and Native Californians. As detailed by Hackel, missionaries in Alta California initially believed the conversion of native people too precarious to warrant the last rites in general and final communion in particular. This notion is evidenced in the increasing rate of viaticums performed over time, particularly after the 1790s.[24] Yet, the uneven distribution of viaticums noted in the records of Payeras as late as the 1810s, as well as in the investigation of death records at particular missions like Santa Clara, suggests that the Franciscans likely adopted localized practices regarding the administration of the last rites to adult neophytes. Practical concerns, such as the availability of unleavened bread and wine, may also have been an issue at some missions. For their part, indigenous neophytes probably exercised some agency regarding whether they would receive the final sacraments. The uneven administration of the last rites and universally low rate of viaticums to neophytes suggests that certain individuals avoided the sacraments once death was imminent.

Archaeological Evidence

Given the long history of archaeological research at California mission sites, surprisingly little information has been published on mission cemeteries. Although variation exists, the general pattern appears to be that the mission cemetery, or *campo santo*, was adjacent to the church. Most neophytes were buried in shrouds, often with their arms folded over their torsos.[25] In the mid-twentieth century, a woman who illicitly disturbed more than two dozen

---

22. Ibid., 361.

23. Donald Cutter, ed. and trans., *Writings of Mariano Payeras* (Santa Barbara, CA: Bellerophon Books, 1995).

24. Hackel, *Children of Coyote*, 170–181.

25. Skowronek, "Sifting the Evidence," 686.

Native American graves in a cemetery possibly associated with Mission Sonoma noted that the burials were in the extended position and contained numerous glass beads and other imported objects.[26] Archaeological testing was conducted at one of the cemeteries at Mission Soledad in 1969, and information was also collected at that time regarding the numerous graves disturbed during agricultural grading of the cemetery in 1940. Glass and shell beads were both present, as were redwood coffins, although the results were difficult to interpret given the amount of disturbance to the cemetery and the possibility of post-mission interments.[27] At Mission San José, earth-moving activities associated with the reconstruction of the mission church in the early 1980s revealed some beads and mission tiles associated with neophyte burials, and both shell and glass beads are occasionally brought to the surface through rodent activity in the post-1811 mission cemetery about a mile west of the mission.[28]

Missions Santa Clara, San Diego, and La Purísima offer the best evidence for neophyte burial practices. At Santa Clara, two cemeteries have been investigated archaeologically. In the earlier cemetery, adjacent to the third mission compound (ca. 1781–1818), two archaeological mitigation projects documented the remains of a minimum of twenty-four individuals. Although many of the burials had been previously disturbed, the cemetery contained large quantities of grave goods, including shell and glass beads and abalone pendants, as well as mission tiles.[29] The second cemetery is associated with the fifth mission church (ca. 1825–1851), and was the site of a small archaeological mitigation project after several clusters of human bone, grave goods, and possible redwood coffin fragments were discovered in construction activities.[30]

---

26. Treganza, Adan E., "Sonoma Mission: An Archaeological Reconstruction of the Mission San Francisco de Solano Quadrangle," *Kroeber Anthropological Society Papers* 14 (1956): 13.

27. Donald M. Howard, "Archaeological Investigation at Misión Nuestra Señora de La Soledad, MNT-233, Monterey County, California," *Monterey County Archaeological Society Quarterly* 1(3) (1972): 1–10.

28. Andy Galvan, personal communication.

29. Mark G. Hylkema, Archaeological Investigations at the Third Location of Mission Santa Clara de Asís: The Murguía Mission, 1781–1818 (CA-SCL-30/H) (Oakland: California Department of Transportation, 1995); Alan Leventhal, Diane DiGiuseppe, Melynda Atwood, David Grant, Rosemary Cambra, Charlene Nijmeh, Monica V. Arellano, Sheila Guzman-Schmidt, Gloria E. Gomez, and Norma Sanchez, Final Report on the Burial and Archaeological Data Recovery Program Conducted on a Portion of the Mission Santa Clara Indian Neophyte Cemetery (1781–1818): Clareño Muwékma Ya Túnnešte Nómmo [Where the Clareño Indians Are Buried] Site (CA-SCL-30/H), Located in the City of Santa Clara, Santa Clara County, California (Report to Pacific Gas and Electric Company, 2011). The earlier cemetery may have been in use as late as 1825.

30. Russel K. Skowronek and Julie C. Wizorek, "Archaeology at Santa Clara de Asís: The Slow Rediscovery of a Moveable Mission," *Pacific Coast Archaeological Society Quarterly* 33(3), (1997): 54–92.

Together, more than 5,000 shell and glass beads, as well as 18 abalone pendants and pendant fragments, were recovered from the two cemeteries.

Excavations at Mission San Diego have also revealed significant numbers of indigenous burials dating to the mission period. Archaeological work in 1989, for example, resulted in the discovery of between eighteen and forty burials in one of the mission cemeteries. Out of respect for the descendant communities, the remains were only minimally studied, but investigators noted the presence of modest quantities of grave goods, including glass and shell beads, phoenix buttons, and incised clay tiles.[31] Archaeologists have also investigated the cemetery associated with the second site of Mission La Purísima (ca. 1813–1849), home to a large Chumash population. There, over fifty individuals were noted during excavations, although this total is far less than the number of neophytes recorded in the mission's burial records during the period in question.[32] Nevertheless, the La Purísima interments stand in contrast to the patterns seen at Santa Clara, San Diego, and other missions in that they were almost devoid of grave goods.[33] One individual at La Purísima was associated with 120 glass beads, but the excavators believed the burial to post-date the primary use of the mission cemetery.

The La Purísima cemetery can also be compared to the historic-era Chumash cemetery at Humaliwo (present-day Malibu), a village that sent more than one hundred individuals to nearby missions during the late eighteenth and early nineteenth centuries. Archaeological investigations of the cemetery revealed thousands of glass beads and other historic-era grave goods, items conspicuously lacking at La Purísima. The Humaliwo cemetery, moreover, departed from native burials at mission sites in that they were primarily in the flexed position with the head oriented to the west, both important components of Chumash mortuary practices.[34] For comparison, the La Purísima burials were all extended and oriented to the northeast.[35] Although Gamble suggests Humaliwo residents were more

---

31. Richard L. Carrico, Remnants Pulled from the Fire: Report on the 1989 Spring–Summer Mission San Diego de Alcalá Archaeological Excavations (manuscript on file with Richard Carrico, 2014).

32. Richard Humphrey, "The La Purísima Mission Cemetery," *Annual Reports of the University of California Archaeological Survey* 7 (Los Angeles, 1965), 179–192; Philip L. Walker, John R. Johnson, and Patricia M. Lambert, "Age and Sex Biases in the Preservation of Human Skeletal Remains," *American Journal of Physical Anthropology* 76 (1988): 183–188.

33. The available responses to the Interrogatorio of 1813–1815, which may shed light on this issue, do not include Mission La Purísima.

34. Terisa M. Green, "Archaeological Evidence for Post-Contact Native Religion: The Chumash Land of the Dead," *Journal of California and Great Basin Anthropology* 23 (2001): 319–327.

35. Humphrey, "The La Purísima Mission Cemetery."

closely aligned with secular ranching operations than they were the missions,[36] the cemetery data nonetheless demonstrate that native people there ignored Catholic burial customs while simultaneously incorporating Euroamerican objects such as glass beads into dynamic indigenous mortuary traditions.

The archaeologically documented burials of so-called *gente de razón* who were interred at Alta California missions and presidios provide an additional angle of comparison with indigenous burials from mission cemeteries. At Mission Soledad, for example, several individuals were buried within the mission church, including José Joaquin de Arrillaga. Howard excavated two burials there, which he interpreted as possibly being the remains of a mission mayordomo and his wife.[37] Both were interred in redwood coffins, and the male individual was buried with a copper crucifix. Indeed, coffins may have been more commonly used for *gente de razón* throughout Alta California. In San Diego, a higher percentage of individuals were interred in coffins at the presidio than at the mission where neophyte burials included mass graves.[38] Coffins were also used for burials in the chapel of the Santa Barbara Presidio.[39] At Mission Santa Clara, redwood coffins were apparently not used for neophyte burials until the final years of the mission's occupation.[40] Although no systematic review has yet been completed, information on mortuary practices for Spanish officials and other colonial settlers indicates significant differences between *gente de razón* and mission neophytes.[41]

Archaeological research also has the potential to illuminate indigenous mourning practices that took place outside of the mission cemeteries. Recent archaeological excavations within the neophyte *ranchería* at Mission Santa Clara, for example, raise the intriguing possibility that native people continued to practice some form of mourning ceremony at the mission. Archaeologists have noted several pit features each containing hundreds of burned shell beads, as well as other items that would have been highly valued such as shell

---

36. Lynn H. Gamble, *The Chumash World at European Contact: Power, Trade, and Feasting among Complex Hunter-Gatherers* (Berkeley: University of California Press, 2008).

37. Howard, "Archaeological Investigation at Misión Nuestra Señora de La Soledad."

38. Carrico, Remnants Pulled from the Fire; Patricia Mitchell, Summary of Findings for a Portion of the Human Remains Recovered from ERCE's 1989 Excavation at San Diego Mission de Acalá, San Diego, California (Report to the Kumeyaay Cultural and Historical Committee, 1993), 48.

39. Julia G. Costello and Phillip L. Walker, "Burials from the Santa Barbara Presidio Chapel," *Historical Archaeology* 21 (1987): 3–17.

40. Skowronek and Wizorek, "Archaeology at Santa Clara de Asís."

41. See also Richard L. Carrico, "The Identification of Two Burials at the San Diego Presidio," *Journal of San Diego History* 19 (1973): 51–55; and Paul Ezell, "The Excavation Program at the San Diego Presidio," *Journal of San Diego History* 22 (1976): 1–19.

ornaments.[42] One feature, discovered adjacent to an adobe neophyte barracks, included over 1,800 shell beads, nearly all of which appear to have been burned *in situ*. The feature, which was only partially excavated, also contained 30 glass beads, an iron spur rowel, large portions of two ceramic vessels, a ceramic gaming disk, a brass finger ring, a raptorial talon, a small bird bone tube, two abalone pendant blanks, and over 2,500 native tobacco seeds, among other materials. I interpret this feature, and others like it, to represent either the remains of annual mourning ceremonies and/or evidence of the ritual destruction of property belonging to recently deceased individuals.[43] The location of these features within the neophyte *ranchería* suggests that native people maintained or modified traditional mourning practices within their own neighborhood even as most individuals were buried in accordance with Church doctrine in the *campo santo*.[44]

Conclusion

The combination of ethnographic, documentary, and archaeological data offer evidence of accommodation and negotiation regarding indigenous mortuary practices in the Franciscan missions of Alta California. Native people accepted, perhaps reluctantly, some of the Franciscans' teachings, but nonetheless succeeded in maintaining and rearticulating other aspects of their pre-Contact mortuary practices under the constraints of colonialism. The Franciscans, for their part, intended to alter Native Californian beliefs and customs, but also appear to have accommodated certain indigenous practices regarding death and mourning. Across the province, the evidence suggests both local variation as well as general trends in the conditions under which native deaths occurred, the location

---

42. Rebecca Allen, R. Scott Baxter, Linda Hylkema, Clinton Blount, and Stella D'Oro, *Uncovering and Interpreting History and Archaeology at Mission Santa Clara* (Report to Santa Clara University, 2010); Lee M. Panich, Helga Afaghani, and Nicole Mathwich, "Assessing the Diversity of Mission Populations through the Comparison of Native American Residences at Mission Santa Clara de Asís," *International Journal of Historical Archaeology* 18 (2014): 467–488; Panich, "'Sometimes They Bury the Deceased's Clothes and Trinkets'"

43. The latter practice was referenced by Franciscans at Mission San Francisco in the Interrogatorio of 1813–1815. They wrote, "The effects belonging to the deceased are, as a rule, burned or are placed with him in such a way that no one will make use of anything which had come into contact with the dead person." Geiger and Meighan, *As the Padres Saw Them*, 120.

44. Archaeologists recently documented a feature related to indigenous mourning ceremonies at Mission San Gabriel. John Dietler, Heather Gibson, and Benjamin Vargas, "A Mourning Dirge was Sung: Community and Remembrance at Mission San Gabriel" (Paper presented at the 80th Annual Meeting of the Society for American Archaeology, San Francisco, CA, 15–19 April 2015).

and method of burial, the presence of grave goods, as well as associated mourning traditions.

As the documentary record from Missions Santa Clara and San Francisco demonstrate, some native people may have avoided the last rites while others actively sought to die outside the mission walls where culturally appropriate burial and mourning could take place. Within the missions of Alta California, however, most neophytes were buried in the extended position in the *campo santo* adjacent to the mission church. While this practice conformed to the missionaries' expectations, indigenous neophytes also would have considered appropriate the placement of formal cemeteries within or on the margins of village communities. The use of extended burials was not unknown to Native Californians, although it was only occasionally employed outside of the missions. As important aspects of most indigenous mortuary practices, grave goods were likely a more significant arena of negotiation and accommodation. Neophytes throughout Alta California clearly continued to offer goods such as beads and seeds during burials at many missions, and some individual Franciscans appear to have either tolerated the practice or at least turned a blind eye to its persistence. Native people continued other important mourning practices, such as wailing, bodily adornment, and dietary restrictions, with variable reactions from the Franciscans. Native neophytes may also have continued to celebrate annual mourning ceremonies and/or the ritual destruction of the deceased's property, as evidenced by archaeological features discovered at Mission Santa Clara.

The evidence presented here offers multiple perspectives on how Franciscan missionaries and diverse groups of Native Californians negotiated each other's tightly held cultural beliefs about death and mourning. Similar patterns of accommodation can be seen in other regions of the Spanish Borderlands, such as La Florida.[45] There, archaeologists have also noted that many indigenous people buried in colonial-era cemeteries associated with Franciscan missions were accompanied by large quantities of grave goods. At Mission Santa Catalina de Guale, in Georgia, nearly seventy thousand glass beads were found associated with the graves of more than four hundred native individuals, likely representing Franciscan accommodation of persistent indigenous traditions. As in California, these goods may have marked individual or group status

45. Elliot H. Blair, "The Role of Beads on St. Catherines Island," in *The Beads of St. Catherines Island*, edited by Elliot H. Blair, Lorann S.A. Pendleton, and Peter Francis Jr., 167–178, American Museum of Natural History Anthropological Papers, no. 89 (New York: American Museum of Natural History, 2009); Bonnie G. McEwan, "The Spiritual Conquest of La Florida," *American Anthropologist* 103 (2001): 633–644; David Hurst Thomas, "Saints and Soldiers at Santa Catalina: Hispanic Designs for Colonial California," in *The Recovery of Meaning: Historical Archaeology in the Eastern United States*, edited by Mark P. Leone and Parker B. Potter (Washington, DC: Smithsonian Institution Press, 1988), 73–140.

within the mission's native population. The spatial structure of mission cemeteries in La Florida also appears to be related to group membership and/or status, a topic not well studied in Alta California. Together, the mission cemeteries of La Florida and Alta California provide similar stories of negotiation that span the North American Borderlands.

Mission cemeteries also remain important places within the modern cultural landscape. In Alta California, many cemetery sites have been lost to agricultural activities or modern development, but they have not been forgotten by the descendants of the indigenous people who lived, worked, and too often died in the California missions. Active lobbying by local native people successfully saved the Ohlone Indian Cemetery, associated with Mission San José, from being destroyed during highway construction in the 1960s.[46] In the 1980s, widespread protest by an alliance of indigenous groups helped preserve a cemetery associated with Mission San Diego.[47] And in the 2000s, the Muwekma Ohlone Tribe succeeded in gaining control of archaeological mitigation in the largest of multiple cemeteries associated with Mission Santa Clara, eventually renaming the site in their own language as the Clareño Muwékma Ya Túnneŝte Nómmo [Where the Clareño Indians Are Buried] Site.[48] Yet the public interpretive programs at most California mission sites downplay or ignore the presence of large colonial-era cemeteries,[49] leaving invisible not just the tragic toll that the missions exacted on indigenous peoples in colonial California, but also the complex processes of resistance, negotiation, and accommodation that unfolded there.

Acknowledgments

I thank the organizers and other participants in the Franciscan borderlands conference for a stimulating intellectual exchange. In particular, this chapter benefited from conversations with Elliot Blair, Andy Galvan, John Johnson, Vincent Medina, Jack Robinson OFM, and David Hurst Thomas. Back home in Alta California, Luis Calero SJ, Richard Carrico, John Dietler, Alan Leventhal, and Sarah Peelo each contributed to my understanding of the diverse issues surrounding indigenous mortuary practices in colonial California.

---

46. Vincent Medina, "Our Cemetery, Our Elder: Hope and Continuity at the Ohlone Cemetery," *News from Native California,* 29 (1) (2015): 16-19; Randall Milliken, Laurence H. Shoup, and Beverly R. Ortiz, Ohlone/Costanoan Indians of the San Francisco Peninsula and Their Neighbors, Yesterday and Today (Report to National Park Service, 2009), 224–225.

47. Clifford Trafzer, "Serra's Legacy: The Desecration of American Indian Burials at Mission San Diego," *American Indian Cultural and Research Journal* 16 (1992): 57–75.

48. Leventhal, et al., Final Report on the Burial and Archaeological Data Recovery Program.

49. Deana Dartt-Newton, "California's Sites of Conscience: An Analysis of the State's Historic Mission Museums," *Museum Anthropology* 34 (2011): 97–108.

Chapter 16
"Suffering hunger and a thousand labors in the mountains…": The Archaeology of Indigenous Resistance, Runaways, and Refuge in Spanish Alta California

Tsim D. Schneider[1]

Sparked by the beating of a baptized Indian visiting a jailed relative at Mission Santa Inés in February 1824, Chumash Indians torched mission buildings and set upon garrisoned soldiers with bow and arrow and stolen rifles.[2] Chumash messengers quickly traveled the seventeen miles from Mission Santa Inés to Mission La Purísima and twenty-five miles to Mission Santa Barbara to tell of the attack to other Chumash residing at these neighboring missions. In a matter of hours all three missions and the Santa Barbara Channel region were embroiled in armed revolt.

At Mission La Purísima, armed Chumash rebels held out the longest. There, they prepared embattlements to fend off Californio troops, and they sent couriers carrying sacks of beads to relatives and long-standing allies east

---

1. This chapter is an extended version of a paper presented at the conference, "Franciscan Florida in Pan-Borderlands Perspective: Adaptation, Negotiation, and Resistance" (Flagler College, St. Augustine, Florida, March 13–15, 2014). Radiocarbon dates, EDXRF data, and artifact analyses appear in Tsim Schneider, "Placing Refuge: Shell Mounds and the Archaeology of Colonial Encounters in the San Francisco Bay Area, California" (PhD diss., University of California, Berkeley, 2010). I thank Drs. Timothy J. Johnson and David H. Thomas for the invitation to present at the conference, and Drs. Jeffrey M. Burns and Kathaeryne E. Soluri for their editorial assistance.

2. Translated accounts of the 1824 Chumash Revolt appear in Sherburne F. Cook, "Expeditions to the Interior of California, Central Valley, 1820–1840," *University of California Anthropological Records* 20 (1962): 152–158; Lisbeth Haas, *Saints and Citizens: Indigenous Histories or Colonial Missions and Mexican California* (Berkeley: University of California Press, 2014), 116–139; James A. Sandos, "LEVANTAMIENTO! The 1824 Chumash Uprising Reconsidered," *Southern California Quarterly* 67 (1985); and James A. Sandos "Christianization among the Chumash: An Ethnohistoric Perspective," *American Indian Quarterly* 15 (1991).

in the California interior as enticement to "join them in annihilating the soldiers."[3] At Mission Santa Barbara, priests' quarters were pillaged, but Californio soldiers from the nearby Santa Barbara presidio quickly regained control of the mission. Fearing retribution, Indian leaders at Mission Santa Barbara led followers to nearby mountain refuges and then further east and inland to the *tulares*, or the once-vast tule marshes of southern San Joaquin Valley, where they were given safe haven by unbaptized Yokuts.[4] Fifty Chumash from Mission Santa Barbara also fled west in two plank canoes and sought refuge—possibly at familiar villages—for at least eleven weeks on Santa Cruz Island, twenty-five miles offshore.[5]

During the revolt and afterward, Franciscan padres worked delicately to coax Indians back to the missions. For example, Father Antonio Ripoll—who is described as energetic, but also a "disturber of traditional Chumash culture . . . [without] peer" and one possible source of the revolt[6]—sent messages to those who had fled Mission Santa Barbara for the nearby mountains. Unsuccessful, Father Ripoll lamented, the Indians instead pulled out and fled further east, "suffering hunger and a thousand labors in the mountains, carrying the old and infirm, and leaving all my efforts frustrated."[7]

In this synopsis of the 1824 Chumash Revolt, we see that even while residing at the coastal missions—and even relatively late for Alta (Upper) California missions, which began secularization in the 1830s—California Indians kept connections to people and places beyond the mission walls. Contrary to a widely circulated view on the Native American experience at Spanish missions as one that positions missions as inescapable and/or sources of irreversible cultural loss for Native communities,[8] recent ethnohistorical and archaeological research examines missions as venues of culture change *and* loci of cultural resilience and indigenous resistance to colonialism. Kent Lightfoot's comparative analysis of colonial enterprises in California, for example, opened mission archaeology to examine the missions in light of the indigenous groups who built them and constructed their lives at the missions, as well as

3. Cook, "Expeditions, 1820–1840," 152.

4. Sandos, "LEVANTAMIENTO!," 120–126.

5. Dee Travis Hudson, "Chumash Canoes of Mission Santa Barbara: The Revolt of 1824," *Journal of California Anthropology* 3 (1976).

6. Sandos, "Christianization," 78.

7. Cook, "Expeditions, 1820–1840," 152.

8. From one widely circulated volume on California Indians: "The California missions were coercive authoritarian institutions . . . [and] once inside the mission system the neophytes, as converts were called, were not free to leave. Constantly under the absolute control of the Franciscans and soldiers, the Indians were forced to observe a rigid discipline." Edward D. Castillo, "The Impact of Euro-American Exploration and Settlement," in *California*, ed. Robert F. Heizer, vol. 8 of *Handbook of North American Indians*, ed. William C. Sturtevant (Washington, DC: Smithsonian Institution, 1978), 101.

the nuanced living conditions and public and private spaces maintained at them.[9] Through the scholarship of Lee Panich, we have a deeper appreciation for the ways Native peoples in Baja and Alta California creatively maintained technological and social traditions at the missions, and the idea that culture change cannot always be equated with cultural loss but also entails the persistence of some practices.[10] Still others demonstrate that mission archaeology is well situated to elaborate on the cultural and historical particularities that framed indigenous responses to colonialism, including numerous examples of Native resistance to Spanish colonialism.[11]

Still, day-to-day Native and non-Native engagements with the broader landscapes around colonial enterprises remain largely undertheorized in North American archaeology. For Alta California especially, trips away from the missions are mostly colored by historical accounts of failed Spanish expeditions into unknown lands—many expeditions that set out from Spanish colonies were organized around the goal of collecting runaways and culminated in the production of official reports that adopted a "language of fear attributed to Indigenous people in Spanish writing."[12] Building on previous mission research, the latest tide of mission scholarship examines how colonial enterprises often fit into preexisting indigenous political, social, and spiritual systems; how Indians continued to subsist on locally available foods and, in some cases, even supplied European colonies; and, in still other cases, how Indians created and recalled material traditions while at and also away from the missions.[13] For the Franciscan missions of California, again, still more can be done to develop these themes and bring them to bear on the broader indigenous landscapes encircling Spanish missions.

---

9. Kent G. Lightfoot, *Indians, Missionaries, and Merchants: The Legacy of Colonial Encounters on the California Frontiers* (Berkeley: University of California Press, 2005). See also Sarah Peelo, "The Creation of a Carmeleño Identity: Marriage Practices in the Indian Village at Mission San Carlos Borromeo del Río Carmel," *Journal of California and Great Basin Anthropology* 30 (2010): 117–139.

10. Lee M. Panich, "Archaeologies of Persistence: Reconsidering the Legacies of Colonialism in Native North America," *American Antiquity* 78 (2013): 105–122.

11. See, for example, Elliot H. Blair and David H. Thomas, "The Guale Uprising of 1597: An Archaeological Perspective from Mission Santa Catalina de Guale (Georgia)," in *Indigenous Landscapes and Spanish Missions: New Perspectives from Archaeology and Ethnohistory*, eds. Lee M. Panich and Tsim D. Schneider (Tucson: University of Arizona Press, 2014), 25–40; Matthew Liebmann, *Revolt: An Archaeological History of Pueblo Resistance and Revitalization in 17th-Century New Mexico* (Tucson: University of Arizona Press, 2012); Michael V. Wilcox, *The Pueblo Revolt and the Mythology of Conquest: An Indigenous Archaeology of Contact* (Berkeley: University of California Press, 2009).

12. Haas, *Saints and Citizens*, 129.

13. Lee M. Panich and Tsim D. Schneider, eds. *Indigenous Landscapes and Spanish Missions: New Perspectives from Archaeology and Ethnohistory* (Tucson: University of Arizona Press, 2014).

This chapter examines Spanish missions in Alta California from the vantage of the indigenous hinterlands that surrounded them. Specifically, I address the places away from missions where Indians—while also visiting missions and negotiating the challenges wrought by them—returned to seek refuge and reconvene in the company of people, places, and traditions. Following an overview of the Franciscan missions and human agency in the San Francisco Bay region, the chapter focuses on shell mounds as one type of site among others where archaeologists can critically evaluate the reuse, new use, and abandonment of sites by Indians fleeing or on furlough from local missions. Discoveries at three shell mound sites (CA-MRN-114, CA-MRN-115, and CA-MRN-328) are discussed relative to archaeological studies of refugeeism in other parts of California. I conclude with some considerations for future research addressing California's indigenous hinterlands.

Spanish Missions in Alta California: A View from San Francisco Bay

California Indians of the San Francisco Bay were initially visited by Europeans in the late sixteenth century, although Spanish colonists would not return to the area for another two hundred years. In 1769 an expedition led by Gaspar de Portolà relocated the bay and in 1775 Juan de Ayalla anchored at Angel Island. In the following year, Mission San Francisco was established and the first Native Americans from the San Francisco Peninsula were baptized. Between 1777 and the 1830s, Spanish colonists established one military presidio, two civilian pueblos, and five more Franciscan missions—Mission Santa Clara (est. 1777), Mission Santa Cruz (est. 1791), Mission San José (est. 1797), Mission San Rafael (est. 1817), and Mission San Francisco Solano (est. 1823).[14] At the northwest extent of New Spain's colonial frontier, Alta California missions bolstered Spain's claim to lands increasingly encroached upon by Russians and Americans. This was done by transforming through baptism the preexisting Native American population into loyal and Christianized subjects of the Spanish Crown.[15]

A system of *reducción* and *congregación* envisioned for the province ideally "reduced" the many Native villages external to the missions and "congregated" Native peoples at individual mission sites along the California coast for conversion. Yet, at missions throughout Alta California small teams of

14. Julia G. Costello and David Hornbeck, "Alta California: An Overview," in *Columbian Consequences*, vol. 1, *Archaeological and Historical Perspectives of the Spanish Borderlands West*, ed. David H. Thomas (Washington, DC: Smithsonian Institution Press, 1989), 311.

15. Francis F. Guest, *Fermin Francisco de Lasuén (1736–1803): A Biography* (Washington, DC: Academy of American Franciscan History, 1973), 204.

colonists—typically one to four Franciscan padres and a few soldiers—were regularly eclipsed by larger, dynamic, and linguistically and culturally diverse pluralistic communities of Indians who not only contributed to the construction, maintenance, and operation of the mission manifold but also created spaces for themselves within. The mission, as both *place* and *process*,[16] was a setting of daily routines and sundry tasks meted out to Indians and performed under the watchful eyes of the padres to ensure the success of the operation. As Native places "nearly everything grown or manufactured in the missions, presidios, and pueblos resulted from the labor of Indians" who occupied positions in a variety of craft, agricultural, ranching, and domestic jobs.[17]

In addition to creating and participating in the mission place, as a *process* missions were also negotiated and continually redefined by the interested actions, or "agency," of Natives and newcomers alike. Negotiations at times took place under cover of darkness, "between the houses and behind closed doors."[18] At other times, negotiations were more brazen, taking on the moniker of "resistance." Resistance to the missions changed over time and took many forms,[19] ranging from large-scale resistances such as the 1824 Chumash Revolt to other reactions that may have escaped the notice of the missionaries, the historian's pen, or even the archaeologist's trowel. In viewing resistance to the missions simply in terms of Native reaction to colonial dominance, however, Native American agency is stifled and reduced to a handful of violent flashpoints that uncritically reaffirm one-dimensional colonial power structures. Moreover, this line of thinking privileges written forms of history, "filtered through the eyes and inkwells of nonnative interlocutors, in which indigenous perspectives were systematically excluded."[20]

Compared to such overt forms of resistance as thievery, revolt, and attacks on missions and missionaries, other subtler forms of resistance exhibited at the

---

16. Mark T. Lycett, "Archaeology under the Bell: The Mission as Situated History in Seventeenth Century New Mexico," *Missionalia* 32 (2004).

17. Steven W. Hackel, "Land, Labor, and Production: The Colonial Economy of Spanish and Mexican California," in *Contested Eden: California before the Gold Rush*, eds. Ramón A. Gutiérrez and Richard J. Orsi (Berkeley: University of California Press, 1998), 122. See also Finbar Kenneally, ed. *Writings of Fermín Francisco de Lasuén*, vol. 2 (Washington, DC: Academy of American Franciscan History, 1965) and Lightfoot, *Indians, Missions, and Merchants*, 67.

18. Lightfoot, *Indians, Missions, and Merchants*, 113.

19. Robert H. Jackson and Edward Castillo, *Indians, Franciscans, and Spanish Colonization: The Impact of the Mission System on California Indians* (Albuquerque: University of New Mexico Press, 1995).

20. Matthew Liebmann and Melissa J. Murphy, "Rethinking the Archaeology of 'Rebels, Backsliders, and Idolaters'," in *Enduring Conquests: Rethinking the Archaeology of Resistance to Spanish Colonialism in the Americas*, eds. M. Liebmann and M.S. Murphy (Santa Fe, NM: School for Advanced Research Press, 2011), 4.

missions were just as prevalent and at times inclusive of the actions of Natives and Europeans alike. For example, illicit departure from the missions by running away was widespread in the Alta California province. Whereas rates of Native flight vary by mission and by year, and also hinged on the temperament or managerial inexperience of some padres,[21] a recent estimate suggests 5 to 10 percent of baptized Indians illicitly visited the hinterlands throughout the colonial period.[22] An even smaller percentage of runaways fled and remained away as most aborted their flight or were recaptured. Despite the ubiquity of Native runaways in the accounts of many missions, apostasy is commonly overlooked in a dominance-resistance framework as a simplistic response by those who had no choice but to abscond. As discussed above, this thinking also negatively reinforces the generic idea that missions were inescapable contexts of indigenous loss avoidable only through violent acts of overt resistance.

Another way to view Native peoples' illicit absences from the missions is through the lens of practice theory and close inspection of the interrelatedness of running away and the consequences for everyone involved. Practice theory establishes that everyday activities are patterned and can reflect the daily "regulated improvisations" by which people intentionally order and reorder their social conditions.[23] The Franciscan missionaries of Alta California—informed by two hundred years of practical experience with missionizing Native groups on the North American continent—applied a Native recruitment policy and *paseo* system quite unlike that implemented at other missions of North America.[24] This *paseo* system is an overlooked example of resistance that emerged

---

21. For a discussion of illicit and approved departures from the missions, see Schneider, "Placing Refuge," 164–170. For rates of Native fugitivism at the Alta California missions, see Sherburne F. Cook, *The Conflict between the California Indian and White Civilization* (Berkeley: University of California Press, 1976), 58. Robert H. Jackson, *Indian Population Decline: The Missions of Northwestern New Spain, 1687–1840* (Albuquerque: University of New Mexico Press, 1994), 138 suggests a priest's personality factored into the decisions of Native Americans to flee or remain at the missions. See also Mariah Wade, "The Missionary Predicament: Conversion Practices in Texas, New Mexico, and the Californias," in *From La Florida to La California: Franciscan Evangelization in the Spanish Borderlands*, eds. Timothy J. Johnson and Gert Melville (Berkeley: Academy of American Franciscan History, 2013), 294.

22. Steven W. Hackel, *Children of Coyote, Missionaries of Saint Francis: Indian–Spanish Relations in Colonial California, 1769–1850* (Chapel Hill: University of North Carolina Press, 2005), 94-95.

23. Pierre Bourdieu, *Outline of a Theory of Practice* (Cambridge: Cambridge University Press, 1977), 78; Anthony Giddens *Central Problems in Social Theory: Action, Structure, and Contradiction in Social Analysis* (Berkeley: University of California Press, 1979).

24. Jackson and Castillo, *Indians, Franciscans, and Spanish Colonization*, 6. See also Susan M. Deeds, *Defiance and Deference in Mexico's Colonial North: Indians under Spanish Rule in Nueva Vizcaya* (Austin: University of Texas Press, 2003), 90, who also argues that "the local environment was an especially conspicuous modifier of the Spanish blueprint."

in California and reveals how the accumulated and persistent actions of Native apostates could in fact alter the institutionalized constraints of the missions. That is, while the mission "structure" established social constraints, it also simultaneously enabled possibilities for action, and the structure itself was reproduced and transformed—intentionally or not—by indigenous and non-Native imperatives.[25]

Passes given out at some Alta California missions helped curb high rates of fugitivism by allowing Indians to return home to relax and visit friends and family.[26] Yet *paseos* also put mission Indians back in touch with the very places and things flagged for elimination at the missions. *Paseo* facilitated the collection of wild foods, which could be used to supplement mission diets, especially during times of shortage. With or without a pass, Indians at Spanish missions across North America continued to hunt and gather.[27] Shellfish gathering expeditions, fishing trips, and nocturnal duck hunts were a common feature at San Francisco Bay missions. Farther south at Mission Santa Barbara, a single kettle of soup was sufficient to feed the entire mission community in the fall season as most Indians "lived scattered in the mountains," the padres confessed.[28] Persistent fugitivism played a role in how missions were administered in California and, with or without pass in hand, trips to the hinterland likely reinforced connections to Native places and practices routinely viewed as lost at the outset of missionization.

In addition to seeking physical and mental nourishment, reports exist of illicit dances in the mission hinterlands attended by furloughed and unmissionized Indians alike.[29] Chumash are known to have departed missions for the Santa Barbara backcountry to prepare rock paintings.[30] Quincy Newell has even documented the timing of some furloughs from San Francisco Bay missions that correspond with major life events, including childbirth and

---

25. John C. Barrett, "Agency, the Duality of Structure, and the Problem of the Archaeological Record," in *Archaeological Theory Today*, ed. Ian Hodder (Cambridge: Polity Press, 2001), 141–169.

26. Quincy D. Newell, *Constructing Lives at Mission San Francisco: Native Californians and Hispanic Colonists, 1776–1821* (Albuquerque: University of New Mexico Press, 2009), 101.

27. For examples from the California missions, see Maynard J. Geiger and Clement W. Meighan, ed., *As the Padres Saw Them: California Indian Life and Customs as Reported by the Franciscan Missionaries, 1813–1815* (Santa Barbara: Santa Barbara Mission Archive Library, 1976).

28. Maynard J. Geiger, *The Indians of Mission Santa Barbara in Paganism and Christianity* (Santa Barbara: Old Mission Santa Barbara, 1960), 37.

29. See, for example, Sherburne F. Cook, "Expeditions to the Interior of California, Central Valley, 1800–1820," *University of California Anthropological Records* 16 (1960), 256.

30. John R. Johnson, "Indian History in the Santa Barbara Back Country," *Los Padre Notes* 3 (1984), 12.

death.[31] Either the structured lifestyle of mission living for Indians is overemphasized, or many more opportunities to depart the missions existed than have been reported. In short, many California Indian groups retained a mobile lifestyle and sustained traditional forms of subsistence and other cultural practices while still engaging with the missions. At times this behavior was encouraged by the missionaries themselves through the administration of passes. These insights should encourage scholars to turn their eyes away from the missions to the hinterlands beyond.

San Francisco Bay Shell Mounds as Historical Places

There are clear challenges to detecting and studying the archaeological remains of Native American refugees. Key among them are difficulties determining the spatial and temporal extents of where and when specific places or entire landscapes were occupied by Native peoples at the time of the missions. There are also challenges with identifying and classifying artifacts, features, sites, and regions connected to mission-era apostates, as well as broader disciplinary obstacles archaeologists must overcome to improve the ways places—like shell mounds, as I discuss below—and objects are parsed as "prehistoric," "colonial," "historic," and so on.

Archaeologist Nels Nelson recorded upwards of 425 individual shell mounds during a landmark pedestrian survey of the San Francisco Bay area in the early 1900s.[32] Nelson's survey report provides important detail on the locations and composition of mounds in the greater Bay Area, including those found along the Pacific coast at Tomales Bay and Bodega Bay. Local Native American populations constructed shell mounds from many tons of shellfish (e.g., mussel, clam, and oyster) piled up over many centuries.[33] Additionally, most mounds contain deposits of soil, ash, and fire-affected rocks; animal remains; flaked stone and milling tools; cooking features; and, frequently, human burials. Shell mounds also vary in size. Some inconspicuous mounds rise only a few feet above the ground surface. In contrast, one of the largest shell mounds recorded in Cali-

31. Newell, *Constructing Lives*, 161–164.

32. Nels C. Nelson, "San Francisco Bay Mounds," *Collection of Manuscripts from the Archaeological Archives of the Phoebe A. Hearst Museum of Anthropology* 349 (1907). See also Nels C. Nelson, "Shellmounds of the San Francisco Bay Region," *University of California Publications in American Archaeology and Ethnology* 7 (1909), 309–356.

33. Initial construction of San Francisco Bay shell mounds took place approximately 5,000 to 4,000 years ago, and most well-dated deposits from mounds date to 500 B.C.E. to C.E. 300. See Kent G. Lightfoot and Edward L. Luby, "Late Holocene in the San Francisco Bay Area: Temporal Trends in the Use and Abandonment of Shell Mounds in the East Bay," in *Catalysts to Complexity: Late Holocene Societies of the California Coast*, vol. 6, *Perspectives in California Archaeology*, eds. Jon M. Erlandson and Terry L. Jones (Los Angeles: Cotsen Institute of Archaeology, 2002).

fornia, the Emeryville shell mound, once measured an imposing 300 feet wide by 1,000 feet long and it contained no fewer than ten distinct strata spanning over 30 feet in depth and minimally two thousand years of history.[34]

In an era of rapid urban development, shoreline modifications and in-filling, casual collecting, and amateur digs, Nelson's survey notes also describe mound condition and destruction. For example, by 1907 "Mound No. 1" in Sausalito—north of the Golden Gate and the first shell mound recorded during the survey—was already "practically all carted away."[35] Arriving at "Mound No. 84" near San Rafael, Nelson discovered it had already been "culled over . . . and all the relics were shipped to the museum in London."[36] After over two thousand years of gradual accumulation, mounded landscapes have been nearly erased by natural and cultural disturbances, primarily from coastal erosion and construction projects occurring within the past two hundred years. Many other mounds have been picked over, quarried, and repurposed as road base and fertilizer for residential gardens.[37] As a consequence, very few shell mounds are visible on the present-day landscape, and those that linger are often missing large portions, especially their upper (more recent) deposits. Such damages have complicated the ways archaeologists view and understand the long-term use of mounded sites.

Furthermore, very few people see a connection between shell mounds and Native American tribes. Local histories—and the production of "terminal narratives,"[38] as they have been called—uncritically tell of the abandonment of native villages and the disappearance of Native Americans from the landscapes of Marin County, and anthropologists confirmed the extinguishment of the bay's indigenous cultures at the hands of Spanish, Mexican, and American colonial enterprises. Damage to shell mounds amplify such narratives of cultural loss and position the mounds themselves—and their occupants—as fixtures of a far-

34. Jack M. Broughton, ed., "Excavation of the Emeryville Shellmound, 1906: Nels C. Nelson's Final Report," *Contributions of the University of California Archaeological Research Facility* 54 (1996); W. Egbert Schenck, "The Emeryville Shell Mound: Final Report," *University of California Publications in American Archaeology and Ethnology* 23 (1926); and Max Uhle, "The Emeryville Shellmound," *University of California Publications in American Archaeology and Ethnology* 7 (1907).

35. Nelson, "San Francisco Bay Mounds," 19.

36. Ibid., 157.

37. A similar fate is documented for shell mounds in other coastal environments on the west and east coasts of North America. See, for example, Scott Byram, "Shell Mounds and Shell Roads: The Destruction of Oregon Coast Middens for Early Road Surfacing," *Current Archaeological Happenings in Oregon* 34 (2009), 6–14, and Lynn Ceci, "Shell Midden Deposits as Coastal Resources," *World Archaeology* 16 (1984): 62–74. Keith Ashley (this volume) also suggests that shell midden was quarried and added as "sweetener" to postholes at some missions in La Florida to protect wood posts from rot.

38. Wilcox, *The Pueblo Revolt*, 11.

removed prehistoric landscape. Writing against this narrative, I seek to reconnect shell mounds to those Native groups negotiating colonial institutions and to subsequent generations who still live within the landscapes of their ancestors.

Due in large part to their relative isolation on protected State Park property, three shell mounds (CA-MRN-114, CA-MRN-115, and CA-MRN-328) were examined as part of my doctoral dissertation research and found to be largely undisturbed.[39] Archaeologists excavating CA-MRN-115 in 1949 collected artifacts similar to those found at other Bay Area shell mounds, including bone tools, mortars, and flaked stone tools. Some of the more surprising finds collected from a house pit on top of the mound include burned wood house planks, grass thatching, charred basketry, and one *Haliotis* (abalone) ornament and a projectile point both diagnostic of the late prehistoric and historic time periods (C.E. 1500–1800). These discoveries informed the hypothesis that the shell mound's most recent occupants were living there until about 1800, at which point they were "taken to one of the Spanish missions."[40]

Testing this hypothesis, I designed—and am continuing to refine—a theoretical and methodological framework for investigating the possibility of visits to hinterland shell mounds and other sites by Native peoples who also visited Spanish missions. Two key components of this project are now discussed. First, archaeological field investigations involved shallow geophysics to target surface and near-surface archaeological features for excavation and radiocarbon sampling and to avoid human burials (a concern shared with the Native American descendant community in whose ancestral territory the shell mounds are located). Second, my analysis of lithic (stone) artifacts sought to identify and evaluate long-term continuities in artifact styles, material types, and production techniques before and after Contact. Geochemical source data, the focus of this chapter, were also collected from obsidian artifacts and analyzed to better track people's movements across hinterland landscapes. Findings from the radiocarbon and obsidian sourcing studies were then compared to the historical record of opportunities available to Indians to come and go from missions with and without permission.

Shallow geophysics is a proven and increasingly standard practice for limiting destructive archaeological excavation by detecting buried features, such as hearths and compacted house floors, prior to excavation and sampling.[41]

39. For information on all three sites, see Schneider, "Placing Refuge."

40. Clement W. Meighan, "Preliminary Excavations at the Thomas Site, Marin County," *Reports of the University of California Archaeological Survey* 19 (1953), 5.

41. For excellent recent examples of shallow geophysics at shell mounds and Spanish mission sites, see chapters by Ginessa J. Mahar and Elliot H. Blair in *Life among the Tides: Recent Archaeology on the Georgia Bight*, vol. 98, American Museum of Natural History Anthropological Papers, eds. Victor D. Thompson and David H. Thomas (New York: American Museum of Natural History, 2013).

A magnetometer survey at CA-MRN-114 first pinpointed several subsurface magnetic anomalies, which I interpreted as distinct cultural features based on their orientation and systematic spacing horizontally across the site.[42] A second geophysical survey at the same site used an electrical resistivity/conductivity instrument to produce a refined vertical positioning of the features previously detected with the magnetometer. An excavation unit placed strategically atop one feature led to the discovery of a stone-lined hearth and adjacent ash deposit interpreted as hearth rake-out. Prior to its removal for flotation and microconstituent analysis, shell and charcoal samples were sampled from the bottom of the hearth for accelerator mass spectrometry (AMS) radiocarbon dating.

Radiocarbon assays for the three shell mounds included four AMS determinations from CA-MRN-114, two determinations from CA-MRN-115, and two dates from CA-MRN-328.[43] Two samples taken from the bottom of the hearth feature produced conventional radiocarbon ages of 380 ± 40 B.P. and 640 ± 40 B.P., or two sigma (95% probability) calibrated age ranges of cal C.E. 1440–1640 and cal C.E. 1480–1680 respectively. Additional samples from levels above and below the feature produced conventional radiocarbon dates of 870 ± 40 B.P., or cal C.E. 1650–1880 (above), and 1870 ± 40 B.P., or cal C.E. 700–940 (below). Radiocarbon samples from CA–MRN–328 produced conventional ages of 940 ± 40 B.P. (cal C.E. 1540–1720, 1740–1750, and 1790–1800) and 870 ± 40 B.P. (cal C.E. 1650–1880).

Charred basketry and wood plank fragments—both collected in 1949 from the excavated house pit—were sampled from the CA-MRN-115 collection housed at the Phoebe A. Hearst Museum of Anthropology. The basketry sample yielded a conventional radiocarbon age of 280 ± 40 B.P. (cal C.E. 1490–1670 and cal C.E. 1780–1790), while the wood plank produced a conventional age of 260 ± 40 B.P. (cal C.E. 1520–1590, 1620–1670, 1770–1800, and 1940–1950). Importantly, the baskets and wood planks were *not* collected from the top of CA-MRN-115. Archaeologists excavating down to the house floor in 1949 observed at least 12 inches of refuse with an undisturbed shell lens accumulated above the floor "that cannot all be attributed to fill from the raised margins of the [house] pit" and may, in fact, reflect reuse of the house later in time.[44] This is a pattern observed by archaeologists deciphering the ephemeral signatures of mobile groups who visited and

42. For further information on geophysical surveys, see Schneider, "Placing Refuge," 70–74.

43. For further information on AMS radiocarbon sampling and dating, see Schneider, "Placing Refuge," 151–159. Two additional dates are reported by Meighan, "Preliminary Excavations at the Thomas Site," 5.

44. Meighan, "Preliminary Excavations at the Thomas Site," 4.

departed missions in other provinces.[45] The six AMS dates indicate site use during a transitional time period that spans late prehistoric and historic times (the "Late Period, Phase 2," or C.E. 1500–1800). Although discrete components associated with Indian apostates are difficult to pinpoint on the basis of AMS radiocarbon dates alone, the data fall within the realm of possibility and cannot be ignored. Moreover, they provide an instructive scaffolding for additional refinement by researchers addressing the question of refuge at shell mounds and other indigenous places contemporaneous to the missions.

To this end, one component of my lithic analysis involved energy dispersive x-ray fluorescence (or, XRF) spectroscopy to chemically match obsidian artifacts found within the shell mounds to their parent obsidian sources.[46] This was done to interrogate shell mound occupations and identify broad patterns of economic and social exchange across the landscape before and after Spanish colonization. Prior to the missions, obsidian from several North Bay sources circulated widely throughout Central California. For Marin County, a previous sourcing study demonstrates that artifacts made from an obsidian source in the Napa Valley (Napa Glass Mountain) dominate late prehistoric lithic assemblages at sites closest to the San Francisco Bay, while artifacts created from a second obsidian source called Annadel prevail at sites found closer to the Pacific Ocean.[47] Analysis of obsidian artifacts from the three sites reveals that only CA-MRN-115 fits this previously reported pattern (i.e., more Napa Valley obsidian), and that more Annadel obsidian artifacts appear in surface and near-surface components at CA-MRN-114 and CA-MRN-328. One explanation for this pattern—supported by the historical record of heightened recruitment from Native communities at Tomales Bay and Bodega Bay to San Francisco Bay missions after 1800—is that the sites were reoccupied by Native peoples orginally from villages closer to the Pacific coast who arrived at the missions (with either Annadel tools or ties to the Annadel source) and subsequently departed.[48] As observed at the nearby Russian mercantile colony of Fort Ross (est. 1812),[49] a second interrelated explanation for the pattern is

45. Deni J. Seymour, "Contextual Incongruities, Statistical Outliers, and Anomalies: Targeting Inconspicuous Occupational Events," *American Antiquity* 75 (2010), 172–173.

46. For further information on the XRF study, see Schneider, "Placing Refuge," 141–149.

47. Thomas L. Jackson, "Late Prehistoric Obsidian Exchange in Central California" (Ph.D. diss., Stanford University, 1986).

48. Randall Milliken, *A Time of Little Choice: The Disintegration of Tribal Culture in the San Francisco Bay Area, 1769–1810* (Menlo Park, CA: Ballena Press, 1995), 176–179 and 201–203.

49. Glenn J. Farris, "The Russian Imprint on the Colonization of California," in *Columbian Consequences*, vol., *Archaeological and Historical Perspectives on the Spanish Borderlands West*, ed. David H. Thomas (Washington, DC: Smithsonian Institution Press, 1989), 492.

that precolonial flows of obsidian were blocked, or created anew, in the hinterlands of newly established Spanish missions.

Liminal Spaces, Persistent Connections

Native Americans continued to dwell within the landscapes around Spanish missions. Rather than uncritically accept that shell mounds and other places were abandoned at the outset of colonization simply because pieces of these sites were removed or because certain mass-produced materials are missing from them, the historical and archaeological findings presented above open shell mounds to reconsideration. Ceramics, metal items, glass beads, and flaked glass—all typical artifacts found within Native American components of mission-era sites—are indeed noticeably absent from the three sites in this study. Yet, the absence of such artifacts should not be taken as evidence that mounds were vacant, but rather as a challenge to locate the subtle traces of colonialism in indigenous places. Moreover, stone tools and shell artifacts, native house styles, and the remains of native plant and animal species recovered from *within* many mission archaeological contexts—and described in historical documents—underscore the continuation of architectural styles, foodways, and other technologies despite efforts to eradicate them. As an additional thought, Native people wishing to rid themselves of the missions and avoid detection might not carry introduced materials, thus requiring archaeologists to reassess materials and artifact types carried over from precolonial times and not merely search for items introduced by the missionaries.

In contrast to my findings, southwest of Bakersfield, California—and situated between the Santa Barbara Channel and the southern San Joaquin Valley—archaeologists are investigating the San Emigdio Canyon and vicinity as a region comprised of numerous points of refuge for Indians fleeing southern California missions.[50] Long viewed as a stale backwater of degeneracy and cultural loss, historical accounts of dreary punitive expeditions to the *tulares* prepared by Spanish soldiers and missionaries colored the earliest anthropological views of mission hinterlands that, in turn, shored up any doubt that the missions alone were the only places to study missionization.[51] Contrary

---

50. See Julienne L. Bernard, "An Archaeological Study of Resistance, Persistence, and Culture Change in the San Emigdio Canyon, Kern County, California" (PhD diss., University of California, Los Angeles, 2008); Julienne Bernard, David Robinson, and Fraser Sturt, "Points of Refuge in the South Central California Colonial Hinterland," in *Indigenous Landscapes and Spanish Missions: New Perspectives from Archaeology and Ethnohistory*, eds. Lee M. Panich and Tsim D. Schneider (Tucson: University of Arizona Press, 2014); and David Robinson, "Polyvalent Metaphors in South-Central California Missionary Processes," *American Antiquity* 78 (2013): 302–321.

51. See, for example, William J. Wallace, "Southern Valley Yokuts," in California, ed. Robert F. Heizer, vol. 8 of *Handbook of North American Indians*, ed. William C. Sturtevant

to this view, at sites within the San Emigdio region, more traditional precolonial artifact types comingle with iron needle–drilled marine shell beads, faunal remains unique to both coastal and interior locales, and glass beads. Mixed deposits of marine shell beads and glass beads near centuries-old rock art panels also reflect a reinvestment in ancestral places amidst the creation of novel material traditions.[52]

In light of these findings and my own discoveries, additional radiocarbon dates and other analyses can help flesh out the use, tempo, materiality, and evolution of California's indigenous hinterlands. For example, could different assemblages from the three shell mounds versus the San Emigdio region be attributed to different time periods or types of refuge? That is, with time spent at the missions, perhaps glass beads and other items would be more prevalent in hinterland sites later in time? In contrast, few, if any, articles of European manufacture may be associated with shell mound refuges utilized earlier in time. Anecdotally, support for this idea comes from an account of a boat trip heading north from San Francisco in 1811. Sailing past the location of the three shell mounds at Point San Pedro, Father Ramon Abella observed five villages that were "still heathen."[53] Further complicating the issue, however, observations of those who fled during the Chumash Revolt in 1824 indicate some Indians who "took nothing with them"[54] and others who "carried away everything in the shape of clothing and money" and nothing else.[55]

As observed by Kent Lightfoot and Ann Danis (this volume), still another consideration for Marin County is the establishment of Fort Ross by the Russians north of San Francisco Bay in 1812 and the transition of the Marin hinterland to a "middle ground." At this time and afterward, the Marin landscape might be better viewed as a social anchor and transitional space. Whereas Spanish missions are best understood as indigenous artifacts created and inhabited primarily by Indians, perhaps ironically the hinterlands developed as landscapes of cultural perseverance *and* venues to learn and apply new ways of making a living. As Katherine Hayes observes in her archaeological and historical analysis of a Dutch plantation on Long Island, colonial landscapes were

(Washington, DC: Smithsonian Institution, 1978), 460, who writes: "During the early decades of the nineteenth century the southern valley became a rendezvous for Indian converts fleeing from the discipline of steady and directed work at the coastal mission establishments. Their presence had far-reaching consequences, for the fugitives introduced alien practices from their half-forgotten cultures and others they had learned from the padres."

52. Robinson, "Polyvalent Metaphors."

53. Cook, "Expeditions, 1800–1820," 261.

54. Travis Hudson, "The Chumash Revolt of 1824: Another Native Account from the Notes of John P. Harrington," *Journal of California and Great Basin Anthropology* 2 (1980): 124.

55. Sandos, "LEVANTAMIENTO!," 122.

multiethnic spaces as much as contested settings of "spatial proximity and an ongoing negotiation of social distance."[56] This theme is also echoed in research examining the encampments of runaway enslaved Africans who found refuge in Mid-Atlantic swamps while remaining "hidden in plain sight" and participating in emerging commercial lumber enterprises.[57]

For the archaeology of Spanish missions to continue forward, it requires a turn in thinking and simultaneous repositioning of archaeological inquiries that address both the contextualizing possibilities of indigenous hinterlands and, as Lee Panich argues, the realities of Native American survival.[58] In the five years leading up to the Chumash Revolt, major projects at Mission Santa Barbara not only used native labor but transposed traditional Chumash craft guilds into positions as carpenters, masons, roofers, and blacksmiths.[59] With time spent at the missions of Alta California, Native Americans developed specialized skills and gained work experience; some also learned to tack strategically between native and colonial worlds. John Johnson describes the transformation of some hinterland Chumash villages into sheep ranches operated by Chumash shepherds who supplied the missions and, elsewhere, Native men identified as *venaderos* (deer hunters) who were particularly adept at bringing in wild game and consequently well-regarded within the mission community.[60] Perhaps more poignantly, and returning to Father Ripoll's solicitations to Chumash refugees to return to Mission Santa Barbara during the Chumash Revolt, some refused stating: "What are we to do at the mission since the soldiers have robbed all our belongings, seeds, etc.? We shall maintain ourselves with what God will provide us in the open country. Moreover, we are soldiers, stonemasons, carpenters, and we will provide for ourselves by our work."[61]

Conclusion

As varied as the environments and indigenous populations encountered by the Franciscan missions of Alta California were the responses to missions presented by Native peoples. While some accepted the missions, others were more ambivalent to the requirements of relocating and relearning life as they

56. Katherine Howlett Hayes, *Slavery before Race: Europeans, Africans, and Indians at Long Island's Sylvester Manor Plantation, 1651–1884* (New York: New York University Press), 86.

57. Ted Maris-Wolf, "Hidden in Plain Sight: Maroon Life and Labor in Virginia's Dismal Swamp," *Slavery & Abolition* (2013): 446–464.

58. Panich, "Archaeologies of Persistence," 119.

59. Sandos, "Christianization among the Chumash," 78.

60. Johnson, "Indian History," 9; "Comments on Indians, Missionaries, and Merchants: The Legacy of Colonial Encounters on the California Frontiers," *Boletín* 22 (2005), 73.

61. Sandos, "LEVANTAMIENTO!," 124.

knew it. Still others rejected the missions, either withdrawing outright or entering the missions and then later refusing them. Examples of resistance to the Spanish missions range from outright revolt to flight, and also included, as I argue, mission-administered liberties. Varying by time, place, and participants, the examples discussed in this chapter fundamentally showcase the persistent connections California Indians maintained to places across the landscape despite the structural constraints imposed by the missions.

For archaeologists it is important to consider life beyond the relatively isolated confines of the coastal missions, pueblos, and presidios, which for so long have been the sole focus of analysis. Considering findings at the shell mounds and San Emigdio sites discussed above, this also entails rethinking expectations—and an improved accounting—of what one would or would not find at refuge sites. Historical accounts like those of the Chumash Revolt further blur our understanding of what was taken away from the missions and what was left behind. Colonial hinterlands, like missions, were dynamic settings that varied across California and changed through time as people, materials, and ideas entered and exited them. For San Emigdio, mixtures of shell and glass beads indicate links to coastal missions, as well as enduring symbols of social and economic connectivity spanning time and great distances. For other places, like shell mounds, site reuse might not be signaled by obvious sprinklings of glass beads but elucidated instead through other means of site detection and material analysis, including the reanalysis of artifacts regularly classified as "prehistoric." By and large, glass beads or not, the hinterlands were also landscapes inhabited by Native groups whose own histories of managing environmental and political flux in prehistory probably factored into their ability to maintain *and* reconfigure cultural practices during mission times.

At missions and away from them, Indians recontextualized their own ways of knowing and doing things in new arenas. Native apostasy figures prominently in many historical accounts of San Francisco Bay missions and hunting and gathering was evidently encouraged, at times through the administration of *paseos.* By repositioning archaeological inquiries to look beyond the thatched, stone, and adobe walls of Spanish missions in North America, we may start to more fully account for the activities taking place within indigenous hinterlands. As I argue, approved and illicit returns to old villages—like some shell mounds—facilitated reconnections to significant places, gathering areas, and sacred sites and, in doing so, these settings provided contexts for reinvesting in tradition and reordering shattered worlds.

Chapter 17
Franciscans, Russians, and Indians on the International Borders of Alta California

Kent G. Lightfoot and Ann E. Danis

The purpose of this paper is to highlight the importance of examining the broader landscape of Franciscan missions in undertaking archaeological research in the Spanish Borderlands of North America. We argue that a detailed understanding of the spatial and sonic dimensions of colonialism is crucial for examining the kinds of interactions and relationships that took place between Franciscan missionaries, Indian neophytes, and other colonial and Native peoples in the outlying hinterland. The northern frontier of Alta California is employed as a case study for examining the borderland geography of Spanish/Mexican and Russian settlements in the greater San Francisco Bay Area. Building on an earlier study,[1] we outline a spatial-sonic model for the Franciscan missions that consists of four zones: the mission quadrangle, proximal zone (under the mission bell), the outlying hinterland, and the interspaces of colonial regimes (international zones). While California archaeologists have focused most of their research on mission quadrangles, this paper emphasizes the significance of looking beyond the quadrangle walls to examine the full range of economic practices and social relations of mission neophytes.

Further, we argue that to do so we must consider the multisensory differences between various parts of the mission landscape, particularly the soundscape of the proximal zone and beyond. We also emphasize the critical importance of including distant lands and people located many kilometers from mission centers in our archaeological studies of colonialism. This point is especially pertinent in cases where Franciscan settlements were situated along international frontiers in close proximity to other colonial enterprises as illustrated in this paper for Alta California.

---

1. Kent G. Lightfoot, Sara L. Gonzalez, and Tsim D. Schneider, "Refugees and Interethnic Residences: Examples of Colonial Entanglements in the North Bay San Francisco Bay Area," *Pacific Coast Archaeological Society Quarterly* 42, no. 1 (2009): 1–21.

The Northern Frontier of Alta California

The northern borderland of colonial California developed into a dynamic international zone in the late 1700s and 1800s. It was here in the greater San Francisco Bay Area where the Spanish empire in the Americas literally touched the southernmost outpost of the vast Russian mercantile enterprise administrated by the Russian-American Company (Figure 1). The northernmost settlements of Spain's (and later Mexico's) colonial domain consisted of the San Francisco Presidio and three missions—San Francisco de Asis (Mission Dolores), San Rafael, and San Francisco Solano. The southernmost Russian colony in North America consisted of the administrative center of Settlement Ross, a port at Bodega Bay, and several outlying ranches. Situated between these two colonial empires was an international frontier where more than 50 small indigenous polities of Ohlone, Coast Miwok, Bay Miwok, Patwin, Wappo, and Pomo speakers resided. Both the Spanish and Russian colonists attempted to recruit these Native groups to their settlements primarily to work as laborers in agriculture, ranching, and craft production.[2]

The northern frontier of Alta California provides an excellent case study for examining the multifaceted spatial and sonic dimensions of Franciscan missions and highlights the need to shift our attention beyond the walls of the mission quadrangles to the broader indigenous landscapes in which these colonial settlements were embedded. Although considerable archaeological research has been conducted over the years on California missions, the vast majority has focused on the central quadrangles where the church, *convento*, visitors' quarters, kitchens, storage rooms, and *monjerio* (dorms for young girls, unmarried women) were built around a central courtyard.[3] Regrettably,

---

2. For overviews, see Glenn J. Farris, *So Far from Home: Russians in Early California* (Berkeley, CA: Heyday, 2012); Kent G. Lightfoot, *Indians, Missionaries, and Merchants: The Legacy of Colonial Encounters on the California Frontiers* (Berkeley: University of California Press, 2005).

3. The focus on mission quadrangles began in the late 1800s and early 1900s with the reconstruction work initiated at many California missions. Unfortunately, the historical accuracy and scientific rigor of these early reconstructions varied tremendously as outlined by David Hurst Thomas in "Harvesting Ramona's Garden: Life in California's Mythical Mission Past," in *Columbian Consequences: Volume 3, the Spanish Borderlands in Pan-American Perspective*, ed. David Hurst Thomas (Washington, DC: Smithsonian Institution, 1991): 119–157. Recent syntheses of archaeological research undertaken at missions in Alta and Baja California outline the sampling bias that privileges excavations of quadrangles and adjacent features. For example, see Rebecca Allen, "Rethinking Mission Land Use and the Archaeological Record in California: An Example from Santa Clara," *Historical Archaeology* 44, no. 2 (2010): 72–96; Brooke S. Arkush, "Native Responses to European Intrusion: Cultural Persistence and Agency among Mission Neophytes in Spanish Colonial California," *Historical Archaeology* 45, no. 4 (2011): 62–90; Lee M. Panich, "Spanish Missions

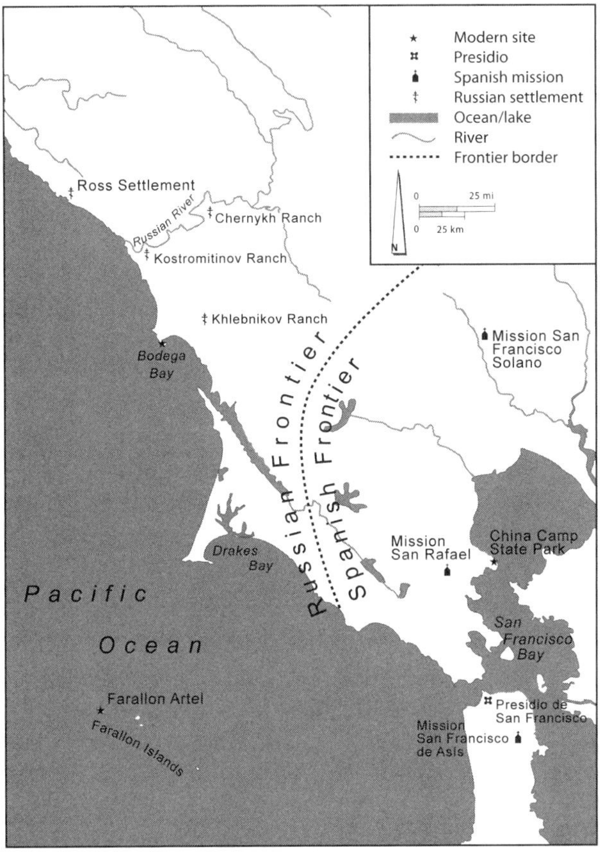

FIGURE 1. Northern frontier of Alta California showing the primary Russian and Spanish settlements (from Lightfoot, Gonzalez, and Schneider 2009: 2).

much less archaeological work has been done outside the mission quadrangles where most of the economic activities and populations of the missions resided. It was beyond the mission walls where agricultural and ranching production took place, where various industrial work areas (pottery kilns, tanning vats, grist mills) were located, and where the majority of Indian neophytes lived.

As a consequence of this sampling bias, our understanding of the broader spatial organization of most California missions outside the central quadrangles and immediate environs is limited. The northern Alta California missions

---

in the Indigenous Landscape: A View from Mission Catalina, Baja California," *Journal of California and Great Basin Anthropology* 30, no. 1 (2010): 69–86.

exemplify this problem. In cases where archaeological research has been undertaken, it has focused primarily on the central quadrangles with minimal work in the outlying hinterland. For example, at Mission San Francisco Solano, where significant archaeological work has taken place in the past, we have a good understanding of the spatial structure of several of the quadrangle buildings and associated architectural features, including the chapel site (original 1824 wooden chapel, replaced in 1840 with an adobe chapel), the *convento* (known as the "Priests' House"), a probable "dormitory for resident Indian neophytes," and the location of tile drains, tile walkways, and remnants of adobe walls.[4] However, beyond this core area, the spatial organization of the mission is largely conjectural based on available archival evidence.[5] Treganza,[6] in undertaking some limited survey of the broader mission area, reported that the specific locations of the cemetery and neophyte village were unknown, a significant lacuna that continues to this day.

There is now growing interest in the study of mission hinterlands to understand more fully how these colonial endeavors operated across space. Archaeologists are now considering how missions were embedded within broader indigenous landscapes and how neophyte Indians maintained relations with outlying lands and people where they continued to obtain wild foods, raw materials, medicines, and dance regalia. This thesis emphasizing the critical importance of studying the external relations of mission neophytes is outlined in a freshly published volume, edited by Lee Panich and Tsim Schneider.[7] This book and other recent publications highlight the importance of examining the outlying environs of the missions to document various agrarian and ranching features, neophyte residences, nearby colonial settlements (such as *visitas* [mission stations], *assistencias* [chapels], and ranchos), and indigenous lands where gentile (non-Christian) Native populations maintained their villages and where

---

4. James Bennyhoff and Albert B. Elsasser, "Sonoma Mission: An Historical and Archaeological Study of Primary Constructions, 1823–1913," *University of California Archaeological Survey Reports* 27 (1954); Adan E. Treganza, "Sonoma Mission: An Archaeological Reconstruction of the Mission San Francisco De Solano Quadrangle," *Kroeber Anthropological Society Papers* (1956).

5. The most detailed reconstruction of the hinterland of Mission San Francisco Solano that we know of is by Robert S. Smilie, *The Sonoma Mission: San Francisco Solano de Sonoma* (Fresno, CA: Valley Publishers, 1975): 37–41. However, even this reconstruction is not tied to any actual geospatial reference points.

6. In writing up his findings, Treganza is obviously puzzled about where the neophyte village and cemetery are located. See Adan E. Treganza, "Sonoma Mission: An Archaeological Reconstruction of the Mission San Francisco de Solano Quadrangle," *Kroeber Anthropological Society Papers* (1956): 2, 12–13.

7. Lee M. Panich and Tsim D. Schneider, eds. *Indigenous Landscapes and Spanish Missions: New Perspectives from Archaeology and Ethnohistory* (Tucson, Arizona: University of Arizona Press, 2014).

mineral, faunal and floral resources continued to be exploited.[8] The number, size, and spatial distribution of villages in Indian lands, of course, remained dynamic with changes in the founding and growth of colonial settlements and as outlying indigenous populations declined in numbers due to disease, violence, and recruitment into the missions.

A landscape-sensory perspective is critical for understanding how Indian neophytes in the missions retained relations with outlying lands and populations. We outline a spatial-sonic model for examining Franciscan missions in Alta California that allows us to integrate previous studies of the central quadrangle with the outlying landscape. Building on an original paper by Lightfoot, Gonzalez, and Schneider,[9] we define three spatial zones beyond the quadrangle—the proximal zone, outlying hinterland, and interspaces of colonial regimes (Figure 2).

Proximal Zone or Under the Mission Bell

The proximal zone, defined by the area within earshot of the mission bells, includes not only the central quadrangle with the church, *convento*, and other buildings, but also the nearby spaces where the regular chiming of the church bells could be heard. The Franciscans of Alta California subjected the neophytes to a rigorous daily schedule of meals, work, and prayers heralded by the incessant ringing of mission bells that started in the morning and continued throughout the day and early evening.[10] The bells themselves were

8. Other studies beyond those included in the Panich and Schneider edited volume include: Rebecca Allen, "Rethinking Mission Land Use and the Archaeological Record in California: An Example from Santa Clara," *Historical Archaeology* 44, no. 2 (2010): 72–96; Julienne Bernard, "An Archaeological Study of Resistance, Persistence, and Culture Change in the San Emigdio Canyon, Kern County, California" (PhD diss., University of California-Los Angeles, 2008); Lee M. Panich, "Spanish Missions in the Indigenous Landscape: A View from Mission Catalina, Baja California," *Journal of California and Great Basin Anthropology* 30, no. 1 (2010); Lee M. Panich, "Assessing the Diversity of Mission Populations through the Comparison of Native American Residences at Mission Santa Clara De Asis," *International Journal of Historical Archaeology* 18 (2014): 467–488; Tsim D. Schneider, "Placing Refuge: Shell Mounds and the Archaeology of Colonial Encounters in the San Francisco Bay Area, California" (PhD diss., University of California-Berkeley, 2010); Tsim D. Schneider, Sara L. Gonzalez, Kent G. Lightfoot, Lee M. Panich, and Matthew A. Russell, "A Land of Cultural Pluralism: Case Studies from California's Colonial Frontiers," in *Contemporary Issues in California Archaeology*, eds. Terry L. Jones and Jennifer E. Perry (Walnut Creek, CA: Left Coast Press, 2012), 319–337.

9. Kent G. Lightfoot, Sara L. Gonzalez, and Tsim D. Schneider, "Refugees and Interethnic Residences: Examples of Colonial Entanglements in the North Bay San Francisco Bay Area," *Pacific Coast Archaeological Society Quarterly* 42, no. 1 (2009).

10. For example, see Jean Francois de La Pérouse, "The Journals of Jean Francois De La Pérouse," in *Monterey in 1786: Life in a California Mission*, ed. Malcolm Margolin (Berkeley, CA: Heyday Books, 1989), 81; Douglas Monroy, *Thrown among Strangers: The*

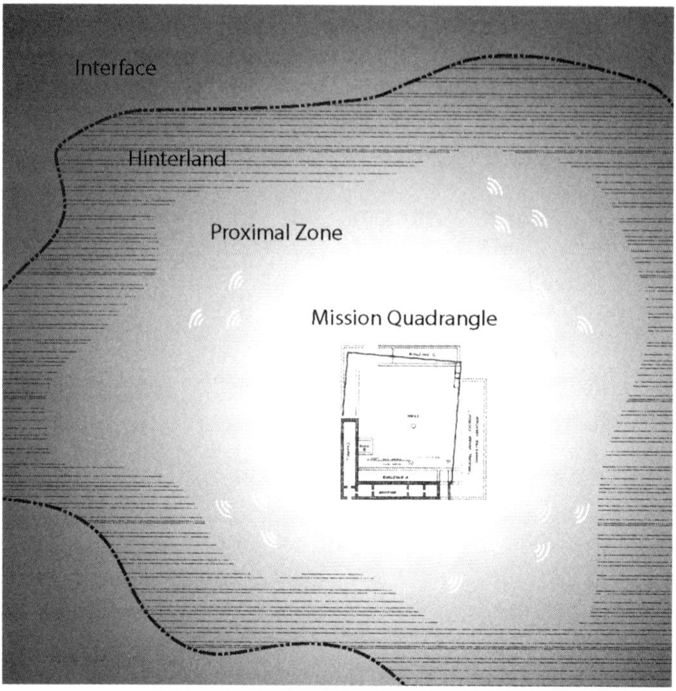

FIGURE 2. Spatial-sonic model for a Franciscan mission. Quadrangle illustrated is from Mission San Francisco Solano showing the location of existing (dark lines) and suggested (dotted lines) buildings and walls based on ethnohistorical and archaeological research (see Treganza 1956, map 2).

considered by some as an important part of Catholic doctrine; bells were personified through baptism and thought to have a physical relationship to heaven through the sound of their ringing.[11]

A critical component of the proximal zone is that these spaces were typically kept under surveillance by the Franciscans and could be reached by the mission guards in relatively short order. The neophyte villages associated with the Franciscan missions in California were probably situated within range of the mission bells so that people could be roused to report for roll call, worship,

Making of Mexican Culture in Frontier California (Berkeley, CA: University of California Press, 1990), 53.

11. Alain Corbin, *Village Bells: Sound and Meaning in the Nineteenth-Century French Countryside*, European Perspectives (New York: Columbia University Press, 1998); Matthew Liebmann, "Catechesis and Catachresis: Bells in the Mission Pueblos of 17th Century New Mexico" (paper presented at annual meeting of Society for American Archaeology, Austin, April 27, 2014).

mealtimes, and work activities. The area under the mission bell probably also contained the facilities for craft production (pottery, textiles, bricks, etc.), places where crops were processed and stored (granaries), and nearby irrigated fields, gardens, orchards, and vineyards.

Francisco Palóu, a Franciscan friar and colleague of mission leader Junípero Serra, wrote in the mid-eighteenth century of the perceived importance of the spatial and sensory aspects of enculturation enforced by mission bells:

> They [Native Californians] can be conquered first only by their interest in being fed and clothed, and afterwards they gradually acquire the knowledge of what is spiritually good and evil. If the missionaries had nothing to give them, they could not win them over. *If the Indians did not live in a town within hearing of the mission bell*, but rather in their villages after the fashion of their pagan days, naked and hungry, the missionaries would not be able to get them to leave off their vicious pagan practices.[12]

This description of the mission bells evokes the idea of a "soundscape"[13] of enculturation. The demarcation of civilized and uncivilized, Catholic and pagan, is not only spatially enforced through the domination and development of landscape, but sonically through the sound of the mission bells—marking out the sensory reach of the mission's influence for both Native and European people, and for archaeologists, the proximal zone.

Depending on the topography and acoustic properties of local places, the extent of the proximal zone varied from mission to mission and potentially from person to person or group to group depending on their relationship to the soundscape. Research can be undertaken today on the acoustic environments of mission sites in order to determine the spatial distribution of the proximal zone considering these variables. A number of novel methods in archaeoacoustics are being actively developed in primarily prehistoric and non–North American contexts that could be applied to the mission case.[14]

---

12. Emphasis is ours, Fray Francisco Palóu, *Palóu's Life of Fray Junípero Serra*, trans. and annotated by Maynard J. Geiger, vol. 4 (Washington, DC: Academy of American Franciscan History, 1955), 232.

13. Here we are following R. Murray Schafer, *The Soundscape: Our Sonic Environment and the Tuning of the World* (Rochester, VT: Destiny Books, 1993), while acknowledging critiques of the term like Tim Ingold's "Against Soundscape," in *Being Alive: Essays on Movement, Knowledge and Description* (New York: Routledge, 2011).

14. For a basic overview of current approaches, see Christopher Scarre and Graeme Lawson, *Archaeoacoustics* (Cambridge, UK: McDonald Institute of Archaeology, 2006); Miriam A. Kolar, "Acoustics, Architecture, and Instruments in Ancient Chavín de Huántar, Perú: An Integrative, Anthropological Approach to Archaeoacoustics and Music Archaeology," in *Music and Ritual: Bridging Material and Living Cultures*, eds. Raquel Jiménez, Rupert Till, and Mark Howell, Publications of ICTM Study Group on Music Archaeology,

Digital modeling of the potential reach of bell sounds across both short and long distances can be combined with pyschoacoustic experimentation in contemporary landscapes to accurately estimate the size and shape of the proximal zone.[15] Sensitivity to the size, type, and location of bells known historically and archaeologically can be accounted for to map changing sizes of this zone over the course of occupation or other variables.[16]

Once the proximal zone has been defined for a specific mission, it should inform the search for particular kinds of mission places (e.g., neophyte villages) and activities found outside the mission quadrangles. As outlined in the chapters by Blair, Jeffries and Moore, and Ashley (this volume), a diverse range of detection methods can be employed by archaeologists to locate architectural features and living spaces in mission landscapes, including surface pedestrian surveys, shovel probes, geophysical surveys, and limited excavations. As Panich (this volume) details, the investigation of these proximal places can provide critical information about neophyte work areas, residences, foodways, and ceremonial activities.[17]

Outlying Hinterlands

The outlying hinterlands extended beyond the quadrangle and proximal zone, but still within regular use of mission populations. Defined by this use, but out of the range of the mission bells, here were located the more distant agricultural fields and free-range lands where mission livestock grazed, as well as mission rancho settlements, *visitas* (mission stations), and *assistencias* (chapels). The lands beyond earshot of the mission bells would have also been used by neophytes for a variety of purposes. These less developed lands would have also provided areas for harvesting wild foods, collecting materials for basket making and textile production, searching for medicines used by Native healers, pursuing paraphernalia for making dance regalia, and for the exploita-

---

vol. 1 (Berlin: Ekho Verlag, 2013); Nicole Boivin, "Rock Art and Rock Music: Petroglyphs of the South Indian Neolithic," *Antiquity* 78 (2004): 38–53; Dianne Scullin and Brian Boyd, "Whistles in the Wind: The Noisy Moche city," *World Archaeology* 46:3 (2014): 362–379.

15. Miriam A. Kolar, "Archaeological Psychoacoustics at Chavín de Huántar" (PhD diss., Stanford University, 2013); Steven Mills, "Sensing the Place: Sounds and Landscape," in *(Un)settling the Neolithic*, eds. Douglass Bailey, Alasdair Whittle, and Vicki Cummings (Oxford: Oxbow, 2005), 79–89; Steve Mills, *Auditory Archaeology: Understanding Sound and Hearing in the Past* (Walnut Creek, CA: Left Coast Press and Routledge, 2014).

16. Liebmann, "Catechesis and Catachresis."

17. Other excellent studies include Rebecca Allen, "Rethinking Mission Land Use and the Archaeological Record in California: An Example from Santa Clara," *Historical Archaeology* 44, no. 2 (2010): 72–96; Lee M. Panich, "Assessing the Diversity of Mission Populations through the Comparison of Native American Residences at Mission Santa Clara de Asís," *International Journal of Historical Archaeology* 18 (2014): 467–488.

tion of lithic sources for making tools. Moreover, Franciscan surveillance and control of the outlying hinterlands would have decreased significantly. Clandestine ceremonies, subversive gatherings, and illicit meetings would have taken place in this zone where the sounds of singing and dancing would not carry back to the mission quadrangles. This is not to say that these kinds of surreptitious activities did not also take place in the proximal zones, but that they were probably performed behind closed doors, whereas in the outlying hinterlands they may have been more open and accessible by larger numbers of people. Considering the land and soundscape of both the proximal zone and hinterland allows us to investigate both clandestine and overt expressions of Native agency. Having a spatio-sensorial model of the mission landscape may allow us to understand the persistence of traditional (or formation of hybrid) practices and identities not only "in plain sight" of colonial administrators but perhaps "in earshot" as well.[18]

The hinterlands also provided places where neophytes could go during *paseos* (approved leaves of absence) or when they left the missions without Franciscan permission. For example, Tsim Schneider[19] (this volume) articulates how hinterland spaces in the San Francisco Bay Area served as places of refuge for neophytes from nearby missions. His archaeological investigation of ancient shell mounds that once ringed the bay shows that Native peoples reused these places during the mission period. He suspects that they were probably neophytes from the missions in San Francisco de Asis, San Rafael, or San Francisco Solano who had either escaped from these colonial settlements (adding to the sizeable number of mission fugitives who lived outside the missions) or who had been given short-term passes by the Franciscan friars to visit their homelands.

Many of the mission hinterlands would have also been populated by gentile Indians whose villages may also have provided places of refuge for some neophytes fleeing the missions. However, detecting the colonial occupations of outlying indigenous archaeological sites can be challenging. Ancient sites situated near good sources of water, firewood, and other resources, and which were recognized as meaningful, spiritual spaces to local Indians, would have

---

18. See Jun Sunseri, "Hiding in Plain Sight: Engineered Colonial Landscapes and Indigenous Reinvention on the New Mexican Frontier," in *Rethinking Colonial Pasts through Archaeology*, eds. Neal Ferris, Rodney Harrison, and Michael V. Wilcox (Oxford: Oxford University Press, 2014): 173–190.

19. See also Tsim D. Schneider, "Placing Refuge: Shell Mounds and the Archaeology of Colonial Encounters in the San Francisco Bay Area, California" (PhD diss., University of California-Berkeley, 2010); Tsim D. Schneider, Sara L. Gonzalez, Kent G. Lightfoot, Lee M. Panich, and Matthew A. Russell, "A Land of Cultural Pluralism: Case Studies from California's Colonial Frontiers," in *Contemporary Issues in California Archaeology*, ed. Terry L. Jones and Jennifer E. Perry (Walnut Creek, CA: Left Coast Press, 2012): 319–337.

been likely candidates for reuse during the mission period. Furthermore, if neophytes did not bring many Hispanic goods from the missions with them due to the transportation costs and/or conscious decisions to leave non-indigenous materials behind, then these colonial age deposits may be very challenging to distinguish from earlier prehistoric contexts (see Schneider, this volume).

Interspaces of Colonial Regimes

The interspaces between competing colonial regimes and tribal groups add another important dimension to the study of indigenous landscapes. The creation of international frontiers that encompassed diverse colonial and Native polities presented considerable challenges and opportunities for both Franciscans and indigenous peoples. Shifting power dynamics between colonial enterprises and outlying Native populations made these regions particularly volatile and fluid in space and time. As this volume nicely documents, the Franciscan missions dispersed across the Spanish borderlands in North America were marked by significant variation in how frontier relations unfolded in the sixteenth through early nineteenth centuries.

For example, as discussed in the chapters by Thomas, Blair, and Bossy (this volume), the frontier zones between the Spanish and British in the American Southeast were among some of the most dangerous and heavily contested in the Spanish Borderlands with significant implications for both colonists and tribal groups alike. The outcome of these entanglements in the sixteenth and seventeenth centuries eventually forced the remnant populations of the Franciscan missions to retreat southward to Saint Augustine, Florida.[20]

In California a very different kind of international frontier emerged in the indigenous landscape between the northern Spanish settlements and Colony Ross that neither colonial regime fully controlled. Russian and Hispanic relationships in California were a little schizophrenic. On one hand, the Spanish government and later the Mexican government demanded that the Russians abandon their colony that had been placed in lands they claimed, and respective governments never officially recognized the legitimacy of the Ross Colony during its entire operation from 1812 to 1841. On the other

20. See also Jerald T. Milanich, "Franciscan Missions and Native Peoples in Spanish Florida," in *The Forgotten Centuries: Indians and Europeans in the American South 1521–1704*, eds. Charles Hudson and Carmen C. Tesser (Athens: University of Georgia Press, 1994), 276–303; Jerald T. Milanich, *Florida Indians and the Invasion from Europe* (Gainesville: University Press of Florida, 1995); David Hurst Thomas, "The Spanish Missions of La Florida: An Overview," in *Archaeological and Historical Perspectives on the Spanish Borderlands East*, vol. 2 of *Columbian Consequences*, ed. David Hurst Thomas (Washington, DC: Smithsonian Institution Press, 1990): 357–398.

hand, the Russians became key economic partners with the Franciscan missionaries and presidio soldiers. The latter came to rely on black market trade with the Russian merchants to obtain manufactured goods that were no longer being supplied by Spanish ships after 1810 with the eruption of the Mexican war for independence. The Russian-American Company, in turn, traded a diverse range of goods to the Spanish settlements in return for agrarian products, such as wheat, barley, peas, and beans, tallow, butter, dried meat, and salt, which were shipped northward to help provision Russian colonies in the North Pacific.[21]

Interestingly, while construction of Mission San Rafael and Mission San Francisco Solano was supposedly undertaken to keep the Russians from settling along the north side of San Francisco Bay, the founding of these two missions stimulated increased trade across the Hispanic and Russian frontiers. The Russian-American Company supplied materials and goods used in construction of the two missions and frequent visits took place across the borderlands between Russian merchants and Hispanic missionaries and soldiers. Some of the Franciscans even had charge accounts with the Russians in which they placed special orders, such as custom candles and religious materials, and other miscellaneous goods, including brandy.[22]

While we have relatively good written documentation of the interactions that took place between the Russians and Spanish on the northern frontier, much less is known about the implications of the international frontiers between the two colonial regimes for tribal groups.

We believe these borderlands may have provided unique spaces of opportunity for indigenous populations. There are some colonial documents that indicate the international zone between the Spanish and Russian colonial regimes served as significant places of refuge for Native peoples. Here they could disappear into the periphery between the competing colonies. Russian sources suggest a number of neophyte fugitives moved into this region to escape the Franciscan missions. Russian interviews with Native peoples moving into this area indicate that they believed the Russian-American Company would prevent Spanish military excursions from entering this frontier zone. Other documents suggest that Russian administrators actively worked

21. The various economic relationships between the Russian and Spanish/Mexican colonies in Alta California are outlined in Glenn J. Farris, *So Far from Home: Russians in Early California* (Berkeley, CA: Heyday, 2012); Kent G. Lightfoot, *Indians, Missionaries, and Merchants: The Legacy of Colonial Encounters on the California Frontiers* (Berkeley: University of California Press, 2005).

22. See for example, Diane Spencer Pritchard, "Joint Tenants of the Frontier: Russian-Hispanic Relationships in Alta California," in *Russian America: The Forgotten Frontier*, eds. Barbara Sweetland Smith and Redmond J. Barnett (Tacoma: Washington State Historical Society, 1990): 81–93.

to persuade Indian fugitives from the missions and other outlying groups to relocate in the periphery of the Ross Colony, which would help maintain this area as a buffer zone between the Russians and the Spanish.[23]

Conclusion

In conclusion, there is growing interest in California and elsewhere in examining the broader indigenous landscapes that radiated out from colonial enclaves, such as Franciscan missions, and to take a closer look at how the lands and people of these hinterlands influenced the growth and development of colonial centers and vice versa. A critical issue is better understanding the social, political, and economic relationships that existed between people in these pluralistic colonies and in the outlying peripheries. In this paper, we outlined a geosensory model that will allow archaeologists to incorporate their work on mission quadrangles with the spatial-sonic landscape, defined here as the proximal zone, outlying hinterland, and interspace of colonial regimes. We argue that the mission bells and their associated soundscapes are significant considerations in understanding how a diverse range of residential, economic, and clandestine activities may have been mapped onto the proximal zones and outlying hinterlands of missions. We further emphasize that a better understanding of the outlying hinterlands and the interspaces between competing colonial regimes is crucial for examining how both Franciscans and neophytes related to more distant ecological habitats, gentile Indian communities, and other Europeans. As the Franciscan frontiers in California and the American Southeast demonstrate, these outlying lands were dynamic and ever-changing in time and space, offering a mixed assortment of opportunities and troubles to missionaries and neophytes alike.

Our plans for future work are twofold. One is to undertake acoustic experiments with bells at extant mission sites in California. The purpose is to begin to explore the soundscape of mission bells to better define the proximal zone. This includes both investigating existing archival sources for evidence of sound-related strategies of enculturation and information about mission bells, as well as modeling the potential range of these sonic activities. Following such models, coupling experimental bell ringing in contemporary environments and fieldwork ground-truthing the existence of different activity zones would refine the categories and help us understand how people moved between and within zones.

23. See Glenn J. Farris, "The Day of the Tall Strangers," *The Californians* 9, no. 6 (1992): 15; Kent G. Lightfoot, *Indians, Missionaries, and Merchants: The Legacy of Colonial Encounters on the California Frontiers* (Berkeley: University of California Press, 2005), 155–156; Fyodor F. Matiushkin, "From a Journal of a Round-the-World Voyage on the Sloop Kamchatka, under the Command of Captain Golovnin," trans. Stephen Watrous, *Fort Ross Interpretive Association Newsletter* (September–October, 1996): 5–6.

The second part of our plan is to initiate a study of the northern frontier of colonial California that builds on newly published work by Julie Bernard,[24] Sara Gonzalez,[25] Lee Panich,[26] Sarah Peelo,[27] Matt Russell,[28] Tsim Schneider,[29] and others. Our goal is to better understand what happened to the Native polities situated on the outskirts of the Spanish and Russian empires and how they negotiated this international space. Collaborative work with local tribes and state and national parks will involve five major tasks: (1) experimenting with the sonic and spatial landscapes of the northern missions to better define the proximal zones, outlying hinterlands, and interspaces of the colonial regimes; (2) doing a better job of synthesizing previous work in this area, and particularly recent CRM investigations; (3) undertaking selective survey work

---

24. Julienne Bernard, "An Archaeological Study of Resistance, Persistence, and Culture Change in the San Emigdio Canyon, Kern County, California" (PhD diss., University of California-Los Angeles, 2008); Julienne Bernard, David Robinson, and Fraser Sturt, "Points of Refuge in the South Central California Colonial Hinterlands," in *Indigenous Landscapes and Spanish Missions: New Perspectives from Archaeology and Ethnohistory*, eds. Lee M. Panich and Tsim D. Schneider (Tucson: University of Arizona Press, 2014), 154–171.

25. Sara L. Gonzalez, "Creating Trails from Tradition: The Kashaya Pomo Interpretive Trail at Fort Ross State Historic Park" (PhD diss., University of California-Berkeley, 2011).

26. Lee M. Panich, *Persistence of Native Identity at Mission Santa Catalina, Baja California, 1797–1840* (PhD diss., University of California-Berkeley, 2009); Lee M. Panich, "Spanish Missions in the Indigenous Landscape: A View from Mission Catalina, Baja California," *Journal of California and Great Basin Anthropology* 30, no. 1 (2010): 69–86; Lee M. Panich, "Assessing the Diversity of Mission Populations through the Comparison of Native American Residences at Mission Santa Clara De Asís," *International Journal of Historical Archaeology* 18 (2014): 467–488.

27. Sarah M. Peelo [Ginn], *Creating Community in Spanish California: An Investigation of California Plainwares* (PhD diss., University of California at Santa Cruz, 2009); Sarah M. Peelo, "The Creation of a Carmeleño Identity: Marriage Practices in the Indian Village at Mission San Carlos Borromeo del Río Carmel," *Journal of California and Great Basin Anthropology* 30, no. 2 (2010): 117–139; Sarah M. Peelo, "Pottery-Making in Spanish California: Creating Multi-Scalar Social Identity through Daily Practice," *American Antiquity* 76, no. 4 (2011): 642–666.

28. Matthew A. Russell, "Encounters at Tamál-Húye: An Archaeology of Intercultural Engagement in Sixteenth-Century Northern California" (PhD diss., University of California-Berkeley, 2011).

29. Tsim D. Schneider, "Placing Refuge: Shell Mounds and the Archaeology of Colonial Encounters in the San Francisco Bay Area, California" (PhD diss., University of California-Berkeley, 2010); Tsim D. Schneider, Sara L. Gonzalez, Kent G. Lightfoot, Lee M. Panich, and Matthew A. Russell, "A Land of Cultural Pluralism: Case Studies from California's Colonial Frontiers," in *Contemporary Issues in California Archaeology*, ed. Terry L. Jones and Jennifer E. Perry (Walnut Creek, CA: Left Coast Press, 2012), 319–337; Tsim D. Schneider and Lee M. Panich, "Native Agency at the Margins of Empire: Indigenous Landscapes, Spanish Missions, and Contested Histories," in *Indigenous Landscapes and Spanish Missions: New Perspectives from Archaeology and Ethnohistory*, eds. Lee M. Panich and Tsim D. Schneider (Tucson: University of Arizona Press, 2014), 5–22.

in key places, such as Point Reyes National Seashore; (4) rethinking how we work with museum collections from previously excavated sites; and (5) developing a better methodology for dating colonial-aged indigenous sites. We hope to be able to give an update on this project in future symposiums at Flagler College.

Acknowledgments

We appreciate greatly the invitation from Timothy Johnson and David Hurst Thomas to participate in the conference on "Franciscan Florida in Pan-Borderlands." We are grateful for the excellent support provided by Flagler College during the conference, including the use of their fine facilities and bountiful offerings of food and refreshments. Many thanks are extended to Jeffrey Burns and the Academy of American Franciscan History for their generous assistance and expertise in producing and publishing the conference proceedings.

Chapter 18
Moquis, Kastiilam, *and the Trauma of History: Hopi Oral Traditions of Seventeenth-Century Franciscan Missionary Abuses*

Thomas E. Sheridan and Stewart B. Koyiyumptewa

On November 7, 2002, soon after *Moquis and Kastiilam:* The Hopi History Project[1] began, Stewart B. Koyiyumptewa of the Hopi Cultural Preservation Office interviewed Vice-Chairman of the Hopi Tribe Elgean Joshevama in his office in Kykotsmovi, Arizona. Stewart was there to record Hopi oral traditions Vice-Chairman Joshevama had heard about the *Kastiilam*, the Spaniards who conquered and missionized the Hopis between 1629 and the Pueblo Revolt in 1680. "The information that I heard about came from not a lot of discussions, because apparently this was an issue that was very difficult to talk about, and so people were not very willing to even say too much about what happened then," Vice-Chairman Joshevama responded. "But I sense that it was an important time to Hopi because of the

*This chapter originally appeared in *New Mexico and the Pimería Alta: The Colonial Period in the American Southwest*, eds. John G. Douglass and William M. Graves, 239–260, Boulder: University Press of Colorado, 2017. It is reprinted here with the permission of the editors and the University Press of Colorado.

1. The Hopi History Project is a formal collaboration between the University of Arizona (UA) and the Hopi Tribe. Its goals are to tell the story of relations between Hopis and Spaniards during the period when the Spanish empire was attempting to incorporate the Hopi people into its colony of New Mexico. Researchers at the UA's Southwest Center, School of Anthropology and Arizona State Museum have selected, transcribed, translated, and annotated Spanish documents about the Hopis, whom the Spaniards called *Moquis*. The Hopi Cultural Preservation Office of the Hopi Tribe has interviewed Hopi elders to gather their oral traditions about the *Kastiilam*, the Hopi term for Spaniards. The University of Arizona Press published *Moquis and Kastiilam: Hopis, Spaniards, and the Trauma of History, 1540–1679*, Vol. I, in 2015. The second and final volume is in preparation. The project has been partially funded by a series of grants from the National Historic Publications and Records Commission (NHPRC) and a Collaborative Research Grant from the National Endowment for the Humanities.

disruption of our lives and how it later on impacted our lives. And even today, I think, we're still struggling with some of those issues that, that the Spaniards inflicted on us."

As the interview proceeded, Vice-Chairman Joshevama reflected on his work at the Hopi Guidance Center with Hopi children who had been sexually abused. "And, and as I was working with them I was curious to see how these victims of abuse had a lot of feelings. And, these feelings included anger," he continued. "A lot of feelings of being sad, sometimes some signs of depression, some signs of helplessness, guilt." Vice-Chairman Joshevama went on to say:

> And, and the more I worked with them trying to help get them past these kinds of feelings, trying to help with what they had been going through, to get them to a point where they might now be able to talk about it easier, the more I began to think that these children were showing me, and showing us who were working with them, to me were similar to the way that we in the villages were behaving too.
>
> We had a lot of suspicions of each other. We were angry at each other. We weren't very happy. We were sad sometimes and a lot of times these kinds of feelings of anger, sadness, would come out in different ways in our villages. And, then I recalled this part of our history that something happened to us a long time ago, and in particular, that period between about 1630 and 1680 when the Spanish were here and from the stories that we learned, they forced our people to do things that was against our way of doing things.[2]

Spanish conquest and missionization were profoundly traumatic for the Hopis, shaking the very foundations of Hopi society and provoking Hopis to carry out acts of violence that still haunt them today. The Franciscans never asked, "Could we be your guests here," Vice-Chairman Joshevama observed:

> They just simply intruded into Hopi lives and then enslaved us, slaved our people, and then subjected Hopi to a very foreign way of life. But Hopi, all this time, had already had its own way of life. We had our own initiations, we had our own rituals, we had our own ceremonies, we had own spiritual beings that we would talk to and pray to those. And, then here comes a foreign intruder and totally tells us that that's not right. This is the way your life has to be lived. And, so they forced that kind of idea or that concept on us. And, when any time anybody does that to somebody, it's, it's going to create a lot of feelings. It's going to create anger but at the same time fear because what can you do about it when these people have the might of the weapon, the modern weapon at the

---

2. Thomas Sheridan, Stewart B. Koyiyumptewa, Anton Daughters, Dale Brenneman, TJ Ferguson, Leigh Kuwanwisiwma, and LeeWayne Lomayestewa. 2015. *Moquis and Kastiilam: Hopi Indians, Spaniards, and the Trauma of History*, Vol. I, *1540–1679* (Tucson: University of Arizona Press, 2015), 236.

time, and that they could kill you without any kind of respect given to whether you agree with them or not.

See they, they just took completely away our freedom to live the kind of life that we had up to that point. So, those were the things that I thought about when I saw the similarities between the victims of sexual abuse of children, and then when I look at our villages and how they were behaving, and that behavior was pretty much the same as what these children were showing as victims of abuse. And, I concluded then that we, we must have been victims of abuse at some point, and that's when I thought back on our history and I thought of that period. That's when this abuse happened to us.[3]

Abusive Guests: Franciscan Missionaries on the Hopi Mesas

Like the other Pueblo peoples in southwestern North America, the Hopi Indians first encountered Europeans in 1540, when Francisco Vásquez de Coronado's expedition passed through the region like a brief but brutal plague. Spanish accounts of this initial contact between Kastiilam and Moquis, the term the Spaniards used for Hopis, paint a relatively benign picture of the interactions. More than four centuries of Hopi oral traditions, in contrast, report that Coronado's soldiers destroyed a Hopi village (Sheridan et al 2013; Sheridan et al 2015). For the next nine decades, contact between Hopis and Spaniards was intermittent, but in 1629, the governor of New Mexico led six Franciscans and thirty soldiers to establish missions among the Ácomas, Zunis, and Hopis. The leader of the Franciscans, custodio Padre Fray Esteban de Perea, claimed that the Ácomas and Zunis welcomed the Spaniards. But the Hopis at Awat'ovi, the easternmost Hopi pueblo on Antelope Mesa, received them "with some coolness" because an "apostate Indian of the Christian pueblos" had told them that the Spaniards "were coming to burn their pueblos, rob their haciendas, and behead their children." The Franciscans later accused Hopis at Awat'ovi of poisoning their first missionary, Padre Fray Francisco de Porras, in 1632.[4]

Despite Hopi resistance, however, Franciscan missionization proceeded. Missionaries established *cabeceras* (headquarters) with resident priests at Awat'ovi on Antelope Mesa, Songòopavi on Second Mesa, and Orayvi on

3. Ibid., 237

4. "Padre Fray Estevan de Perea's Account of the Grand Conversion of New Mexico, 1632," in ibid., Real Academia de la Historia, Madrid. Papeles de Jesuitas, Tomo 86, fol. 578. Our translation is from a transcript by historian Herbert Eugene Bolton. Charles Lummis published an English translation in *Land of Sunshine*, November and December, 1901. Lansing Bloom made slight revisions and published his version in *New Mexico Historical Review* 8 (1933): 211–235.

Third Mesa, with *visitas* (subsidiary churches) at Wàlpi on First Mesa and Musangnuvi on Second Mesa. The primary purpose of the religious mission in New Spain was to convert Native peoples to Roman Catholicism and transform them into vassals of the Spanish Crown. This usually involved prohibiting them from practicing their own religious ceremonies and beliefs. At Awat'ovi, for example, the sanctuary of the mission church—that most sacred of Catholic ritual spaces—was constructed on top of a perfectly preserved kiva.[5] Building the church above one of the Hopis' sacred underground chambers proclaimed that the Christian God was superior to Hopi gods, that Christian sacred spaces were submerging Hopi sacred spaces.

Conquest and colonization took an unrelenting material toll on the Hopis and other Pueblo peoples during the seventeenth century as well. Demands for labor and tribute under both missions and the *encomienda* system, which granted prominent Spaniards the right to extract foodstuffs and textiles from Pueblo households, increasingly burdened the Pueblos as their populations plummeted because of Old World diseases. At the beginning of the seventeenth century, when Juan de Oñate's expedition was establishing the colony of Nuevo México, Barrett estimates that there were about 81 occupied pueblos along the Rio Grande and its tributaries.[6] That number had plummeted to about 31 when the revolt broke out eight decades later. Her figures do not include either Zuni or Hopi communities. Population figures are more difficult to calculate because not all rooms in a pueblo may have been inhabited at any one time. Spanish observers provided population figures, but those were no more than educated guesses, colored by where the Spaniards went and for whom they were writing. Barrett speculates that there may have been perhaps 60,000 Pueblo inhabitants when Oñate arrived. By 1678, that number had dropped to 17,000. She argues that the greatest losses of both pueblos and people took place in the late 1630s and early 1640s, when smallpox decimated the Pueblo world.[7] More recent studies contend that even greater declines occurred after 1650, with another wave of disease ravaging the Pueblos in 1671.[8]

---

5. Ross Gordon Montgomery, Watson Smith, and John Otis Brew, *Franciscan Awatovi: The Excavation and Conjectural Reconstruction of a 17th-Century Spanish Mission Establishment at a Hopi Indian Town in Northeastern Arizona*. Vol. 36, *Papers of the Peabody Museum of American Archaeology and Ethnology, Harvard University*. Reports of the Awatovi Expedition, Peabody Museum, Harvard University, No. 3. Cambridge: Peabody Museum, 1949.

6. Elinore M. Barrett, *Conquest and Catastrophe: Changing Rio Grande Pueblo Settlement Patterns in the Sixteenth and Seventeenth Centuries* (Albuquerque: University of New Mexico Press, 2002), 64.

7. Ibid., 65, 78.

8. Matthew Liebmann, *Revolt: An Archaeological History of Pueblo Resistance and Revitalization in Seventeenth Century New Mexico* (Tucson: University of Arizona Press, 2012), 40.

Climate change compounded epidemics. In the mid-1660s, the third worst drought between 622 and 1994 A.D. seared the northern Southwest.[9] It was a cold drought, with cooler temperatures reducing the growing season for corn, the staple of Pueblo peoples. In the words of Carla Van West and her colleagues, "These harsh conditions initiated around 1664 and continued, almost unbroken, through 1678."[10] For three straight years—1667, 1668, and 1669—summer monsoons failed to moisten the parched fields of the Salinas pueblos, forcing their abandonment over the next decade. The Piro pueblos of the southern Rio Grande basin also drained away. The smallpox epidemic of the early 1640s had savaged the southern Pueblos most, causing the abandonment of eleven of fourteen Piro pueblos and five of eleven Salinas pueblos. Drought provided the coup de grace three decades later.

The same drought that afflicted the Pueblo World in New Mexico withered crops on the Hopi Mesas. From 1650 to 1680, the Palmer Drought Severity Index (PDSI) for the Southwest was negative, indicating poor conditions for agriculture for all years except seven; between 1664 and 1670, the drought was particularly harsh, with negative PDSI ranging from –1.632 in 1666 to –3.303 in 1668.[11]

An even more sensitive indicator of agricultural conditions on the Hopi Mesas is the PDSI for the month of June, when the all-important spring crops were ripening. Between 1660 and 1679, June PDSI was negative for fourteen of twenty years; from 1666–1670, June PDSIs reveal why famine stalked the Hopi pueblos as one dry year slid into another: 1666 (–2.232), 1667 (–3.407), 1668 (–3.542), 1669 (–1.095), 1670 (–4.954).[12] What little

9. Henri D. Grissino-Mayer, Christopher H. Baisan, and Thomas W. Swetnam, *A 1,374-Year Reconstruction of Annual Precipitation for the Southern Rio Grande Basin* (Final report submitted to the Legacy Program of Defense, El Paso, Texas. Laboratory of Tree-Ring Research, University of Arizona, 1997); J.A. Parks, J.S. Dean, and J.L. Betancourt, "Tree Rings, Drought, and the Pueblo Abandonment of South-Central New Mexico in the 1670s," in *Environmental Change and Human Adaptation in the Ancient American Southwest*, eds. D.E. Doyel and J.S. Dean, 214–227 (Salt Lake City: University of Utah Press, 2006), 214–227.

10. Carla Van West, Thomas C. Windes, Frances Levine, Henri D. Grissino-Mayer, and Matthew W. Salzer, "The Role of Climate in Early Spanish-Native American Interactions in the U.S. Southwest," in *Native and Spanish New Worlds: Sixteenth-Century Entradas in the American Southwest and Southeast*, eds. Clay Mathers, Jeffrey M. Mitchem, and Charles M. Haecker, Amerind Series in Anthropology, John Ware, series editor (Tucson: University of Arizona Press, 2013), 81–98.

11. E.R. Cook, Southwestern USA Drought Index Reconstruction. International Tree-Ring Data Bank. IGBP PAGES/World Data Center for Paleoclimatology Data Contribution Series #2000-053. NOAA/NGDC Paleoclimatology Program, Boulder, CO, 2000.

12. Southwest Paleoclimate Project, June PDSI, Hopi Mesas, AZ. Courtesy of Dr. Jeffrey Dean, Laboratory of Tree-Ring Research, University of Arizona.

household surpluses were left after the demands of missionaries and *encomenderos* had been met would have been quickly exhausted.

The final blow may have been a hard freeze during the growing season in the summer of 1680, as evidenced by a "frost ring" in the tree-ring chronology for the San Francisco Peaks and other sites in western North America. "Given that bristlecone pines in the Rocky Mountain region put on new growth from late June to late August or early September, we suspect that this destructive frost took place at a point in the corn-growing season when it was too late to replant," Van West et al surmise. "The frost-damaged section of the SFP ring of 1680 is located within or near the latewood rather than the early wood. It is likely that this destructive freeze took place in July or early August within a year *and* multi-year interval of exceptional cold. Our guess is that this 'event' was a contributing factor in the timing of the revolt."[13]

It is a truism in the social sciences that there are no "natural disasters." Mission and encomienda exacerbated cold and drought, grinding the Hopis and their Pueblo neighbors down. During these decades when famine and abuse haunted the Hopi mesas, many Hopis who may have converted to Christianity returned to the beliefs of their ancestors. Similar patterns of nativistic resistance and rebellion aggravated by drought wracked colonial Sonora in the mid-eighteenth century as well. Hopis and other Pueblo peoples were forced to carry out their religious ceremonies in secret, far from the prying eyes of missionaries. "Whose religion had been taken away? Whose ceremonies had been stamped down?" Vice-Chairman Joshevama asked rhetorically. "It's no wonder that we understand that in order for a Hopi person, or a Hopi people to do something that would bring back those kinds of things that had been important to them, that they had to steal themselves away in secrecy." Later in the interview, he added, "So that they would not forget. So that they could maybe teach the younger ones who might have been there with them those kinds of things that they needed to have them remember."[14]

The Investigation of Padre Fray Salvador de Guerra

When we began the Hopi History Project, Hopi colleagues, teachers, and elders expressed a great deal of interest in how Spanish colonial officials and missionaries portrayed colonial abuses. They wanted to see how those representations articulated with, or silenced, the Hopi people's long memory of missionary abuses during the seventeenth century prior to the Pueblo Revolt. One case in particular captured their attention because of its horrific details.

13. Van West, et al., "The Role of Climate," 9.
14. Sheridan et al., *Moquis*, 239.

In 1655, a Hopi named Juan Xiveni appeared before Padre Fray Antonio de Ybargaray, the *custodio* of New Mexico. As custodio, Ybargaray was the highest ranking Franciscan in charge of New Mexico's missions. Xiveni represented the Spanish-appointed Hopi *gobernador* (governor) of Orayvi and its *naturales*, or native inhabitants. They sent him to lodge a formal complaint against Padre Fray Salvador de Guerra, missionary in the pueblo of Orayvi on Third Mesa, "because of the terrible and inhuman punishments that [Guerra] has given to some natives, whipping them extremely cruelly in all parts and limbs of their bodies, and afterwards scalding them and anointing them with boiling turpentine." Ybargaray, Guerra's superior, took the charges seriously enough to travel to the Second Mesa village of Songòopavi and conduct a formal investigation, which is how and why the case made its way into the Spanish colonial record.[15]

Guerra's worst abuse involved a Hopi named Juan Cuna, whom Guerra had caught in an unspecified "idolatry." During the first stage of the investigation, Ybargaray heard the testimonies of three Hopis from Orayvi—Joseph Ocheguene, a *fiscal* (native official who carried out the policies of the *gobernador*) and two *capitanes de guerra* (war captains) from Orayvi, Francisco Quera and Juan Cocpi. All three confirmed that Guerra kicked and punched Juan Cuna just outside the door to Orayvi's mission church until he was "bathed in blood." Then, inside the church, Guerra tied Cuna to a ladder and whipped him severely "on the back, belly, and all of the other parts of his body." Finally, the Franciscan "scalded him from head to foot with a large lump of turpentine, and he burned him with it." After these grisly punishments, Cuna and "other idolators" were dispatched to Awat'ovi under the charge of Joseph Ocheguene and other Hopi fiscales. Cuna died, "unconscious and speechless," along the trail between Orayvi and Songòopavi.

Guerra denied that he kicked or punched Cuna, stating that he only gave him a slap on the face from which "six or seven drops of blood came out of his nose." He admitted to having Cuna tied up and whipped, but claimed that he did not do the lashing, that "the lashes did not exceed twenty, and he gave him no lashes on the belly." As for the turpentine, "seeing that [Cuna] was old and sick, he had thrown on him no more than ten or twelve drops, and not all [over] his body, as the witnesses state." Guerra then accused fiscal Joseph Ocheguèni of whipping Cuna to death because he "did not want to walk."

In light of Guerra's testimony, Ybargaray ordered Ocheguene, Quera, and Cocpi to ratify their statements. Ocheguene could not be located because Franciscan lay brother Fray Pedro Moreno, who "loved him well," had told Ocheguene to hide because of Guerra's counter-accusations. So Ybargaray

15. Archivo Histórico-Nacional (AHN), Inquisición 1729, exp. 2, n. 3, ff. 34–38, 44–51. Madrid, Spain.

took Moreno's testimony. Moreno stated that Ocheguene only hit Cuna "with a switch or branch on the legs so that he would move along." Quera and Cocpi swore that their original statements were true and also testified that Ocheguene did no harm to Cuna.

While at Songòopavi in June, Ybargaray also investigated other charges against Guerra brought by Hopi leaders from Orayvi, Songòopavi, and Musangnuvi. The Hopis said that Guerra "compelled them to make many cotton mantas, for which the aforesaid father would give them half the cotton that was necessary to finish them. And the harshness of the aforesaid father obliged them to finish [the mantas] with cotton they had in their homes within eight days. Because of this rush, they could not plant their cotton [fields] or cultivate their milpas [corn fields]." As to his "harshness," the Hopi officials accused Guerra of "whipping them terribly and giving them up to forty and fifty lashes, and scalding and smearing them with burning-hot turpentine." Ybaragaray took the testimonies of nine Hopis who confirmed those charges. Guerra denied them. Ybargaray called the Hopis back in again, and they all ratified their original charges. They also declared that Guerra was only entitled to less than a third of the mantas he demanded of them.

Mission Indians were supposed to supply their missionaries with food, cloth, and other basics. These provisions were in addition to the annual stipend the missionary received from the Spanish crown. But missions were not parishes and the Franciscans were not secular clergy who could own property or receive benefices. Nor could they charge mission Indians for administering the sacraments to them.[16] Franciscans like Guerra tried to justify the extraction of mantas from their neophytes by claiming that it was in the support of the mission, not the missionary. But Guerra clearly violated the moral economy of the Hopis by forcing them to produce an excessive amount of mantas at a time when they needed to plant their fields.

The investigation then moved to Santo Domingo where, in July, Ybargaray and five other Franciscans found Guerra guilty of killing Cuna and the other charges. Clearly shocked by his behavior, they concluded that Guerra not only had to be removed from Orayvi but sent to Mexico City as well. Ybargaray and the others therefore sentenced Guerra to seclusion in the convento of Quarai until he could be deported to Mexico City for punishment by Franciscan superiors of the Provincia de Santa Evangelio. Guerra was also prohibited from saying mass or administering the sacraments.

But Guerra may never have traveled to Mexico City. In 1659–60, he was stationed at Taos. A year later, he was posted to Isleta. In 1661, he served at

16. Nancy Farriss, *Crown and Clergy in Colonial Mexico, 1759–1821* (London: Athlone Press, 1968); William Taylor, *Magistrates of the Sacred: Priests and Parishioners in Eighteenth-century Mexico* (Stanford: Stanford University Press, 1999).

Ácoma and then at Jémez, where he was notary to Fray Alonso de Posada, comisario of the Holy Office of the Inquisition. During the 1660s, Guerra was Posada's right-hand man during his crusade against governors Bernardo López de Mendizábal and Diego de Peñalosa. Guerra remained at Jemez at least until 1668, when he described himself as "preacher, difinidor actual, commissary of the Santa Concordia, secretary of the Holy Custodia of the Conversion of San Pablo of New Mexico, and minister-guardian of the congregation of San Diego de los Jemez."[17] In 1672, he was in charge of the supply train itself. Guerra's fall from grace was short indeed.[18]

The Torture and Death of Sitkoyma

Most Hopi oral traditions of missionary abuses are generalized accounts. The most common concerns were having to haul beams for mission churches from distant mountains or of priests abusing Hopi women, often after sending their husbands away to fetch water from distant springs. Occasionally, however, precise details emerge. One afternoon in October 2009, during a three-day workshop with members of the Hopi Tribe's Cultural Resources Advisory Task Team (CRATT), Leigh Kuwanwisiwma, director of the Hopi Cultural Preservation Office, led a field trip to a natural amphitheater in the mountains south of Third Mesa known as Katsina Buttes. There, while talking about how Hopis had to hold their ceremonies in secret during the mission period, Kuwanwisiwma gave another version of what may have been Juan Cuna's punishment. Four years later, on October 19, 2012, Stewart B. Koyiyumptewa recorded Kuwanwisiwma's narrative of the incident at greater length.[19]

After discussing the "pretty systematic . . . suppression of Hopi religion," including the burning of Hopi paraphernalia and altars "necessary to conduct ceremonies and initiate members," Kuwanwisiwma talked about how the missionaries were called away from the Hopi missions to attend a meeting in Santa Fe:

> So one individual by the name of Sitkoyma from Orayvi thought about quickly sponsoring a katsina Home Dance—we call it *Nimàntikive*—and that was because his son had recently married and had gone through the Hopi wedding ceremony so I guess you would think that at least those kinds of ceremonies were not forbidden by the church.
>
> And as he looked throughout the village of Orayvi and other villages, he knew that other traditional weddings had also been completed. But

17. Translated by France Scholes in France Scholes, "Documents for New Mexico Missions," *New Mexico Historical Review* 4, Number 2 (1929): 196.

18. Lansing Bloom and Lynn Mitchell, "The Chapter Elections in 1672," *New Mexico Historical Review* 13, Number 1 (1938), 85–115.

19. See Sheridan et al, *Moquis*.

because the katsina ceremonies were never completed, they could never conduct the Home Dance, which is a really major part of the Hopi wedding ceremony. There's many things that occur between both sets of the family and, particularly—and of the ceremony—there's an exchanging of different kinds of personal vows between the bride and husband and you know of course because the katsinas were forbidden, none of the brides that had gone through—over a period of years—never completed that part of the Hopi wedding ceremony. So, he thought that maybe he could take advantage of the absence of the priest, the church and the military to quickly conduct—sponsor and conduct—a katsina ceremony, Home Dance, so that that last piece of the ceremony would be offered to the couple and then subsequently work towards concluding the Hopi ceremony.

So he probably sought advice and got support and they say that it was out of season—the katsina season had ended—but he took that opportunity to quickly call together some people. Men and I'm sure women, and said this is what I want to do. And that was to hold a katsina ceremony and Home Dance for his new bride, his new daughter in law. So they said that they quickly convened out of season—and yes, they still remembered the Home Dance songs—so they quickly put together their own types of paraphernalia and then because they really didn't want to have a big, big public show because they were afraid that would be very well be immediately known by the Spanish priest and the military, they took refuge into what we now call Katsina Buttes or *Kaktsintuyqa*. So that's where the men practiced the katsina Home Dance and then when they were ready then they announced it and Sitkoyma, Sitkoyma was the guy in charge of it.

And so he invited other villages that if in fact they were able and willing. He invited all the brides that had gone through the ceremony to go there so that they could conclude a part, and part of the last parts of the Hopi wedding ceremonies. So they say that brides from throughout the mesas, they'd accept the invitations, so the dance was held. And we now call it over in the Hopi Buttes area about maybe half an hour away from Old Orayvi due east, we call it now that whole landscape *Kaktsintuyqa* but we also call this one alcove that they used as a plaza we call it *Tipkya* and *Tipkya* is a very important place in a village and that's where the final Home Dances are danced—where the bride is shown publically to everybody, the audience. So that's what happened. They danced the Home Dance and then towards the evening, all the brides were dressed up in their robes and then they were presented to the people witnessing it and then of course to the katsinas, the katsina spirits. So that's what happened and of course everybody I'm sure with that happening and then ending successfully everybody liked all of our dances was pretty happy about it.[20]

20. Ibid.

After returning from Santa Fe, however, the priest at Orayvi found out about Sitkoyma's sponsorship of the forbidden Home Dance. Hopis referred to that missionary in particular, and missionaries in general, as *Tota'tsi*: Kuwanwisiwma defined *Tota'tsi* as "a spiritual person that you can never ever please and if you don't please him, *Tota'tsi* will do whatever it can to get its way." The missionary ordered Sitkoyma to be arrested and interrogated. Then, in Kuwanwisiwma's words:

> The Tota'tsi told the military to announce and also make sure that on a particular day he wanted all of Orayvi to converge on the plaza. So that's what happened. It was announced that on a certain day no one would be allowed [to leave] the village and the military of course I'm sure, made sure of that. I'm sure they had units watching the village outside the village, making sure. And what the Tota'tsi now had decided was that because he [Sitkoyma] was convicted of violating this decree of the ban on Hopi ceremonies that he had to be publically punished and that was the intent of having the whole village come to the Orayvi plaza where when Sitkoyma got there, the posts had already been put into the plaza there and he was led there and then tied there with his frontal body tied, strapped. Hands were tied. And then he was tied to this post. So the priest, they say, who was fluent in Hopi, then announced the charges, the conviction and now the punishment. So the punishment was flogging by horsewhip. So that's what happened with the whole village present there. The priest and the military commander ordered the whipping of Sitkoyma.
>
> So he received some initial slashes they say and of course quite literally the horsewhip with the amount of force landing on human skin simply cut it open. And there were more slashes they say until Sitkoyma, because of the amount of whipping he took, was literally covered in blood from throughout his body and they say he was screaming. The point was that if there were any further violations of different kinds of decree, such as the one that Sitkoyma and others violated, this would be the kind of punishment that they would receive
>
> So while Sitkoyma was still strapped there, still alive, then Tota'tsi then ordered the military to show Sitkoyma and the village really what he meant when he said you will suffer the consequences if you dare violate church and military decrees. So what he ordered then was to have the military people pour turpentine on Sitkoyma, on his wounds. And you can imagine what Sitkoyma was going through. So based on the turpentine and everything else that happened, they say that Sitkoyma died there in Orayvi plaza still strapped you know to the post that was there in the village. And so when you look back to that incident you can see probably the kind of horrific trauma the whole village witnessed and suffered. And also what Sitkoyma also went through.[21]

21. Ibid., 173–74.

The Pueblo Revolt and the Destruction of Awat'ovi

The torture and death of Sitkoyma, may have been one of the tipping points that pushed the Hopis to rebel. Kuwanwisiwma continued:

> So one Hopi informant said that was what Sitkoyma went through—what he did and was killed there—the decision on whether to join the Pueblos in the revolt was being debated and the Hopis being pacifist people, against the taking of life, were not really wanting to participate in the Pueblo Revolt that the Pueblos were planning. But they say that when the Hopi chiefs and leaders witnessed this thing of Sitkoyma, that's when Orayvi said we will participate in the Pueblo Revolt. We just simply need to get rid of the church and the military and when Orayvi decided to do that then because it was one of the biggest ceremonial centers, largest in population, very influential, then that's where other Hopi villages, particularly Songòopavi, Musangnuvi, Wàlpi, and Awat'ovi, decided to join Orayvi in the Pueblo Revolt.[22]

We do not know if the torture and death of Sitkoyma was the same incident as that of Juan Cuna. Some of the details are different, particularly the location of Sitkoyma's death in the Orayvi plaza. Juan Cuna supposedly died on the trail to Awat'ovi. The possibility that more than one Hopi individual was killed by whipping and scalding with turpentine would only strengthen our contention that missionary abuses profoundly traumatized the Hopis and drove them to rebellion. If Sitkoyma and Juan Cuna were one and the same, however, Hopis waited twenty-five years to throw off the Spanish yoke.

What we do know is that rebellion was simmering throughout the Pueblo world long before the coordinated uprising of August 10, 1680. After the revolt erupted, Sargento Mayor Diego López Sambrano stated that he had witnessed sorcery, rebellion, and punishment for "more than forty years" since the administration of Governor Fernando de Arguello (1644–47), "who hanged, and lashed, and imprisoned more than forty Indians."[23] Pueblo peoples, including the Hopis, clearly had been contemplating rebellion for a very long time.

During the early days of the revolt, the Hopis killed the three missionaries stationed among them. In Fray Padre Silvestre Vélez de Escalante's "Extracto de Noticias," written nearly a century after the revolt, the Franciscan chronicler includes the interrogation of a Pueblo rebel named Bartolomé de Ojeda, who was captured during Governor Domingo Jironza Pétris de Cruzate's

---

22. Ibid., 178–79.

23. Charles Hackett and Charmion C. Shelby, *Revolt of the Pueblo Indians of New México and Otermín's Attempted Reconquest 1680–1682, Part 1*, Coronado Historical Series, Vol. VIII. Coronado Cuarto Centennial Publications, 1540–1940., ed. George P. Hammond (Albuquerque: University of New México Press, 1942), 298–99.

siege of the pueblo of Zia in 1689. Ojeda provided an account of the missionaries' execution:

> This fatal news [the murder of Padre Fray Agustín de Santa María by the Zunis] reached Moqui, and the Moquinos immediately undertook to kill the friars who administered them. And they were Father Fray José de Espeleta (he had been a missionary for 40 years), Fray José Trujillo, and Fray José de Figueras. An Indian named Francisco, also a Moquino, whom Father Espeleta had reared, defended them. And seeing this, the apostate rebels said to him: "Now you must kill them yourself, and if not, we must kill you." In order to save his life, although against his will, he gave up the charitable office of advocate for the three blameless priests, and agreed to be their executioner. They placed the three friars together as a target (for their rage) and Francisco, impelled by fear, went on shooting at them with a musket until all three died of the bullet wounds. Then some compassion entered them, which could also have been a horrible manifestation of such execrable evil at seeing the three bodies stretched out, and they carried them to a church and burned them in it. The same Moquino Francisco related this long afterwards to this witness, Bartolomé de Ojeda, with tears in his eyes.[24]

Francisco was the same Francisco Espeleta who served as chief spokesperson for the Hopis who refused to allow the Franciscans to return in 1700. He also may have organized, if not masterminded, the destruction of Awat'ovi in late November of that same year. If Bartolomé de Ojeda's account of young Francisco's reluctance to kill his namesake is accurate, Espeleta must have had a radical change of heart over the next two decades of Hopi independence. Taught to read and write by his namesake, Padre Fray Espeleta, whom he killed during the Pueblo Revolt, Espeleta emerges from Spanish pages as the foremost opponent to the Franciscans. Wily, intransigient, and fluent in Spanish, he embodies Hopi resistance to the Spaniards.

During his reconquest of the Pueblo world, Diego de Vargas visited Awat'ovi, Wàlpi, Musangnuvi, and Songòopavi, where the Hopis appeared to "reconcile" themselves to God and King.[25] But that was just an example of one Hopi strategy: to tell the Spaniards what they wanted to hear so they would go away. When the Franciscans returned to stay, Hopi resistance hardened. The rejection of the missionaries appears unequivocal everywhere except Awat'ovi in Narvaez y Valverde's account, written in 1730.[26]

---

24. In Sheridan et al, *Moquis,* Vol. II, in preparation.

25. See Carlos de Sigüenza y Góngora, *Mercurio Volante, con al noticia de la recuperación de las provincias del nuevo méxico* (México: Antuerpia, 1693). An English translation can be found in *Mercurio Volante of Don Carlos de Sigüenza y Góngora.* An Account of the First Expedition of Don Diego de Vargas into New Mexico in 1692. Trans. with an Introduction by Irving Leonard (Los Angeles: The Quivira Society, 1932).

26. In Sheridan et al, *Moquis,* Vol. II, in preparation.

The standard interpretation of the destruction of Awat'ovi is that Espeleta and other Hopi leaders razed the pueblo and killed its men because its inhabitants had invited the Franciscans to return. Bandelier provides one of the first and most detailed published accounts of it—an account that largely shaped subsequent non-Hopi understandings of the event:

> In the meantime, Ahua-tuyba [Awat'ovi] had virtually become again a Christianized pueblo. In the last days of the year 1700, or in the beginning of 1701, the Moquis of the other pueblos fell upon the unsuspecting village at night. The men were mostly killed, stifled in their estufas [kivas], it is said; the women and children were dragged into captivity, and the houses were burnt.[27]

Hopi accounts paint a much more complex picture, one in which leaders of important ceremonial societies at Awat'ovi were spared in order to keep those societies from dying out. There were also accusations of witchcraft and disorder (*koyaanisqatsi*) at Awat'ovi and a desire to wrest control of important initiation societies like the *Wuwtsim*, which originated there, from Hopis who were considered to be corrupt.[28] Anthropologist Peter Whiteley argues that the Hopis in 1700 were engaged in a cultural revitalization movement that was redefining what it meant to be Hopi.[29] Like other Pueblo peoples, the Hopis had endured decades of forced labor and religious persecution. Some may have converted to Christianity; others were compelled to attend mass and allow their children to be baptized. But the Spaniard's God had not brought them prosperity. Instead, pestilence and drought stalked the land. Hopis conspired with the other Pueblos to kill their missionaries and drive the Spaniards from their homelands. When the Spaniards returned to Nuevo México, many Tewas, Tiwas, Tanos, Jemez, and Keresans sought refuge on their mesas. Those desperate, uprooted people must have stiffened Hopi resistance. Never again, they may have told one another as they revived their ceremonies. Never again would the katsinam or the corn mothers be driven away by the gray-robed Franciscans.

---

27. Adolph Bandelier, *Final Report of Investigations Among the Indians of the Southwestern United States, Carried on Mainly in the Years from 1880 to 1885, Part II* (Cambridge, MA: John Wilson and Son, University Press, 1892), 372.

28. Edward Curtis, *The North American Indian.* Vol. 12, *The Hopi* (Cambridge, MA: University Press, 1922); Harold Courlander, ed.and trans. *Hopi Voices: Recollections, Traditions, and Narratives of the Hopi Indians.* Recorded, transcribed, and annotated by Harold Courlander. Albuquerque: University of New Mexico Press, 1982); Ekkehart Malotki, ed. and trans. Michael Lomatuway'ma, Lorena Lomatuway'ma, and Sidney Namingha Jr. (narrators), *Hopi Tales of Destruction* (Lincoln: University of Nebraska Press, 2002); Peter Whitely, "Re-Imagining Awat'ovi," in *Archaeologies of the Pueblo Revolt: Identity, Meaning, and Renewal in the Pueblo World*, ed. by Robert Preucel, pp. 147–66 (Albuquerque: University of New Mexico Press, 2002), 147–166; Sheridan et al in prep, Vol. II.

29. Whitely, "Re-Imagining."

Whatever their motivations, however, the destruction of one of their own communities and the killing of their own people still sear Hopi memories today. The covenant that the Hisatsinom (Hopi ancestors) made with Màasaw, Guardian of the Fourth World, required them to be a humble, peaceful people. As Vice-Chairman Joshevama explained, "We have this basic value of respecting all forms of life. Human life is respected. Animal life is respected. The spiritual life, the plant life. All of these are respected. And, that's what our ceremonial events are based on." The forced labor, the suppression of their religion, the sexual exploitation of their women, and the shocking brutality of a Padre Fray Salvador de la Guerra, drove the Hopis to kill their missionaries during the 1680 Pueblo Revolt and then, twenty years later, to destroy the village of Awat'ovi itself to prevent the missionaries from returning. "But what they left us though was with the consequence," Vice-Chairman Joshevama observed. "They left us with us having to deal with the guilt of destroying our own people. And, then the anger we have to deal with of those who survived it, the survivors of Awatovi probably felt a lot of anger. And, what do they do with that anger? A lot of it is suppressed."[30]

Historical Trauma, Social Memory, and Healing the Soul Wound

Vice-Chairman Joshevama was expressing what a growing number of researchers and clinicians have observed among American Indian and Alaskan Native (AIAN) peoples: "historical" or "intergenerational" trauma.[31] Maria Yellow Horse Brave Heart, a pioneer in the identification and treatment of historical trauma, defines it as the "cumulative emotional and psychological wounding, over the lifespan and across generations, emanating from massive

30. Sheridan et al, *Moquis*, 242.

31. Eduardo Duran and Bonnie Duran. 1995. *Native American Postcolonial Psychology* (Albany: State University of New York Press, 1995); Maria Yellow Horse Brave Heart-Jordan, "The Return to the Sacred Path: Healing from Historical Trauma and Historical Unresolved Grief among the Lakota." Doctoral Dissertation, Smith College for Social Work, 1995, "Gender Differences in the Historical Trauma Response among the Lakota." *Journal of Health and Social Policy* 10, Number 4 (1999):1–21, and "Oyate Ptaleya: Rebuilding the Lakota Nation through Addressing Historical Trauma among Lakota Parents," *Journal of Human Behavior in the Social Environment* 2 Number 1–2 (1999b), 109–26, and "Wakiksuyapi: Carrying the Historical Trauma of the Lakota," *Tulane Studies in Social Welfare* (2000), 245–66; Maria Yellow Horse Brave Heart and L. M. DeBruyn, "The American Indian Holocaust: Healing Historical Unresolved Grief." *American Indian and Alaska Native Mental Health Research* 8 (1998), 56–78; Bonnie Duran, Eduardo Duran, and Maria Yellow Horse Brave Heart, "Native Americans and the Trauma of History," in *Studying Native America: Problems and Prospects*, edited by Russell Thornton (Madison: University of Wisconsin Press, 1998), 60–76.

group trauma experiences."[32] Examples of historical trauma experienced by American Indian and Alaskan Native (AIAN) peoples include "community massacres, genocidal policies, pandemics from the introduction of new diseases, forced relocation, forcible removal of children through Indian boarding school policies and the prohibition of spiritual practices."[33] For the Hopis, those systematic assaults began in 1540 when, according to Hopi oral traditions, Coronado's soldiers destroyed a Hopi village on Antelope Mesa.[34]

Substance abuse is one of a "constellation of features" Brave Heart describes as "historical trauma response (HTR)." Others self-destructive behaviors include "suicidal thoughts and gestures, depression, anxiety, low self-esteem, anger, and difficulty recognizing and expressing emotions."[35] One of the consequences of such trauma—a consequence Vice-Chairman Joshevama himself acknowledged—is "historical unresolved grief," which may be "impaired, delayed, fixated, and/or disenfranchised."[36] Unlike posttraumatic stress disorder (PTSD), historical trauma is collective rather than individual, passed down from one generation to another. Research on survivors of the Jewish Holocaust, African-Americans, and Cambodian refugees identify similar patterns of what many Native Americans call the "soul wound."[37]

The two volumes of *Moquis and Kastiilam: The Hopi History Project* tell the story of that trauma, and the Hopis' resistance to it, from both Hopi and

---

32. Maria Yellow Horse Brave Heart, "The Historical Trauma Response Among Natives and Its Relationship with Substance Abuse: A Lakota Illustration," *Journal of Psychoactive Drugs,* 35 Number 1 (2003), 7.

33. Tommie Begay, "Toxic Stress: Linking Historical Trauma to the Contemporary Health of American Indians and Alaskan Natives," Department of Teaching, Learning and Sociocultural Studies (Disse., Tucson: University of Arizona, 2012), 11.

34. Sheridan et al, *Moquis,* and Thomas Sheridan, Stewart B. Koyiyumptewa, Anton Daughters, Dale Brenneman, T.J. Ferguson, Leigh Kuwanwisiwma, Dale Brenneman, and Lee Wayne Lomayestewa. 2013. "Moquis and Kastiilam: Coronado and the Hopis," *Journal of the Southwest* 55 (2013): 377–434.

35. Brave Heart, "The Historical Trauma Response," 7.

36. Ibid., 7.

37. Eva Fogelman,"Intergenerational Group Therapy: Child Survivors of the Holocaust and Offspring of Survivors," *Psychoanalytic Review* 75 (1988): 621–40, and "Mourning without Graves," in *Storms and Rainbows: the Many Faces of Death,* ed. A. Medvene (Washington, D.C.: Lewis Press, 1991); R. Yehuda, *Risk Factors for Posttraumatic Stress Disorder* (Washington, D.C.: American Psychiatric Press, 1999); Carol Kidron, "Surviving a Distant Past: A Case Study of the Cultural Construction of Trauma Descendant Identity," *Ethos* 31 (2003): 513–544; William E. Cross, "Black Psychological Functioning and the Legacy of Slavery," in *International Handbook of Multigenerational Legacies of Trauma,* Ed by Y. Danieli (New York: Plenum Press, 1998), 387–400; Ron Eyerman, *Cultural Trauma: Slavery and the Formation of African American Identity* (Cambridge: Cambridge University Press, 2002); William Sack, Gregory Clarke, and John Seeley, "Post-Traumatic Stress Disorder Across Two Generations of Cambodian Refugees," *Journal of the American Academy of Child and Adolescent Psychiatry* 34 (1995): 1160–66.

Spanish points of view. For nearly five hundred years, the story has been overwhelmingly one-sided. Historians and anthropologists have relied upon documents written by representatives of the Spanish empire. Hopi voices have been silenced, ignored, or relegated to "myth." Those of us on the project have attempted to restore a balance to the historical record by presenting not only Spanish documents about the Hopis but interviews with Hopi elders about the Spaniards carried out by members of the Hopi Cultural Preservation Office. We argue that these Hopi oral traditions are living records of the past that have just as much, if not more, scholarly validity as the letters, court records, and reports of Spanish officials and Franciscan missionaries. Both are lines of evidence—"texts" in the parlance of literary and cultural criticism—that need to be interrogated. Both have their strengths and limitations that need to be understood.

The testimony of the Vice-Chairman Joshevama offers a historical memory distinct from colonial documentary representations in content, form, and voice. As noted at the beginning of this chapter, the abuses of the missionaries were "very difficult to talk about, and so people were not willing to even say too much about what happened then." In other words, the Spanish presence in the Hopi pueblos was still a sensitive subject more than three hundred years later.

The vice chairman's testimony also reveals that some Hopi memories of trauma are grounded in a generalized identity of descent; no particularities are mentioned. Instead, Hopis are referred to as a single group who suffered and were abused by Spaniards. Other narratives like Leigh Kuwanwisiwma's narrative about Sitkoyoma, reference specific persons, places, events, landscape features, or supernatural beings, often foregrounding clans or villages rather than the Hopi Tribe, which in many respects was a creation of the Indian Reorganization Act of 1934.[38] The juxtaposition of Kuwanwisiwma's very specific account with more general stories of missionary abuse suggest the depth, richness, and diversity of Hopi narratives about the past. There is no single Hopi oral tradition about the Kastiilam. On the contrary, Hopi chronicles about the past are like underground rivers that flow together and break apart, surfacing only when the moral topography of speaker and audience comes together and the narratives issue forth as small springs.

Accounts like that of Vice-Chairman Joshevama also meld past and present together in a way that fosters an "imagined community" based on the intergenerational memory of colonial trauma. A frequent use of "we," "our people," and "our way of life" reflects this sense in the vice chairman's testi-

38. Peter Whiteley, *Deliberate Acts: Changing Hopi Culture through the Oraibi Split* (Tucson: University of Arizona Press, 1988), and *Rethinking Hopi Ethnography* (Washington, D.C.: Smithsonian Institution, 1998).

mony. Moreover, this generalized identity of descent emphasizes, and is reinforced by, disruption and interruption. In the words of Vice-Chairman Joshevama, the missionaries "didn't ask, 'Could we be your guests here?' They didn't ask if they could build the churches or their missions in our villages." On the contrary, "They just simply intruded into Hopi lives and then enslaved us, slaved our people, and then subjected Hopi to a very foreign way of life. But Hopi, all this time, had already had its own way of life." The disruption and interruption of the "Hopi way of life," then, is remembered as more than simple transgressions or individual acts of violence on the part of the colonizers. On the contrary, the Spaniards attempted to destroy or transform many domains central to the social reproduction of the Hopi people: their subsistence activities, their spiritual practices, their gender relationships, and their political organization. "And, when any time anybody does that to somebody, it's, it's going to create a lot of feelings," Vice-Chairman Joshevama noted. "It's going to create anger but at the same time fear because what can you do about it when these people have the might of the weapon, the modern weapon at the time, and that they could kill you without any kind of respect given to whether you agree with them or not."[39]

Along with anger and fear, an even more powerful trope of guilt also emerges. Although the Hopis rebelled by carrying out their rituals in secret, and by participating in the Pueblo Revolt, they had to destroy the village of Awat'ovi to keep the missionaries from reestablishing missions among the Hopi and suppressing the Hopi way of life once again. "They never returned to have that, have that influence again. But what they left us though was the consequence. They left us having to deal with the guilt of destroying our own people. And, then the anger we have to deal with of those who survived it, the survivors of Awat'ovi probably felt a lot of anger. And, what do they do with that anger? A lot of it is suppressed."[40] Past injustices continue to cause contemporary ills.

Missionary abuses during the 1600s and the destruction of Awat'ovi in 1700 remain open wounds among the Hopis today. The enduring experience of these emotive memories accounts for the Hopi Tribe's response to a formal apology for past abuses issued by the Diocese of Gallup. When Bishop Donald Pelotte, a Native American whose father was of the Abenaki/Algonquin Nation, met with them in 2000, he reported, "they are still cautious and uncertain about efforts at reconciliation. Nonetheless, they are open to allow us to prove that we are indeed serious about healing the past by asking us for support of their efforts to have justice regarding treaty rights, land and water rights, education, housing, health care, social services, training in jobs, and

---

39. Sheridan et al, *Moquis*, 237.
40. Ibid., 242.

the use of sacred lands."[41] The Hopi Tribe also replaced Columbus Day with Hopi Independence Day—August 10, the anniversary of the outbreak of the Pueblo Revolt—as a paid tribal holiday.

Nevertheless, Hopis still debate whether or not those memories should be exhumed. Perhaps because of his experience dealing with sexually abused children, Vice-Chairman Joshevama believes that the traumatic past has to be confronted:

> How can we do a healing from that event, from those events? How can we heal? So, what they did, what the Hopi did, start doing from that point is they just took those kinds of feelings and put them under here, stash it away somewhere else, but you know what happens when you stash something, you hide it. At some point it starts to creep back out and it surfaces. And that, that's what happens. And, that's what's happening even to this day. And, then the younger people would learn from this, they carry it on. And, it's like telling our children that this is the way you're going to have to be because this is what somebody did to your family a long time ago instead of saying, we need to talk about this and let's, let's try to find a way to resolve it so that we don't carry it onto the next generation. To me, that's the step we need to take. And, that's what I have been hoping can happen, that people can understand and, and not practice that kind of intergenerational abuse.[42]

41. Donald Pelotte, "Seeking Forgiveness, Building Communion: A Time for Atoning and Reconciling." Encuentro 2000. United States Conference of Catholic Bishops, July 6, 2000.

42. Sheridan et al, *Moquis*, 243.

Chapter 19
Personal Missionary Reflections

Sister Theresa Chato, SBS

I'll introduce myself in the traditional Navajo way meaning that I'll tell you what clans make up my life. Since the Navajos are matrilineal, our clans come through our mothers. My name is Sr. Theresa Chato. I was born into the *Tábąąhá* clan (edge of the water), my mother's clan and I was born for the *Tsi'naajinii* clan (black streak wood people), my father's clan. My maternal grandfather's clan is the *Tódich'ii'nii* clan (bitter water) and my paternal grandfather's clan is the *Haltsooí* clan (meadow people). Our clans tell other Navajos how we are related to one another. We are not just individual persons with our own identity. We are also in relation to other Navajos; we are part of a larger community of people.

Most of the presentations at this conference have been about the early Spanish friars and their encounter with the native peoples of this country upon their arrival. I'll share about my experiences of the friars with my people, the Navajos that are more contemporary.

I understand that the early Spanish friars tried to establish contact with the Navajos around the time they established missions among the pueblo peoples. However, the Navajos didn't live in villages as the pueblos did. They were more nomadic, moving where they could find food for their animals and people. The early Spanish friars didn't succeed in establishing any missions among the Navajos.

In the late 1800's the foundress of my community, the Sisters of the Blessed Sacrament, St. Katharine Drexel traveled to the Navajo reservation and learned there was no Catholic presence among the people. Upon returning to the motherhouse in Pennsylvania she wrote to several men's missionary groups. The Franciscan friars from Cincinnati responded that they would be willing to minister among the Navajos. Katharine was able to purchase private land and helped to established the first Franciscan mission among the Navajos in 1898. St. Michael the archangel was a special saint for the Drexel family. Thus she named this first mission, St. Michael Mission. Today the community where the Mission is located is called St. Michaels, AZ. Katharine also established the first Catholic school a mile from the Mission in 1902, St. Michael Indian School, where my community ministers. The school (K–12) still continues to this day.

The Navajo reservation is vast about the size of West Virginia, located in the northwestern part of New Mexico, the northeastern part of Arizona, and a little portion of Utah. The entire reservation is in the diocese of Gallup. After the establishment of St. Michael Mission there followed other parishes where the Franciscan friars served. In 1998 the diocese celebrated 100 years of Catholic presence among the Navajos. Unlike the pueblos and other native peoples who had very early contact with the friars, the Navajos have had a short history with them. In many ways the Navajos are still learning about their Catholic faith. People often ask me why there are no Navajo priests and very few Navajo sisters and brothers. My people value marriage and grandchildren so there is little encouragement for one to consider going into the priesthood or religious life knowing that the person will never marry or have children.

My people are a spiritual people. Many of them practice both our traditional spiritual way and the Catholic way. In earlier times the Church discouraged the people from practicing their traditional ways but today there is no such discouragement. Navajos find great strength in both ways; they don't see the two as opposites but rather as a whole with different aspects. Both are harmonious with the other. They realize that they can still be Navajo and Catholic.

The early friars realized that they needed to know the people, especially their language in order to be effective missionaries. They took the time to know the people by observing and becoming speakers of Navajo. It is a difficult language to learn. I know this from first hand experience since I don't speak Navajo. Having been raised in Albuquerque, NM my parents taught my siblings and me English. I've tried to learn Navajo. It's my hope that now living and ministering in Chinle, AZ where more Navajo is spoken that I'll learn basic phrases.

It is important for those ministering among the Navajos that they take and make time to know the people—not bringing a "packaged program or prepared agenda" without getting to know the people. Getting to know doesn't mean asking questions but being a keen observer with a sincere interest in the people and learning some basic Navajo words and phrases.

The present reality of Catholic presence is a challenge for the Navajos with fewer and aging priests, both diocesan and Franciscan, as well as fewer women and men religious ministering among the people. As we face the future, missionaries, the diocese of Gallup, and the Navajo people need to come together to talk about the future of Catholic presence. Action planning needs to take place—how will the church continue to be a sacramental presence among the people.

Blessings Brought—Blessings Received

Blane Grein

I am Fr. Blane Grein, OFM, a Franciscan priest, ordained in 1962, belonging to the Province of St. John the Baptist, headquartered in Cincinnati, Ohio. Practically, for all my priestly ministry, I have lived in a minority situation. I lived in the Zuni Pueblo for three years; spent ten years in the Philippines in a rural setting in the Province of Leyte; served for two years in a black parish south of New Orleans, Louisiana; and for the past thirty-four years lived on the Navajo Indian Reservation in Chinle, Arizona; and presently trying to semi-retire in Jamaica, Westmoreland. In each ministry, paraphrasing Fr. Richard Rohr, OGM, I had to learn to see anew, live in a world I did not know and leave a world that I knew and had things under control and live in a culture where I was poor and powerless in order to be converted anew. That was the goal and motivation in all of my ministry.

While in Chinle I had the unique experience of working with six Navajo church members to build a new church structure. Once sufficient funds were raised to meet Diocesan requirements and permission was obtained to build, we had a parish workshop for about twenty-six parishioners to discuss the theolog and the importance of the five foci in a church; namely, the altar, the presider's chair, the ambo or lectern, the baptismal font, and the tabernacle. After this workshop six people volunteered to be a committee to plan the new church, to be the architects as it were. All were strong both in their Christian belief as well as in the traditional ways; all were very vocal; two were quite artistic.

All agreed that the structure should be a female Navajo hoghan, a place for life and prayer even till today, made from huge, roughly hewn logs, having chinking in the cracks, must be eight sided, with the door facing east. Facing the church east was a little problem. We consulted the entire parish community about it and they determined that main door face, not the magnetic east, but the rising sun on the day construction began. We also determined the height of the walls (9 feet), the diameter of the church (70 feet), the pitch of the roof (2–23). We agreed on the type of light canisters, the type of and number of individual chairs (250), we put a cushioned bench around the entire church except for the wall behind the altar, we agreed on some indirect lighting near the roof line around the entire church except for the wall behind the altar. We also came up with a floor plan for the entrance of the church, with dimensions, for a cry room, one rest room, a sacristy, work room, a reconciliation room, and a mechanical room. We wrote down every item that we agreed on to eventually give to the architect once one was chosen.

As people walk into church they are greeted by a male and female Navajo yei that are approximately four feet tall that are etched in the two glass interior doors. These yeis are the holy people of the Navajos and they roam throughout the entire reservation. They walk good ways and they remind us that we, too, are to walk the good way, the pollen path of harmony and righteousness and peace.

Once inside the church one notices on the east, south, west, and north walls six by three foot paintings done by local artists, of the four sacred mountains of the Navajo people in their sacred colors; namely, white, turquoise, yellow and black. These are real mountains outlining the Navajo Reservation and the medicine people go to these mountains often to pray and to gather items that they will use in their ceremonies, e.g. water, herbs, dirt, bones (for whistles), teeth of animals. The Navajo people feel blessed living within the boundaries of these sacred mountains. If they are living outside the boundaries of the mountains and bad things start to happen, like sickness or accidents, often many will return back to the reservation where they are protected by the sacred mountains, blessed by the yeis, and united with their departed elders and loved ones. The committee people said that they felt blessed worshipping in church with the four sacred mountains surrounding them.

The center of church was our next topic of discussion. I suggested that we put the altar in the center of church, but all six members were against it. Their reasoning: when a medicine person comes to a hoghan for a ceremony he/she always sits against the west wall with the patient immediately in front of him/her. The priest is to do his thing at the west wall of the church, and that is where the altar should be placed. The idea of the entire floor of the church being dirt, as is the case with all hoghans, was voted down. But all agreed that the church should be grounded to mother earth in some way. It was decided to have a six-foot diameter hole right in the middle of the floor, one step down, showing the compacted dirt to ground it to mother earth. Then it was agreed upon that the six-foot hole could represent the emergent hole in the Navajo tradition whereby all the talking animals were in the four underground worlds (white, turquoise, yellow and black) and the flood waters were rising. They all feared that they would drown until one animal got a reed and punched it through the heavens and it gave an opening to this present world. All the animals were able to climb up the reed and be saved. We decided to place our baptismal font in the center of the six-foot hole proclaiming that god's people are saved through the waters of baptism. And what better place to have the baptismal font than under the spirit hole of the hoghan—the opening in the center of the roof. Around the large baptismal bowl are images of the four stages of Navajo life; namely, a little baby in a

The Navajo Church at Chinle, Arizona.

cradle board, a teen age girl, an older woman weaving a rug, and an old man on a horse. I suggested that we make our baptismal font an immersion pool by going down another step or two. That idea got nowhere. We are not ready for that was the answer.

All of the furnishings in the sanctuary are made of juniper stumps or branches. The altar is covered with a deer skin. A medicine person will bring items for the ceremony wrapped in a deer skin. We thought that it would be fitting that the items that the priest uses at Mass also rest on a deer skin. Facing the altar to the right is the ambo or lectern. It is a large juniper stump about four and a half foot tall. The presider's chair behind the altar is all made from slabs and branches of juniper wood with the seat and back covered with a sheep's skin. To the left of the altar is a stump of juniper wood that has a cedar burning bowl sitting on it with various Navajo scenes involving fire carved out on it. Hanging from this same juniper log is an eagle feather used to move the cedar smoke around and also two pollen pouches for the Navajo people to pray with. They use white corn meal to pray with in the morning and yellow in the evening. The crucifix in the sanctuary is a resurrected Christ having Navajo look, feathers, and the hair done up in a traditional male way.

To the left of the altar is the tabernacle. It is a wooden box with both Christian and Navajo symbols carved in the door. This box is covered with a symbol of a summer home of the Navajos—logs leaning against a frame on

The Navajo Church at Chinle, Arizona.

three sides and branches covering the top. It is only about fifteen inches tall. This tabernacle rests on what is meant to be a Navajo prayer shrine. A traditional prayer shrine is started by a medicine person. A twig is broken off, a rock is found, and the rock is placed on the twig lest it blow away. As others use the prayer pile by doing the same thing it grows. After getting approval from a medicine man that it is permitted to use a piece of petrified wood on a prayer pile we asked the parishioners to bring to church a piece of petrified wood, the bigger the better, and from them we made a prayer pile. The one difference, we cemented our rocks together. We added two ledges in front so that some green plants could rest there symbolizing the green twig.

Hanging on the walls to the left and right of the altar are objects that you will often find in a Navajo home. On one side there is a Navajo woven basket and a water jar. On the other side there is a Navajo broom/brush/comb made out of the stems of yucca leaves. There is a set of large stirring sticks that a young girl uses to mix her cake that is baked in the ground when she has her kinalda ceremony—shortly after her first menstrual period. There is also another water jar hanging there. Up in the sanctuary there is a grinding stone that is used to grind corn for ceremonies and to pray with.

Between the north and east wall towards the rear of the church there are four statues, all wood carvings and standing three feet tall. The saints of the catholic church that we have depicted there are: St. Francis of Assisi, a Navajo Blessed Mother Mary with the child Jesus on a cradle board, St. Kateri Tekak-

The Navajo Church at Chinle, Arizona.

witha, and St. Katherine Drexel, SBS. The parish has been under the care of the Franciscans since its beginning in 1905 till now. Mary as a Navajo woman reverences the Navajo people. St Kateri is the first and only native person till now that has been officially declared a saint in the church and she is greatly loved by the native peoples. St Katherine actually visited Chinle several times and she is the one who got the Franciscans to minister among the Navajo people in 1898. So, there are reasons why these four statues grace the wall of the church. Behind these four statues there is a yellow arch, representing the pollen path. The yeis walked the pollen path of peace and harmony and these saints, the holy people of the catholic church, likewise walked that same good path.

On the wall between the east and the south wall of church there are the fifteen stations of the cross. The resurrection was added to the usual fourteen. Each depiction is done in a Navajo sand painting art form. Each station is about ten inches square. Arching over the stations, in a stylized form, is a red and blue Navajo rainbow. The rainbow is the body of the yei and it could, but doesn't, have a head and feet of a yei on it. The Navajo rainbow represents peace and harmony and the stations of the cross proclaim the restored peace and harmony that Jesus accomplished by his way of the cross and crucifixion.

On one wall in the cry room there is a Navajo cradle board, a means of carrying a baby that is still very much used today. And in the reconciliation room there is a beautiful juniper table, a lamp with a juniper base that has a large copper shade with cuts in it to show mesas, sun rays, and corn stalks. On one of the walls is a beautiful two foot by three foot picture of a Navajo

Good Shepherd that was made from a fifteen foot painting in the sanctuary of St. Mary's Catholic Church in Tohatchi, New Mexico.

Through this enculturation effort we are saying that there can be a blending of the Navajo traditional way and the Catholic Christian way. Meaning that you don't have to give up one to receive the other. Nor are we saying that this is the only way or necessarily the best way. It is just our way and I was happy to be part of the wonderful discussions and sharings that took place during the course of almost a year. When we finally chose an architect his comment was—you certainly made my job pretty easy. And that was our purpose, have a church that reflected our wishes and not that of some architect, and a church that reflects the respectful blending of the Catholic way and the Navajo traditional way.

Chapter 20
Indian Memorials at California Missions

Andrew Galvan and Vincent Medina

A note about the authors Andrew Galvan and Vincent Medina. Both Andrew and Vincent are descended from Avelina Cornates, a Mission Indian common ancestor who was baptized at Mission San Jose in 1864 and buried at the Ohlones Cemetery near Mission San Jose in Fremont in 1904. Avelina's grandfather, Liberato Culpecse was baptized in 1801 at Mission San Francisco de Asís (Dolores), but eventually moved to Mission San Jose. Liberate Culpecse's mother and father, Jobocme, and Poylemja, are buried at the Mission Dolores Cemetery in San Francisco. Both Andrew and Vincent descend from this lineage that stretches back hundreds of years in a post-contact world, but thousands of years in a pre-contact world.

The California Mission Cemeteries are the final resting place of nearly 70,000 Indians. "*The Mission Cemeteries were always incomprehensibly small,*" E.B. Webb wrote, "*As a consequence, in time they all became very much overcrowded.*"

Acknowledgement of these Native peoples is nearly non-existent, save for the occasional wooden marker. In this paper we will address challenges, and meaningful changes we are implementing at Mission Dolores, San Francisco to bring dignity and respect to our Indian ancestors buried at the Mission. Our objective is that the story of Native people at Mission Dolores be told in a truthful manner. Sometimes the inaccuracy is all in the words on the numerous plaques and exhibits throughout the Missions.

For generations Indian cemeteries at California Missions have been neglected places where little dignity or acknowledgement is given to the burials of California Indian people, which typically number in the thousands. Furthermore, thousands of Indian burials at California Missions are often relegated to a simple marker that generically gives recognition to all Native burials present. Many Native people see these mass grave markers as an inaccurate, albeit an attempt, to give recognition to Native people resting in mission cemeteries.

At most of the California Missions people often associate mission history with the early Spanish invaders. The Ohlones and other peoples whom lived in communities surrounding the missions are often left out of the story. The native world of our ancestors was overwhelmed—the environment was changing, epidemics were very destructive. It was a time of survival and native people came into the missions to survive. But, that is not the whole story. Time and time again we emphasize at Mission Dolores that people came to the missions in order to survive and that the Mission was built by Indian people. We are determined to tell that neglected history.

Often romanticism and Mission folklore takes hold in tangible ways at California Mission cemeteries fueling notions and misconceptions that Native people are no longer present in the larger society. Reality is far more complex than what is typically presented in California Mission cemeteries. Indian people, still present in modern times, have a deep and often painful, connection to the cemeteries at the twenty-one California Missions. Efforts are underway to begin to share the story of Indian burials at Mission Dolores in more accurate, fair, and just manners.

Andrew Galvan, Curator at Mission Dolores, often says "*I have two goals for my tenure as curator: to tell the accurate story of my ancestors and to give that story an academic slant. To reach these goals, I decided to develop a strong educational program using the museum's potential to focus on public interest on the history of Mission Dolores and especially of the Indian people whose lives the mission impacted and changed.*"

Vincent Medina, Assistant Curator of Mission Dolores, sees also the Mission as a unique place to be able to share history, tell a truthful story, claim the Mission as a uniquely Indian cultural space, all while seeing the Mission cemetery as a sacred space—one that Indians successfully resisted colonial oppression and kept cultural values—language, religious and political beliefs—alive in spite of attempts to Hispanicize Ohlone cultures. To Vincent, recognizing the Native presence in the cemetery is an aspect of telling a truthful and accurate story of the Mission, as well as pre-contact and post-contact Indian experience.

Our current goal is to recognize the 5,700 Indian people in unmarked graves buried in the Mission Dolores Cemetery. Our plan is to project digital images of individual names recorded in the Mission Dolores death registers onto the walls of the Old Mission. The challenge is to motivate other California Missions to likewise acknowledge the Native peoples buried at the sites they administer in meaningful ways.

Many California Missions have made scarce attempts to tell the story of Native burials. A number of Missions, such as Mission San Carlos Borromeo (Carmel), Mission Santa Ynez, and Mission San Luis Rey have simple, generalized crosses to represent the Indian burials present. Mission San Francisco de Asís (Dolores) has a statue of the Mohawk Saint Kateri Tekakwitha along with the words "*To Our Faithful Indians.*"

Fantasy and romanticization take hold in tangible ways with memorials for Indians at many Missions; by giving lone recognition to individuals said to be the last of their people, and negating Indians in the Missions as being faithful converts. Reality teaches a more honest story. We are aware that generations of Indian people persevere into current days, and that California's Native people are part of contemporary society, far from being *a dying race* as a casual visitor at most missions could easily interpret without accurate context. Also, we are aware through oral histories of Native people, Spanish documentation, archaeology, and reports from outside visitors to California during the Mission Period that many California Indians were not, in fact, faithful to the Catholic religion being imposed on their communities. Many individuals and tribal communities actively resisted the Catholic Church, missionization, and colonial occupation. Many California Indians continue to resist this spiritual oppression, even in the present-day.

What appears to be the most extensive, thorough, and far-reaching attempt for an Indian memorial is the memorial that exists for Native American Mission neophytes buried at Mission San Francisco de Solano, popularly known as Mission Sonoma. Bronze tablets are raised in the street adjacent to the Mission and recount the 800-plus names of the population of Mission Indians buried at that Mission researched from the Mission period death records. Each name represents a person who is buried at Mission Sonoma and shows visitors the multitude and immensity of the Native burials present. Each person buried there has a name, a story, and a presence at that Mission.

Efforts to begin to tell a story of Natives buried at Mission Dolores began around 1991, in the early stages of the Mission Dolores Restoration Project. Plans involved three life-sized bronze statues of an Ohlone man, woman, and a child in a reflective circle in the center of the Mission Cemetery. Due to rising costs and what some viewed as an aesthetic issue of having linear objects in an otherwise flat cemetery the plan was cancelled. For over a decade, the reflective circle was in place with no memorial to Native people present.

In the Spring of 1991, Curator Andrew Galvan received an invitation from the then Pastor of Mission Dolores, Monsignor John J. O'Connor to visit the Mission so he could share his vision for the soon to begin Restoration of the Old Mission Church, Museum and Cemetery. The Mission Church, completed in 1791 was constructed with adobe bricks. After the Loma Pieta Earthquake of October 1989, there was a renewed effort to retrofit the unreinforced adobe brick building. Monsignor O'Connor had plans to upgrade the exhibits in the one room museum which had been set up in 1976 for the Mission's Bicentennial. Finally, many of the Mission Cemetery's granite and marble tombstones were in need of repair. The overgrown plantings in the cemetery were in need of attention. As part of the cemetery restoration project, Monsignor O'Connor wanted to find an appropriate way to acknowledge the thousands of Mission Period Indians buried there between the years 1782–1834.

The Project's General Contractor, Mr. Frank Portman, Jr., knew Andrew and his father from the time his firm built the Mission San Jose Church during the years 1981–1985. Frank suggested to Monsignor that he'd be happy to make an introduction on his behalf to Andrew and his father. Finally, in late February 1992, Monsignor O'Connor and Andrew met at Old Mission Dolores. Monsignor explained his plans for the Mission Restoration and then he asked for Andrew's thoughts on what would be the best way to acknowledge the Indian people buried in the Mission Cemetery.

Monsignor O'Connor's question took Andrew by surprise. Usually, Native People are called in after all the decisions have been made about a project, any project, and aren't asked for input. This was a breath of fresh air for Andrew.

At Mission San Francisco de Solano (Sonoma) Andrew Galvan was part of a group that had worked to install three bronze plaques with the names of all the known Indians buried at that Mission. About 825 individuals died and were buried in the Mission Cemetery, a small number compared to other earlier Missions as the Mission was the last in the chain established in 1823. Mission Dolores in San Francisco was established nearly 50 years earlier in 1776 and counted 5,700 Indian interments in the Mission Death Register. Andrew suggested a wall similar to the Vietnam War Memorial in Washington, DC be placed at the edge of the Mission Dolores Cemetery. Monsignor O'Connor threw himself behind the idea. There was immense hope of the possibilities, until there was a telephone call for the General Contractor Frank Portman, Jr. Frank told our Curator "Andy please don't give Fr. John anymore expensive ideas such as the Indian Memorial Wall. It will cost about one million dollars." Frank was supportive of an Indian Memorial but was also mindful of the ever-increasing budget for the entire Restoration Project.

Over the next three years, until his death from cancer just a week before the Restoration Project was completed in March 1995, Frank suggested ideas for a way to acknowledge the Indian people buried in the Mission Cemetery.

As with the Sonoma Mission Memorial to the Neophytes buried there, the decision at Mission Dolores was made to make a listing of the names of those who died and were buried in the Mission Cemetery. Some had suggested to use the names listed in the Baptismal Register, however Andrew was not in favor of that; and he would recall telling people that he preferred the names from the Death Register, as no one can escape death. The Baptismal Register is a listing of the names of individuals who were baptized into the Roman Catholic Faith. In many cases, if not in most cases, an individual had not freely selected to be baptized. So, it was decided on the names from the Death Register.

The Mission Registers (Baptism, Marriage and Death) at Mission Dolores date from 1776. They are parchment pages bound in leather and the words in many cases are difficult to read as the ink has bled through the pages. The first project to be completed was to make a computer data base of the Mission Dolores Death Registers. Ethnohistorian Dr. Randall Milliken was called upon for assistance. His plan, and it was the plan used, was to reach out to a local University and obtain some student interns to go through the registers line by line and to record all the information. Most entries in the Death Register included the following information: Christian name of the individual, date of death, perhaps a narrative such as career information, and in many cases a cross reference to the individuals Baptismal entry, which often included Native names.

After two years, a computer print out was available. The names of those who had died at Mission Dolores were sorted by village, sometimes language, or origin. 5,700 names in all. Immediately the print outs were placed in a binder in the Mission Museum on a podium that bore a small plaque that read "A listing of those Neophytes buried in our Cemetery between the years 1782–1850." This effort was a monumental task. While the names were now available on the computer, the average visitor on a limited time schedule did not have the opportunity to review each name. And often, if the one room Museum was crowded the ledger was neither visible or available.

As part of the Cemetery Restoration, a large granite Grotto dedicated to Our Lady of Lourdes erected in the 1920's was demolished and removed – it was determined to be out of place in the Mission Cemetery. It was at this now cleared location that it was decided to place a Memorial to the Indian people buried in the Mission Dolores Cemetery.

As previously mentioned, the Memorial to Indian peoples did not become a reality, and for nearly a decade a memorial circle to a project that never occurred sat empty in the center of the Cemetery with the only indicator that Indians were ever buried at the Mission being the aforementioned statue of Saint Kateri Tekakwitha with the inscription *In Memory of our Faithful Indians.* This served as a painful reminder of the challenges Indian people faced in creating a memorial that was accurate, inclusive and fair.

After his installation as Curator of Mission Dolores in 2004, Andrew Galvan, while reminding himself that he was in charge of interpretation of the Old Mission including the Mission Cemetery, decided that a grave marker to his direct ancestors should be installed. Our ancestors were baptized at Mission Dolores, and were buried there after their Christian funerals in the Old Mission Church. Soon after the idea came into Andrew's mind, and he realized the unique ability he had as Curator of the Old Mission to make this a reality. He began that project.

Redwood boards were purchased from a local Home Depot, and archival information was hand carved onto the redwood boards, and created into the shape of double wooden grave markers.

It was decided that using the Mission period archives as a basis for the research of the names of our ancestors who this wooden grave marker was being installed to honor and give respect. The Spanish had a policy of documenting traditional names of Indians who would become neophytes. After their traditional names, and villages were documented in the baptismal record then, the policy of the Spanish Missionaries was to change the Indians' traditional names and force them to adopt a Christian name. The reality, however, is that most Indian people did not relinquish their traditional names. They often continued using traditional names, sometimes in clandestine ways, and sometimes in outright defiance against the will of the Spanish.

On the wooden grave marker that was constructed it was decided to use Native names as the primary names inscribed on the wooden grave marker—we engraved first *Jobocme* and *Poylemja*. Jobocme is an Ohlone woman from an East Bay village named Jalquin and adopt a new Catholic name after baptism—which was Obulinda. Jobocme's husband, Poylemja, came to Mission Dolores in 1794 from a village in the East Bay foothills named Saklan. We are certain, that while their lives were being affected and the Spanish trying to change the Indian cultures of the Mission that Native people kept using their traditional names; just as they kept other aspects of culture alive—such as their languages, religious beliefs, dances, arts, and political beliefs.

The grave marker in the center of the cemetery is a tangible piece that visitors, community members, and family members can visit that gives proof to specific Native people buried at Mission Dolores. It gives recognition to two of the individuals that are interred there, and even without much label-copy tells a story that is necessary to tell. It reminds the casual visitor to Mission Dolores Cemetery that Indian people are in fact buried in that place. The wooden grave marker has been very popular, as it stands out among the stone grave markers of the names of Europeans. Its central location, across from a traditional Ohlone house called a *ruwway* helps remind visitors understand that there truly is an Indian presence at Mission Dolores.

In early 2009 Vincent Medina was hired at Mission Dolores, and took the title of Assistant Curator. He leads popular tours to school children, explains colonization from a Native perspective, has worked to develop museum exhibits, and helped with the general upkeep of the Mission itself. Vincent Medina and Andrew Galvan are cousins, sharing common ancestry, including Jobocme and Poylemja, who are buried at Mission Dolores. It is a unique relationship to have two direct descendants of Mission Indians in direct control of the daily operations at a Mission their ancestors were once in.

Both Andrew and Vincent often wondered of ways to incorporate a large memorial for the 5,700 other Indian people buried in the Mission Dolores Cemetery. One that shows the humanity and brings recognition to those whose final resting spot is the Old Mission. With no funding for a "Vietnam

Style" memorial wall, with the names of nearly 6,000 individuals—thoughts began to come into our minds of other things that could be done.

One day Vincent and Andrew were in the Mission Dolores Cemetery watering and tending to the roses as they often do. Vincent suggested that perhaps, using technology, a digital memorial project could be created—setting up canvases in the Mission Cemetery and digitally projecting the names of each Indian person buried at the Mission. Andrew, thinking very quickly, looked up at the whitewashed, adobe Mission walls and suggested that the very white walls of the Mission Church itself be a canvas for this proposed projections of names.

It felt powerful to have this idea, and also symbolic factors began to be felt. Andrew and Vincent made a conscious decision to use only the Native names that were recorded as much as possible, but only in cases of there not being a Native name listed, or the children of first-generation Mission Indians who only adopted European names would we use their Christian names. The symbolism previously described is that we would be projecting Native names onto a building where those names were once banned inside. After an Indian person was baptized, it was the policy of the Spanish to make that individual adopt a new Spanish name that would be used for the rest of their lives by the Spanish in the Missions. The reality is that, even under those circumstances, Indian people refused to relinquish their traditional names. Symbolically projecting those once banned names onto this institution of colonization sends a powerful message that traditional, Native names matter and that they are not forgotten.

Beginning in the Fall of 2010 and again in the Fall of 2011, we began to submit Grant Requests to the California Missions Foundation for funding for our proposed digital Indian Memorial.

In October 2010, Tina Foss, Chair of the Grant Committee of the California Missions Foundation informed us that the guidelines for the committee limited funding to Preservation, Conservation and Restoration projects only. And that our request for funding of digital projectors, as well as a budget to fund the tedious data entry process of 5,700 names did not fall under any of those guidelines.

A year late, a new proposal that suggested that at one time every Native person buried in the cemetery would have had a grave marker was submitted. We requested funding for our Indian Memorial as a restoration project. Tina Foss reported that the Grant Committee was not sold on this project of restoring grave markers for Indians as deserving of funding. Foss also informed us that many of the Grant Committee members were concerned that the Indian Memorial project was unfair and actual racist in that it did not include the names of the Spanish and/or Mexicans buried in the Cemetery during the Mission Period. Frustrated Andy blasted Tina saying "what part of *Indian Memorial* don't those Grant Committee members understand?"

A year later, in the Summer of 2012, the outgoing California Missions Foundation Executive Director, Dr. Knox Mellon, was able to provide a Grant of $2,000.00 to Mission Dolores for the Indian Memorial. Dr. Mellon apparently had access to funds that the Grant Committee did not.

In the early Spring of 2013, another donor provided a check in the amount of $1,000.00 towards the Indian Memorial project. Up and down the State of California, we discussed our project with friends and colleagues. Many had some thoughtful suggestions. The proposed presentation underwent several changes—from using high powered out door projects at a cost of $90,000.00 for two, with a monthly fee of lightbulb replacement at $300.00 per month to projection by means a laptop and viewed on a Flat Screen Monitor in the Museum. The first difficult task was how to prepare the nearly 6,000 names on slides for projection.

While at a consultation meeting in southern California in the late Fall of 2012 for a planned exhibit in commemoration of the 300th Birthday of Junipero Serra, OFM, we shared our ideas of a projection of the names of those buried in the Mission Dolores Cemetery with Historian Steve Hackel. Dr. Hackel was co-curator of the upcoming exhibit to be showcased at the Huntington Library—as well as developer of the Early California Populations project. The Early California Population Project is a computerized tool that can be used to search the Baptism, Marriage and Death Registers of the 21 California Indian Missions. Dr. Hackel told us that he would be able to assist us in sorting the names—but at that time he was occupied with the upcoming exhibit and we would need to wait for his assistance to after the exhibition was completed in early 2014.

In September 2013, there was a Scholars' Symposium at the time of the opening of the exhibit in commemoration of Padre Junipero Serra. The Serra Exhibit included a nine hour long slide presentation of each name of the over 100,000 individuals who were either baptized or buried at a California Mission between the years 1769–1835. While viewing the exhibit in the company of Archivist Emeritus Lynn Bremer of the Santa Barbara Mission Archive Library, we shared with Lynn our hopes of making a similar names presentation at Mission Dolores as a Memorial to Indians buried in our cemetery. Gently, Lynn asked "Andy, how much money do you think it would take to make the Indian Memorial happen at Mission Dolores?" Andy thought about it and replied "maybe $10,000.00." At the end of the day's luncheon, Lynn asked Andy for a private moment in the rear of the auditorium where the symposium was in session. Lynn quietly handed Andy and Vincent a check in the amount of $10,000.00 for our proposed Memorial Project.

Of course, there will be challenges and difficulties that will rise in the future; but we are confident that those future hurdles will be overcome. In July of 2014, Andrew and Vincent met with Dr. Steve Hackel and Victor

Solomon. Victor is a multimedia, digital artist who shared with us a realistic vision of what a projection might look like, how much it will cost, and ways to make this project a reality. The projection idea for an Indian Memorial is indeed feasible and possible. As this paper is written, Andy and Vincent are anticipating their next move and their options.

With a combination of public interest, generous donations such as Lynn's, a desire from Indian communities for social justice and recognition, and support from the Church administration we have begun to see success in reaching our goal for an Indian Memorial Project become a reality. Of course, as unprecedented of an action this Memorial Project will be, it is to be said that the humble beginnings of this project stem from a deep love for our Indian ancestors, both at the Mission and from a time before these painful places of colonization entered our world.

Index

Names

Places

Themes